KW-019-333

THE NEW MARKETING

Building strong marketing strategies in South Africa today

STEVEN M. BURGESS

Professor of Marketing
Association of Marketers Chair
School of Economic and Business Studies
University of the Witwatersrand, Johannesburg

ZEBRA

Published by Zebra Press
(a division of the New Holland Struik Publishing Group (Pty) Ltd)
PO Box 3103, Halfway House, 1685
Tel: (011) 315-3633
Fax: (011) 315-3810
Email: zebrastaff@icelogic.co.za

First edition, first impression 1998

© Zebra Press
Text © Steven M. Burgess
Illustrations © Steven M. Burgess except where otherwise credited

Figure 2.3 and Table 5.2 from *Consumer Behaviour* (Eight edition) by Engel, J.F., Blackwell, R.D. & Miniard, P.W. Copyright © 1995 by The Dryden Press, reproduced by permission from the publisher.

Table 4.1 from *Human Development Report*. Copyright © 1997 by the United Nations Development Programme. Used by permission of Oxford University Press, Inc.

All rights reserved. No part of this publication may be reproduced, stored in a retrieval system or transmitted, in any form or by any means, electronic, mechanical, photocopying, recording or otherwise, without the prior written permission of the copyright holders.

Editor Sean Fraser
Designer Patricia Moloney
Cover design Crazy Cat Designs

Reproduction by PG & A (Gauteng)
Printed and bound by Colorgraphic, Durban

ISBN 1 86872 142 6

THE NEW MARKETING

DEDICATION

To my lover, partner and wife.
Colleen, you are a gift of sweetness lighting every corner of
my life.

To our children Ariel, Alethe, Richard and Jonathan.
May they prosper and enjoy the fruits of the digital age.

REVIEWERS

The following busy academics and executives read the draft manuscript of this book and improved it by sharing their frank comments. Any deficiencies remain my sole responsibility:

Prof. Roger Blackwell
  Professor of Marketing and Consumer Research: The Ohio State University.
Ms. Rose Blatch
  Executive Director: International Trade Institute of Southern Africa (ITRISA). Director: International Association of Trade Training Organisations.
Mr Derrick Dickens
  Executive Director: The Association of Marketers.
Mrs Sue Grant
  Chief Executive Officer: Markinor. Member of the International Board of Directors: Gallup Research (USA).
Prof. Warren Keegan
  Professor of Marketing and International Business, Lubin Business School. Director of the Institute for Global Business Strategy, Pace University, New York. Visiting Professor on Executive Programs, Wharton Business School, University of Pennsylvania.
Mr Keith Rosmarin
  Partner: KPMG Management Consulting.
Mr Theo Rutstein
  Director: Jasco Electronics Holdings Ltd. and founder of Teljoy.
Mr Roger Sinclair
  Faculty: School of Economic and Business Studies, University of the Witwatersrand.
Mr Arie van der Zwan
  Executive Director: Southern Life.
Mr J. Len Van Zyl
  Chairman: Lindsay-Smithers FCB.
Dr W.P. Venter
  Chairman: The Altron Group.
Mr Graham Warsop
  CEO: The Jupiter Group.

FOREWORD

The sweeping changes taking place in marketing practice may be even more important than the political changes that attract so much attention in South Africa today. Companies that have thrived for more than a hundred years are being buffeted in a turbulence created by technology, innovation and globalisation that is blurring industry boundaries and changing the nature of competition. No company can escape.

Our work at the Association of Marketers (ASOM) today is very different to that of just ten years ago. Although we remain busy with the issues that have always demanded our attention, we find ourselves protecting the interests of marketers in new arenas today. Restrictive legislation and other threats to advertising and direct marketing practice are examples of the new arenas in which ASOM seeks to defend or extend its members rights.

Internet advertising and promotion, which is rising on the horizon as a substitute for traditional mass media advertising, promises even more challenges in the future.

The problems that marketers face also have changed. Marketers in many industries confide to me that the traditional marketing mix (the so-called 4Ps) has diminished in importance in the new environment and that they find themselves experimenting with new ideas and innovative approaches to marketing. They tell me strategic management issues now take up more time.

In a sense, marketers have become the victims of their own successes. We sold the notion that marketing is everyone's job very effectively. Marketing is no longer a department that turns out 'pretty pictures' to drive sales.

Now, we find ourselves managing marketing as a cross-functional set of activities throughout the enterprise and through others. Our skills and abilities, once used to influence customers only, must now be used to influence others in the organisation to do what they should be doing to satisfy customers.

What I like about *The New Marketing* is that it addresses this complex new world.

I have known Steve Burgess for many years. He has achieved international respect as a marketing practitioner, company director, consultant and academic. *The New Marketing* captures his experience and knowledge in these aspects of marketing practice. It is a fresh, insightful look at marketing today and tomorrow. Leaving the 4Ps behind, the author weaves a picture of marketing as a cross-functional activity and develops a methodology and process for instilling the new marketing into any company.

What I find most appealing about this book is that it is undeniably African. It surveys the latest thinking globally and makes it understandable and appropriate for African and Indian Ocean Rim marketing.

I firmly believe that any company director or marketing manager who hopes to be running a successful business in the year 2010 needs to read this book, absorb the principles and begin implementing them immediately.

Mr Derrick Dickens
Executive Director
The Association of Marketers
Sandton
April 1998

PREFACE

Losing 35 cents changed my life. Twenty-five years ago, I lost my bus fare and a friend offered me a ride home from Ohio State after his marketing class. I tagged along to a lecture by Professor Roger Blackwell. Blackwell was already one of America's hottest and most entertaining marketing authorities but I had no idea who he was and prepared to complete my engineering homework. I never finished it.

Blackwell was exploring product innovation and his premise was that good marketing is the animating force behind the world's most exciting new products. Every glimpse of the future that Blackwell presented — from palmtop computers and electronic funds transfer at the point-of-sale to cellular telephones and mobile offices — was unknown then, but is now a part of our lives. That future Blackwell spoke of so many years ago is the present that threatens so many South African companies and careers today.

More than 20 years later, I sat at the speaker's table in Boston with Roger Blackwell and Philip Kotler preparing to present a paper at the opening session of the American Marketing Association's Summer Educator's Conference. As we discussed the changing nature of marketing before the presentations, my beliefs about the need for practical relevance in academic marketing and for a new marketing paradigm were confirmed. That discussion probably planted the seed for this book. I have asked myself some penetrating questions since. If every marketing proposal to a customer is a request for change, why isn't marketing undergoing meaningful change? When it has never been so needed, why does marketing appear to be losing influence? When lasting stakeholder value has never been so difficult to build, why do companies take actions that weaken marketing and destroy their company's value?

If one takes a step back, a major trend is evident. Marketing is slipping from the grasp of marketing managers and into the hands of others who often do not know what to do with it. This is a good thing that can be observed in the increasing trend to distribute the responsibility for traditional marketing mix elements (product, promotion, distribution and pricing strategies) widely in many enterprises. Nevertheless, companies need marketing people like never before. Marketing needs a new paradigm consistent with this trend and appropriate to the new digital economy.

It has become fashionable to suggest that the world is now changing so fast that there is no longer any time for analysis or planning. This may comfort some managers who lack these skills but the comfort will be cheap and short-lived in the face of the failure that must soon follow. Cast in the kindest light, such guidance is no more than a harmless snake oil sold by well-meaning merchants on the sides of the digital highway. If this is the proper course, why are none of the great minds championing it?

Things are changing fast and the digital economy requires more analysis more frequently. Analysis must be automated where possible so that people are free to focus on the important things that build sustainable superior customer solutions. This book presents tried and trusted analysis techniques and suggests new ones. I believe that the five disciplines presented in this book are the 'new marketing', and that these disciplines represent a paradigm that offers a way to build strong marketing within companies. There is no option in the digital age except to build strong marketing following the principles outlined in this book.

This is not a book written for managers who wish to 'plan the market' from behind a desk at corporate headquarters. It is for directors, senior managers and fast-trackers who plan to master the details of strong marketing in order to empower their companies and careers to reach new heights.

Please feel free to contact me to share your experiences with the new marketing. In-house seminars are available.

Dr Steven M. Burgess

The Association of Marketers Professor
School of Economic and Business Studies
Private Bag 3
University of the Witwatersrand
2050
Johannesburg, South Africa

Telephone: (011)716 5563
Fax: (011) 339 7385
International: Dial your international access code plus 2711 and the last seven digits of the above numbers.
E-mail: Steve.Burgess@pixie.co.za

APPRECIATION

Writing this book has been the most difficult thing I have ever done. In Africa, people say that 'A person is only a person through another person'. In America, people say that one achieves things in life because someone else takes an interest in them. I have benefited from the friendship and guidance of many over the years. No one has influenced my thinking about marketing and consumer behaviour more than my mentor, friend and colleague Roger Blackwell of The Ohio State University. The many awards for his seminal contribution to consumer behaviour and marketing literature and his teaching excellence fail to honour the decency and altruism of this man. He is responsible for much that I have achieved and I cherish my friendship with Roger and his beloved Tina.

Warren Keegan, of Pace University and Wharton Business School, is considered by many to be the father of global marketing. His advice and friendship have been an important influence on my thinking about globalism and the requirements for global competitive advantage. Shalom Schwartz of the Hebrew University of Jerusalem and the late Milton Rokeach shared their time to help me understand the values literature. I have learned much from collaborating with Shalom over the years. Jan-Benedict E.M. Steekamp of the Catholic University of Leuven and Richard Bagozzi of the University of Michigan have been helpful friends during my transition back to academia. Andy Andrews of The Graduate Institute of Management and Technology has always been willing to tell me when he thought I was losing focus on the practical issues of management. My friend Michael Bond of the Chinese University of Hong Kong also influenced my thinking about cross-cultural values. Michael Greenacre, formerly of the University of South Africa, was instrumental in helping me appreciate the value of nonparametric statistical techniques. Bede Doherty and Bernard Potgieter of SPL have always been ready to share their knowledge about data warehouse technology. Neil Higgs and Butch Rice of Research Surveys, Tony Sham of Analogue Marketing and Glenn Milligan of The Ohio State University were other influences. Wilhelm Crous of Knowledge Resources often encouraged me to write a book over the years. Marilyn Chaplin of ICMD is another to whom I am indebted. My thanks to Ann Morgan and the SAFTO library staff for their assistance with access to less widely available data sources, particularly for the appendix. Rose Blatch and Ali Parry of the International Trade Institute of South Africa, and David Graham of International Trade Projects pointed me towards the Indian Ocean Rim.

I would not have entered academia if Tim Bester and Sue Lerena, then of McCann-Ericksen, had not believed in me and if Russel Abratt had not supported my appointment at the University of the Witwatersrand (Wits). Tim provided much-needed financial support and guidance in the first year. Duncan Reekie and Rob Vivian also supported my research at Wits and made it a rewarding place to work. Sue Grant of Markinor and Teddy Langschmidt of Integrated Marketing Research have been friends and trusted colleagues. The late Wally Langschmidt of Market Research Africa also influenced me. My understanding of the influence of GIS systems is largely due to Lindsay Welham and Anthony Poorter of Maps and Data, Fred Barber, Roger Trythall and Dirk Beukes at MarketMap, and to David Coupe at Experian Marketing (UK). One way to learn is to model yourself after effective executives whom you observe. I learned from David Dowds and Sam Abramson at Glicks, Alan Rains, Lawrie Golding, Wayne Munro and Carl Spalding at J&J, Dr Bill Venter and Craig Venter at Autopage, and Jean-Michel Trousse, Lovelle Henderson and Barry Cowden at Experian Scorex. A special word of thanks to Kate Rogan who took over this project as she came on board at Zebra. Her guidance and hard work have made this a much better book.

My parents created an environment that encouraged me to think independently and to be entrepreneurial and I thank them here. Over the years – in undergraduate and graduate classrooms, in executive seminars and in consulting relationships – I have received kind hospitality and acceptance from South Africans from all cultural backgrounds here in my adopted homeland. I am proud that many consider me to be a South African.

CONTENTS

INTRODUCTION

Would global business strategies change if the Americans fell from the top ten countries according to per capita GNP[1]? Would global consumption patterns of your products change if 35 per cent to 50 per cent of the population were over 65 years of age in America, Japan and Western Europe? Would today's developing nation markets be more attractive if illiteracy, innumeracy, war and illnesses (from tooth decay to tuberculosis and most forms of cancer) were eradicated? Consider the implications of a global currency, perhaps even a world government. Imagine connecting to anyone else in the world – family, friends, top professors or consultants – for the cost of a postage stamp. Imagine watching any sporting event, movie or programme televised in the world whenever you wanted to see it. How would your company's long range strategies change if you thought the Indian and Chinese economies would grow to be five times, perhaps as much as eight times, their present size? Or if the Indian Ocean Rim (IOR)[2] contained some of the world's most desirable markets (where many consumers would enjoy a similar living standard comparable to that of the Republic of Korea today)?

As improbable as it may seem, this is a most likely scenario for the world just 20 years from today[3]. In 2020, after two decades of investment in people and infrastructure, fast growth will continue in the IOR. Regional businesses will participate fully in globalised high-tech industries and invent new technologies. Population growth will slow everywhere.

THE GROWING IMPORTANCE OF THE INDIAN OCEAN RIM

During the past 25 years, I have read more than 2 000 articles and books concerning effective marketing and management. Many of these publications focused on the implications of business globalisation trends and offered regional analyses and company examples 'from around the world'. However, it was not my world: Africa and the developing nations of the IOR do not feature much in discussions about global markets. Even when the region is mentioned, it appears to be as an uncomfortable afterthought confined to a small separate section. It is the common failing of a marketing literature that fails to acknowledge the wealth of intermarket segments or the potential of this fast-growing region.

In academia, business practice and consulting, I have thought about these questions and what they mean to companies attempting to build strong marketing in South Africa and other IOR countries. I have written this book to answer those questions. Although the lessons in it apply around the world, I have made a special effort to explore how strong marketing is built in this important point of entry into the IOR.

In the classroom, in the boardroom and on the shop floor, we have begun to explore the unique character and diversity of the IOR. We have discovered that the majority of the world's peoples have access to resources and live a lifestyle comparable to our own. We are questioning whether products and services developed in response to an ageing, wealthy and post-modern marketing environment are appropriate for our young, poor and mass-consumption environment. We are concerned about the effect of products and lifestyles on our resources and environment. We have started redefining 'world-class' and stopped pretending that the more industrialised countries have a monopoly on marketing excellence. We have learned that the process and skills required to build strong marketing in a developing nation environment may differ to those required in the more industrialised countries. This book includes examples from Europe, Japan, the United States and from daily marketing practice in the IOR. It has been especially rewarding to mention South African firms that leveraged experience in the region to beat the world's best – not just survive. This book explains many of the management skills that make those firms winners.

THE IMPORTANCE OF CHANGE

> It is not too much to say that in these respects more has been done, richer and more prolific discoveries have been made, grander achievements have been realised in the last 50 years of our own lifetime than in the previous lifetime of the race[4].

Consider this quote from *Scientific American* about humanity's progress in building civilisation and providing the comforts of life to the masses. Few would disagree with such a quote and few did when it was first published in 1868!

So many have written about the 1990s as a time of great change, turbulence and chaos that many people believe change is unique to our times. In decade after decade since the 1960s, writers have bemoaned the pace of change and pointed to the relative stability of the previous decade. If we reflect on the Great Depression, the World Wars and the onset of the Cold War, the turbulence of our age fails to overshadow that faced by preceding generations. What we must ask is whether change is really affecting the conduct of our businesses or whether we are hanging onto the past and failing to recognise and embrace change. It is clear that winning firms must embrace change in an age of converging technologies and massive socioeconomic and political change. Turbulence will accelerate. Marketing complexity and competitive intensity will increase with the continued emergence of the IOR as a global trading powerhouse – perhaps much more than many suggest. This book illustrates how winning firms learn to recognise change and see it as an opportunity.

THE IMPORTANCE OF THE ENVIRONMENT

Today, too many firms fail to consider the impact of basic environmental trends. Managers struggle to keep pace with change, and increased information about day-to-day affairs does little to help them understand the basic environmental trends that influence success in their markets – many companies fail as a result. Most South African managers I know would have difficulty accepting the possibility that the world in 2020 will resemble the world I sketched at the opening of this chapter – even though the vision suggested is a very likely scenario.

The failure to identify basic trends leaves management unprepared to ask the right questions about the business. This is the bedrock issue behind the crisis of indecision gripping many enterprises today – a crisis made worse by the authoritative management legacy that characterises so many companies in the IOR. Marketing cannot provide solutions when core issues elude senior management. How many times must we read about companies where effective guidance from the boardroom evaporated while senior management floundered, unable to grasp core issues? Pity the shrinking middle management teams implementing tactics at odds with the long-term survival of the company while they wait for a solution from on high! This book helps explain how to monitor the environment and thrive within today's changing circumstances.

THE PROMISE OF THE NEW MARKETING

In companies practising the new marketing, no one is really surprised that proven strategies become irrelevant in a fast-changing marketing environment. Associates at all levels understand the impact of various environments on the firm. Management prepares itself for changing industry boundaries in a world characterised by the convergence of new communication, computing and content technologies. Everyone expects companies from slower-growing industrialised countries to enter the faster-growing developing regions, and competitors in mature product markets to move into growing product markets requiring similar skills. No one is astonished when these new competitors upset the balance of competitive advantage and force management to reconsider the nature of competition and co-operation. After all, they reconsider such things on a regular basis anyway.

Of course, all is not smooth sailing in firms that practise the new marketing. They also face dynamic trading environments. They work hard to achieve the strategic insight necessary to master the nuances of daily business and to set and achieve realistic short-term targets. They recognise the inherent challenge in building strong marketing: the job is never finished.

Building strong marketing is a continually renewing process of global understanding about sources of demand, sources of supply and methods of effective management. It is not an event or a destination, and this book examines the challenges facing regional managers in the light of the most recent developments in marketing. Strong marketing is not a department – it is an underlying foundation upon which all strategies and tactics must be built. It is the foundation from which firms must embrace the new converging technologies and incorporate them into their businesses. Firms that refuse to accept this new reality ultimately choose to perish.

Those who were protected by tariffs and regulations already know the challenges of massive transformation that lie ahead. However, the most successful firms are most at risk in the new marketing environment. It is these firms where complacency is the quiet enemy threatening survival.

Don't think so? Consider how many leading companies have disappeared or suffered severe reversals of fortune in recent years. Who would have thought these companies would face the problems that caused them such difficulty? This book helps explain how to monitor the environment and thrive within today's changing circumstances.

THE FIVE NEW SURVIVAL SKILLS

Most businesses have systems in place that more or less ensure that people are doing things right. The new environment also forces management to focus on doing the right things. *The New Marketing* is organised about the five disciplines required to build strong marketing in the new IOR consumer, services and business-to-business marketing environment.

MANAGING PURCHASE AND CONSUMPTION BEHAVIOUR

No management team can build strong marketing and deliver sustainable shareholder value growth without an intimate understanding of purchase and consumption behaviour. What skill could be more important than competent management of the purchase and consumption environment? What asset could be more valuable than an intimate understanding of purchase and consumption behaviour in key market segments? Managing the purchase and consumption environment requires careful analysis of consumer characteristics and behavioural trends as well as the social influences and environmental factors that influence behaviour. Strong marketing requires an empathy with the customer that permeates the entire organisation. It is not enough to understand a local market in isolation. Consumption and purchase behaviour must be understood at a local, regional and global level.

MANAGING THE COMPETITIVE ENVIRONMENT

Sound management of consumption and purchase behaviour provides a foundation for analysing and managing the competitive environment.

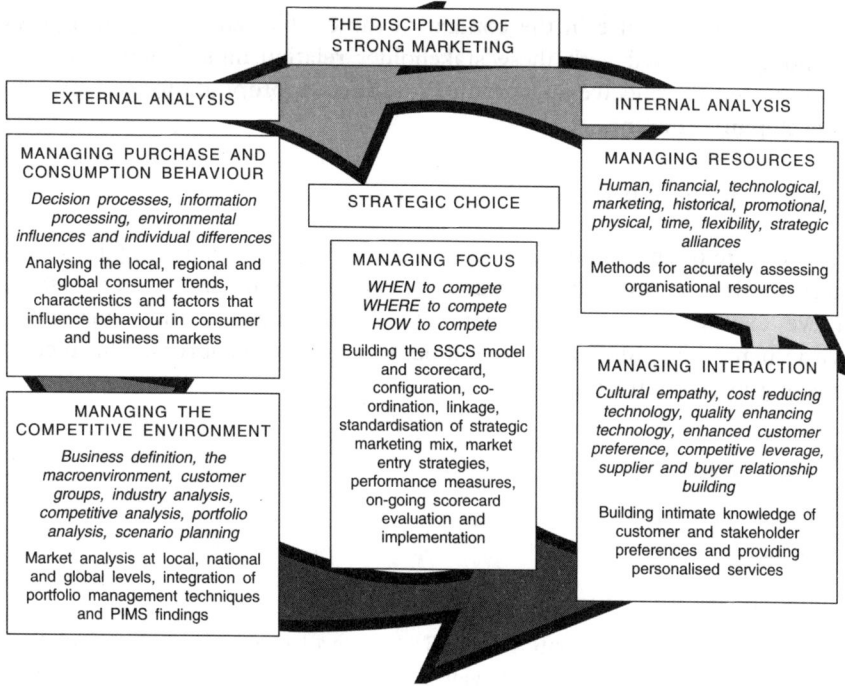

Figure 1.1 *The five disciplines of the new marketing*

Structures in industries and product-markets evolve in response to unique historical events and influences. Strategies employed by local market participants are a product and a source of these evolving forces. It is important to develop a competent understanding of evolving technologies and business processes, market structures, value chains and sources of competitive advantage at local, regional and global market levels. Management must also contemplate how alternative strategies will influence the playing field that the team must defend or conquer tomorrow.

MANAGING RESOURCES

Managing people, capital and infrastructure have always featured as key management functions. However, the changing nature of resource management demands new skills. Perhaps the most significant change concerns the ownership of resources. Government, special interest groups and strategic alliance partners often own or control key resources. A new model of competition pits value chain against value chain, marketing network against marketing network. Many managers have difficulty refining and influencing resource access and use in the context of the conflict and divergent interests commonly associated with these stakeholder relationships. There is also the pressing need to conceive and produce products appropriate for the resources of developing economies.

MANAGING INTERACTION

Resources are often shared with value chain and strategic alliance partners. An enterprise that cannot manage interaction will eventually fail, even if it should achieve excellence in its management of the purchase and consumption environment, the competitive environment, focus and resources. This includes managing interaction with

- customers;
- the public at large;
- business partners;
- staff; and
- public policy influencers.

Interaction has become a survival skill. New and dramatic interactive digital technologies are multiplying the ways that companies model and respond to customer requirements.

MANAGING FOCUS

Focus is the enabling discipline of strong marketing. Through the haze of the emerging competitive environment, the idea that a business is a collection of a few core competencies is gathering momentum. Effective companies focus keenly on developing the core competencies required to meet their overall objectives and to satisfy the market. Managing the core competencies that deliver superior sustainable competitive advantage has become a necessity for enduring achievement. In addition, a set of general competencies has become increasingly important. These include cultural empathy, business partnering, alliance creation and management and stakeholder relationship management. Kaplan and Norton have recently popularised the balanced scorecard approach[5]. The new marketing employs a similar approach, culminating in the construction of a performance model and scorecard that focus management attention on doing the right things and doing those things right.

MORE THAN A MARKETING AUDIT

Introduced in a 1959 American Management Association publication and popularised by Kotler[6], the marketing audit has become an accepted starting point for marketing strategy in the region. The marketing audit answers the questions 'where are we today?' and 'what are we doing about it?'. Strong marketing has one objective: building superior sustainable customer solutions (SSCSs). The process advocated in this book makes it easier to conceive and implement marketing strategies appropriate to these objectives. Firms that incorporate these processes are also more likely to determine a balance between flexibility and entrepreneurship that stimulates the business without threatening the sound financial business practice so necessary for survival.

ENDNOTES

1   Gross National Product per person, the most common measure of individual prosperity.
2   The IOR begins in South Africa and ends along the south coast of Australia. It includes South Africa, Singapore, Australia, Indonesia, Thailand, Malaysia, India and other countries.
3   See United Nations (1995). This report presents a vision of a world struggling towards social maturity and was called 'thorough and thought-provoking' and 'a timely work deserving our full attention' by President Mandela.
4   Quoted by Mintzberg (1994). Mintzberg argues that turbulence may be more illusion than fact on pages 203-209. I believe that steadily increasing turbulence would explain the phenomenon he discusses as well.
5   Kaplan & Norton (1992: 71-79).
6   Kotler, Gregor & Rogers III (1977: 25-43). Schuchman (1959: 11-19).

PART ONE

Managing Purchase and Consumption Behaviour

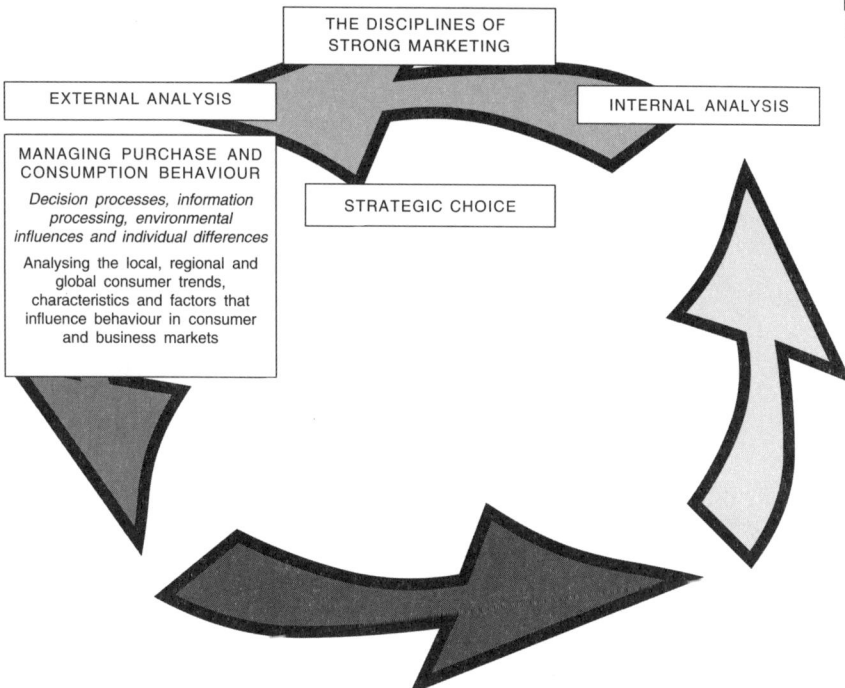

THE DISCIPLINES OF
STRONG MARKETING

EXTERNAL ANALYSIS

INTERNAL ANALYSIS

MANAGING PURCHASE AND
CONSUMPTION BEHAVIOUR

*Decision processes, information
processing, environmental
influences and individual differences*

Analysing the local, regional and
global consumer trends,
characteristics and factors that
influence behaviour in consumer
and business markets

STRATEGIC CHOICE

1 Managing Purchase and Consumption Behaviour

There is no substitute for understanding customers

Most executives spend their time trying to answer basic questions: How can we grow the market? How can we grow our market share? How can we earn higher margins? How can we get more business from every customer? These may be the most important questions any manager ponders. Managers who practise the new marketing realise the answers to these questions are beyond the reach of companies that stop managing when the order is delivered. It is not enough to understand buyer behaviour and the purchase environment. Emphasis is shifting rapidly to understanding consumption.

Group Africa of the Amavulandlela[1], a promotional services and communications company founded with a commitment to authentic African roots, is a company that understands consumption. Group Africa has become an integrated communications company communicating face-to-face with over three million South Africans every month and learning about consumption preferences in those interactions. The company staff mirror the racial and geographic mixture of South Africa and operate in deep rural areas. With an almost evangelical bent, Group Africa espouses the commercial value of doing what is African and doing it well. The results — a compound growth rate exceeding 60 per cent annually for over ten years[2].

Across the world from Africa, 200 American males of all descriptions lather up at Gillette's plant in South Boston every working day to evaluate new razor designs for blade sharpness, smoothness and handling ease, while women do the same in nearby shower rooms[3]. Can there be so much to learn about something so basic as shaving? Warren Buffet and other Gillette investors apparently think so — the share trades at a price to earnings multiple of 33 and boasts a return on sales second only to Coca-Cola. Gillette markets a number of brand names that consumers know and trust, such as Parker Pen, Braun consumer electronics, Oral-B and Right Guard. Every one of these businesses is number one in its industry worldwide and every one rests on a sound technological base.

3

Group Africa and Gillette demonstrate a wisdom of the new day: product innovation delivers fleeting competitive advantage when compared to the sustainable advantages derived from understanding consumption. The best technology and resources are not enough. The power of market leadership in the distribution channel is not enough. There is no substitute for understanding customers in periods of rapid social change. Companies must develop a burning passion for managing the purchase and consumption environment.

Part 1 of this book includes chapters on purchase decisions and environmental forces which shape consumer decisions. These chapters summarise the strategic implications of over 30 years of research into why people and companies choose and use products. This part of the book constitutes the basic building block of the marketing concept – knowing your customers.

ARE WE REVISITING THE SIXTIES?

Marketing entered its childhood during another period of rapid social change – the 1960s – when managers believed they needed new theories and models to understand the environment and to craft effective strategies. Read a marketing text from the early 1960s and you may be surprised about how much of the content remains relevant today[4], especially in the IOR. You may also notice a similar disquiet amongst marketers concerning the future.

There are many parallels between the 1960s and the 1990s. Change characterised both periods. Political realignments (and European reconstruction) pressurised existing patterns of trade. Although the marketing concept was not a new idea (South African economist, William Hutt, referred to consumer sovereignty first in the early 1930s), post-war consumption was booming and the 1960s were ripe for the emergence of a new science. The subsequent leap forward in the 1960s is paralleled in the emergence of the new digital technologies of the present. The rapid social change of the 1960s encouraged pioneering. Behaviourists such as Katona[5] had already begun exploring consumer behaviour with psychological research tools during the 1950s. Katona was championing an eclectic blend of psychology and economics. Ernest Dichter's motivational research theories became very popular with marketers[6]. New York's McCann-Erickson advertising agency boasted a five-person motivational research department by 1955[7]. Marketers were able to advance quickly by 'borrowing' but they learned some important lessons about using tools developed for other scientific applications. For instance, Franklin B. Evans concluded that personality had little influence on brand choice when he used a borrowed standardised personality instrument to predict American consumers' choice of Ford or Chevrolet vehicles[8]. Researchers today know that Evans erred by using a psychology tool to infer customer behaviour for which it was not designed.

Pioneering always awakens fear of the unknown in some people. Fears today that marketers will use data to invade and control consumers' lives also have a parallel in the 1960s when people suspected psychological manipulation by big business. First Packard[9] frightened consumers and government officials around the world with tales of hidden meaning and stereotypical class behaviour. Then social psychologist James Vicary fanned the flames further by reporting increased sales of popcorn (+52 per cent) and Coca-Cola (+18 per cent) when a subliminal message was flashed to consumers on the big screen. Although Vicary later confessed to faking the results in order to shore up his flagging research business, and even though his results were never replicated[10], legislation against subliminal persuasion was implemented in many countries and remains in statutes regulating advertising to this day in many IOR countries. The contemporary legislative debate about data privacy, data ownership and information usage is certain to continue and to result in every bit as much legislation as the subliminal persuasion debate created in the 1960s.

Summary

The new environment challenges marketing to take another great leap forward. Again today, we sometimes have more questions than answers. The emerging developing economies, slow growth in the developed world, easy access to information and technology and changing influence of social institutions, present pressing questions to business leaders that require a competent understanding of purchase and consumption behaviour.

Marketers will not succeed in this challenging environment unless the new tools give them greater insight into consumer needs and preferences. Managing purchase and consumption behaviour has become the most important managerial activity in any enterprise. The next chapters explore the nature of consumer decision making and the influences that shape consumer behaviour.

ENDNOTES

1 Amavulandlela is a Zulu word for pathfinders.
2 Boon (1996).
3 Grant (1996: 133-135).
4 For a good example of books of the time, see Holloway & Hancock (1968). Today's most popular marketing texts often trace their roots to that time. These include Engel, Kollat & Blackwell (1968); Kotler (1967); McCarthy (1960).
5 Katona (1951).
6 Dichter (1964).
7 Packard (1957: 31).
8 Evans (1959: 340-369).
9 Packard (1957; 1959).
10 See Engel, Warshaw & Kinnear (1991: 106). Weir (1984: 46).

2 | The Two Types of Purchase Decisions

Understanding involvement is a key to winning strategies in IOR marketing

Most IOR marketing strategies focus activities on pricing competitively, appealing to basic needs, gathering distribution and enticing purchase. There seems to be less recognition that strong marketing must influence consumption behaviour and shape perceptions of satisfaction after the purchase (encouraging future purchases). Many companies do not analyse and record with any sophistication what they learn about the environment and consumer response to the marketing mix over the years. Not enough companies take the time to distil experiences into simple principles of lasting value. Such companies deny themselves the benefits of disciplined learning.

THE BENEFITS OF DISCIPLINED LEARNING

Stew Leonard is a man who became known for many sayings of the following kind in the 1990s: Eye-level is buy level. Retail is detail. Pile 'em high and watch 'em buy. Winners focus, losers spread.

Stew Leonard's Dairy Store[1], situated in a suburban location on America's eastern seaboard, became one of the largest retail food outlets of its type. Carrying only 800 stock control units (SKUs)[2] instead of the traditional 15 000-20 000, Stew Leonard's sales exceed $100 million every year – enough to make his the world's largest dairy store. Limiting his product line to only specific items ensures that Leonard's customers must shop at a competitor's outlet every week. Still, the business continues to grow.

The Dairy Store is often cited for the tall stone tablets outside its front door announcing, Rule 1: The customer is always right. Rule 2: If the customer is ever wrong, reread Rule 1! Animated 3D figures throughout the store sing greetings to customers and kids get a thrill out of the extensive play area, the petting zoo or the interactive cow that moos on demand.

Stew Leonard's is a perfect example of what can happen when a retailer understands consumer behaviour.

TWO TYPES OF DECISION MAKING

Every person makes decisions based on the influence of individual characteristics (such as age, wealth, experience, personal values and attitudes), and the
influence of environmental factors (such as family, reference groups, social
values or culture). These differences affect the type of decision process the
individual acts out.

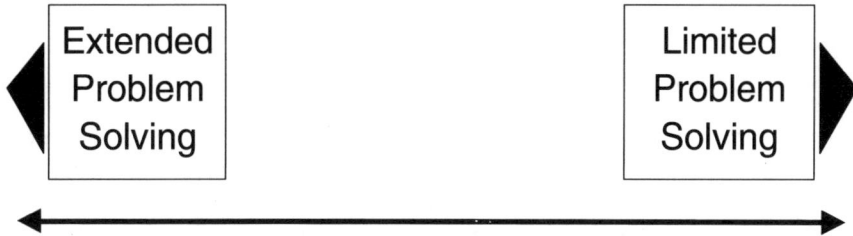

Figure 2.1 *The EPS–LPS continuum showing the two types of decision making*

BUYING FRUIT AND VEGETABLES OR A HOME COMPUTER?

Ever had the choice of four soggy tomatoes at the supermarket? Almost
everyone in the business understands that 80 per cent of supermarket sales
come from 20 per cent of the items.

Leonard's strategy reflects his mental model of consumers. He believes that
focusing exclusively on a small product range allows him to build larger displays
that offer wider choice and better prices for each item. He thinks that many
consumers consider fruit and vegetable quality to be very important.

Recognising that grocery shoppers prefer merchants who cut out the frills
and keep it simple, he also recognises the need for entertainment and diversion
for the small children of his main customers — mothers. He knows that grocery
shoppers do not go through the same kind of rigorous decision process that they
might go through when buying a home computer or motor car. Somewhere, at
the heart of his strategy, is the belief that the quality of the shopping experience
is important to consumers.

American retail economics discourages hypermarkets[3], South African retail
economics does not. Responding to very different environmental factors but
many of the same consumer preferences, South Africa's Pick 'n Pay
Hypermarkets find success by selling more items, not less. Pick 'n Pay
Hypermarkets respond to a similar desire for selection by building huge
displays, but they also recognise the desire of South Africans to buy a wider
range of products at a specific outlet. However, some lessons appear to
transcend nationality. Despite working for a much larger chain than Stew
Leonard's, Pick 'n Pay managers have a universal appreciation of good fruit and

vegetable marketing, honed during an extended stint as a fruit and vegetable section manager during training and regulated by strict procedures.

Now consider the purchase of a home computer. How would you measure quality? What factors would you consider? Would a three-year guarantee be important? Where would you look for information about computers? Would you consult a knowledgeable friend?

Home computers and weekly food shopping are good examples of the two types of decision making shown in Figure 2.1 (page 7):

1. extended problem solving (EPS) and

2. limited problem solving (LPS).

EPS and LPS can be thought of as the extremes of a continuum. What type of decision process are consumers active in your product categories acting out? Judith Zaichkowsky's measuring tool should help you decide (see Figure 2.2). You may wish to customise the survey by adding factors such as importance to the family or significance to tribes or clans, if these are appropriate to your market.

EXTENDED PROBLEM SOLVING

It is easy to believe that most consumers contemplating the purchase of a personal computer for business use in the home would score above 100 on Zaichkowsky's scale. In addition to wasting money, buying the wrong computer wastes time and lowers productivity during the computer's ongoing use (if it can be used at all). These outcomes increase the perceived risk that consumers feel at the time of purchase. The importance and salience of the decision are high. Buyers need more information and they search extensively for it. This example demonstrates the importance of understanding involvement[4]. Consumers are said to be involved when they feel a particular product is important in their life. Products seen by others, products related to values and culture, products associated with social class or wealth, products with aspirational brand names – these are the types of products likely to engender high involvement.

High involvement is the first clue that a computer purchase is probably an EPS situation for many consumers. However, you should answer three more questions before characterising the purchase of a personal computer for business use in the home as an EPS purchase for most consumers.

- Is the consumer choosing between product alternatives which (s)he believes are significantly different?

- Does the consumer have adequate time to choose between alternatives without feeling pressure to make a decision before (s)he is ready?

- Is this an irregular purchase? In other words, is there evidence that this is not a habitual or routine purchase and that a similar purchase was not made recently?

Every time your consumers answer yes to one of these questions, you should gain more confidence that those consumers experience extended problem solving in your purchase category.

Consider each of the following descriptive terms. You will note that they are opposites. If you have evidence that consumers feel your product is closely related to the descriptive word, then check the box closest to that word. If you think that the descriptive word is quite closely related to one or the other descriptive word (but not extremely), then check the next closest box to the middle of the scale. If you think the descriptive word is only slightly related to your product, then check the box next to the middle box that is closest to the descriptive word. If you think there is no relation between the descriptive word and your product in the consumer's mind, then check the middle box:

important	□ □ □ □ □ □ □	unimportant*
of no concern	□ □ □ □ □ □ □	of concern to me
irrelevant	□ □ □ □ □ □ □	relevant
means a lot to me	□ □ □ □ □ □ □	means nothing to me*
useless	□ □ □ □ □ □ □	useful
valuable	□ □ □ □ □ □ □	worthless*
trivial	□ □ □ □ □ □ □	fundamental
beneficial	□ □ □ □ □ □ □	not beneficial*
matters to me	□ □ □ □ □ □ □	doesn't matter*
uninterested	□ □ □ □ □ □ □	interested
significant	□ □ □ □ □ □ □	insignificant*
vital	□ □ □ □ □ □ □	superfluous*
boring	□ □ □ □ □ □ □	interesting
unexciting	□ □ □ □ □ □ □	exciting
appealing	□ □ □ □ □ □ □	unappealing*
mundane	□ □ □ □ □ □ □	fascinating
essential	□ □ □ □ □ □ □	nonessential*
undesirable	□ □ □ □ □ □ □	desirable
wanted	□ □ □ □ □ □ □	unwanted*
not needed	□ □ □ □ □ □ □	needed

Now you are ready to arrive at a measure of consumer involvement in your product. Start from the left and score each box from 1 to 7. Where the descriptive word on the right is followed by a *, score the boxes in reverse order, that is, start from the left and score from 7 to 1. Add up the total score which should be between 20 and 140. The higher the score, the higher the involvement. When you complete the exercise, ask some consumers to complete the inventory. The results may surprise you!

Figure 2.2 *Zaichkowsky's personal involvement inventory* [5]

LIMITED PROBLEM SOLVING

In EPS, consumers are likely to process actively at every decision stage shown in the Engel, Blackwell and Miniard (EBM) model (Figure 2.3, page 13).Consider most of the purchases you made in the last week outside your work. Would your score on the Zaichkowsky scale exceed 70 points in many categories? Most people report that their score would not (and research showing that most product categories do not present consumers with an EPS situation supports this). LPS is very different to EPS.

Consider the grocery shoppers at Stew Leonard's or your local supermarket chain. What is the worst that can happen when a typical shopper buys tomatoes that very soon turn rotten? It depends. Shoppers with higher levels of disposable income will feel the loss of a small amount of money and may have to change meal plans. Risk is relatively low. The importance and salience of the decision is low. Buyers feel they know what they need to know about tomatoes most of the time. They do not need more or feel the need to search for more information about tomatoes. Buyers in the lower economic strata may react very differently, feeling the loss of much-needed money, and the change of menu may lead to embarrassment in the home. Involvement is higher.

One quick cautionary note: many issues influence involvement. If the tomatoes were to be served as part of a meal marking a special occasion, such as a wedding or funeral, consumers might well enter EPS. Usage occasion is a very important situational influence on behaviour.

THE MYTH OF BRAND LOYALTY

Do consumers repeatedly buy your product? Does your management team think this makes it harder for competitors to enter your market (because yours is the 'tried and trusted brand')? Firms should expect a life-threatening surprise if they do not know the difference between habitual purchase and brand loyalty. Consider the well-established market leaders — companies that can trace purchases of their product by generations of families — that have suffered dramatic market share losses when relatively unknown competitors have launched brands into regular purchase categories. How can you be sure this will not happen to your firm?

When consumers are involved in a regular purchase category, they are much more likely to be brand loyal. Involvement can be encouraged in traditionally low involvement markets by associating the brand with deeply held values and emotions, by widening the spectrum of the total purchase and consumption experience, by expanding the shopper's product and brand knowledge and by developing relationships between consumers and brands.

Consider the brand loyalty that Johnson's Baby Powder enjoys. Mothers are more involved with their babies than anything else. Johnson's employs teams of researchers to understand the physiology of touch and the psychology of parent-child interaction so that they can associate the Johnson's brand with these deep feelings. Stew Leonard actively encourages shopper involvement by creating a fun experience. Pick 'n Pay places managers and customer care advisors on the retail floor so shoppers develop relationships with the associates at each outlet. These relationships improve Pick 'n Pay's understanding of what shoppers want and give Pick 'n Pay associates an opportunity to link the brand with local community values and to share product knowledge at the point of purchase. In each case, competitors find the going tough because involvement leads to increased brand commitment.

When consumers are not involved, brand use over a long period may be little more than habitual behaviour. Johnson's Baby Shampoo is not participating in a product category that seems very different to Johnson's Baby Powder. Nevertheless, although both products may be toiletries, the product categories differ greatly.

Can you think of a shampoo brand that evokes the emotive response of the smell of Johnson's Baby Powder? It is not likely. The average consumer has a number of shampoo formulations in the home at any one time. Although cornstarch and moisturising powders are available, there has been little support by consumers for any niche baby powder formulations and there is likely to be only one brand in the home. In comparison, hair care requirements are diverse. Shampoo manufacturers have responded with hundreds of compelling products for small niche markets. However, the niches and specialised product offerings are often too small to differentiate the brand meaningfully in the eyes of most consumers, and brands are forced to continually reinvent themselves in order to maintain share.

Some consumers are highly involved in hairstyle and haircare products. For those who are not, loyalty is probably not the driving force behind regular purchase of a shampoo brand. Instead, habit is a more logical motive.

BREAKING HABITS

Habits can be broken. Competitors find market penetration easier in stable markets characterised by habitual purchase behaviour. Concentrate on breaking habits if you are marketing a new product into a habitual purchase category. Every customer who leaves the market leader as a result of your marketing is a success, even if they move to a third brand that's not yours. Once you break the habit, chances are greater that they will come to you.

Can involvement be borrowed? Yes! Many brands under attack defend themselves with borrowed involvement. How? When Nestlé launched its baby toiletry range in South Africa in the eighties, they had a significant overall size advantage on Johnson & Johnson (J&J). Senior J&J executives quickly instructed marketing management to produce a counter-attack strategy.

The first component of the plan was designed to increase consumer loyalty to Johnson's baby products by borrowing involvement. J&J launched a major integrated marketing communications campaign and sales promotion benefiting South Africa's largest non-racial charity at the time, the National Council for Child and Family Welfare. Television, radio and press advertising, and public relations coverage was critical. Consumers 'popped out' a 20-cent coin from a 20-cent coupon at the point of sale. The 20-cent coin represented a donation to Child Welfare and it was dropped into a donation box. The coupon led to an immediate 20-cent deduction in the purchase price. The campaign linked J&J to Child Welfare's caring image, further reinforcing Johnson's baby products brand image. As consumers loaded their cupboards with J&J products at a good price that included a donation to Child Welfare, Nestlé withdrew their launch team from the field.

Whether intended or not, the campaign may have quietly drawn attention to J&J's long-standing social responsibility and cuddly baby brand images at a time in the 1980s when consumer groups' criticism of Nestlé's infant formula marketing policies in some parts of Africa were still fresh in many consumers' minds.

J&J's counter-attack strategy produced a year of record-breaking sales and market share performance across the Johnson's baby range after years of stagnant growth. J&J South Africa won its first Strategic Planning Award for J&J's best strategic planner of the year worldwide. Nestlé, one of South Africa's top consumer goods marketers, battled valiantly for distribution but eventually gave up after J&J continued their aggressive counter-attack strategy.

Charity promotions should be linked to important interests of the target market. A pet food manufacturer might consider fund-raising for facilities improvement at a local animal protection agency. Indian marketers serving Hindu or Sikh communities would be wise to consider special activities during Divali. Marketers serving the Muslim community might focus on charitable acts during Ramadan. South Africa's Pick 'n Pay supermarket chain is always involved in socially responsible projects in local communities around an outlet. Nedbank has developed a range of affinity cards that link donations to environmental, sports or other trusts[6]. ABSA offers a range of affinity cards linked to sports teams. Toiletry manufacturers often consider promotions featuring low involvement products banded to related higher involvement packs. The key is understanding when customers are being loyal and when they're just buying out of habit.

HOW CONSUMERS DECIDE

A brief introduction will set the stage for discussing the strategic implications for strong marketing presented by consumer behaviour research. Simply put, the consumer decision process follows a progression from need recognition, to search, to pre-purchase alternative evaluation, to purchase, to consumption, to post-purchase evaluation — ending with feelings of satisfaction or dissatisfaction. People are not computers and they do not think or behave like computers. Our brains are capable of analysing many more inputs than a computer and our emotions often produce irrational thoughts and behaviour. So, the various stages of this process do not always happen in a neat and ordered way.

In extended problem solving, consumers are more likely to process actively at every stage of the EBM model (Figure 2.3), and to process in the order of the model. That means they search actively for information, processing what they remember from previous exposures to information as well as marketer-dominated information (such as advertising, promotion and public relations), and other stimuli (a recommendation from a relative or a consumer magazine comparison article). Extended processing is distinguished by the evaluation of alternatives prior to purchase and consumption and by more rigorous post-purchase evaluation. In limited problem solving, consumers are likely to evaluate brands only after purchase, especially when the price is relatively low.

Environmental influences and individual differences affect the decision process. Our environment is more influential during the early stages of the decision process. Individual differences are more influential during purchase and consumption.

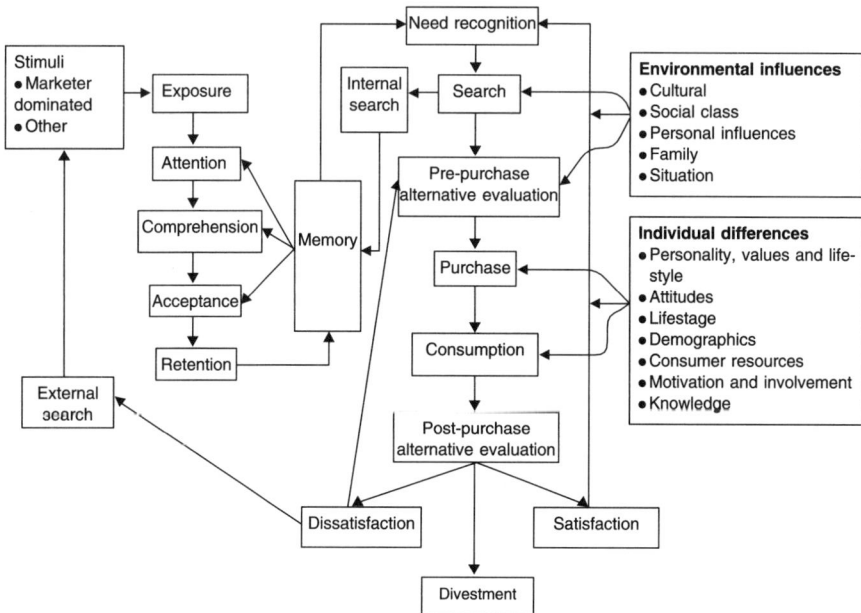

Figure 2.3 The Engel, Blackwell and Miniard (EBM) model [7]

13

Also, according to the EBM model, consumers are constantly exposed to information about products. The marketer dominates some information sources but not most. Information processing occurs when consumers are exposed to a message, give it their attention, comprehend the message, accept the message as they understand it and retain what they have understood. Astute marketers realise that this suggests five stages of understanding where something can go wrong! Consumers are more likely to process information when they are involved in a product category.

Summary

The new marketing demands that companies understand purchase and consumption behaviour. This chapter introduced the concept of problem solving and showed how consumer involvement can help marketers determine whether customers are loyal or are buying simply out of habit. Not all consumers, or segments of consumers, approach a particular product category with the same type of problem solving. Knowing how extended the consumer decision process is in a specific segment is an important first step in successful marketing strategy development. The next chapter examines how the environment influences consumer behaviour.

ENDNOTES

1 The material here is drawn from a number of sources but predominantly from an interview conducted by Paul Hawken, a well-known American business writer, as part of the Hawken, 1988 television series.
2 Each size of every thing sold in an outlet counts as one SKU.
3 See Keegan & Green (1997: 338).
4 See Engel, Blackwell, & Miniard (1995: 157-158).
5 Zaichkowsky (1985: 341-352). Other researchers have produced involvement measurement scales. Among the better known are the CIP scale: Laurent & Kapferer (1986); and the GSMI scale: Traylor & Joseph (1984). Astute marketers will work with market researchers to review as many scales as possible and test product specific beliefs in order to develop the most effective scale for a particular product.
6 An affinity card can be a debit or credit card that is linked to a third party, such as an environmental group, a sports team or a charity organisation. Usually, the bank pays a small percentage of transactions or a flat monthly fee to the third party.
7 Engel, Blackwell, & Miniard (1995: 154).

3 Environmental Forces Shaping Consumer Decisions

The environment shapes every consumer

Individual characteristics and environmental influences shape consumer behaviour. These two forces have been the objects of much consumer research. Many environmental influences and individual characteristics have been linked to brand preference, new product adoption, information processing – almost any aspect of purchase and consumption behaviour which might be of interest to managers. This chapter focuses on environmental influences on consumption and purchase behaviour.

Environmental influences consist of external forces that shape the behaviour of consumers. Although the consumer may participate in the shaping of those forces, such as the expectations of a reference group of peers, environmental influences are generally considered to be outside the direct control of the consumer. Culture, social class, personal influences, household and family influences and situation are powerful influences on every element of consumer behaviour.

CULTURE

Culture is the common values, attitudes and meaningful symbols that help individuals to interpret, communicate and evaluate as members of a society. Few regions can boast the cultural diversity that characterises the IOR. Culture influences consumer behaviour powerfully, especially in this region of multi-ethnic countries such as South Africa, and other countries where sharp differences exist concerning religious beliefs, language and other environmental influences[1].

Culture is a pervasive influence that affects the firm's internal and external publics. Organisational culture, an important research topic in recent years[2], is discussed later in this book. The discussion here concerns culture as an environmental influence on consumer behaviour outside the organisation, that is, the cultural forces influencing consumer behaviour in the marketplace. No one is completely immune to cultural influences.

Culture is everywhere. Consider the case of the distillers attempting to end the self-imposed moratorium on American liquor advertising in the electronic media that has existed since the 1940s[3]. Makers of distilled spirits are keen to reverse the consumption decline of more than 40 per cent since 1980 and they see Generation X'ers[4] as an opportunity to regain momentum and growth. TV is the most effective medium for reaching America's Generation X consumers, and a recent court case held that liquor advertisers could advertise on TV and radio, citing commercial free speech rights.

With the battle seemingly won, liquor executives quickly called an end to the moratorium. Within days, organisations such as Mothers Against Drunk Driving and the Center for Science in the Public Interest (CSPI) were mobilising against the industry. The CSPI sent out community action kits to 750 action groups across the USA. Legislators, in a rare bi-partisan show of unity, prepared a host of countermeasures that could include increased alcoholic beverage taxes, point of sale constraints and content restrictions. Attention has also focused on liquor advertisements in *Spin, Rolling Stone, Allure* and other youth-oriented print media.

Industry spokespeople suggest the furore will die down and everyone will accept the change 'once they realise there is nothing to fear'. Opponents suggest that the campaign may signal the beginning of the end for all alcohol advertising. Social values lie at the heart of culture and at the heart of this debate. Although social psychologists have been enamoured with the concept of individual and collective value types[5], recent research carried out by Schwartz in 41 countries[6] supports the organisation of seven main cultural value types. Table 3.1 (page 17) shows the cultural level value types which emerged from Schwartz' considerable international research concerning values.

Using this model, one senses immediate value differences in the liquor debate: Conservativism vs Affective Autonomy and Mastery vs Harmony. Schwartz' values present marketers with a list upon which to test consumer and brand value differences. Marketers must always be sensitive to such value priorities. Social institutions shape personal values. In Western culture, the family, religious and educational institutions play the major value-shaping roles. Western culture is a strong influence on many IOR cultures. However, IOR marketers must consider the influence of other value-shaping institutions and experiences, such as the elaborate ceremonies marking the passage into adulthood, healing ceremonies and observance of traditional African religions[7].

Successful companies doing business across cultures acknowledge and value the diversity of the market segments they approach by understanding the 'emic' and 'etic' distinctions of each culture. **Emic distinctions** mark differences within a culture. Understanding how inter-market segments differ from other local groups would be an example of emic knowledge about a market. **Etic distinctions** concern differences between cultures.

Managers must constantly question their assumptions about culture in target segments. The popular international press often suggests that American or British pop culture is becoming more universally accepted[8]. For instance, Asian countries have been quick to point out that wearing Disney clothing and listening to American pop tunes does not imply wholesale acceptance of Western culture. In fact, a growing trend towards anti-Westernism may emerge as the millennium approaches and IOR consumers begin to re-explore their cultural roots[9]. This trend is becoming especially influential in some Islamic countries.

CULTURAL-VALUE TYPES	VALUE EXAMPLES
CONSERVATIVISM	Family security, national security, respect for tradition, social order, clean, moderate, honour elders, politeness, protecting public image, reciprocation of favours, self-discipline, devout, obedient, wisdom
HARMONY	Protect the environment, unity with nature, world of beauty
EGALITARIANISM	World at peace, social justice, honest, helpful, responsible, freedom, accept my portion in life, equality, loyal
INTELLECTUAL AUTONOMY	Broadminded, creativity, courageous
AFFECTIVE AUTONOMY	A varied life, an exciting life, pleasure, enjoying life
MASTERY	Ambitious, independent, choosing my own goals, capable, daring, successful
HIERARCHY	Humble, influential, wealth, social power

Table 3.1 Single values representing Schwartz' cultural level value types

On a related note, many business authors have focused on the topic of doing business across cultures in recent years.[10] This is discussed later in this book (see Chapter 8).

SOCIAL CLASS

Many societies divide into strata or levels which separate people with similar socio-economic characteristics. People in a social class often share similar values, attitudes, interests and behaviours. Social class is a more important influence when product consumption or purchase is visible to others. Brand names that imply status or social class membership to some reference groups, such as Rolex, Billabong, Pringle, Fender, Cross Creek, Cartier, Polo, BMW, Mercedes, Marshall or Stussy, may imply nothing at all to others.

Social class is generally broken into six groups: Upper Upper, Upper Middle, Upper Lower, Lower Upper, Lower Middle, Lower Lower. The likelihood of social class membership is often measured with surveys such as the Coleman Computerised Status Index or the Nam and Powers Index[11]. Geodemographic surveys such as Experian, Claritas, Donnelley's or Equifax have become quite popular in the industrialised nations where postal codes contain as few as 15 residences, where extensive, accurate demographic information is freely available and where people migrate to relatively homogeneous neighbourhoods containing people of similar affluence. The link between neighbourhood, wealth and consumer behaviour often evaporates in IOR regions because people do not always move to neighbourhoods that are more affluent.

Marketers in developing countries must be careful when applying foreign social class models to local markets. Characteristics such as income and education are relative. A person who can read English may be considered well educated in some communities. The perceived wealth and excitement of urban life can impart much status to a coal-mine labourer returning to his rural African village. Bank tellers, bus drivers, traditional healers and truck drivers may enjoy high status in certain communities for the same reason.

PERSONAL INFLUENCES

The people in our lives help us choose and use possessions. Reference groups are people with whom we identify and interact. Reference groups can influence behaviour by playing normative, value-expressive and informational roles. Personal influence is sometimes referred to as word-of-mouth advertising but it includes much more.

The pressure for conformity and compliance is called *normative influence*. Normative influence is strongest

1. when strong normative pressures exist,

2. when social acceptance is a strong motivation and

3. when the product is conspicuous when it is purchased or consumed.

Appeals to follow fashion trends or to do the 'in-thing' are normative appeals. The breakdown of traditional society around the world has contributed to the declining importance of normative influence. However, normative influence remains strong throughout the IOR.

Sometimes the purchase of a product indicates acceptance of a group's values and norms. This is the **value-expressive** role of personal influence. Value-expressive appeals are much evident in cigarette and alcohol advertising targeted at aspiring consumers, such as teens, women and the historically disadvantaged. South African Breweries began targeting value-expressive advertising at the emerging black middle class as early as the mid-1980s. The advertisements featured multiracial friends closing out the day in their favourite pub at a time when such a scene rarely happened in South Africa. The advertisements were well liked by black consumers.

The **informational** aspect of personal influence may be the strongest. When it comes to some products, we respect the opinions of certain people around us. Sipho may know much about motor cars but we may not ask his opinion of the likely winner of the America's Cup Yacht Race.

Certain conditions increase the likelihood that consumers will seek **word-of-mouth information** to aid in a purchase or usage situation:

1. The consumer lacks sufficient information to decide. This is often true in the least developed and educated IOR segments. The product is complex or difficult to evaluate with objective criteria.

2. The person feels unable to make the decision, regardless of how much information is available. Other sources of information have low credibility with the consumer.

3. An opinion leader is readily accessible and easier/cheaper to consult than other information sources.

4. The individual has a high need for social approval.

Marketers can achieve great success by understanding how personal influence is communicated through a market segment[12]. The trickle-down theory holds that lower classes emulate the behaviour of the upper class. Thus, the upper classes are more aware and more able to afford innovations. Over time, the price of an innovation declines and the lower classes are able to participate. Some theorists question the value of the trickle-down theory because of the availability of mass media and the growing middle class. IOR marketers approaching developing market segments would be wise to consider its effects.

The multistage interaction theory holds that mass media influence opinion leaders and information seekers. Mass media interaction can influence information seekers to approach the influential for advice or to seek advice from other sources. Thus, the information seeker can be the source of information for the influential.

It seems logical that marketing strategy should focus on opinion leaders in less developed segments but that strategy should include communication strategies capable of reaching a wide spectrum of potential segment participants.

FAMILY AND HOUSEHOLD INFLUENCES

Families and other household members affect purchase and consumption behaviour in many product categories. You may find it useful to think of families as organisations or businesses. Like company staff, family members play different purchase and consumption roles. Every family is unique and families go through life cycles.

ROLES

Family members play a number of roles in family purchase behaviour. The *gatekeeper* is responsible for gathering information and initiating family communication about a proposed purchase. *Influencers* share personal opinions that influence deciders. *Deciders* make the purchase decision and decide about financing arrangements. *Purchasers* make the purchase. *Users* use the product and often act as influencers.

Family members can play one role, many roles or no roles in a specific product category or purchase decision. In traditional family structures, the elder male may be the major decider for motor car accessories, and the influencer for food purchases, but may play no role in the purchase of cleaning products. However, gender egalitarianism has growing influence and markets must be alert to changing roles. Australia, Singapore and South Africa are examples of IOR countries where women often play non-traditional roles in all phases of society, especially business.

Ever wondered why baby advertising appeals to parenting (as opposed to mothering) more often than in the past? Observe how many men are shopping for baby products in your area these days and you will understand why. The increasing impact of career women on family life has also influenced many other product markets, such as financial services. The more educated, more affluent market segments probably feel gender equality more strongly. Even where traditional family roles dominate the market, marketers should be sensitive to the changing status of the historically disadvantaged.

FAMILY LIFECYCLES

Traditional thinking suggests that adolescents leave the home, live as single adults, marry, have children, live as a more mature family, watch their children leave the home, retire, live together as a couple again, bury a spouse and then die. In many IOR societies, this model still describes life. Divorce, remarriage and the growing acceptance of alternative lifestyles such as cohabitation or homosexuality bring traditional family definitions into question in more affluent areas. Because marketing research and the academic literature use the term family lifecycle, I will use it here. Traditional family lifestages include:

- *Singles* (low earnings but higher discretionary income due to low commitments);
- *Newly-Married Couples* (purchases to set up the home, high discretionary income becoming more constrained toward end of the stage);
- *Full Nest I* (first child arrives, one parent likely to reduce or quit work, money tight);
- *Full Nest II* (youngest child now six, income increasing, likely to purchase economy size packs and family entertainment);
- *Full Nest III* (children now almost ready to leave home, income continues to increase, consumption shifting to education and luxury items);

- *Empty Nest I* (most disposable income, luxury purchases, travel and recreation increase, children gone from home);

- *Empty Nest II* (one or more retired, income more constrained, consumption shifting to health and medical, likely to move to a smaller dwelling);

- *Solitary Survivor* (consumption similar to other Empty Nest consumption but income may be higher if still working);

- *Retired Solitary Survivor* (loneliness drives participation in travel and club activities, constrained consumption).

	Young Singles	Young couples	Young parents	Distant member households	Mid-life families	Mid-life households	Older households
URBAN							
Upmarket							
Middle market							
Down market							
PERI-URBAN							
Upmarket							
Middle market							
Down market							
RURAL							
Upmarket							
Middle market							
Down market							

Table 3.2 A proposed grid for plotting family lifestage influences

It is also important to note that the concept of families taking care of their elders has almost disappeared in America and other industrialised nations. Such behaviour is still an important part of the responsibilities of life in many IOR regions.

Management Horizons, the highly rated American retail and consumer marketing consultancy, recommends the use of a modified matrix that contrasts lifestage with household buying power[13]. Table 3.2 does not include divorced households, and where divorce affects purchase and consumption, it should be included. Nevertheless, Table 3.2 portrays IOR lifestyles more accurately than the Management Horizons matrix for South African marketing by

1. recognising the differences in family purchase behaviour in urban and more traditional rural family structures;

2. the addition of a new class called *Distant Member Households*, which recognises rural or peri-urban households supported by a family member living in a separate, more urbanised setting some distance away. Distant member households may feature more than two spouses and may be in a state of transition from or to rural life. Migrant labour for agriculture and on the mines has made distant member households a significant factor in sub-Saharan Africa.

Young Singles, *Young Couples* and *Young Parents* compare with the first three lifestages above. In *Mid-life Families*, the head of household is 45 to 64 years old and children are present or supported financially by the household. *Mid-life Households* are the same except that there are no children present or financially supported. *Older Households* feature a head of household older than 65. Families and their structures are dynamic in many IOR market segments and successful marketers follow their changing nature carefully. Would your strategy differ for the various groups of consumers?

SITUATIONAL INFLUENCES

Consumers choose and use possessions within three types of situation:

1. the purchase situation,

2. the communication situation and

3. the usage situation.

Unlike most other environmental influences, marketing strategy can often influence situations.

THE PURCHASE SITUATION

Strong marketers realise that every situation has five aspects that require careful planning to ensure consumers experience each situation in a way that encourages purchase[14]. These aspects include the

- *physical surroundings* the consumer experiences, such as light level, temperature, sounds or smells;

- *social surroundings*, such as the presence or absence of other people;

- *time*, such as the time of day, time in the month, time since the last purchase, time to make a decision;

- reason, goals, objectives and object of the *task*;
- *antecedent* states the consumer brings to the situation.

Thus, a well-conceived marketing strategy will recognise task differences that suggest different needs and values (i.e. buying a computer for home use vs buying one for the office).

The purchase situation probably offers the most immediate chance of influencing purchase and consumption. For instance, Coca-Cola and South African Breweries are especially hard targets because of their dominance at the point of sale in the South African informal retail sector.

Asking the right questions often helps to shape informational content and delivery at the point of sale. Marketers need to ask probing questions about consumers that indicate the consumers' informational requirements.

- What should we be telling customers to ensure that they understand the benefits we offer?
- Who should communicate these benefits?
- Is there a technical, size or format question in the consumer's mind?
- How should we format the information — in unit prices; with or without sales or value-added tax?
- How can we communicate in a way that makes it easier for consumers to make decisions?

In retail settings, the right colours, styles, music and shop layouts can influence purchase. The behaviour of salespeople is another important factor to consider. The delicate balance between informing, influencing and closing the sale must be weighed against negative consumer perceptions of 'pushy' behaviour. Good sales-training programmes help salespeople become more sensitive to the time shoppers require to make a decision, and to shoppers' informational requirements. Good salespeople ask the right questions and listen to ascertain consumer needs.

Extending usage situations for a product is a primary way to add shareholder value to a company. Consider the remarkable story of Arm & Hammer baking soda (bicarbonate of soda in most IOR countries). Many people would consider baking soda to be a commodity product. Two decades ago, it was a minor ingredient in some baking recipes and considered to be a mature product with little chance of growth in the American market. It was not always that way — environmentally-friendly baking soda enjoyed use as a dentifrice before the development of toothpaste, and many people claimed that it had deodorising properties when dashed under the arms. Arm & Hammer's management decided to focus strategy on extending the usage situation.

The time predated the widespread adoption of reusable plastic food containers or plastic food wrap for the refrigerator. Arm & Hammer's strategy focused on a common household problem: uncovered foods in the refrigerator often pick up the flavour and scent of other foods. Onion-flavoured chocolate birthday cake was not a hit in most households!

Baking soda's mild anti-bacterial and non-toxic nature allowed Arm & Hammer to position the product as an odour destroyer. The campaign focused on convincing Americans to put an open box of baking soda in the refrigerator to absorb odours. Consumers did and sales nearly doubled. Having established an odour-fighting position, Arm & Hammer researched other odour problems. Subsequent campaigns convinced consumers to place a tablespoon of baking soda down the drain to fight odours in the kitchen sink[15].

Today, baking soda is back in the dental care market as a toothpaste ingredient, in the deodorant market as an ingredient in deodorants, body powders and women's sanitary care products, and in a host of other products.

THE COMMUNICATION SITUATION

Communication situations require careful planning, as the discussion concerning information processing later in this section shows. Choosing the right communication situation can be the difference between gaining exposure and getting lost in the clutter. The IOR offers unique communication situations that require careful planning. Consider the many IOR consumers who live from paycheque to paycheque. They shop for essentials primarily at month-end. They are a large and important market for many products. Many of these consumers listen to battery-powered portable radios and televisions. Do you think advertisements flighted in mid-month would be more likely to be heard than those flighted in the week before month-end? When would batteries be most likely to run down?

Conducive media is important to communication. Baby product advertisements generally receive more attention in baby magazines than they do in sports magazines or magazines directed at executives.

THE USAGE SITUATION

Marketers should be careful to plan strategies to take the specific benefits sought by different types of consumers in different situations into account. Constructing a matrix of consumer types and situations can be a very powerful tool to uncover unexpected interactions between market segments and specific requirements in usage situations. For instance, men might be more interested in a sun protection product that contains an insect repellent while women might seek greater moisturising benefits[16].

Summary

Strong marketing responds to the environmental influences influencing consumer behaviour. It adapts by integrating these influences into the policies, activities and other aspects of the marketing mix. Consumers experiencing strong marketing feel that the company is part of their community and part of their lives. Situations often offer an opportunity to combine sales and promotional strategies with channel partners or other non-competitive firms. The sale of computer software with personal computers is one common example of this. Purchase and consumption are also influenced by individual characteristics which offer a rich vehicle for building strong marketing and provide the topic of discussion for the next chapter.

ENDNOTES

1 McCracken has made a most meaningful contribution concerning culture and consumption in recent years. See McCracken (1986; 1988).
2 See Kotter & Heskett (1992), Schein (1992), Thomas (1991) for excellent reviews of topical issues in organisational culture and leadership.
3 Leonhardt & France (1996: 51-4).
4 Generation X refers to the children of the post-World War II baby boomers. Many X'ers realise that slowing economic population growth, an ageing population and technological advances in developing nations may make theirs the first generation to do less well than their parents. Born in the late 1970s, researchers portray X'ers as cynical and angry. Drug use, domestic violence, alcohol abuse and cigarette usage are more common among X'ers. There is little evidence to suggest that the Generation X culture is widely dispersed or influential throughout the Indian Ocean Rim. However, its influence can be felt in affluent communities such as Johannesburg's northern suburbs.
5 See Schwartz (1990) for an excellent review.
6 Schwartz & Ros (1995). Burgess, Schwartz & Blackwell (1994) explored the structure of Schwartz' values in South Africa. For a commercial application of values research in South Africa, see Burgess & Blackwell (1994). Hofstede (1984) is an alternative study which received much interest. However, Hofstede studied the values of employees of an information technology multinational in 40 countries. It is hard to imagine that his sample was representative or that his findings represent the values of nations he studied.
7 South Africa is attempting to overcome traditional Eurocentric-bias toward traditional healing. However, health care marketers have much to learn. See Berglund (1989); Hammond-Tooke (1989) for an exposure to some of the many cultural issues facing rural health care marketers in Africa.
8 Articles of this nature appear regularly. For instance, see Anonymous (1996).
9 Elliott (1996) has written a very nice summation of this trend.
10 For instance, see Lewis (1996), McCall & Warrington (1989), Trompenaars (1993).
11 Engel, Blackwell & Miniard (1995: 688-695).
12 Engel et al. (1995) See especially pages 726-727.
13 Engel et al. (1995: 753-755).
14 Belk (1975).
15 American homes often feature a garbage disposer under the kitchen sink. The appliance grinds up unwanted food that is poured into the sink drain and washed down the sewage pipes. Garbage disposers can be an especially strong source of odour during the cold North American winter when houses are closed to ventilation.
16 This example draws on Dickson (1982: 56-64).

4 | Individual Differences Shaping Consumer Decisions

Understanding individual diversity can pay off in marketing success

People are born with individual characteristics, such as wealth, health, race and gender. The environment, life experiences and maturation also shape individual characteristics. Wealth is one individual characteristic that requires no introduction to managers from any discipline. This chapter introduces a range of individual characteristics linked to purchase and consumption and proposes a new belief system model of consumer behaviour.

RESOURCES

Anna Modise had clearly had enough. Having waited over 45 minutes to deposit her monthly cheque, she flew into a fit of rage and withdrew all of her money from her account when she reached the teller. She opened an account across the street at another bank. Was it the interest rates that attracted Anna? Was it the bank's service charges? Was it the new advertising campaign? None of these. Anna's final, angry words to the teller were, 'I've got one day to shop at month-end and I'm tired of spending it in this bank because of your slow service'.

Anna is an example of what can happen when firms fail to understand and manage consumer perceptions about resources. Consumers spend more than money at the point of sale. They also spend time and the mental effort required for understanding and agreeing to the purchase. A sale is an exchange of resources of equal value and, at one time or another, we have all felt as short-changed as Anna.

WEALTH

Ohio State's Roger Blackwell delights in telling audiences about Willie Sutton, the great bank robber, who said, 'I go where the money is and I go there often'.

IOR wealth is concentrated among the top 20 per cent of the population in most countries. Consider South Africa, an average IOR country and the median country for reported per capita GNP and very near the median for human development[1]. If 20 per cent of the population enjoys 63.3 per cent of the per capita GNP, they probably enjoy a living standard comparable to the average person living in a country where per capita GNP is more evenly distributed and equal to approximately \$9 621[2]. The top 10 per cent would enjoy a standard of living equivalent to \$14 379 by the same rationale. This suggests that significant developed nation opportunities exist within the developing IOR region.

Such calculations may lack elegance but the adjusted statistics provided are more useful and accurate for comparisons of consumer wealth across transnational segments[3]. Astute IOR marketers make other adjustments. For instance, most also adjust per capita GNP for annual spending on winter clothes and central heating in most industrialised regions[4].

Understanding when people have money is also important. In segments living subsistence lifestyles, cash flows may be very seasonal, such as at harvest time. In poorer segments throughout the IOR, cash disappears quickly after month-end. In less skilled employment, people often receive wages on a daily, weekly or monthly basis, thus, if wages disappear fast after pay-day, consumers are less likely to have money just after month-end. This can impact on many elements of the marketing mix. For instance, Teljoy found that rental television advertising flighted just after month-end was most effective – possibly because consumers had fresh batteries in their radios.

Many IOR governments target poorer communities for development initiatives. For instance, Indonesia reduced the number of people living in absolute poverty to 14 per cent by targeting 20 633 less economically developed villages for direct grants to people in need. The United Nations Development Programme assisted with the project.

TIME

Anna Modise is not the first person to close a bank account or to lose her temper because of wasted time. The rapid pace of change, the emergence of globalised media and trade and other issues have brought the time pressures of the industrialised world to the region. In particular, upwardly mobile segments of the population experience severe time pressures.

Traditionally thought of as work vs play, contemporary researchers study three types of time:

- working time (time spent travelling to and from, and at work);
- non-discretionary time (time spent doing the things that have to be done outside the workplace);

- leisure time (time spent watching television, listening to radio, attending burial society meetings and sporting events, going on vacation or whatever one wishes).

The advent of the multiple-income household has a major influence on the timestyles[5] of the more educated economic strata as people have less leisure time and spend more time shopping, cleaning and taking care of other non-discretionary activities. Working time does not appear to be declining appreciably for many IOR segments. Even where it is declining, non-discretionary time demands make life more hectic.

Consumers with little leisure time are potential targets for *time-saving goods*, i.e. goods that save time in use, in the use of other products or in installation, for example, convenience food products, prefabricated products and pre-loaded computer software packages.

Time-using goods such as television, radio, burial society meetings and sporting events provide activity or diversion during leisure times. Vacation, holiday and travel are important opportunities for international trade in the IOR.

Travel and tourism marketers constantly monitor industrialised nation consumer timestyles for marketing opportunities. Segments with lots of leisure time often possess considerable financial wealth that they enjoy spending on time-using goods such as travel. In the IOR, time-wealthy consumers are often financially impoverished, but may well be targets for appropriately priced time-using products.

Foreign aid workers often express amazement about rural communities which ignore new, modern piped-water schemes to go to a local stream to manually collect water and wash clothes. Many people in the lower socio-economic IOR segments have plenty of leisure time on their hands, and collecting water often presents a good chance for social contact and relief from boredom.

Marketers need to be conscious that social pressures often require time to be spent on activities that could be done faster if desired. For instance, in the sub-Sahara, the amount of time spent preparing meals such as mealie meal is often taken as a sign of one's love and caring for the family. The unemployed and under-employed represent a large proportion of the population. Convenience products are not likely to do well in such segments.

COGNITIVE EFFORT

The Human Development Index is an overall statistic that allows the comparison of human development across borders. It may also be an indicator of cognitive-processing abilities. The index comprises three basic measures: longevity (life expectancy), knowledge (adult literacy and mean school years) and standard of living (per capita GNP measured for purchasing power parity)[6].

As Table 4.1 shows, human development does not always correlate with per capita GNP.

COUNTRY	PER CAPITA GNP (PPP) 1994	WEALTH HELD BY		HUMAN DEVELOPMENT INDEX RANK (174 TOTAL COUNTRIES)
		TOP 10% IN 1994	TOP 20% IN 1994	
AUSTRALIA	19 285	25.8	42.2	14
SINGAPORE	20 987	33.5	48.9	26
BAHRAIN	15 321	–	–	43
UNITED ARAB EMIRATES	16 000	–	–	44
KUWAIT	21 875	–	–	53
QATAR	18 403	–	–	55
THAILAND	7 104	37.1	52.7	59
MALAYSIA	8 865	37.9	53.7	60
MAURITIUS	13 172	–	–	61
IRAN	5 766	–	–	70
OMAN	10 078	–	–	88
SOUTH AFRICA	4 291	47.3	63.3	90
SRI LANKA	3 277	25.2	39.3	91
INDONESIA	3 740	25.6	40.7	99
SWAZILAND	2 821	–	–	114
ZIMBABWE	2 196	46.9	62.3	129
MYANMAR	1 051	–	–	131
KENYA	1 404	47.7	62.1	134
LESOTHO	1 109	43.4	60.1	137
INDIA	1 348	28.4	42.6	138
PAKISTAN	2 154	25.2	39.7	139
BANGLADESH	1 331	23.7	37.9	144
YEMEN	805	–	–	148
TANZANIA	656	30.2	45.4	149
MADAGASCAR	694	34.9	50.0	152
MOZAMBIQUE	986	–	–	166
BURUNDI	698	–	–	169
ETHIOPIA	427	–	–	170
SOMALIA	–	–	–	–
AVERAGE OF REPORTED VALUES	6 261	32.55	47.7	101

Table 4.1 *Selected indicators of human development for IOR countries (1997)*[7]

It can be difficult to adapt marketing strategy to the basic differences underlying human development, such as in literacy, numeracy and cognitive ability. In work and leisure, IOR executives interact with well-educated people. This isolates managers from the influences felt by the poorer consumers who constitute their markets. The nature of this separation goes beyond race and culture. It finds its genesis in the differences of education, wealth and access to resources in daily life experience. When people from all economic strata comprise management teams, and all associates have input into strategy development, such isolation need not impede consumer understanding. This points to the wisdom of Tom Peters' admonishment to managers to get out from behind the desk and interact with the market in daily life.

Focusing cognitive effort is called attention (see also page 54). Marketing strategy must ensure that the nature of marketing communication does not exceed the capacity of the listener. It is difficult for many marketers to understand that '25 per cent off' may not be fully understood by many innumerate consumers in the market. Offers should stick to the basics when targeted at the mass market in many IOR regions. 'Free', 'lowest price this year' and 'save R2.10', often constitute better advertising copy than '25 per cent off'.

THE BELIEF SYSTEM: VALUES, LIFESTYLE & PERSONALITY

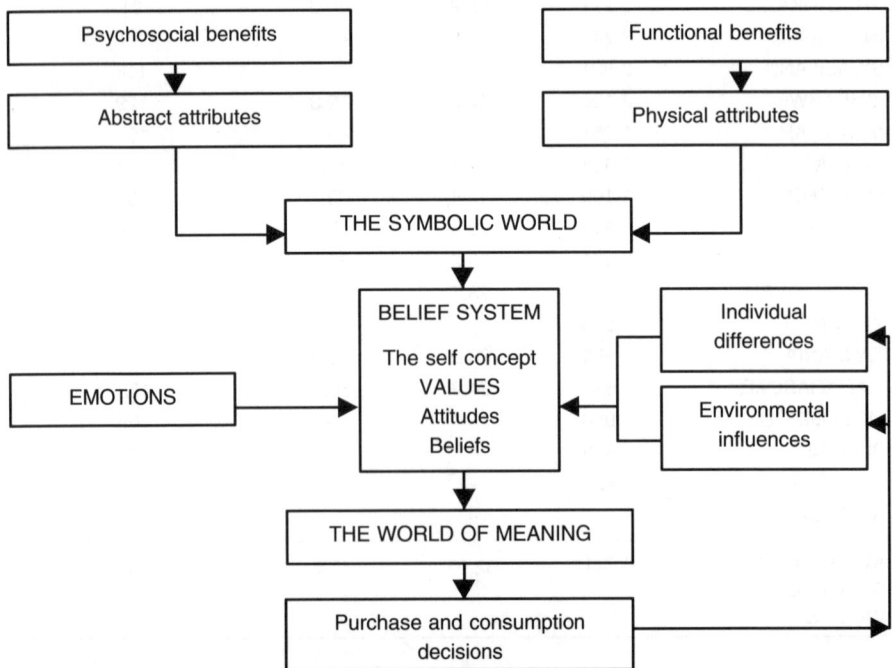

Figure 4.1 *A belief system model of consumer behaviour*

Understand a person's belief system and you have all the knowledge you need to create an especially strong product offer. The belief system includes personal values, attitudes and brand-specific beliefs. Values are included or implied in most psychological theories and have been a hot topic for consumer research [8]. The next few pages discuss some of the findings from this exciting research.

Consumer behaviour research concerning personal values has been influenced most by Rokeach[9]. Rokeach defined values as core elements of the human belief system which includes the end-states for which people strive (such as equality, a comfortable life and self-respect) and the modes of conduct they employ to achieve those end-states (such as ambition, logic, love and honesty). Although Rokeach believed that end-states and modes of conduct represented two types of values, research by Schwartz [10] has now diminished the importance of this notion and called the existence of this distinction into question.

What is a personal value and why are personal values so important to strategy development?

A personal value is a specific kind of belief that transcends objects or events. The belief that race, class or gender discrimination is wrong is an attitude. Value importance is relative, not absolute. We learn to place more or less importance on a value through experience, through growing more mature and through social influence. The relative importance of personal values can change, depending on the situation. The importance of equality might be felt very strongly when observing another person being unfairly discriminated against. It might be less strongly felt when dishing out your favourite pudding to others at the end of a meal.

Our values tell us what 'is right' and what we 'ought to do'. They give us our sense of the good life. They tell us what is wrong.

Rokeach[11] suggested that we all possess the same small number of values but hold them in differing degrees of importance. Values transcend objects and events. The importance of values can be traced to individual differences and environmental influences. Values are the cognitive representation and transformation of needs. They are organised in the belief system ready to be consulted when forming an attitude toward a product, brand or event.

People have thousands of attitudes. Attitudes toward marketing mix elements can often be predicted from a thorough understanding of a target segment's values. Values probably number less than 75, and only two or three are activated in a particular decision on average. This small number of values makes values research quite appealing to marketers.

UNDERSTANDING THE SYMBOLIC WORLD OF THE CONSUMER

Consumers perceive physical and psychosocial aspects of the world around them – what I call the symbolic world – as seen in Figure 4.1 (page 30).

Consider a product-market – motor cars for example. A Ford and a BMW may each have similar physical attributes, such as four doors, an ABS braking system, a sunroof and leather seats, that deliver similar functional benefits such as a smooth ride, fast stopping and a durable and luxurious seating compartment. Yet, a host of abstract attributes ensures that the cars remain differentiated in the consumer's mind.

Anna Modise may believe a BMW is a German-made luxury sports car implying psychosocial benefits of success, impeccable styling, safe engineering, status and desirability. To Anna, Ford is an American-made family car implying durability, rural ruggedness and economy. You may perceive these cars very differently but, to Anna, this is the nature of the symbolic world in which she lives. Anna's perceptions are Anna's reality. Every company must appeal to Anna within the context of her reality.

Beliefs about products and brand are attitudes, not values. Much values research focuses on linking values, attitudes and other beliefs[12].

Laddering is an especially useful methodology for exploring the consumer's perception of the symbolic world that encourages researchers to explore the linkages of values, attitudes and product features and benefits[13]. A researcher performing a laddering analysis would guide Anna to consider her brand-specific beliefs, her attitudes and her values. As Anna tells you how she feels about each brand, she reaches deeper and deeper into her symbolic world. Each recounted perception is constructed from the bits and pieces of sensual information recalled from her memory[14]. Many factors influence Anna's ability to remember and relay her perceptions. She may feel more definite about less central beliefs, describing those beliefs in more absolute terms than the values that she recalls. However, her attitudes and other less centrally held beliefs change more quickly than values and she may report them differently tomorrow with the same degree of commitment.

As Anna probes more deeply into her belief system, she enters a world of symbols and metaphors where it is harder to report self-perceptions accurately. This is because Anna is verbalising the constructed combination of remembered sights, sounds and other senses. These cognitive structures do not always fit neatly into words when she tells the researcher how she feels about each brand. She may also recall other sensual information that would change the way she described her feelings, depending on her mood and other factors she is experiencing at the time, such as stress or tiredness.

We do not know many things about the human mind but we know it does not operate with the clinical preciseness of a computer. We also know that market segments are generalisations into which no one fits exactly. One should always realise that research revealing 'eight types of bread users', or the 'seven emerging segments' may not be relevant to every market. One should always be suspicious of researchers who talk about consumers or their beliefs as if they are precise, highly rational or unchangeable.

CHANGING CONSUMER BELIEFS

Values, attitudes and brand-specific beliefs are very different kinds of beliefs operating in a hierarchical system. The self-concept and deeply-held needs are often held at a level beyond the awareness of many consumers. Values transform these often subconscious cognitive structures and act as the basis for affect (liking), behaviour (doing) and cognition (knowing). At each level of the system, the relative importance of a belief is learned through experience and maturation, and by the resolution of conflicts.

So how can marketers change beliefs about a brand? For instance, how should a brand be repositioned if it conflicts with deeply-held values?

The process by which value priorities change fascinated Rokeach. He found that value priorities could change when people confront inconsistent value conflicts in their belief systems. Consider a white person with racist attitudes who places much importance on the values of national security, family security and loyalty but a low importance on equality. How would such a person feel about the surviving wife of a deceased black war veteran who gave his life in order to save the lives of his all-white platoon by throwing himself on a live hand grenade? Would equality become more important to him?

Rokeach's findings indicated that it would. This example brings the low importance of equality felt by the person with racist attitudes into conflict with his admiration for a man of a different race who also placed high importance on national security and loyalty. The situation immediately brings the low importance placed on equality into conflict with these other value priorities. Rokeach induced long-term value change in people by allowing them to rank values and then compare their value priorities to those of stereotypical groups, such as racists or hippies. The example also highlights the importance of understanding the core values that underlie brand attitudes. Marketers must associate brands with desirable values and disassociate them from values of low importance.

MINING THE WORLD OF MEANING FOR COMPETITIVE ADVANTAGE

In 1992, I was fortunate to present research concerning South African personal values and consumer behaviour to the Society for Consumer Psychology sessions of the American Psychological Association's Annual Conference held in Boston, Massachusetts. This was psychology's biggest conference of the year and B. F. Skinner, the renowned Harvard academic and champion of the behavioural approach to psychology, was also on the programme – making what was to be his final public appearance before his death.

Skinner believed that the environment shaped the individual[15]. He cared little for values or other internal psychological characteristics, believing instead that anything that might exist in the individual was the product of the environment – a collection of learned predispositions capable of being shaped by manipulating the individual's environment. Skinner reasoned that it made less sense to study nebulous psychological characteristics when one could study the environmental factors that were their genesis.

Skinner strode the world stage for much of the 1950s and 1960s and his behaviourism acquired great influence. His theories about conditioning and learning continue to be core concepts in psychology texts today. From the time he gained fame for teaching pigeons to play ping-pong, Skinner spent his life advocating a world where the authorities would shape and condition everyone's behaviour by shaping their environment.

Skinner was terminally ill when he spoke and I did not meet him personally, but from a few metres away I developed more sense of the man than I ever had from his writings. The point of Skinner's short talk was that psychology should reconsider his theories. He did not want to be remembered as the man who taught pigeons to play ping-pong but rather as the man who had proposed behaviourism as an answer to the world's problems[16]. As I listened, I thought of how attention shifted to the humanistic theories of Maslow, Rogers and others in the 1970s, and of the advent of post-modernist thinking in more recent times. These movements had already robbed Skinner of the influence he once held. He was doggedly clinging to his beliefs when they wheeled the grey and frail man off the stage to a more than polite standing ovation recognising his career. As I surveyed the room three minutes later, it seemed as if Skinner had never been there.

A few months later, I was invited to Pretoria University to hear a public address by the great humanist psychologist Viktor Frankl[17]. Frankl, an Austrian Jew, survived internment in the infamous Nazi death camp at Auschwitz. The acts of individual heroism and stoic capitulation he witnessed there provided a fertile breeding ground for Frankl's rejection of Freud's will to pleasure and Adler's will to power, in favour of a new theory of personality which he based on the human will to meaning and called logotherapy. The existential school of psychology emerged from Frankl and his followers.

Once again, from metres away, I had the opportunity to experience momentarily the gestalt of a great psychologist. His body frail, bent and nearly broken by the life he had led, his eyes so bad that he hunched less than ten centimetres above the reading surface, straining to read through a magnifying glass and eyeglasses as thick as the bottom of a soft drink bottle, Frankl addressed a packed and hushed auditorium with a spirit that outshone the two bright reading lamps he used to see his notes – lights so bright that they hurt one's eyes at the back of the auditorium.

Frankl's talk concerned the will to meaning. He articulated an elegant theory built around the central theme that meaning is found in the attainment of values[18]. He shared recollections about people finding meaning in the most trivial aspects of life at Auschwitz, such as attaining independence by feeding or cleaning themselves. Frankl acknowledged the importance of the environment without ignoring the importance of individual differences. He talked about confronting his utter loss of meaning when Nazi authorities found and destroyed the scraps of paper upon which he had written his original concepts of logotherapy just days before the camp was liberated, as he learned later.

Watching Frankl was exhilarating and the auditorium was alive with energy. The vibrancy remained long after Frankl departed the stage. I stayed afterward to meet Frankl, to touch him very briefly, as did many others. I was surprised to find recently that Frankl continues to be an active contributor to psychology in 1996 at 91 years of age – a living monument to the futility of racism.

These two brief encounters stand in my memory as defining moments for my own beliefs about the nature of consumer behaviour.

One does not need to conduct expensive marketing research in order to begin understanding how a product or brand helps consumers to achieve meaning in life. However, there is little doubt that mining the world of meaning for comprehensive competitive advantage requires substantial spadework, and that an understanding of the intricacies of marketing research can unlock information capable of providing lasting competitive advantage.

LINKING BRANDS, MEANING AND VALUES: METHODOLOGIES

Thus, as Figure 4.1 (page 30) shows, the belief system translates symbolic world stimuli into meaningful thoughts and motives. The world of meaning answers questions such as, 'Is this the brand for me?', 'Is this the type of product I should use?', or, 'Is this really worth this much money?'.

If one accepts that meaning is the attainment of values, then laddering methodologies produce rich data to interpret and model consumer meaning systems. Thus, by modelling symbolic world relationships, laddering suggests links between product attributes, consequences and values that are of relevance to consumers. More directly put, laddering identifies values that consumers may be fulfilling when they use a product.

Asking consumers to associate values with brands may provide interesting and useful but less detailed information about values and brands.

Laddering and other means-end analyses provide information about specific values activated by brand and product associations. However, these techniques do not establish the importance of one value to another or explore the nature of value priorities to consumers that are not related to the research at hand. Such research questions are normally explored using standardised values scales, such as the Schwartz Value Survey, which have been tested for reliability and validity[19].

Researchers typically use a standardised values scale in the following way. A random sample is drawn from the target population and respondents complete the values scale and an additional battery of awareness, attitude and usage statements about the brand[20]. Respondents are partitioned into value segments based on their responses to the values scale, using cluster analysis or another technique. The value segments are then used as a classifying variable, and the battery of awareness, attitude and usage questions is featured in most questionnaires, as would normally be the case with the standard battery of demographic questions. A number of appropriate data-modelling techniques, such as logistic regression or log-linear modelling, might also be used to provide a deeper understanding of overall value priorities and brand-specific information.

PERSONAL VALUE TYPES	VALUE EXAMPLES
SELF DIRECTION	Freedom, creativity, independent, choosing own goals, curious, self-respect
STIMULATION	An exciting life, a varied life, daring
HEDONISM	Pleasure, enjoying life
ACHIEVEMENT	Ambitious, influential, capable, successful, intelligent, self-respect
POWER	Social power, wealth, authority, preserving my public image, social recognition
SECURITY	National security, reciprocation of favours, family security, sense of belonging, social order, healthy, clean
CONFORMITY	Obedient, self-discipline, politeness, honouring of parents and elders
TRADITION	Respect for tradition, devout, accepting my portion in life, humble, moderate
SPIRITUALITY	A spiritual life, meaning in life, inner harmony, detachment
BENEVOLENCE	Helpful, responsible, forgiving, honest, a world at peace, loyal, mature love, true fellowship
UNIVERSALISM	Equality, unity with nature, wisdom, a world of beauty, social justice, broadminded, protecting the environment

Table 4.2 Single values representing Schwartz' individual level value types

BRAND EQUITY

One of the areas receiving a lot of attention from researchers these days is brand equity[21]. Brand equity has been measured in many ways and is often considered to be the difference between a brand's asset value and its market value. Brand equity is closely related to brand identity, another term subject to various definitions[22].

Brand identity has been measured by the perceptions of consumers toward the brand's characteristics. Researchers often find it useful to personify the brand in order to measure brand identity, for example, if Coke were a person, what would that person be like?

Brand identity is the sum of the symbolic world and meaning world associations with the brand. Brand equity is the sum of assets and liabilities that add or detract from the consumer's valuation of the brand during purchase and consumption. The assets comprising brand equity include brand loyalty, brand awareness, perceived quality, brand associations and other proprietary brand assets[23]. We will return to the management of brand equity in Chapter 10.

LIFESTYLE

Personal values come alive in consumer lifestyles. Lifestyles are the patterns in which people choose and use possessions and spend their time. Research measuring lifestyles generally measures a target population's psychographics, that is, their activities, interests and opinions. The analysis of psychographic statements can provide useful market segmentation information. Lifestyle has much influence in marketing strategy as can be witnessed by the advent of affinity credit cards, the content of awards in most loyalty programmes and the increasing value of sports sponsorship.

Many research firms offer commercialised values and lifestyle segmentation schemes, such as the Stanford Research Institute's (SRI) Values and Lifestyles Study (VALS)[24] and VALS2, or Market Research Africa's Sociomonitor. Such programmes provide rich descriptions of generic segments. Many companies claim to have discovered valuable insights from such research.

Merrill Lynch changed brand positioning as a result of a VALS analysis. The research revealed that Merrill's advertising, featuring a charging herd of bulls and the slogan 'Bullish on America', was incompatible with the upwardly mobile and individualistic segment Merrill wished to attract. A change to a lone bull emerging from the herd and to the slogan 'A breed apart' yielded much-improved sales.

Generic lifestyle segmentation schemes are controversial and should be used with caution. Commercial research companies often do not provide enough detailed information about the research behind their segmentation scheme to allow users to evaluate it, often citing the need to protect proprietary findings. Academic researchers are often critical of such research and suspect that poor reliability and validity may be the real reasons behind the failure to disclose basic information about the research.

Consider the response of academic researchers to VALS and the subsequent re-launch of VALS2 after Mitchell and SRI failed to answer basic questions about the research. Although Mitchell claimed to measure values, he equated values with attitudes, behaviours and other beliefs that are not values[25]. Researchers questioned the rationale behind reporting only 87 of the 'over 800' questions asked in the VALS survey[26]. They wondered why Mitchell didn't indicate exactly how many statements were tested, exactly how many respondents completed the survey, how many failed to complete it because of its length or the statistical significance for the reported results. After all, 40 questions would appear to be significant, by chance anyway at a .05 level of confidence, even if no statistical difference existed. How could a survey asking only nine value statements and demographic questions (List of Values) predict brand choice better than VALS? Why doesn't Mitchell report adequate validity and reliability information?

Thus, although expensive generic segmentation schemes may provide results that appear useful, it is possible that superior results could have been achieved at a lower cost using a simple values scale.

Companies would be wise to use the new geodemographic segmentation schemes with the same level of caution. Geodemographic information linked to lifestyle information has become very popular these days. Among others, CCN, Claritas, Donnelly's, Equifax and others link individual characteristics to specific neighbourhood information. These schemes offer an advantage over many segmentation concepts: prospects can be identified. Unfortunately, these programmes often suffer from the same problems as other lifestyle schemes. For instance, geodemographic segmentation programmes work well in developed nations where postcodes refer to as few as 15 homes, and where population growth and migration behaviour is more stable. The lack of such highly detailed information in IOR countries may present a special challenge, and these programmes should be used with caution subject to proof about reliability, validity and utility in the product class being segmented. Results should be compared against other segmentation methods where possible.

PERSONALITY

Personality is our learned predisposition to respond to the world around us. It describes the way other people experience our value priorities and us. Our own belief system influences the way we perceive other personalities. A person who is seen to be 'willing to stand up for what he believes' may be viewed as 'arrogant, combative and inconsiderate' by others.

Although the personality literature is rich and many research scales have been developed for measuring personality [27], personality scales have not been designed for consumer research and personality has not been a particularly useful tool for predicting consumer behaviour or segmenting markets [28]. The trait-factor approach to psychology was influential in the late 1960s and early 1970s but it has been much maligned and is no longer a central concept in influential consumer behaviour research. Nevertheless, some valuable personality research does emerge. Research concerning the personality variable *need for cognition* or tendency to enjoy thinking, has revealed interesting differences in the response to advertising [29].

However, personality does retain much influence in the area of product positioning. Brand personality refers to the characterisation of the brand in the consumer's mind. People answering our earlier question about the personification of Coca-Cola might highlight qualities such as light, young, exciting and fun. These qualities are the result of years of experience with the Coke brand and Coke's branded communication strategies. Characterisation may be related to physical or abstract attributes. Nevertheless, if people relate to brands in a similar way to the way they relate to people, as many advertising executives suggest, then it makes sense to think of personality as an entirely different aspect of the brand.

KNOWLEDGE AND ATTITUDES

Attitudes have dominated research concerning individual differences. Usage and Attitude studies (U&A studies, also called AAU or Awareness, Attitude and Usage Studies), are probably the most popular ad-hoc research studies in IOR marketing.

Two types of attitudes have been most influential:

1. attitude toward the brand and

2. attitude toward company communications.

Knowledge is generally probed to discover the unaided and aided awareness of products, brands and their uses. Unaided awareness is measured by asking consumers to name products and brands without the benefit of any aid from the researcher. Many people believe that the product and brands mentioned in unaided awareness constitute a consideration set of brands from which consumers are likely to choose when contemplating purchase (discussed in more detail in the next chapter). Aided awareness is measured by asking consumers about products and brands while providing them with a list from which to choose.

Taking reports of consumer knowledge at face value can be a dangerous thing. In some cultures, respondents believe that it is rude to leave a question unanswered or that the failure to answer reflects on the interviewer's evaluation of the respondent's intelligence. 'I can answer any question' bias is a serious consideration in cross-cultural research[30].

It's surprising that consumers are willing to interrupt their lives to share their opinions when they often have little to gain immediately from the exercise. Some of the opinions they share can be even more surprising. For example, there are numerous reports of American respondents providing opinions on detailed questions about issues such as the 'Non-Metallic Metals Act', the 'Green Bottle Act' and 'the new TV programme, Space Doctor.' The answers given seem well-reasoned enough. Unfortunately for the respondents, the 'Non-Metallic Metals Act', the 'Green Bottle Act' and the 'Space Doctor' did not really exist – they were created to see if respondents made up opinions about things when interviewed[31].

Such bias can extend to professionals, as well. Over 96 per cent of American lawyers surveyed expressed their degree of agreement to the statement, 'The National Bureau of Consumer Complaints provides an effective means for consumers who have purchased a defective product to obtain relief', when no such bureau existed[32].

Consumers can, however, provide detailed, accurate and useful information about product knowledge. It is important to understand consumer knowledge about products, where products are purchased and how products are used, and to understand the content, source and organisation of each[33]. Don't forget to consider different kinds of knowledge:

- **Declarative knowledge** can be about subjective facts, such as how much a call costs or the features of different cellular handsets. It consists of *episodic knowledge* which includes information bounded by time (i.e. when is the last time you made a call on your cellphone?), and *semantic knowledge* which contains generalised knowledge used to make sense of the world (i.e. you can use a Nokia GSM handset anywhere in the world).

- **Procedural knowledge** concerns the way things work (i.e. you can use any GSM phone anywhere in the world so long as your service provider approves your account for international roaming prior to your departure for another country).

	SOURCE	CONTENT
PRODUCT	A friend who got a nasty shock when her first bill arrived.	Network operator and service provider range of products
	Advertising and newspaper articles	How a cellphone works
		How cellular accounts operate
PURCHASE	Has seen advertisements and learned from friends	Where to buy
		When to buy
USAGE	A friend who got a nasty shock when her bill first arrived.	How to use
		When to use
		Cost of calls versus fixed wire network

Table 4.3 *Selected knowledge about cellular telephone service providers*

Consumers organise knowledge in associative mental networks. It is important to know how consumers relate various pieces of knowledge in this mental organisation. Do they think that all service providers are expensive? Or do they think that only the service providers that advertise are expensive? Do they associate your brand with unique call tariffs? Which elements of the cellular offer are most important to them and how are these linked from their perspective? How important is each element in choosing a service provider?

Organisation can be probed effectively by understanding the symbolic world relationships as perceived by the target market.

ATTITUDE TOWARD THE BRAND

Successful companies often influence consumer knowledge about brands. Knowledge can be the basis of favourable attitudes toward a brand that pay off in increased sales. Three elements of attitudes with strategic relevance have emerged from the wealth of attitude research:

1. attitude multidimensionality,

2. attribute salience, and

3. attribute importance.

Attitude Multi-dimensionality

Attitudes are multi-dimensional. Like values, they are beliefs with affective, behavioural and cognitive components. Unlike values, they are linked to objects or events. Multi-attribute models attempt to represent the impact of various attitude elements on the overall attitude toward a brand. Many multi-attribute models have been proposed and readers wishing more depth are referred to Engel, Blackwell and Miniard[34].

Attribute Salience

Perhaps the most important management implication of multi-attribute attitudinal research concerns the way consumers choose among brands. Consumers consider the salience of various brand characteristics and then rank various brands on those salient characteristics. Returning to our angry bank client, Anna Modise may assign much importance to fast service by her bank and she rates her bank poorly on this characteristic.

Attribute Importance

The major theories differ concerning the mental process whereby consumers evaluate performance. Theories suggest that brands may be rated either on a continuum or against an ideal point. There is merit to examining both approaches. Regardless of the method of arriving at an overall attitude score, the implication of multi-attribute attitudinal research is that it is not important that the brand win on every attribute consumers might evaluate. As Figure 4.2 on page 42 shows, knowledge of the importance of attributes and the firm's performance versus competitors can provide powerful strategic direction. Thus, marketing strategy may focus on changing beliefs about a brand, changing the importance of attributes or changing ideal points.

IOR marketers must remember some special conditions when contemplating attitude measurement. First, although consumers can rate or rank the importance of various attributes in almost any product category with which they are familiar, many consumers in emerging markets lack sufficient familiarity to allow consistent evaluation. Second, the nature of the research process across cultures requires careful consideration of questionnaire design, survey method and statistical analysis procedures. Even though most multi-attribute models are produce-data, appropriate for parametric statistical analysis procedures, differences in meaning and rating across cultures may suggest reliance on nonparametric techniques.

ATTRIBUTE IMPORTANCE	OUR PERFORMANCE	COMPETITOR'S PERFORMANCE	STRATEGIC IMPLICATION
HIGH	Poor	Poor	Neglected opportunity
		Good	Competitive disadvantage
	Good	Poor	Competitive advantage
		Good	Head-to-head competition
LOW	Poor	Poor	Null opportunity
		Good	False alarm
	Good	Poor	False advantage
		Good	False competition

Figure 4.2 *The simultaneous importance-performance grid*[35]

ATTITUDE TOWARD COMPANY COMMUNICATIONS

Advertising, sales promotion, public relations and other elements of the promotional mix are often employed when firms attempt to influence favourable attitudes about products. There is a wealth of research supporting the notion that the success of such campaigns often depends on the consumer's attitude toward the communication itself.

There is also evidence that advertising which is not liked can be effective. For instance, South African furniture retailer Morkel's ran a very effective campaign during the 1980s featuring a woman who many people found irritating. Nevertheless, the campaign communicated Morkel's unique two-year guarantee and was a significant contributor to Morkel's market leadership position at the time. The attitude toward company communications is discussed more in the following chapter.

Summary

This chapter explored the influence of individual differences on consumer behaviour. Individual characteristics can be innate or can be shaped by the environment and social interactions of everyday life. Consumer resources include wealth, time and cognitive effort. Few companies adequately consider the impact of the latter two resources. Companies that focus on value-for-money fail to capture much of the magic that is the basis of compelling product offerings.

A thorough understanding of the symbolic and meaning worlds of the target market often allows the crafting of truly sustainable competitive advantage. These worlds include many different types of beliefs, including values, attitudes and knowledge. Cross-cultural issues greatly increase the difficulty of mastering a true understanding of these belief systems.

Marketing strategy often focuses on changing attitudes toward brands. The multi-attribute theories suggest that two major dimensions shape attitudes toward brands. Marketers must seek to understand the values underlying brand beliefs and attitudes because these more central beliefs are more resistant and act as the basis for the more transitory brand perceptions and attitudes. The following chapter explores the decision process shaped by these individual characteristics.

ENDNOTES

1 See United Nations Development Programme (1996).
2 $(\frac{63.3\%}{20\%})=\$3040$
3 See World Bank (1994: 230-231).
4 As compared to most Indian Ocean Rim countries where people wear comfortable, light clothing in open air, and live in homes without central heating or cooling.
5 The way people allocate their time to various activities, see Engel, Blackwell, & Miniard (1995: 313-322). Values and time orientations interact to influence product choice in time related product markets, such as insurance and financial services products, according to Usunier (1991).
6 United Nations Development Programme (1996: 91).
7 Source: United Nations Development Programme (1997), World Bank, 1996.
8 Burgess, 1992 contains a most extensive review of research concerning values and consumer behaviour.
9 Rokeach (1973).
10 See Schwartz (1992).
11 See Rokeach (1973) especially pages 3-5.
12 Burgess (1992) reviews the major methodologies with the exception of the Schwartz Value Survey.
13 See Reynolds & Gutman (1988) for an excellent review of the laddering methodology.

14 The process of cognition and memory is complex. Two excellent sources for more information are Klatzky (1980) and Matlin (1989).

15 Skinner (1976).

16 Skinner articulated this point of view as early as 1976, see the introduction to Skinner (1976).

17 Frankl (1986).

18 Frankl (1984).

19 Standardised scales generally require certain methodologies. Users should be familiar with these methodologies and research in general, or a qualified professional should be consulted. My experience suggests that many marketing researchers do not understand the values research methodologies that they use very well.

20 See Schwartz (1992).

21 Zinkhan & Pereira (1994). Brand equity has been popularised most by Aaker, see Aaker (1991; 1993; 1996).

22 Zinkhan & Pereira (1994: 211) reviews the major contributions toward a definition of brand image.

23 Aaker (1991).

24 Kahle, Beatty & Homer (1986: 405-409).

25 See Burgess (1992) especially pages 60-61.

26 See Mitchell (1983).

27 Hjelle & Ziegler (1987) and Mischel (1986) review many of the major theories. However, both omit Frankl, covering Maslow and Rogers instead. Most university libraries include copies of Hall & Lindzey (1970).

28 See Engel et al. (1995: 437-439).

29 Haugtvedt, Petty, & Cacioppo (1992: 239-260).

30 See Brislin (1986) especially page 163.

31 Brislin, Lonner, & Thorndike (1973: 60-61).

32 Hawkins & Coney (1981: 373).

33 Chapter 10 of Engel et al. (1995) discusses most of the relevant research concerning knowledge for readers wishing more depth.

34 See Chapter 11 of Engel et al. (1995: 368-382).

35 Adapted from Burns (1986: 49-56).

5 The Consumer Decision Process

Aligning strategy with consumer thinking

Strong marketing aligns the entire organisation with the consumer's world of meaning. This alignment requires companies to understand the seven stages of the consumer decision process well enough to craft effective strategies for each stage. Strong product offerings hold such appeal that the target consumers feel compelled to share their resources, their hearts and their souls with the company. Such consumer loyalty is not easily won and cannot be accomplished unless the firm embraces each decision process stage for its unique opportunities to develop or extend superior sustainable customer solutions – an original concept explained later in this book.

PROBLEM RECOGNITION

Unless the consumer recognises a need for a product, no sale will take place. Problem recognition is a process whereby consumers recognise potential problems, opportunities and needs that emerge from their symbolic world. Every branded communication, every sales presentation, every public relations exercise potentially confronts consumers with a request to change some aspect of their life requiring an evaluation of meaning and a consumption decision. The will to meaning is the primary motive behind every purchase and consumption decision. Even in the seemingly meaningless purchase of a yo-yo, the child attains the values of mastery, independence and an exciting life (and the parent the value of a world at peace!). Meaning occurs when values are realised. Thus, the primary motivating factor of all behaviour presents the individual with the greatest problem of life, i.e. 'How can I realise meaning in life', and its corollary, 'Will the purchase or use of this product help me to realise meaning in life?' Those who practise strong marketing realise that these questions may be asked at a mental level below the awareness of the individual, leaving the consumer with only the perception that deciding in favour of the product 'feels right'. Nevertheless, consumers ask these questions when making purchase and consumption decisions hundreds of times a day.

THINK OF CONSUMERS AS PROBLEM SOLVERS

When I visit a company to consult or speak for the first time, I sometimes ask staff members about the company's way of visualising consumers. The reason? Companies that practise the new marketing are all in the same business – the business of providing customer solutions. When a lower level staff member tells me that the company thinks of customers as problem solvers, I know that company focuses on providing solutions. I cannot remember one company that has not been successful when everyone was taught how the company solved customer problems and the individual's role in solving those problems. Companies that achieve this world-view have established a firm foundation upon which strong marketing can be built.

ESTABLISHING SUPERIOR SUSTAINABLE CUSTOMER SOLUTIONS (SSCS)

We will review the process of achieving sustainable competitive advantage in the second section of this book. Building strong marketing strategies for the problem recognition stage requires an understanding of an equally necessary basic strategy concept also discussed in greater depth later in the book. Survey your industry, talk to people working in supermarkets and pharmacies, talk to the waiter, the till operator, the service station attendant – few companies think of consumers as problem solvers and fewer yet plan to solve customer problems better than their competitors. Unable to understand customer problems, such companies flounder from crisis to crisis or travel through life blissfully unaware of the impending doom that must eventually come.

The new marketing requires the firm to achieve superior sustainable customer solutions (SSCS). A holistic knowledge of consumers and their preferences, as stressed throughout this book, is the normal basis for achieving an SSCS. Companies that win achieve meaningful SSCSs.

WHAT HAPPENS DURING NEED RECOGNITION?

To paraphrase Frankl, every consumer is unique and every situation happens just once in life. Every consumer brings unique lifetime experiences to every situation where an interaction with the company takes place. This diversity is evident in the unique basket of problems that consumers try to solve with every transaction.

Global problems apply to every problem-solving situation[1]. Examples of global problems include the need to overcome feelings of low esteem, lack of love from others, or the need to feel acceptance and approval. Global problems typically emerge from the consistent failure to attain a value in a certain situation but may emerge when values are not attained in any situation in life. So, the failure to achieve a comfortable life is the problem to be solved, not a tight financial budget. The failure to achieve peace or leisure is the problem, not a lack of time. The need to overcome a feeling of inadequacy might be activated when using or choosing financial services. Global problems transcend particular product purchase and consumption decisions.

Domain-specific problems apply only in the case of a specific purchase or usage decision. For instance, allergies to certain dyes could affect food product purchases or use of hair-colouring products, but would not apply to the purchase of a home computer. Sensitivity to tartrazine or another food additive would apply only to the foods that contain these additives.

Both kinds of problems should be investigated thoroughly when attempting to manage consumption behaviour. The problems in Table 5.1 (page 48) emerged from in-depth interviews with prospective bank customers. Bank staff brainstormed about underlying values and solutions to the customer's problems, and produced a list of solutions.

In the actual brainstorming session, many more solutions emerged. Many were impractical. The session leader was wise enough to encourage as many ideas as possible without judging, criticising or ridiculing, realising that bad ideas often become good ideas with further discussion.

Strong marketers must identify the perceived domain-specific needs that influence a target segment's purchase and consumption, the global needs that could become influential if activated, and other needs that may apply to others target segments but not the segment at hand.

Casio is a company that understands need recognition. Although digital cameras have been around since the early 1980s, the prices have been astronomical. Thanks to increased use of the Internet (digital photos can be downloaded and posted directly onto the Web) and an advance in chips, Casio was able to produce a digital camera for less than $300. More than a dozen Japanese companies are jumping on the bandwagon and 1998 sales are expected to top 1.4 million units. IDC Japan estimates sales will top 11 million units by the end of the decade[2]. Yet Casio knows that many consumers need to fit such discretionary product purchases into tight budgets, and that this has implications for competition.

The purchase of a related product often activates need recognition for related items. Roller-blade users are more likely to require kneepads. New editions of software make people aware that Intel's new Pentium Pro chips allow PCs to do more than slower chips were designed to do. Internet usage makes one more likely to want to communicate visually, and Casio's QV-series digital cameras provide a vehicle for that communication.

TYPE	PROBLEM (AND UNDERLYING VALUES)	SOLUTION
GLOBAL	Cost of living being eroded by inflation. Will my savings last? (Personal and family security)	Offer retirement planning advice by suitably trained staff.
GLOBAL	Crime increasing. I am afraid when I visit the ATM machine. (Personal security)	Install closed-circuit TV cameras and bright lights from parking to ATM.
GLOBAL	High-tech and white-collar fraud increasing. I do not trust banks as I used to. I suppose money is as safe in one bank as another, isn't it? (Social justice, honest, sincere, truthful, family security)	Put a sign on a desk near the teller's window which says 'internal auditor'.
GLOBAL	I've overspent my budgets and I'm paying too much on credit cards every month. I'm really struggling. (Protecting public image, self-discipline, family security)	Offer budget planning advice by suitably trained staff. Offer debt consolidation loan.
DOMAIN-SPECIFIC	I do not have time to reconcile statements but my wife likes her statement to be balanced to the cent. We argue about it sometimes. (World at peace, mature love, capable, respect)	Offer separate accounts with reduced service charges. Make statements easier to balance by including a balancing worksheet already filled out, except for items not yet produced for collection.
DOMAIN-SPECIFIC	The banks all agree on interest rates. What difference does it make? (Wisdom)	Show that a wide range of interest rates are available, depending on the needs of the account holder.
DOMAIN-SPECIFIC	All banks have good and bad branches. You just get used to a manager and they move her. (Loyal, reciprocation of favours)	Manage service quality in all branches intensively and post the score of each branch every month where customers can see it.
DOMAIN-SPECIFIC	I get so angry with my bank. They put through debits on different dates throughout the month. I can never plan and I often get caught with an overdraft. (Social justice, sincere, honest, truthful)	Help by consolidating debits with client vendors so that they come through on one day.
DOMAIN-SPECIFIC	I never get statements. The post office is so unreliable these days. (Capable, competent)	Offer an electronic banking service.

Table 5.1 *Consumer problems and solutions from a brainstorming session*

Here are some other times when people are more likely to be re-evaluating purchase or consumption:

- A major change in circumstances occurs, such as moving home, marriage, divorce, the birth of a child, graduation from high school or university, death of a spouse or parent.

- The person or a family member, friend or close associate acquires the product or a related product.

- Consumption of the product or a related product. The empty pantry is often all the motivation necessary to stimulate need recognition.

- Influential individual differences become active. The active awareness of certain values or group affiliations can stimulate the purchase of products, such as was the case with Johnson & Johnson's Child Welfare promotion (see page 12).

- Information processing occurs. One sees an advertisement on TV or a friend tells how much satisfaction he or she is getting from a recent purchase.

Consumers often do not act to improve their lives although they are aware of solutions offered by companies. Golf lessons with Ernie Els, Vijay Singh or Jack Nicklaus would improve one's golf game, but few people can afford it. It would be wonderful to learn a foreign language and visit an exotic foreign country, but few people have the time. It would be great to understand the technical analysis of stocks, bonds and investments, but few people have the required mathematical background.

These cases demonstrate examples where individuals may perceive an opportunity to realise values and gain meaning in life, but in which they perceive a resource deficit. Consumers weigh the benefits to be gained against the cost of acquiring or experiencing a product. Consumers constantly strive to attain a desired state characterised by a meaningful existence. When the perceived gap between the actual and desired states is large, consumers feel tension and become more likely to act to close the gap. When the perceived gap is small, consumers probably will not.

WHEN CONSUMERS ACT

This suggests three possible strategies for activating problem recognition that are available to firms that build strong marketing:

- Lower the perceived cost in the consumer's mind.

- Demonstrate that the actual state is more unacceptable than the consumer thinks it is.

- Demonstrate that the desired state is more advantageous than the consumer thinks it is.

South Africa's Ellerines masters need recognition strategies. To the casual observer, Ellerines is a furniture retailer serving upper and middle income customers. They operate under numerous brand names, from no-frills showrooms often located side-by-side in high-traffic areas near mass transportation to CBDs in towns across the country.

WHEN CONSUMERS ACT

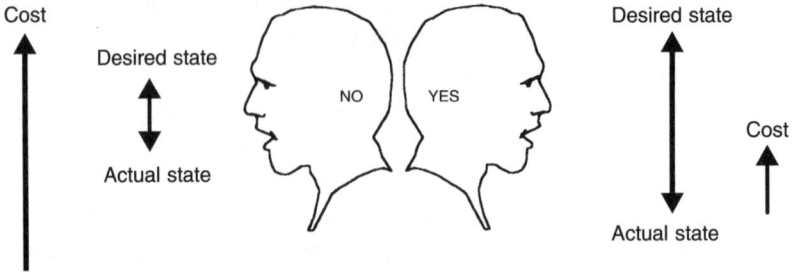

Figure 5.1 The comparison of cost and the potential reward determines action

Ellerines sells mainly on credit, recognising that all consumers are a reliable credit risk so long as repayment amounts are manageable – a fact documented in many studies[3]. Ellerines assigns representatives to specific areas for selling. The representatives, often recruited from the communities they serve, build relationships with customers and perform collection and customer services functions. They are known to the family and to friends. If necessary, they can repossess the furniture. This intensive relationship management allows Ellerines to build customer files on lower income consumers that the leading credit bureaux would dearly love to have.

Lower income customers generally measure affordability based on monthly payments. When loans are nearing repayment, the representatives sometimes bring a matching piece of furniture and their monthly catalogue to the home and offer a second account for the new furniture. Ellerines maintains a share of monthly spending by lowering the perception of cost. By delivering a needed piece of furniture, Ellerines shows that the desired state is more advantageous than the consumer thinks it is.

Ellerines showrooms feature attractive, budget-priced home furnishings and accessories and the company has also developed an in-house selling strategy that sells mostly from the showroom floor.

Ellerines strategies have translated into industry leading profits for decades. Between 1994 and 1996, sales grew 31 per cent, profits before tax grew 60 per cent, and return on capital employed by the long-term debt-free company grew from 18.6 per cent to 22.2 per cent[4].

SEARCH

Once consumers recognise a problem, they tend to search for information about possible solutions. Consumers often scan their memory for relevant knowledge as part of internal search. They may search no further for information and may proceed to evaluate alternatives if they feel they have adequate knowledge about a product decision and the ability in the present situation to retrieve and consider that knowledge. Recent satisfactory purchase or consumption in a product category frequently leads to satisfaction with internal search.

HOW CONSUMERS SEARCH

Internal search can be more than a simple memory scan, requiring processing to associate thoughts to provide meaningful input to the purchase decision. The time available for search also determines the amount of search. Severe time limitations may force consumers to terminate after internal search, even when they feel inadequately prepared to evaluate alternatives retrieved from their memory.

Nevertheless, having searched internally, many consumers do not feel adequately informed to make a decision and so begin external search. External search can encompass marketer-dominated communications, independent media communications and personal sources such as family and friends. External search can be motivated by an impending purchase or can be on-going. If you have a teenage daughter, you know that fashion and beauty product search can be ongoing and the sources of information can be infinite!

Search behaviour is related to problem solving. Extended problem solving leads to deeper search, visits to more shops and information sources and more time spent searching for information. Relatively little search happens during limited problem solving. Three dimensions of search need to be understood for strong marketing:

1. the degree of search,
2. the direction of search and
3. the sequence of search.

Consider the strategic relevance of each of these dimensions in the following example.

Beneath the Blue is a leading scuba diving and travel company in Johannesburg's northern suburbs. With so many competitors offering training that leads to the same internationally recognised Professional Association of Diving Instructors (PADI) qualifications, Beneath the Blue attempts to differentiate by stressing professionalism, knowledge of diving sites and related accommodation, as well as its exceptional safety record. Their limited advertising budget does not allow the company to advertise in every media source where it would like to, and so management take careful steps to answer each of the questions in Table 5.2 on page 52.

Beneath the Blue advertises in *DiveStyle*, a popular diving magazine, sharing its advertising space with three other shops that have joined it in a buying and advertising co-operative. Rosebank shop customers are encouraged to write their contact information into a registry. A similar exercise takes place every week at the upmarket Rosebank flea market. Beneath the Blue maintains a customer database and continually probes consumers to understand search behaviour and changing preferences.

SEARCH DIMENSION	TYPICAL RESEARCH QUESTIONS
DEGREE OF SEARCH	How many brands are considered? How many stores are visited, contacted? How many attributes are considered? How many information sources are used? How much time is spent on search?
DIRECTION OF SEARCH	Which brands are considered? Which stores are visited, contacted? Which attributes are considered? Which information sources are used?
SEQUENCE OF SEARCH	In what order are brands considered? In what order are stores visited, contacted? In what order are attributes considered? In what order are information sources used?

Table 5.2 Dimensions of consumer search[5]

Many companies fail to realise that salespeople are leading sources of information when people are unfamiliar with a product, such as scuba diving. Only people who demonstrate a love of scuba diving, travel and a genuine care for others are hired. Beneath the Blue trains salespeople to listen, probe for concern and provide appropriate information. The work has paid off in a larger than expected market share and lasting customer relationships, leading to repeat business for Beneath the Blue. As this market matures, the company is finding that its travel packages, built around local and international travel and diving packages, are a hot growth area.

INFORMATION PROCESSING

Firms that practise strong marketing reap many benefits from information processing – benefits that exceed those available to firms that practise only good media planning. With the advent of the Internet, the blurring of traditional media and the importance of informal communication in the IOR, I use the term 'commercial message' to indicate all forms of commercial advertising and promotion communications.

Media dominated by marketers, such as television, radio, print, outdoor media and salespeople, offer hundreds of invitations to change one's purchase and consumption behaviour every day. Advertising and the other elements of the promotional mix are sources that are influenced by the company. More invitations to change come from personal influence, press reports and evaluations by independent consumer groups beyond the control of marketers. From these often contradictory messages and fragments of messages, consumers construct their symbolic world.

Many companies are disappointed when a major advertising and promotional campaign yields few results. There are many reasons why this happens. Many messages appear in media that target market consumers do not consume. Some messages do not get the attention of consumers. Even messages that are processed often fail to be understood or accepted. The result is that what is remembered often is not what the company intended to say.

Think of the last time that you watched television. Name the last ten advertisements broadcast on the programme. Now write down the content of each commercial message. Who were the advertisers and what were they trying to say? If you are like most people, you will be unable to remember more than three or four advertisements and you will be lucky to remember the content of two accurately[6]. You can improve your company's advertising and promotion effectiveness by focusing on the five steps of information processing. These steps are included in Engel, Blackwell and Miniard's model[7]:

- exposure
- attention
- comprehension
- acceptance
- retention.

EXPOSURE

Consumers who are not exposed to a message cannot remember it! The objective of every strategic communication programme is to communicate with a target population – and only that target population. Media planning has developed many tools to assist marketers to achieve this goal. Information is available to assist in targeting media likely to be read, seen or heard by the target. These media consumption profiles often include information concerning product usage and some measure of conducive media content (i.e. consistent with the target population's interests and values). While this information provides a good starting point, it is not detailed enough to measure promotional effectiveness.

ATTENTION

One thing that media consumption profiles do not measure is the ability of the advertisement to rise from the clutter to gain attention. Media consumption statistics measure audience, not the ability of a communication to emerge from the clutter and achieve attention. Considering the amount of clutter these days – advertisements, advertorials, tens of thousands of packages in every supermarket – strong marketing requires careful planning to maximise the attention gained from every exposure.

The consumer's adaptation level is your biggest enemy. Adaptation is what happens when six advertisements go by on your radio and you cannot remember one a few moments later. These proven techniques will improve your communication effectiveness and get attention:

- Make sure the communication fits the motivations the consumer feels at the time it is received. Food advertisements will gain the most attention when people are hungry. Travel advertisements gain attention when consumers are caught in rush hour traffic.

- Take advantage of the consumer's need to reduce tension in the belief system[8]. Keep the message content consistent with target consumers' values and attitudes.

- Break out of the clutter. Be novel. Turn up the sound, the colour or cause consumers to think of different sensations that stand out from the crowd. A print advertisement that says 'FEEL THIS' may cause readers to pause to consider how the product might feel. Be creative.

- Make it easy to understand the point of the message quickly. Consumers are very selective about giving attention and they do not generally waste time processing 'creative' messages that are difficult to understand. If your agency says something like, 'Oh don't worry. Let's be creative. They'll read the headline and then they'll have to read the copy so that they understand. People like to work through copy', take your agency representative aside and explain you never want to hear such nonsense again.

- Remember to use aspects of the message itself that draw attention to the message. Relative size is important and a full page gets more attention than a half page. Use interesting colours. Use intensity: bright colours and relatively loud sounds.

- Make sure your message contrasts. If everything is colour, then consider black and white with spot colour on the product. Crack through the adaptation level barrier. Use learned attention-getters, such as ringing telephones, opening doors or other similar props at the beginning of the message.

- Use as many senses as possible. Embed scents in plastic supermarket displays or magazine advertisements, put video and sound in your hardware store display with a DIY video. Use call-in numbers so that people dial a number. The more senses people use, the more likely they will be to remember your message.

- Choose a good position and take advantage of the primacy (to the front) and recency (to the back) effect. Be among the first or last, unless a particularly appealing location in a magazine or radio/TV programme is available. Avoid being in the middle of other advertisements.

- Use directionality to make message elements point to your main message. Movement and isolation also bring attention by standing out from the clutter, but can also be used to highlight a main message.

- Attractive spokespeople, especially people viewed as authoritative by the target market, are also a wise choice – especially when the product offer is complex.

Using these strategies will stimulate attention and result in much increased advertising efficiency. However, attention is not enough if your message cannot be understood.

COMPREHENSION

The best designed media plan and best design of attentive elements can still fail to deliver the message if consumers fail to understand message content. It is most important to maximise comprehension of an advertisement[9]. There are three main concepts that require understanding:

1. symbolic categorisation,

2. symbolic elaboration and

3. symbolic organisation[10].

Symbolic Categorisation

During comprehension, consumers attempt to understand what they have experienced. They do so by associating the symbols they have perceived with elements held in their long-term memory – that is, a process of categorisation takes place in the consumer's symbolic world. As you read this page, you are symbolically categorising the printed images. With almost no conscious effort, your mind sees the lines and recognises them as letters and then as words.

Symbolic Elaboration

You are also practising symbolic elaboration as you associate the symbols you interpret with words you know, and the words with other related symbols, images and ideas. This associative process lacks the neat and tidy consistency of your personal computer database. Personal factors, such as mood or tiredness, and environmental factors, such as noise and other people, can interfere with the process.

Symbolic Organisation

Consumers then organise what they have perceived into recognisable patterns and ideas. That process of symbolic organisation seeks to order the perception into a meaningful whole. The belief system makes value judgements and colours the perception. Other antecedent factors such as mood add additional colours. People have a strong inclination to simplify their perception. In the IOR, where many people are emerging into lifestyles that are more complex and cross many cultures, this may result in a failure to comprehend the actual commercial message.

Your commercial messages will become much more effective if you understand the process of comprehension and organise the elements of your message so that comprehension is maximised. The consumer identifies figure (the consumer's perception of what is most meaningful in the message) and ground (everything else). Information processing often focuses on dominant message elements, such as well-known actors, while missing elements such as the brand name and message content. Design your message elements to direct attention to the core concepts you wish consumers to take away from the communication.

We all practise closure (finishing unfinished sentences and ideas). Konica used closure effectively in a South African advertisement that recited a number of awards and market leadership statements while slowly showing the K and then the O letters on the screen. Consumers expected the Kodak brand name to appear, and were surprised when the Konica brand appeared instead.

Here are some things you can do to increase the effectiveness of your message[11]:

- Recognise that expectations, motivations and knowledge influence perception and are all important in the IOR because of the cross-cultural diversity and emerging markets found here. Understand what they are in your target population and present messages that are consistent with them.

- Linguistics is also important. Remember that IOR consumers speak many languages and have historic disadvantages concerning education. Even consumers in the better educated, less culturally diverse and more affluent industrialised nations more easily comprehend and remember familiar words from everyday language usage.

- Be positive. Words like not and never are less likely to be perceived accurately. Passive sentences (The new feature was manufactured by Acme) are less easily remembered than active sentences (Acme manufactured the new feature).

- Use order effects. Get the message elements you want understood and remembered to the front (primacy) or the end (recency) of your communication. The order in which you present ideas and concepts should be tested. Order is very important.

- Use design elements that feature the right context. The context is right when the target population feels the communication depicts a scene in which they would participate. People want to feel that your product and your message are 'real', that is, consistent with their world of meaning.

- Realise that non-verbal elements also influence comprehension and plan those elements wisely[12].

ACCEPTANCE

Messages that are inconsistent with the consumer's world of meaning fail to be convincing. *Notice that I did not say that consumers will reject false messages and accept truthful messages.* Messages must be consistent with previous beliefs or present a message that changes beliefs convincingly – in other words, be believable.

Strong marketers know that consumers do three things when they see an advertisement and two of them are not good: they generate supportive arguments, they generate counter-arguments, and they disparage the source of the argument. 'Yes, I did see someone remove a nasty stain with Brand X.' 'No, I don't ever want to be embarrassed because I forgot to use Brand X deodorant.' Your message content should encourage supportive arguments by tapping into prevailing supportive attitudes and beliefs. The salesman outside the circus or carnival knows that if you can get people nodding in agreement on minor points early in the message, he'll be much more likely to generate supportive arguments in favour of the message content at the end of the message.

Concentrating on the positive message content minimises the tendency to counter-argue. Do not be afraid to correct misperceptions in the marketplace with facts, but be aware of the emotional response people feel when confronted with a message that requires a change in existing beliefs. Strong marketers understand and plan for affective responses to communications[13]. Affect can influence the amount of elaboration about message content.

According to the Elaboration Likelihood Model (ELM), some consumers lack the ability or desire to process, or do not have strong feelings about a message or the brand it depicts. These consumers are more persuaded by peripheral cues in the communication, such as likeable message content or design elements[14]. Peripheral route attitude changes are temporary, susceptible to change and unpredictive of behaviour.

Consumers with the ability and motivation to process are more persuaded by the rational arguments. Rational arguments cause central route persuasion to occur, which is longer lasting and more predictive of behaviour[15].

Thus, the cultural diversity and emerging lifestyles of the IOR suggest important challenges to marketers wishing to effect long-term attitude change. The ELM implies that IOR marketers must understand ability and desire to process product knowledge in order to get lasting effect from promotional spending.

RETENTION

Retention is the final stage of information processing. As your message is comprehended, it enters the sensory memory where it is held for a quarter to half a second. It then enters the short-term memory where symbolic categorisation begins. The short-term memory is very limited and decay begins within 30-60 seconds if an idea is not moved to long-term memory. This is one reason why messages placed between other messages, as is so often the case in the electronic media, can be less effective. There are a number of techniques available to enhance the chances that your message will enter the long-term memory.

- Repeat essential message elements three times or more in your advertisement. Rehearsal is the main way in which consumers remember. High frequency advertising can have a similar effect, so long as the message is conducive to memorisation. Repeated showings of a message that is unmemorable, or one that has not cleared the four hurdles (i.e. exposure, attention, comprehension and acceptance) before retention, will not lead to efficient gains in memorability.

- Encourage people to elaborate about message content. In my teenage years I was quite interested in anything automotive and a local car parts distributor had an advertisement that caused much elaboration. Every advertisement ended with the spokesperson saying (in his best gruff New York accent), 'That's Kar, as in what you drive but with a K, Part as in what you do to your hair and Outlet as in what you stick a plug in. Kar Part Outlet'.

- Put your message into information sources where people are seeking information. One reason the Yellow Pages are so effective is that people are looking for information about the subject at hand. Baby advertisements may be retained better when placed in a baby magazine instead of a magazine serving the needs of career women.

- Try to design interrelations between words in the message and between the words and visual or auditory elements. Old Spice men's fragrances often feature sea-going images that tie into the wooden ship icon on the bottle. J&J's Reach toothbrushes saw dramatic share increases around the world when a 'Flip-Top Head' cartoon character demonstrated another way to reach back teeth as effectively as the Reach toothbrush.

• Avoid general words such as efficiency or effectiveness. Use concrete words such as clean, best, fast, quick, potent, etc. The Matex Company launched Thixo-Tex, a rust-inhibiting product for motor cars that achieved $2 million in annual sales. Changing the name to Rusty Jones and creating a hard-working character to go along with the product increased sales to over $100 million in a few short years[16].

• Use message elements that cause people to relate the message to themselves and their world of meaning. 'Are you the kind of person who gets an occasional headache?' 'What time of day are you at your best?'

• Use memorable rhymes and jingles.

MANAGE THE SEARCH PROCESS INTENSIVELY

Building strong marketing requires intensive management of consumer search. In addition to the five stages of information processing laid out above, it is important to know the degree, the direction and the sequence of search. There are important opportunities to be gained by getting your message to consumers at the right time, the right place and in the right format.

PRE-PURCHASE ALTERNATIVE EVALUATION

The stage following search is pre-purchase alternative evaluation. If you are contemplating purchasing a business aircraft, chances are that Pete Agur can help you to make a decision[17]. Agur is the President of The VanAllen Group, a management consulting firm specialising in corporate travel. Agur contends that corporations must think about two kinds of travel, i.e. operational and strategic trips.

Operational trips, those trips required for day-to-day management issues, are served by commercial airlines when the destinations are on established routes. Strategic trips, those important trips demanding on-time arrival or extra-ordinary secrecy, are served best by private aircraft. Agur bases his contentions on five important factors that he believes are important decision criteria: confidentiality, cost-effectiveness, safety/security, service and time-effectiveness. A study was carried out where key passengers were asked to rate expectations for strategic and operational trips. The results show that these passengers had very different expectations for the two types of trips.

Although rarely with the rigour of someone contemplating an aircraft purchase, consumers evaluate alternatives in a similar way after search. In general, pre-purchase evaluation rarely occurs in habitual purchases and is severely curtailed in most limited problem-solving decisions.

Pre-purchase alternative evaluation consists of four main components:

1. determine choice criteria,
2. choose alternatives for consideration,
3. evaluate alternatives using the choice criteria, and
4. apply a decision rule.

DETERMINE CHOICE CRITERIA

Thinking of the situations in which they will use a product[18], consumers evaluate many aspects of the brands that exist in their symbolic world. Important aspects emerge as choice criteria. Price, quality, brand name, the availability of after-sales service and country of origin are just some of the attributes which can be choice criteria for many products. As discussed earlier, IOR consumers choose and use products in more diverse situations than their industrialised nation counterparts.

Situational differences can cause very different choice criteria to emerge. The salience of evaluative criteria determines their weight in the decision process. Salience is not always realised, in part because consumers do not always have the knowledge required to understand the potential benefit of a product to them. Utilitarian considerations will cause consumers to examine functional attributes and benefits. Hedonic considerations will result in examination of psychosocial attributes and benefits.

Strategies can influence which choice criteria emerge and the weight consumers place on each criterion. In addition to situation and knowledge, the similarity of choice alternatives and the motivation for the purchase or consumption offer opportunities for marketing programmes to influence choice criteria.

CHOOSE ALTERNATIVES FOR CONSIDERATION

The consideration set consists of all brands that the consumer considers as possibilities for purchase or consumption. If internal search is the only search undertaken, then the consideration set will consist of remembered brands only, i.e. the retrieval set. A test of unaided awareness reveals the retrieval set. Companies that urge consumers to 'try us first' or to 'try us last' are attempting to gain an advantageous position in the consideration set (e.g. through offers such as 'we'll beat any price' or 'visit them and then come and compare our better offer'). One thing is certain, if you're not in the consideration set you won't make the sale. It's also likely that the third or fourth brand considered won't get as much business as brands that stand out from the others in the consideration set. Knowing your brand's position in the consideration set is important.

EVALUATE ALTERNATIVES

Consumers generally employ cut-offs when choosing between competitive brands. When considering a watch purchase, a consumer might decide to consider only those alternatives priced below a certain price or those which have a luminous dial for reading after dark. Alternatives which do not meet these criteria are not considered further. Companies with products outside the cut-off can try to extend the cut-off or minimise the importance of the cut-off criterion so that other criteria can take more weight in the decision.

Consumers use signals as cues when they feel incapable of evaluating alternatives. A relatively high price or a strong guarantee and return policy can signal quality. Packaging can signal which type of people use a product. Deciding which signals to use starts with comprehensive knowledge of the consumer's world of meaning and a systematic analysis of the consumer's experience of the product.

APPLY A DECISION RULE

Knowing how consumers actually decide between alternatives is another key to designing effective marketing strategies[19]. Yet, knowledge of the mechanics of consumer decisions seems to elude most marketers. Companies that believe consumers are always willing to make trade-offs of one benefit for another may be placing their market share at risk.

As Table 5.3 (page 62) shows, the names of the various decision rules can be confusing. However, the rules become easier to understand when you realise that it is important to know four things:

- whether consumers generally process by brand (PBB) or process by attribute (PBA),
- whether they allow strong performance on one criterion to compensate for poor performance on another,
- whether they employ cut-offs, and
- how they eliminate brands from consideration.

Consumers employ non-compensatory rules when they are unwilling to offset a shortcoming on one evaluative criterion with a strong offering on another. When the main usage occasion planned for a personal computer is games, then hi-resolution graphics, a fast video card with adequate ram, a serial port to host a joystick, and a fast co-processor chip will probably not be offset by an extra-large hard-disk or other built-in extras.

The salience of attributes often suggests the order of attribute processing. For instance, order of mention in an unaided brand awareness test should give a good indication of the order in which brands are processed. Some consumers process by brand, others by attribute and others employ a combination of the two approaches.

61

If target consumers generally employ lexicographic rules, the firm must ensure that it does best on the most important criteria. Focus is extremely important in this case. Regular market research is important as well. Brands that do not score well on important criteria can attempt to change the relative salience of attributes, but this can be quite expensive.

When consumers employ cut-offs, product strategy must ensure that minimum performance meets minimum evaluative criteria. If target consumers practice elimination by aspects, then focus must be on the most important criteria. However, conjunctive decision rules require the company to jump the hurdles on every important criterion.

DECISION RULE	COMPENSATORY		NON-COMPENSATORY	
	PBB	PBA	PBB	PBA
Most important on each salient criterion in order of importance				Lexicographic
Impose cut-off on all attributes and compare on each salient criterion in order of importance				Elimination by aspects
Impose cut-off on all attributes and compare brands on all criteria			Conjunctive	
Count number of times brands are judged favourable on salient criteria	Simple additive			
Count number of times brands are judged favourable on salient criteria but assign more salient criteria more weight	Weighted additive			
Any combination of the above	Phased decision	Phased decision	Phased decision	Phased decision

Table 5.3 *Typical decision rules that consumers employ*

There is little research available concerning decision rules in the IOR, but there is evidence that consumers with motivational or ability processing limitations are more likely to use simple additive rules.

PURCHASE

Once a brand is chosen, the consumer attempts to carry out the intention to buy. If the purchase intention is not quickly carried out, many factors can intervene so that it is never carried out. Changing circumstances, such as the loss of a job or news of a pregnancy, can affect the ability to pay. The need can be filled by another product or other needs can become more dominant, and thereby divert the funds intended for the purchase. New information can come to hand that favours an alternative purchase. Suppliers can run out of stock.

Of course, not all purchases are planned comprehensively in advance. The product and brand may be planned; or the product may be planned while the brand decision is left to the time of purchase; or no shopping may be planned at all (impulse purchasing). It is important to understand what kind of planning people do because each of the three alternatives above suggests emphasis on different marketing mix tools.

For instance, when shoppers plan to purchase a product but leave the choice of brand for the point of sale, then packaging, special pricing and sales promotion activities may become especially important. Trade marketing, the intensive account management approach to distribution, may become more important as well for manufacturers facing more intensive category management on behalf of retailers. Purchase is also moving into non-traditional areas, such as the home and the Internet (see Chapters 15 and 16).

CONSUMPTION

Consumption behaviour has become the focus of much research these days. There is a growing recognition that the entire life of a product offers opportunities for marketing activities. The advent of easy-to-use and maintain computerised databases and geographical information systems has given the marketer competencies which did not exist just ten years ago. New technologies enable marketers to record previous interactions with the customer, to understand consumption rates and preferences and to model consumer behaviour with incredible accuracy. The advent of this digital age, this age of addressability, has instilled relationship marketing with a new vibrancy and excitement, especially in services marketing.

What has been the most important outcome of these new technologies? The realisation that the new technologies allow even the largest companies to build and maintain relationships that are as intimate as those enjoyed by the small neighbourhood grocer in many areas of the IOR. A new kind of market researcher records customer behaviour in databases, measures preferences, attrition rates and lifetime values of customers – often automatically. For the first time, we have the ability to measure and manage the profit of every individual customer. Post-modern consumption research has been a major influence in recent years[20]. Consumption which is more closely related to the self and which seems to create significant, powerful and extraordinary moments, is called sacred consumption. That which is ordinary and unlikely to inspire such emotional response is considered profane. Consider the products you consume during those sacred moments of your life. You may be thinking of a significant place, such as the kitchen in most homes, or of a tangible thing, such as a chair, a piece of clothing or a person or pet. Marketers do not create these moments for consumers, rather consumers learn that certain moments are sacred as a result of:

- *Ritual*: Those repeated, expressive and symbolic behaviours which express values and meaning in life. Usually learned through experience and internalised. Rituals may feature exchange, the showing of possessions, grooming and care of a product or self, the marking of an emotional divestment in a favoured product or the celebration of a special time such as a holiday or a special sporting event.

- *Pilgrimage*: Return to a place of consumption, such as a place where one met a loved one or the site of a cherished memory.

- *Quintessence*: The feeling that a product is perfect in every way. The celebration of its design and function.

- *Collection*: The acquisition of related products, such as coins or stamps, but also commemorative packaging and other items seen to be historic or to mark an occasion. Collection can have a negative and compulsive side. Marketers can stimulate purchase and consumption by linking products to the sacred consumption experiences of consumers.

Modelling and understanding consumption and disposal behaviour will be a major research interest for the near future for another reason, especially in the IOR. Humankind must decide how to confront a number of consumption-oriented problems on a global basis. For instance, if all humankind were to achieve the industrialised nations' standard of living, we would exhaust the earth's resources in but a few years. There is simply not enough to go around to duplicate that lifestyle. Over the past 30 years, the rich nations have become richer and the poor nations poorer[21]. IOR firms are ideally placed to understand how the majority of humankind live, as well as to conceive, produce and deliver appropriate products for those markets.

POST-CONSUMPTION ALTERNATIVE EVALUATION

In the case of limited problem solving, especially routine purchases of inexpensive articles, pre-purchase evaluation of alternatives is often skipped. In all cases, consumers evaluate products after consumption. Firms who believe they have comprehensive customer satisfaction programmes in place may be surprised to find that customer satisfaction is much more than simply meeting the consumer's expectations[22]. Consumers do not enter the purchase and consumption equation with the same expectations. Some seek equitable performance (relative value for the money, time and other resources exchanged, measured against some universal scale in their minds). Others seek ideal performance (measuring the brand against an ideal performance they perceive). Still others seek expected performance (the perception of what the performance will be).

When performance equals the expectation (simple confirmation), consumers do not feel satisfied. Rather, they feel neutral – neither too positive or too negative. Positive disconfirmation, when performance exceeds expectations, leads to feelings of satisfaction. Negative disconfirmation, on the other hand, is certain to lead to feelings of dissatisfaction. Marketers often increase the number of dissatisfied customers by encouraging consumers to have unrealistically high expectations.

Most people do not tell the company when they are dissatisfied. However, they tell many others. Strong marketers have programmes in place to query customer satisfaction at key moments during service delivery and after consumption. Chapter 15 explores these programmes more fully.

Engel, Blackwell and Miniard recommend the following steps to alleviate customer dissatisfaction[23]:

- Make individualised marketing a reality.
- Institute a total quality control policy.
- Introduce an early-warning satisfaction feedback system.
- Build realistic expectations.
- Provide warranties/guarantees.
- Provide information on product use.
- Solicit customer feedback.
- Reinforce customer loyalty.

Whatever steps your company takes, the most important cultural value that you can inculcate is genuine concern for customer satisfaction. Study after study shows that *it is cheaper to keep an existing customer than it is to find a new one*. You build strong marketing by consistently exceeding customer expectations and by providing incrementally better service every day.

Summary

A comprehensive understanding of the consumer decision process is a powerful impetus to crafting strong marketing strategies. In companies practising strong marketing, everyone focuses on understanding and solving customer problems. Strategies must be crafted to account for the direction, content and extent of consumer search. Communication strategies must be designed to facilitate exposure, attention, comprehension, acceptance and retention. All forms of information must be considered.

This chapter also explored the nature of alternative evaluation and choice criteria, decision rules and consideration sets. The increasing trend toward new forms of purchase and consumption behaviour was noted. The next chapter focuses on purchase and consumption behaviour in business marketing.

ENDNOTES

1 Vinson, Scott & Lamont (1977: 44-50). I have borrowed and adapted terminology from Vinson et al.'s value concepts to describe the product-specific and transcendent levels of needs that are felt by consumers. The classification proposed here is ripe for research in the Indian Ocean Rim.
2 See Brull (1996).
3 World Bank (1994: 40).
4 See Joubert (1996).
5 Source: Engel, Blackwell, & Miniard (1995: 185).
6 There is an extensive research literature supporting the failure to comprehend advertisements, see Engel et al. (1995) especially Chapter 14.
7 This model is based on McGuire (1976).
8 There has been much research concerning the consumer's need to maintain cognitive consistency or balance in the belief sysem. See McGuire (1972).
9 Those wishing to develop a better understanding of cognition should consult specialist publications. Two of my favourites are written at the practical level most executives prefer: Klatzky (1980) and Matlin (1989). Chapter 14 of Engel et al. (1995) includes references to many practical issues and academic articles that would be of interest.
10 I have abandoned the traditional terms of stimulus categorisation, stimulus elaboration and stimulus organisation for pedagogical reasons and because I feel the new terms more accurately represent what is occurring during comprehension.
11 Engel, Blackwell & Miniard (1995: 493-497).
12 Hecker & Stewart (1988) is an excellent source for non-verbal communication influences on advertising.
13 Engel et al. (1995) lists a number of sources. The Society for Consumer Psychology of the American Psychological Association devoted its annual conference to the topic and the papers were reprinted in Cafferata & Tybout (1989).
14 Petty & Cacioppo (1986). The theory is widely supported and is covered in detail in Engel et al. (1995), especially pages 560-563. The role of affect in the theory is well covered in Cacioppo & Petty (1989).
15 Cacioppo & Petty (1989).
16 Reported in Engel et al. (1995: 520).
17 See Agur (1996).
18 See Dickson (1982) and Miller & Ginter (1979).
19 See Engel et al. (1995) especially pages 222-227.
20 It all started with a cross-country journey by three American consumer behaviourists, see Belk, Wallendorf & Sherry (1989). There is an exceptionally well-written and succinct review in Engel et al. (1995), beginning on page 268.
21 See United Nations Development Programme (1996).
22 Research has been influenced most by a seminal article by Oliver (1980). For a later review and extension, see Tse & Wilton (1988).
23 Engel et al. (1995: 278-282).

6 | Understanding Business Markets

Behaviour also plays a big role in industrial marketing success

As chairperson and CEO of Enron, a Houston company, Barbara P. Marks may be ready to claim an award for the world's most advanced understanding of the influence of the legal and political environments on IOR business marketing strategies.

Since signing a contract to supply a $2.5 billion power plant in India, Enron has had its contract cancelled, has secured approvals from three successive governments and won no less than 24 lawsuits! Circumstances forced Enron to solve a number of unanticipated problems. Consider some of Marks' perceptions:

- *Culture*: Indians perceived Enron as pushy, aggressive and unwilling to do things the 'Indian way'.

- *Communication and persuasion*: The parties had great differences of world-view, with some Indians believing the plant design was too grandiose and that liquified natural gas was inappropriate in a country where coal-burning was still the most popular method of creating energy.

- *Legal and regulatory*: Enron encountered repeated inconsistent application of customs duties.

- *Different rules*: Enron felt unfairly criticised and unable to respond to the allegations.

Noting that multinationals with local partners had made no progress, Marks still wonders whether things would have gone more smoothly with a local partner. However, Marks remains bullish on India, saying 'The fact that Enron was able to win 24 lawsuits in India should give comfort to other investors coming into India[1].'

Enron's experience demonstrates the growing level of complexity and the continued requirements for flexibility that characterise business marketing in the IOR.

NEW BUSINESS MARKETING IS DIFFERENT

At a very general level, marketing theory applies to all types of marketing. However, business to business (BTB) marketing differs substantially from consumer marketing and requires specialised skills. Some important differences include[2]:

- *Functional interdependence*: Business marketing strategy often requires a more integrated input by operations, manufacturing and other functions because of the nature of investment or technology decisions.

- *Product complexity*: Business products are often complex and highly technical. Technical competence is often a prerequisite to crafting successful marketing strategies in business marketing.

- *Buyer-seller interdependence*: Business products are often components in the business customer's final product or a critical part of the operations that deliver the end product to the customer's customer. There is a high degree of interdependence between business marketers and their customers and a stronger after-sales relationship. Strategic alliance building, a key element discussed in Chapter 14 is essentially a business marketing phenomenon.

- *Buying process complexity*: The nature of the negotiation process, the more formalised buying criteria, the explicit roles played by participants and the size of average purchases are but a few of the major differences characterising business marketing. Business buyer behaviour is about organisations, not individuals, and business marketers have to understand organisational behaviour in order to survive.

This chapter focuses on six essential influences on the process of building strong business marketing (see Figure 6.2, page 69).

Consumer behaviourists constructed their discipline by borrowing and testing theories from psychology, sociology, anthropology, political science and other behavioural sciences[3]. Organisational behaviourists constructed their science in a similar way. Thus, the two disciplines share many concepts. The study of organisational purchase and consumption has drawn from both disciplines and given back some compelling research findings.

The approach suggests that firms develop strategy along three dimensions, primarily: the *buying centre*, the *decision process stage* and the *task type*. Environmental and individual influences must also become firmly entrenched aspects of sales strategies. Most importantly, the approach reveals many opportunities for the enhancement of sales, margins and shares that become available when firms practise marketing after the sale is made.

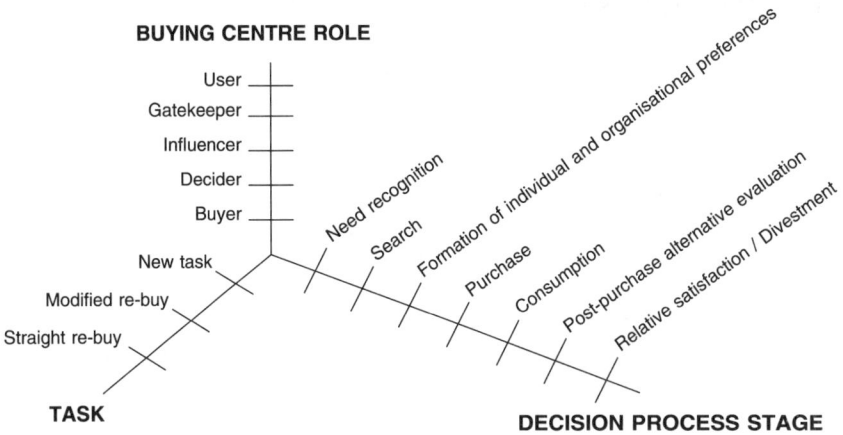

Figure 6.1 *A matrix approach to three key dimensions of business marketing strategy*

THE ENTERPRISE

Purchase and consumption behaviour in an enterprise is shaped by the nature of the purchasing task, organisational structure, mission, values and objectives, personal values of the individual players and technology.

Figure 6.2 *Six influences on the business marketing strategy process*

THE BUYING TASK

Marketing strategy must be sensitive to the unique nature of the buying task for every prospective client. Using consumer behaviour terminology introduced in prior chapters, organisational buying decisions are 'more extended' by nature. People often play prescribed roles with assigned levels of authority, and buy and consume according to established guidelines.

The two extreme types of consumer behaviour decisions have counterparts in business buyer behaviour. The *new-task buying situation* is comparable to the extended problem-solving situation in consumer behaviour. Preferences for many aspects of the product are probably not well formed and the firm actively seeks information from as many sources as possible. The purchase of a new computer system might be a good example of a new-task buying situation in most companies. A particular purchase may stimulate new-task behaviour in one firm and re-buy behaviour in another.

Certain strategies are most effective in *new-task* environments[4]. Established suppliers should constantly monitor changes in emerging purchasing requirements in the industries that they supply. All suppliers should isolate specific needs and participate actively in the early phases of purchase activity. Firms that help prospective clients to write specifications have the opportunity to lower overall costs to the end-user and rarely lose orders!

The *straight re-buy situation* resembles the limited problem-solving situation in consumer behaviour. Buyers feel they have adequate knowledge about the product, conduct minimal search and often standardise the buying process or disperse it throughout the organisation. The purchase of stationery often represents a straight re-buy situation to most companies.

Established suppliers must be sensitive to changing needs and to transaction costs in *straight re-buy* situations. Responsiveness and relationship management are critical. The challenging supplier should concentrate on three objectives:

- convincing the buyer of the net potential benefits to be gained from changing specifications,
- convincing the buyer of the net potential benefits to be gained from changing suppliers and
- becoming appointed to the official buying list as an alternative supplier. Another type of purchasing is a *modified re-buy* situation — in other words, a re-buy situation in which some characteristics of a repeat or regulated purchase have changed.

These characteristics may be within the buying firm (new specifications, new buying procedures, new needs, etc.), or within the selling firm (new product characteristics, new finance terms, new delivery procedures, new information systems, etc.).

The *modified re-buy* requires a re-examination of the client's requirements by the established supplier. Careful management of service quality and immediate action to remedy problems is also vitally important. Problems with the established supplier offer the challenger an opportunity to seize the momentum. Offering trial usage and performance guarantees, and being sensitive to buyer feelings about being pressured while considering a change of a long-term established supplier, can be effective strategies.

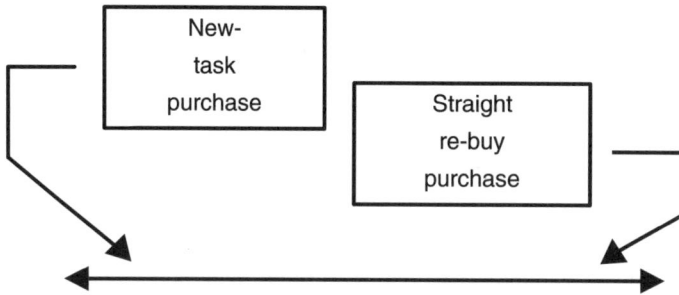

Figure 6.3 *The two extreme types of business purchase and consumption decisions*

THE BUSINESS MARKETING ENVIRONMENT

The business marketing environment influences all the stakeholders in the business – organised labour, shareholders, customers, governmental agencies and staff. However, not all trends may influence business marketers and their clients alike.

CULTURAL ENVIRONMENT

Culture influences business marketing in two ways:

1. as an environmental factor, and
2. as an organisational factor.

Culture as an environmental factor

Organisations consist of individuals. Individuals bring more than work clothes and a briefcase to the office everyday — they bring their personal lives with them into the workplace. Cultures where individuals expect to negotiate the price of every purchase may be more likely to negotiate price strenuously in business. Cultures where ties between individuals are stronger than loyalty to products may require much work to achieve insider status before making a sale. Communication styles and time organisation can be particularly influential in effective marketing strategy. Cultures have been classified into three rough categories[5]:

- *Linear-actives* are task-oriented, highly organised planners, characterised by the Swiss-Germans and American WASPS.

- *Multi-actives* are people-oriented, loquacious inter-relators, more common to populations including Africans, Arabs, Indians, Latin Americans and Pakistanis.

- *Reactives* are introverted, respect-oriented listeners such as the Japanese.

Classifying cultures according to value orientations may be very useful in strategy development. The findings of Shalom Schwartz discussed in Chapters 3 and 4 are particularly interesting, and include a wide range of values from which a picture of value differences and similarities may be drawn. Trompenaars' five value dimensions[6] may also be very useful:

- universalism vs particularism (rules vs relationships),

- collectivism vs individualism (the group vs the individual),

- neutral vs emotional (the range of feelings expressed),

- diffuse vs specific (the range of involvement), and

- achievement vs ascription (how status is accorded).

Much of the discussion of culture in Chapters 3 and 4 is relevant to business marketing. It is key that marketers understand the influence of social values on the business environment, especially when contemplating cross-cultural marketing issues such as entry or participation strategies in foreign markets.

Culture as an organisational factor

Culture is also the way in which people in an organisation solve problems and relate to one another. More formally, organisational culture is the pattern of shared basic assumptions learned by the members of an organisation as the organisations solve problems and internalise solutions into integrated business practices. Culture is distinctive and it permeates organisations, producing distinctive organisational cultures. Units of a larger organisation may have unique cultures. New members learn culture as the correct way to perceive, think and feel in relation to the problems encountered by the organisation and the solutions to those problems[7].

Organisational culture is a major influence on business and is discussed at length later in this book. It is a major influence on the organisational determinants of buyer behaviour and on the buying centre. The centralisation or decentralisation of purchasing, the priority of short or longer term outcomes and the desirability of lower prices or higher quality are all aspects of an organisation's culture. Culture is not the personality of the organisation.

Organisational climate[8], another important influence, is the related characteristic that refers to the overall personality of the organisation.

ECONOMIC ENVIRONMENT

Economic factors influence sales and profits in many organisational markets. Changes in the economic environment are often monitored using indicators. New housing permits, new office construction permits and the prime lending rate are three economic indicators which enterprises use as indicators. For example, new housing permits have a major impact on sales of cement, electrical wiring, brick-making, plumbing, telecommunications, carpeting and floor tiles. New office construction may influence all of those industries but also architectural services, insulation, legal, security, information technologies, project planning and janitorial services. Government policies, bank prime lending rates, the availability of skilled labour and confidence in government policy may all affect new housing permits or the construction of office space. Some traditional economic indicators include:

- rates of change in consumer and wholesale prices;
- personal and institutional saving and borrowing;
- sales of new cars, commercial vehicles, cement and other commodities linked to commercial activity;
- new building plans passed and buildings completed;
- new housing permits;
- manufacturing and production indices;
- imports and exports;
- immigration and emigration; and
- energy usage and sales (electricity, gas, petroleum products).

The significance of economic indicators may differ from country to country. The price of gold is probably much more important to South African business marketers than it would be to Singaporean marketers. The significance of economic indicators also differs from industry to industry. To continue with the example, the price of gold is probably more important to jewellers, mining machinery manufacturers and oil exploration firms than it is to firms producing food products.

Economic indicators can change trends some time before sales and profits in an industry change. When this happens, the economic indicator is said to lead the trend. For example, the rate of inflation can be a leading trend for bank overdraft rates. Business marketers in the IOR would be wise to invest time and effort into leading indicator identification in existing and potential markets.

LEGAL ENVIRONMENT

The legal environment influences business marketing strategy in three ways:

1. Laws and regulations determine possible strategies in an industry. For instance, regulations requiring certain accounting procedures, affirmative action, local content, labour practices or safety precautions may raise administrative costs to an extent that competitive price constraints may no longer allow acceptable profitability.

2. Legal and regulatory barriers can preclude entry by potential competitors to an industry. At the time of writing this book, the South African government is in the process of selling strategic equity shares in parastatals to prospective international alliance partners. There is much speculation that the final agreements will include certain periods of exclusivity and barriers to certain forms of competition.

3. Laws and regulations increasingly determine international product specifications and standards. Japanese regulations requiring compliance with local standards have become legendary (and often inflated). Requiring parts in English measurement units, rather than metric units, may be another regulatory issue in markets such as the United States.

Increasingly, non-product issues such as affirmative action also require careful consideration in the marketing plan. Trade legislation has become much more internationalised during the nineties.

PHYSICAL ENVIRONMENT

Desert dust, extreme coastal humidity or incidence of salt in coastal air can affect the performance and maintenance of equipment. Time awareness and urban density are important considerations in after-sales service promises. Diversity in physical environments characterises the Indian Ocean Rim.

Temperature	Altitude	Humidity
Infrastructural development	Urban density	Forestation
Desertification	Time awareness	Transportation
Agricultural development	Health care	Safety

Table 6.1 *Selected characteristics of physical environments*

POLITICAL ENVIRONMENT

The IOR political environment is also characterised by great diversity. This diversity is evident in the stability of governments in the region. The governments of Australia and Singapore are long established. More recently elected governments in South Africa and Pakistan appear to enjoy significant majority support. The situation in Somalia and some other countries in the region is far less stable. Support for all governments grows and subsides as the political events of the day unfold. Government instability is a source of risk many marketers consider important, especially when making the sizeable investments often required in business marketing.

Business marketers competing for government tenders, for sizeable contracts in industries considered strategic by the government or for business in foreign countries, often find that various political stakeholders in the political arena can exert significant influence in the buying decision. It is important to understand the world-view and objectives of the government's key supporters and their relative influence on purchases in your industry.

International conflict is also important to understand. Some governments in the region have long-standing ideological differences or disputes with other countries that can affect marketing strategy. For instance, marketers visiting India and Pakistan should be sensitive to the historic differences that exist between the two countries.

Casual and seemingly harmless comments about politics have been responsible for losing many major contracts when business marketers have unwittingly offended someone. In many IOR countries, it is fair game to take an opposing side of an argument to test a prospective supplier's political views. It is wise to avoid political discussions. Few people are offended if you courteously say that you feel it is improper to express political opinions as you are an outsider who is unaware of all the facts.

TECHNOLOGICAL ENVIRONMENT

The technological environment is most daunting and often requires intensive management these days. The advent of office automation, business re-engineering, CAD/CAM (computer-aided design and computer-aided manufacturing) technologies, decentralised organisational structures, transaction processing, more intensive strategic alliances with value-chain partners, integrated process analysis and quality control systems, and artificial intelligence and expert systems, signals a major change in the needs and conduct of business practice in many business markets.

INFORMATIONAL ENVIRONMENT

Increased environmental uncertainty leads to greater demands for information in the organisation[9]. Much of the change in the technological environment concerns information. Business marketers are among those realising that Information Technology (IT) gives a company a competitive advantage in logistics, marketing and sales, operations, corporate infrastructure management, human resource management, technology development and procurement[10].

The complexity of information technology development challenges many marketers. New database designs, such as client-server, resource sharing and distributed database systems, are replacing teleprocessing applications. These new alternatives, offering distributed processing and data storage, must be evaluated for their ability to deliver appropriate parallelism, independence, flexibility and availability within the cost, complexity, control and security objectives of the firm[11].

The interface of various network protocols, file structures and data communication links requires adjustments to marketing strategy and the development of competencies that were unimportant a few years ago. American business now spends 63 per cent more on computers and communications hardware (and untold billions more on software) than it does on industrial machinery[12]. For firms that can get it right, information technology clearly provides superior, sustainable customer solutions of great power.

IT can have a major impact on marketing and production as business clients adapt to fast-changing markets. Manufacturing and production uses IT to improve efficiency, cut costs, cope with complexity and co-ordinate processes. Reactions to change, relationship management and provision of differentiation have all made IT an integral part of marketing strategy these days.

INDIVIDUAL INFLUENCES

THE BUYING CENTRE: ROLES PEOPLE PLAY

People play various roles within the organisation. Strategy must address each player's needs in the context of the player's role (see Table 6.2, page 77). The buying centre influences the purchase decision in three major ways[13]. It is a source of information from which the consideration set is chosen. It is the source for the evaluative criteria that steer individuals when forming brand preferences. It acts as an interaction structure through which organisational preferences form.

One of the most important challenges which strong marketers have to overcome is the challenge of providing information to people throughout customer organisations. This often requires bypassing gatekeepers with great diplomacy. A frequently used technique is to mail company newsletters, excerpts from trade and academic journals, or invitations to attend functions at trade shows to customers that are difficult to reach otherwise.

Technical people can help to influence sales most when buying centres are slow to decide, uncertain about needs or required benefits, and more interested in the right solution than a low price and after-sales continuity. By contrast, purchasing personnel play a stronger role in re-buy situations.

ROLE	DESCRIPTION
USERS	The people actually using a product are often removed from the purchasing process. Users are those people who actually use or consume a product. Often play the dual role of influencers.
GATEKEEPERS	Gatekeepers control access to other buying centre members and control the information they see. A secretary often plays the role of gatekeeper, so do buyers.
INFLUENCERS	Influencers may not use or buy the product. Their role is to amend the purchase decision by supplying information that aids in the evaluation of products and buying criteria. Influencers often reside outside the firm.
DECIDERS	Deciders make the actual purchase decision, although they may sometimes need rubber stamp approval from higher levels of the organisation.
BUYERS	Buyers make the actual purchase, sign documents and negotiate terms.

Table 6.2 *The buying centre*

THE INDIVIDUAL PLAYERS

The individual players of the buying centre and their inter-relationships probably contribute more complexity to business marketing than any other characteristic. The individual's role perception is a very important influence. So, too, are the buyer's perceptions of personality, value and attitudinal congruity with the supplier, the representative or the product.

Demographic fit between prospects may also enhance rapport and lead to increased sales. However, enterprises need to ensure that race, gender and cohort fit are not used as an excuse to perpetuate a lack of diversity in the sales force or to frustrate trends towards equal opportunity.

Individuals always have limitations concerning product knowledge and awareness. Companies always attempt to stretch those limits. Strong business marketers train sales personnel to recognise the individual prospect's resource limitations and to work within those limits when presenting product features, benefits and advantages. Astute business proposals always contain executive summaries in simple language that can be repeated comfortably by the buyer when liasing with other buying centre members.

Individual players respond to organisational and personal motivations. Organisational motives can be rational or emotional.

Rational motives can be more important in business marketing because of the formalised nature of the buyer process. They include characteristics such as price, quality, service, logistics, delivery, continuity of supply and reciprocity.

Emotional motives often concern personal issues. For instance, status and reward, the opportunity for promotion, perceived risk and friendship are all important personal motives that are essentially emotional in nature. Business marketers ignore emotional motives at their peril.

RELATIONSHIPS

Business marketing relationships of many kinds exist[14]. This section concerns relationships with two kinds of customers: always-a-share and lost-for-good customers. All customers share characteristics of these idealised customer types although most tend toward one extreme. Companies invest resources (time, money and effort) into building supplier relationships. It is very important that companies regularly review the nature of costs and benefits associated with these relationships.

ALWAYS-A-SHARE CUSTOMERS

Markets with short time horizons are characterised by many always-a-share customers. These markets generally have lower switching costs, relatively smaller resource investments and lower perceived risk. They consist of products which buyers consider to be of less relative importance to their business. Such markets require transaction marketing, emphasising an immediate and compelling product offer targeted to the customer's needs.

LOST-FOR-GOOD CUSTOMERS

Lost-for-good customers are generally found in industries with high switching costs, large resource investments and high perceived risk. The product may be mission critical and certainly has strategic, operational or personal importance to influential members of the buying centre. Lost-for-good customers, called that because once landed they become long-term customers but once lost they are gone forever, can take years to tie down due to the relatively long time horizons. Such markets require relationship marketing epitomised by much activity and contact before the sale.

Chapters 8 and 9 address the issues of business definition and bases for segmenting business markets.

THE DECISION PROCESS

The decision process consists of the eight stages shown in Figure 6.4 on page 79. Many business marketers' clients sell to consumers, and strong business marketers understand their customers' customers.

The determination of task type, while rarely formalised as a selection from new-task, modified re-buy or straight re-buy types, nonetheless is generally established formally by the policies and procedures which govern organisational procurement. Task type is a fundamental influence on need recognition and constitutes a first step in the model.

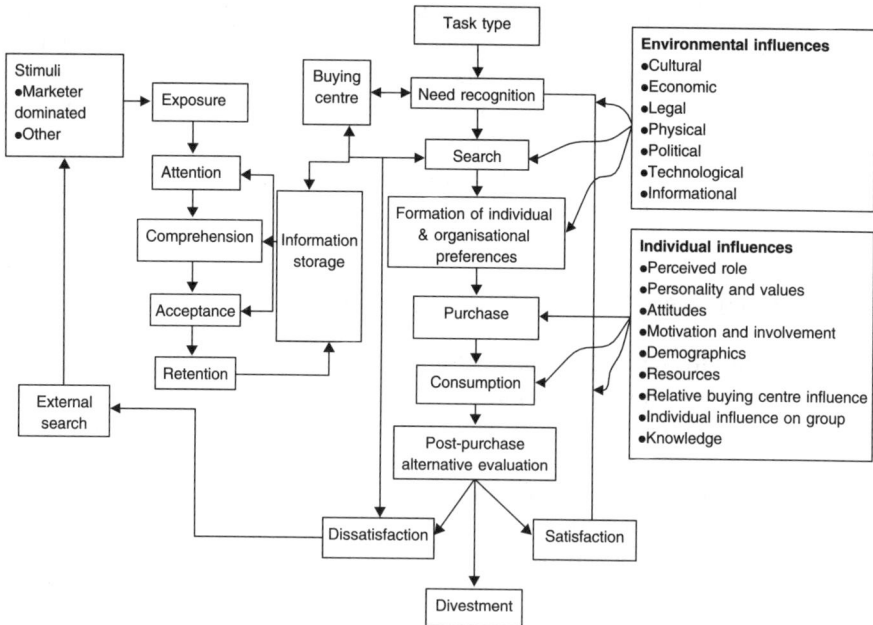

Figure 6.4 *A model of business purchase and consumption*[15]

NEED RECOGNITION

Need recognition occurs as a result of changes in environmental influences, individual differences or buying centre influences.

In straight re-buy situations, out-of-stock or low stock situations are important activators of need recognition. I am constantly amazed by companies that spend so much to attract people to place orders and then leave a bureaucratic bumble in place that makes it hard to actually buy something. Marketing plans should include tactics directed toward assisting customers with ordering and maintaining adequate stock levels. Constant monitoring of industry trends and supplier industry trends should help the business marketer to stimulate need recognition in modified re-buy situations. If strong marketers suggest new product features, advantages and benefits, and weak marketers wait for a customer to ask, then many industries must be characterised by weak marketing[16].

A word on commodity markets is appropriate. Many IOR business marketers find themselves selling commodities. Selling commodity products is a recipe for low margins and unnecessary hard work – two things many of us would like to avoid. Firms selling commodities often fail to realise that the product includes the totality of its features, advantages and benefits. At first glance, there may not be much scope in the sale of stainless steel once specifications are met in a tender. However, there is scope for differentiation in stainless steel companies that can include *information management systems* (stock re-ordering and inventory management), *logistical support* (transportation and distribution management) or *cost-saving technologies* (process-related skills). Such companies would no doubt command higher mark-ups, win more business and enjoy a higher share price on the stock exchange because of the enhanced bundle of end-user benefits. Thus, need recognition is much more than activating awareness of a need to replenish stock.

SEARCH AND INFORMATION PROCESSING

Search is more formalised in business marketing. Industry trade reports, trade associations, trade shows and opinion leaders can play important roles. Mass communication is generally unavailable to business marketers and promotional funds are often relatively small. Efficient allocation of promotional funds requires a comprehensive understanding of the degree, direction and sequence of search (see Figure 6.2, page 69).

So what do you do when your promotional funds are limited? You become even more creative. You do the things that hold special value to your target market. You build even better relationships with the customers most likely to benefit your bottom line.

Communicating features, advantages and benefits to all members of the buying centre is a common problem in business marketing. Many firms use newsletters or direct mail for this purpose. One firm regularly orders reprints from *Harvard Business Review* and a host of engineering journals and includes these with newsletters that are finely targeted at customers and prospects. The articles address technical and management issues of interest to their customers' senior managers. Confessing that he did not understand much of the mathematical gobbledegook in the articles, the firm's CEO told me he is delighted nonetheless with the effort because it positions the company as knowledgeable and expert in the field. He gets many personal calls thanking the company for the articles and says that buying centre members fight to get onto the distribution list. More importantly, he believes the campaign significantly enhances bottom-line profits. This strategy has the added benefit of communicating brand image and message content in an environment that is conducive to customer interests and likely to overcome any barriers raised by selective cognition[17].

Another firm selling to the motor car industry regularly arranges test-drives at a race track where companies can test-drive competitive brands. The firm also maintains an extensive library on the industry and makes it available to customers.

Some firms are known to hold after-hours board meetings at their customers' premises, right on the shop floor. Of course, this requires co-ordination and a willing supplier, but customers feel honoured that the business thinks so much of them that they are willing to hold a board meeting at their premises in order to get a feel for the business. A logical outcome is that both boards meet before or afterwards in a friendly atmosphere, information is exchanged and mutually beneficial ideas emerge from the discussions.

EVALUATION OF ALTERNATIVES

Alternative evaluation hinges largely on adherence to specifications in many markets. This suggests the importance of focusing marketing activities on influencing specification content before finalisation of the specifications. This can only be accomplished if the firm reaches a wide enough spectrum of buying centre roles.

Marketing strategy must respond to differences in the relative importance of criteria to individuals playing different roles[18]. Salespeople must also be sensitive to different risk perceptions, and be aware of the strategies that firms employ to lower risk[19].

Scheduling trips to the firm's premises is one way in which buyers use *external uncertainty reduction*. *Internal uncertainty reduction* is the strategy employed when buyers contact other buyers. Stressing that the firm is well known, tried and trusted through the judicial use of credible endorsements is a very effective strategy which strong marketers use to appeal to *uncertainty reduction*.

Buyers employ *external consequences reduction* strategies when they use multiple sources. Stressing service levels and customer satisfaction may be effective in reducing the use of other suppliers. Strong marketers strive first to become the primary supplier, and then offer a sufficient endorsement to overcome buyer risk perceptions concerning susceptibility to reduced price competitiveness or service as a result of single sourcing with the firm. Loyalty bonuses can be effective inducements to overcome *external consequences risk*. However, in my experience, loyalty bonuses are most effective as annual payments about 30 days before the buyer's financial year-end. I would never offer to pay such bonuses on a more frequent basis, nor would I pay any bonus without a statement from the firm's auditors verifying the share of business my company received. *Internal consequences reduction* strategies include consulting top management. This stresses the importance of communicating with top managers in buyer firms. There is evidence that the offers of established suppliers and challengers are perceived and evaluated differently[20]. The reputation of established suppliers may be more strongly related to the salesperson and product attitudes held by organisational buyer firms than for challengers. Challengers need to understand that extrinsic cues, such as the salesperson's appearance, the quality of a sales brochure or apparent fit with culture take on more importance as summary evaluative criteria in the absence of direct previous experience.

PURCHASE

Purchase in business markets generally occurs when an order is placed with a salesperson. A comprehensive discussion of sales management and strategy is beyond the scope of this book. However, sales management is so important to the purchase of business products and services that I will address some of the emerging trends[21].

CHANGING NATURE OF PURCHASE

The advent of integrated communication, content and computing technologies is making it easier to contemplate selling strategies that avoid the expense of direct sales visits. Telesales, on-line and dial-up systems and direct mail have become favourite strategies for reaching smaller accounts with complex needs. This trend will accelerate as companies begin providing services over the Internet.

MORE INTENSIVE SALES PLANNING

Sales has lost its shotgun approach and joined the marketing movement. Sales planning is playing a more important role and information is the currency of success. Sales planning is conducted at the rock face. Which customers will buy, when, and why? Who plays what role in the buying centre? Management must know the answers to these questions[22]. This suggests that salespeople not only require more information about customers and prospects, but also about their customers' and prospects' customers and prospects!

SALES LEADS REQUIRE GREATER MANAGEMENT

Lead management systems are becoming more widespread with the advent of computerised databases and the automated office system[23]. Sales leads will have to be better qualified in the future. Much effort will be expended in understanding and modelling the ultimate business derived from sales leads so that the effectiveness of the enterprise and its staff can be understood and new product ideas generated.

The organisation of the sales force is another important consideration. Popular organisational styles[24] include organising by

- major account (where account size is large and account complexity is low),
- national account (large and complex accounts), or
- more traditional geographic or broad industrial classes (small and relatively simple accounts).

Strong business marketers have specific programmes in place to generate leads, to compile and store leads, and to manage selling follow-through to leads, and they organise the sales force appropriately.

BETTER INTERPERSONAL INFLUENCING AND NEGOTIATION SKILLS

Consider the buyer's office in coming years. Salespeople will arrive with extensive information about customers and prospects and their markets. They will have extensive buying centre information and will be armed with comprehensive strategies for the various participants in the buying centre. In such an environment, interpersonal influencing and negotiation skills may often close a sale. Firms that concentrate on learning sales-closing techniques by rote are not building the kind of competence required for the new adaptive sales environment. The new environment requires empowered salespeople who understand influencing strategies and how to adapt them during the give and take of negotiation[25].

CONSUMPTION

Many business marketers consider the marketing effort to be complete when a sale is made and the product delivered. Such beliefs stifle an important source of innovation by limiting the firm's ability to learn from lead users[26]. In essence, such beliefs also take away a major opportunity to grow the market and gain market share. If one studies business practices at successful companies, such as The Limited, Banc One or Worthington Steel, one quickly observes a standard rule — *every senior manager* (regardless of functional discipline) *spends one half-day each week with customers.* Every week, without excuse, without exception. Such a practice would give business marketers many good ideas about how to get people to use more products and to buy more products!

POST-PURCHASE ALTERNATIVE EVALUATION

Business customers generally review the performance of major purchases. Thus, post-purchase evaluation is a major concern in new task and modified re-buy situations. Straight re-buy situations may not provoke regular and systematic reviews, yet post-purchase alternative evaluation remains a concern.

Challenger firms can use post-purchase evaluation as a powerful tool to gain new customers. Consider the case of Walton's, named South Africa's leading stationer and company of the year a number of times in the 1980s. Walton's had a very effective direct selling programme that targeted heavy users and major corporate accounts. The Walton's representatives visited companies and spoke directly to secretaries, forming useful relationships and handing out promotional pieces and illustrated stationery catalogues. In this relationship with the customer, they operated from 100 stores countrywide in most businesses and were able to secure national stationery contracts. Discussion earlier in this chapter would suggest that stationery is a low involvement, straight re-buy situation. Walton's apparently found relatively less pressure on margins than many more competitive industries because of their competitive prices and quick delivery. When Makro and Office Mart launched into the cash-and-carry wholesale stationery market, their direct mail pieces immediately called Walton's pricing into question, despite legal impediments to comparative advertising. This post-purchase alternative evaluation did not favour Walton's and the company's overall profitability was affected. Excellent company that it is, Walton's fought back and has learned the cash-and-carry wholesale stationery trade after a rocky period. The firm recently acquired Office Mart when it went into liquidation.

RELATIVE SATISFACTION AND DIVESTMENT

Strong business marketers understand what leads to satisfaction because they participate with the customer at all stages of the buying process. Astute firms constantly measure the level of satisfaction that competitors' clients report. They know when their competitors have problems that can become opportunities to take accounts away. Such market knowledge becomes extremely important when considering lost-for-good customers.

Divestment is also an opportunity to gain business. Many customers would like to trade up to a new purchase but are limited because of previous investments. Opportunities often exist in the IOR to sell used equipment to firms in less developed markets. Strong business marketers understand the importance of this and have programmes in place to take advantage of these opportunities.

Business also can be won when firms offer a complete service to business markets where hazardous materials form a part of the process. Firms that can dispose of such products safely have a stronger position than those that cannot. Products that do not require specialised disposal, so-called environmentally friendly products being an example, are in a strong competitive position.

Summary

This chapter has presented a behavioural approach to business marketing focused on three dimensions (see Figure 6.1, page 69). The belief that buyer perceptions, needs and requirements should guide business marketing strategy is fundamental to the approach.

This chapter ends the first section of the book — a section that has focused on managing the purchase and consumption environment. Much of competitive analysis concerns discovering ways in which competitors are not managing the purchase and consumption market well. Unless firms manage the purchase and consumption environment well, they will not be successful over the longer term, no matter how well they might manage the competitive environment. The next section of this book deals with managing the competitive environment.

ENDNOTES

1 Kripalani (1997).
2 The discussion relies heavily on Webster Jr. (1991: 11-17).
3 Robbins (1991), presents an overview of the science of organisational behaviour. The first chapter discusses contributions from other sciences to the field.
4 Hutt & Speh (1992: 75).
5 Lewis (1996) Chapters 3 and 4. McCall & Warrington (1989).
6 Trompenaars (1993).
7 This definition is summarised from the discussion on pages 12-15 of Schein (1992).
8 Qualls & Puto (1989) explore the link between organisational climate and decision making.
9 Spekman & Stern (1979: 56).
10 See Porter (1985: 39-43).
11 Kroenke (1995) is an excellent introductory text concerning database issues.
12 Mandel (1996).
13 Choffray & Lillien (1979), especially the figure on page 22. Spekman & Gronhaug (1986: 50-63).
14 This section is based on Hutt & Speh (1992), Jackson (1985a), and Jackson (1985b).
15 This model is original but draws on the major models of business buyer behaviour and the EBM model.
16 Von Hippel (1988), presented compelling research findings suggesting that most innovation is undertaken by customers, not by marketers.
17 See Matlin (1989) and McGuire (1972) for a discussion of cognitive consistency theory.
18 This is discussed in detail in Choffray & Lillien (1979).
19 See Puto, Patton III & King (1985) and Sweeney, Matthews & Wilson (1973).
20 Brown (1995).
21 For more comprehensive treatments of sales management, see Abratt, van der Westhuizen & Blem (1989), Bolt (1987), Churchill, Ford & Walker (1997) and Johnson, Kurtz & Scheuing (1987).
22 This element is becoming more important and is covered in most comprehensive texts. See Churchill et al. (1997) and Johnson et al. (1987). Miller, Heiman & Tuleja (1988) advocate a system of selling based on rigorous planning. If you can find a copy of Craven (1983), grab it!
23 Donath, Dixon, Crocker & Obermayer (1995) is devoted to a selling system based on comprehensive lead management.
24 See Shapiro & Moriarty (1982).
25 I am very fond of Conklin (1979), and Kimball (1994), well-written and practical coverages of influencing issues. Fisher and Ury have produced two influential books on negotiation skills: Fisher & Ury (1991) and Ury (1991). Lewicki & Litterer (1985), is a more academic treatment of the topic.
26 Von Hippel (1988).

PART TWO

Managing the Competitive Environment

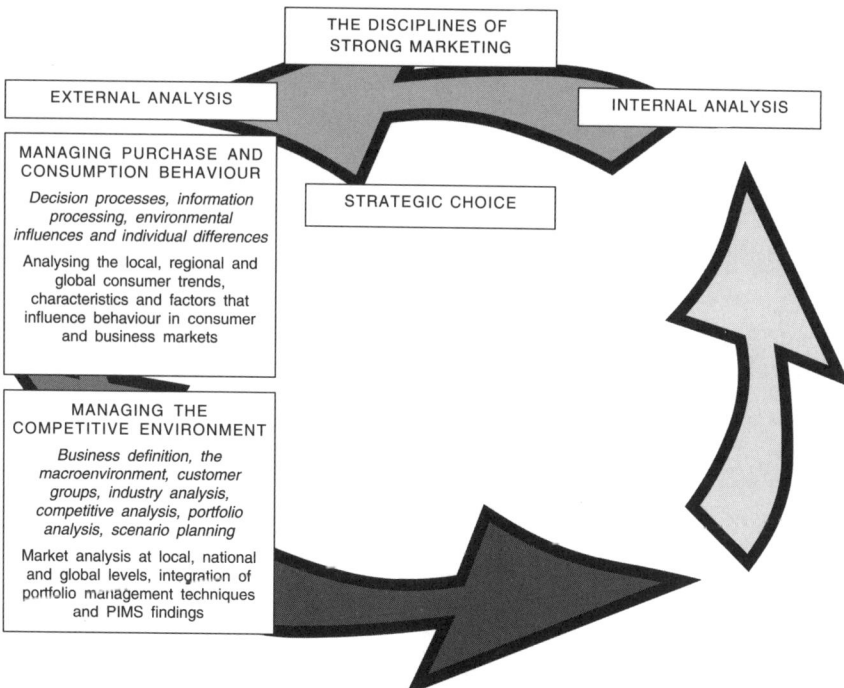

THE DISCIPLINES OF
STRONG MARKETING

EXTERNAL ANALYSIS

INTERNAL ANALYSIS

MANAGING PURCHASE AND CONSUMPTION BEHAVIOUR

Decision processes, information processing, environmental influences and individual differences

Analysing the local, regional and global consumer trends, characteristics and factors that influence behaviour in consumer and business markets

STRATEGIC CHOICE

MANAGING THE COMPETITIVE ENVIRONMENT

Business definition, the macroenvironment, customer groups, industry analysis, competitive analysis, portfolio analysis, scenario planning

Market analysis at local, national and global levels, integration of portfolio management techniques and PIMS findings

7 | Managing the Competitive Environment

Developing and managing the skills required for superior sustainable profitability

If people like Alex Pentland have their way, the pace of change will continue. Pentland's Massachusetts Institute of Technology (MIT) unit is one of the many American think-tanks that brought us the portable computer, graphical user interfaces, the Internet, multimedia and video-conferencing. Pentland teaches computers to do unusual things such as recognising people by voice or the way they walk. Pentland and his team are just one of many teams stretching the new digital technologies to the limit in an effort to find 'the next big thing'[1].

Considered by many to be nothing more than computer geeks dedicated to a world of doorknobs, light switches and clothes hangers incorporating artificial intelligence, Pentland is the kind of person wiser people recognise as having the potential to restructure even the most stable of industries in the wink of an eye.

Not convinced? How will competition be changed if a company like Checkpoint Systems, Inc. can implant a computer chip on packaged foodstuffs and then build a monitor for waste bins to identify what consumers discard in the rubbish? Just think, you could tell the computer that runs the house which items to reorder automatically and your selections could be delivered the next day. Food suppliers would learn how many packs of their product you consume a year, what time of the year, week or month you like to consume their product, how long their product is held in your freezer or pantry, and many other things that might just give them a final edge in conceiving a product offer you just couldn't refuse. What impact would such an innovation have on market segmentation, food transportation and logistics, supermarket sales and retailing management? Could it spell the end of supermarkets?

If one considers the competencies being accumulated by think-tanks such as 'the other Microsoft founder' Paul Allen's Interval Research, such technology is possible today. How long until the cost is cheap enough to justify the expense?

Pentland's world is far away from the mind of Nixon Moyo[2]. Nixon is from a village in Matabeleland near Bulawayo, Zimbabwe. Unable to find work and desperately wishing to provide for his wife and two children, Nixon left his home and illegally entered South Africa in 1984. Nixon bought a South African identity document in 1989 indicating that he is South African by birth and began answering to the new name of Nixon Nkhumalo. He now lives in a township outside Johannesburg with his second wife, Thembi, and three children and works in a motor car repair shop nearby.

Nixon still visits his first wife every year at Christmas and he sends extra money to Zimbabwe when he can, usually through other Zimbabweans who avoid exchange controls in both countries. Nixon is lucky, his Alexandra home is electrified. He has a small black and white television and hopes to buy a refrigerator in 1998. Thembi purchases most of their food from the *sphaza* shop[3] on their street. Most of the food is unpackaged, unbranded and unrefrigerated.

Who competes with whom in Nixon's world? IOR marketers often find themselves straddling the world Nixon lives in and the world Allen and Pentland dream about. This is one of the special challenges of building strong marketing in the region.

THE UNFOLDING IOR MARKETING ENVIRONMENT

So what is this new marketing environment? How will it apply to your business? What kind of implications will it hold for marketing in your industry? What is marketing's contribution to crafting effective strategies?[4] Every industry is different, but there are some common themes that are either being felt or beginning to be felt in most industries.

CUSTOMER RELATIONSHIPS ARE MORE IMPORTANT

The importance of the ability to build and manage customer relationships will determine marketing success in an ever-increasing way. This worldwide trend will grow in importance in the IOR due to the importance of relationships in many IOR cultures.

... *but so is transaction management*

Not every customer wants a long-term relationship. Many customers are one-time opportunities. The marketing literature will realise this when the current infatuation with relationship marketing subsides to a more realistic appraisal. Look for more informed thinking about transactional efficiency and satisfying one-time customers better and more profitably. The trend toward the use of automated transaction processing systems to improve speed of service and flexibility and to prevent fraud will accelerate. Transaction processing will become a very important information source for individualised marketing programmes.

TRANSNATIONAL BUSINESS IS COMMON

Business will be forced to move across borders in the IOR. Slow growth and mature markets will compel many companies in the industrialised countries to invest in the region. They will alter the nature of regional competition significantly.

... but so is cross-cultural marketing at home

Managing across cultures is a strength in many IOR countries. In fact, regional companies may be among world-leading cross-cultural marketers. As the IOR opens, they may become leaders in serving intermarket segments across the IOR which may deliver a tremendous competitive advantage in the emerging globalised market.

IOR WORLD-VIEW IS NECESSARY

The most successful firms will learn to value the diversity of the IOR. They will value the extreme differences in culture, wealth and world-view that characterise the IOR. Successful enterprises will be at home in the great cultures that have arisen from African, Buddhist, Christian, Hindu, Islamic and Taoist values. Only firms with such a world-view will be able to transcend the great differences of the IOR to become truly accepted into local cultures.

... but so is a global viewpoint

Keeping pace with the rest of the world will stretch IOR competitors. The industrialised nations will be bringing innovations into the region using dramatic new distribution sources. IOR winners will balance both worlds, fully understanding the international market as well as the regional market.

STRATEGIC ALLIANCES ARE MORE URGENT

Business partnering will become an ever more urgent requirement as the industrialised nations 'buy into' the IOR. Strategic alliances of IOR firms have the potential to deliver scale economies and other size factors that will contribute to competitive advantage. The diversity of the nations capable of building such alliances does not suggest that this will be an easy task.

FLEXIBILITY IS MORE ESSENTIAL

The nature of change has become increasingly discontinuous. The fall of communism will open the door to experimentation with other forms of government — some inherently socialistic in outlook, others tied to religious or cultural beliefs. Industries will be made obsolete by the quickening pace of innovation and entrepreneurship.

91

ENTREPRENEURSHIP IS MORE VITAL

Entrepreneurship will become more necessary in the prevailing discontinuities. Management will be stretched to think and do more with less. Individual initiative will be required at all levels of the enterprise.

CRAFTING EFFECTIVE STRATEGIES REQUIRES EFFECTIVE STRATEGIC THINKING

Strategic planning and number crunching are practised by almost every enterprise with varying degrees of formality. The existence of formal plans and detailed budgets is no indication of the level of strategic thinking in an organisation.

One difference between companies that achieve sustained growth and excellent performance and those that muddle along, is the ability to craft strategies[5]. Crafting strategy requires more than an analytical, rational approach to business analysis and market planning. It requires a passionate understanding of the intimate details of the business. Crafting strategy is a mastery of process and plan, of opponent and opportunity.

From one viewpoint, the purpose of strategy is to plan interaction with the external environment. Without a comprehensive knowledge of the firm's resources and competencies which constitute its relative weaknesses and strengths or the threats and opportunities in the external environment, the firm cannot craft effective strategies.

DEFINING THE BUSINESS

The process of crafting strategy begins with defining the business. Levitt's seminal article[6] challenging short-sighted business definitions has been standard fare in MBA courses around the world for more than 30 years. Using the example of the railroad, Levitt advocated defining business about an underlying need and suggested that once railroads thought of their '... business as taking care of people's transportation needs, nothing can stop [them] from creating [their] own extravagantly profitable growth[7].'

Levitt raises an essential question concerning the breadth and depth of the product offering. Which is more likely to lead to enduring competitiveness – a business directed at the small passenger car market or a business dedicated to providing mobility to small families on more limited budgets? The success of the VW Beetle was based on the latter. The broader business definition approach has been responsible for some major accomplishments[8] – consider Microsoft's transformation from software developer to provider of business and consumer information solutions.

Nevertheless, there is always the danger of defining the business too widely, as suggested by the sobering experiences of McGraw-Hill, which lost $172 million when widening their business definition from publishing to that of 'information turbine'[9]. McGraw-Hill painfully discovered that business must demonstrate competency in the more widely defined business. A firm's reach must not exceed its grasp.

Simon's innovative study[10] of 500 excellent medium-sized firms suggests a trend toward more narrow business focus in more internationalised markets. Although these firms seem well aware of the competitive risks of 'putting their eggs in one basket'[11], 67.1 per cent of sales come from one market and 60 per cent expect that share of sales to increase[12].

A McKinsey and Company study[13] found that successful manufacturers achieved 80 per cent of their sales from less than half as many customers as the less successful manufacturers (and 100 per cent from about 20 per cent as many customers), at equivalent sales volumes.

Figure 7.1 below demonstrates a useful technique for defining a business, in this case applied to the South African cellular industry. The traditional South African definitions of network operator (Vodacom and MTN) or service provider (Vodac, M-Tel, Teljoy, Radiospoor, Autopage, etc.) are ignored in favour of a multi-dimensional approach plotting services, customer groups and call types.

Figure 7.1 is a plot of three dimensions. The *national emergency services coverage for professionals product market* is the intersection of the three highlighted concepts on the three axes.

The following steps will enable you to plot your own product markets in this way:

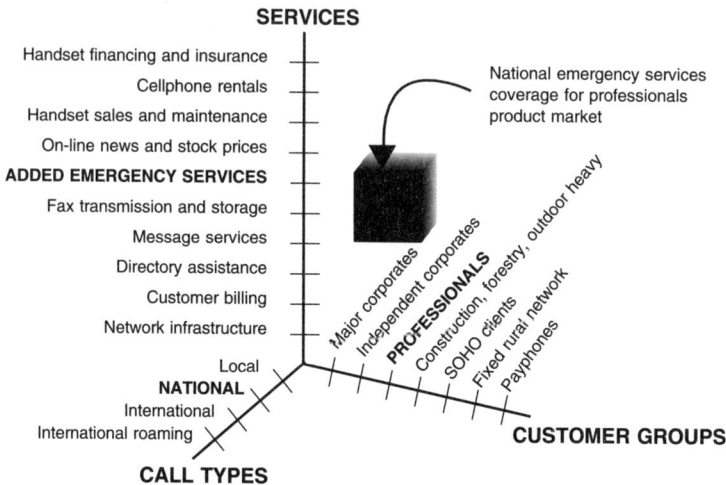

Figure 7.1 *A business opportunity constructed from selected dimensions of the South African GSM cellular industry*

Step 1. Identify products and services offered by the industry as you know it, for example diet colas.

Step 2. Identify products and services offered outside the industry that might be substitutes in various usage situations. Brainstorm about different product forms (regular colas, other diet soft drinks, other soft drinks, concentrates) that offer similar physical attributes and functional benefits, and those that offer similar abstract attributes or psychosocial benefits (see Chapter 4). Then, consider related product categories (hot drinks, wine, beer, juice, bottled water). It may also be useful to consider generic competitors (cigarettes, ice cream). The idea is to build a comprehensive list of possible substitutes at this point. Do not judge.

Step 3. If people had perfect information and no constraints (i.e., ignore resources), would these products or services be substituted if your product did not exist? Focus the list to true substitutes. Do not fall into the trap of thinking of the world as it is. Think of it as it may be by removing from your mind any factors that limit consumers today. Forget about money, awareness or time — these constraints can be overcome.

Step 4. Construct an axis of all these products, services and substitutes and label the axis 'products' or 'services'. In effect, you have just built a model of the consumer's consideration set and considered the consumer's symbolic world.

Step 5. Next, identify customer groups or target segments and the usage occasions in which they use the product or service. In consumer markets, which individual differences and environmental influences affect purchase and consumption in this market? Which of these are important during purchase or consumption? In industrial markets, consider roles (buyer, influencer, gatekeeper, decider or user), usage occasions and task (straight re-buy, modified re-buy, new task). See also Chapter 6.

Step 6. Construct an axis of all these customer groups and label the axis 'customer groups'. In effect, you have just built a model of the influences on the consumer's belief systems.

Step 7. Finally, construct any additional axes. Usage occasion, buyer role, task, time of day, product knowledge, benefit sought, geography (see also Chapter 6) — the list is endless. Of course, you are not limited to three dimensions. You can conceptualise and use tables to analyse more. However, three dimensions are adequate for most products.

Step 8. Finally, consider each business opportunity you have constructed. Quantify your ability to compete in this business. What resources are required to compete in this business? What competencies are required? What experience can you bring to bear?

Defining the business is a process. Many companies find that their definition of the business changes as they audit successive aspects of the competitive environment. The quality of definitions on each axis of the analysis is important. Many companies are not adequately informed about these dimensions prior to conducting the additional analyses detailed in this and other chapters of this book (especially those that follow in this section). This is especially true in industries where communications, information and entertainment are major inputs or influences.

MACROENVIRONMENTAL ANALYSIS

Defining the business opens the door to further analysis of the marketing environment. Macroenvironmental analysis often reveals important environmental trends affecting the business. Discussion in earlier chapters focused on analysing the consumer's environment; the discussion here concerns the greater environment. What trends affect this business? What is the trend in consumer savings? Are wholesale trade inventories excessive? What will happen to the bank overdraft rate? How will the exchange rate vary? Do economists expect inflation to increase?

For many firms, environmental analysis ends when the inflation rate is appended to price increase information in the marketing plan. Of course, this is not enough.

Consider the following questions for each of the product markets and sub-regions in which you hope to do business.

Economic

- What is the rate of increase in prices at the consumer and wholesale levels?

- How do government and banks feel about the economy? What measures are likely from both? Is any change in price regulation likely?

- What is the rate of increase in competitor prices and the price of substitutes? Is this favourable to this business?

- How fast are input prices rising? Are any shortages forecasted?

- Are suppliers vulnerable to environmental trends that might increase prices?

- How fast are all these prices expected to rise during the planning period? What is the longer-term outlook?

- How is overall consumer borrowing changing? How does this compare with your customer's ability to pay? Will credit repayments squeeze consumer buying power?

- Are savings increasing or decreasing as a percentage of GNP per capita?

- Is the government likely to direct resources to any specific sector of the economy or population? How will this impact on the economy? On this business?

- What impact will exchange rates have on inputs? On price competitiveness in foreign markets versus local firms? Versus other foreign companies there and here?

Political/Regulatory

- How do existing laws and regulations affect your product? How are laws and regulations likely to change?
- Is the government likely to change? Is there pressure for change by elements within the government or the opposition that may become more influential? How would this affect this business?
- Which government arenas should be monitored? Will action in labour relations, consumer rights, environmental protection or empowerment of the historically disadvantaged result in new regulations that will affect this product or the profitability of the business?
- Are any cultural groups feeling excluded from influence on government policy? Who are they? What are their aims? How would these aims affect this business?

Legal

- How does the legal system function? Is it effective?
- How much time lapses between the time a suit is filed and final settlement? What does it cost to litigate?
- Are court decisions enforced (are winning litigants likely to receive their award)?
- What is the basis of law (English common law, Roman/Dutch, etc.)? Do your home country lawyers have an affiliate there?
- Is there any aspect of this business that is the focus of legal action in this country?

Technological

- What changes are affecting technology in this business? What technologies are changing as a result, and how are they changing?
- What about process technology? Has business re-engineering affected technologies? How?

- Do traditional competitors in this country use different technologies to those used in the home market? Why? What is the impact on costs and profits? What competencies do these technologies require?

- Are competitors experimenting with or implementing new technologies? What specific advantages do they hope to achieve?

- How will this impact on your price competitiveness?

- How does your technology compare to competitors in all markets? How much would it cost you to improve technology? What would be the return on the investment (not only versus the cost of investment but also versus the cost of doing nothing)?

Summary

This chapter introduced some trends underlying the Indian Ocean Rim macroenvironment and discussed some important points for defining the business.

It is becoming more difficult to craft strategies in the fast-changing environment. Many firms experience problems because of insufficient environmental analysis. Macroenvironmental analysis requires investigation of economic, political/regulatory, legal and technological environments.

Defining the business and performing macroeconomic environment analysis are valuable first steps in crafting effective strategies. The next chapter discusses alternative processes for identifying profitable customer groups. The following chapters of this section address industry analysis, competitor analysis, corporate appraisal, portfolio analysis and scenario planning.

ENDNOTES

1 Ramo (1996).
2 The name and story presented here are fictitious and have been constructed from three similar cases with which I am familiar.
3 A small, informal sector trading outlet. Sphaza means 'hidden' or 'play-play', referring to the times when local traders who were denied licences to trade in the black townships resorted to operating from unmarked houses in the townships so that the police could not spot them. The souks in East Africa are a similar informal sector retail outlet.
4 See Day (1992) for a critique of marketing's role in strategy.
5 Mintzberg (1987) popularised the concept of crafting strategy in strategy research literature.
6 Levitt (1960). See also Kotler & Singh (1980).
7 Levitt (1960: 53).
8 Rappaport & Halevi (1991) demonstrate the thinking espoused by advocates of this approach.
9 Mintzberg (1994: 279-280).

10 Simon (1996).
11 Such as the risk of losing a product's unique position or price premium if more standardised products target the niche, or the risk that higher production prices will result from the failure to capture more economies of scale or scope.
12 Simon (1996) Chapter 3.
13 See Rommel (1995: 38-45).

8 Identifying Profitable Customer Groups

Market segmentation is the basis of marketing

Many textbooks make the marketing concept sound so simple: 1. Find groups of people or companies with similar requirements (market segments). 2. Design an especially enticing total product offer by combining elements of the marketing mix (price, product, promotion and distribution). 3. Implement the strategy.

Unfortunately, no element of this equation is simple in practice. The best firms sometimes fail to define market segments properly, or choose the wrong target segments or assemble an inappropriate marketing mix. Such errors in judgement rob companies and their shareholders of competitive advantage and profits.

ACTIVITY	TASKS
MARKET SEGMENTATION	Identify segmentation variables
	Determine influence on purchase and consumption
	Segment market
	Profile segment
MARKET TARGETING	Evaluate segment attractiveness
	Identify intermarket segments
	Select target segments
PRODUCT POSITIONING	Identify possible positioning concepts for each target segment
	Identify appropriate marketing mix strategies for each target segment
	Finalise positioning strategy with other stakeholders

Table 8.1 Market segmentation, market targeting and product positioning tasks[1]

There is considerable market segmentation literature and volumes of academic journals discuss the relative merits of alternative segmentation criteria, statistical techniques and segmentation methods[2]. This chapter will discuss elements of that literature as they influence marketing in the IOR and the related concepts shown in Table 8.1 (page 99).

Following worldwide trends, finance, research and development (R&D), human resources, operations and other company disciplines are co-operating on marketing strategy development more often. One result of this is that some managers from outside marketing are becoming more intimately involved with segmentation strategies. These managers may find that the identification of profitable customer groups requires knowledge and skills foreign to their 'home' discipline, especially when the topic switches to statistical techniques. The material in this chapter is written to be accessible to these managers, as well as to more experienced marketing professionals.

Market segmentation is a closely related concept to market targeting and product/service positioning as Table 8.1 shows. Market segmentation includes four activities: identifying segmentation variables, determining the influence of segmentation variables on purchase and consumption behaviour, segmenting the market and profiling the segments.

MARKET SEGMENTATION

IDENTIFYING SEGMENTATION VARIABLES

CLASS	CONSUMER MARKETS TYPICAL SEGMENTATION VARIABLES
BEHAVIOURAL	Desired benefits, loyalty, propensity to respond to the offer, readiness to buy, usage occasion, usage rate, user status
BELIEF SYSTEM	Self-concept, values, attitudes, beliefs, symbolic associations, construed meaning
ENVIRONMENTAL INFLUENCES	Cultural values, family size, family life cycle, family decision style, nationality, personal influences, situation, social class, tribe
INDIVIDUAL DIFFERENCES	Ability to pay, addressability, age, attitudes, education, gender, income, involvement, knowledge, lifestyle, lifestage, motivation, need for convenience, occupation, personality, physical characteristics, race, religion, resources, time constraints, values (and other industry-related demographic and psychographic variables)
GEOGRAPHICAL	Region, country, province, major metropolitan area, suburb, trading area, population density, climate, housing type, cyberspace address

Table 8.2 *Selected consumer segmentation variables*

CLASS	BUSINESS MARKETS TYPICAL SEGMENTATION VARIABLES
BUYER CHARACTERISTICS	Buyer-seller similarity, company politics, loyalty, personal ambitions, relationship quality, risk attitudes
DEMOGRAPHICS	Company size, number of employees, industry, location, ownership of office space
PURCHASING APPROACHES	Centralisation of purchasing, negotiating style, organisational structure, power structure, purchasing criteria, purchasing policies
PURCHASING SITUATION	Desired application, order size, task, urgency
OPERATING VARIABLES	Customer capabilities, usage experience, usage occasion, technological capabilities

Table 8.3 Selected business segmentation variables

The identification of segmentation variables has the potential to deliver powerful competitive advantage and there are hundreds of segmentation variables from which to choose. Consider Tables 8.2 and 8.3. There is no one way to segment a market, and thousands of variables have been used effectively by enterprises as a basis for understanding their markets.

THE VALUE OF QUALITITATIVE ANALYSIS

However comprehensive Tables 8.2 and 8.3 may seem, the most useful segmentation variable for a particular objective may not be listed. The relative performance of an individual segmentation variable depends on specific segmentation objectives. So, the best variable for a general understanding of a market may not be the same as the variable selected for new product concepts, a new promotional strategy, an evaluation of pricing policy or a distribution strategy[3].

Adding more complexity, it is common for a particular segmentation variable to correlate with purchase or consumption behaviour for one product, but to add little to the understanding of differences in a closely related product. The same effect can be seen in different cultural groups and in different countries. Thus, the selection of variables for segmenting IOR regional markets can be even more complex.

Qualitative research plays an essential role in eliciting segmentation variables. A wide range of new research techniques and methodologies influences the way contemporary focus groups, in-depth interviews, means-end chain analyses and other techniques are conducted[4]. The new techniques often reveal hidden segmentation variables or suggest the importance of variables one might normally ignore. Qualitative research is both an art form and a science, and requires careful planning and execution that is usually best contemplated with professional assistance.

Ford's entire management team, threatened with ever-sliding American market share and profitability, viewed focus groups from behind the mirrored glass for years in order to build an understanding of what people wanted. The interaction of marketing, human resources, finance and R&D in the viewing suite resulted in much synergy and improved research. The Ford Taurus became the first American car to be Number 1 in America in its launch year, and it maintained this position for over a decade thereafter. Ford credits this success to the customer focus that emerged from this process.

It is important not to make the mistake of assuming that qualitative research has revealed the true nature of a market. Qualitative research samples are normally too small for such a leap of faith and probably are not representative of the total market. Ford tested what emerged from the focus groups in representative samples out in the marketplace to validate these focus groups. A value of qualitative research, and it is great value indeed, is to reveal what the quantitative research should explore and quantify. This is especially necessary when researching across cultures.

SEGMENTING THE MARKET OR THE DATABASE?

Customer database segmentation has become a popular topic in recent years because of the growing popularity of direct marketing. The statistical techniques and methods used for database segmentation differ little from those used for traditional market segmentation. Readers interested in database segmentation will want to consult the focused discussion of direct marketing and database issues in Chapter 15.

THINKING ACROSS CULTURES

The reliability and validity of research often depends on cross-cultural issues in the IOR, even when research is conducted within the boundaries of one country. Much of this chapter details ways to enhance the reliability and validity of cross-cultural research.

A visit to any IOR country often reveals a sameness of cities, shopping malls, television programming and other aspects of culture. However, it would be a mistake to assume a greater diversity does not lie hidden below these surface aspects of culture. The adoption of globalised communications and content do not suggest the adoption of a globalised culture largely rooted in the American cultural experience, in my opinion.

Transnational and regional segmentation strategies require the identification of culture-specific and universal characteristics that represent meaningful differences likely to lead to different product preferences[5]. Cultural-specific characteristics may also transcend national boundaries. Those contemplating pan-IOR strategies would be wise to consider these guidelines:

1. Identify the geographic area and determine the relevant cultures

Always determine the geographic area and the cultures that are resident in an area. The Human Relations Area Files can be consulted to determine not only the cultures of interest but also relevant research on the behavioural aspects of those cultures[6]. The Indian Ocean Rim Virtual Library, resident on Australian university computers, is another possible information source[7].

2. Attempt to identify core meaning issues

Determine all core meaning issues relevant to the marketing strategy. This topic was discussed in detail in earlier chapters. (See page 35.)

3. Design surveys for cross-cultural use

Write cross-cultural surveys in a way that is

- readily translatable into other languages,

- easily understood by all respondents,

- capable of measuring concepts which are important in the cultures under study, and

- free of imposed concepts from the researcher's own culture[8].

4. Ensure culture-free communications

Translation and back-translation procedures are very important. Documents should be translated and then given to a person from the culture in question to back-translate into the original language. The re-translation should be compared to the original document and any differences noted and investigated. The original document should then be re-translated and given to another individual for back-translation into the original language. This process should continue until the back-translation does not differ significantly from the original document[9].

DETERMINING THE INFLUENCE OF SEGMENTATION VARIABLES ON PURCHASE AND CONSUMPTION BEHAVIOUR

The next step of the segmentation process normally begins with the design and execution of field research[10].

An attempt to discuss proper research procedure lies outside the objectives of this management book, but the endnotes to this chapter will direct the reader to many excellent texts concerning marketing research and data analysis.

Managers need to understand some basic issues and to develop an understanding that numbers do not always reveal great truths. The ability to include so many variables in segmentation analysis has encouraged many novices to try their hand at segmentation. This is a trend that is good for marketing and business in general. 'Living with the data' can be a substantial aid to developing a marketing orientation[11] and in-depth understanding of the customer.

However, determining the influence of segmentation variables is the basis of developing target market strategies.

- *Make sure that those conducting segmentation analysis for the firm have adequate knowledge and experience to complete the task properly.* There are many mistakes that can be made and most of them are invisible to the untrained eye. Violating the basic assumptions of statistical techniques invalidates the analysis and leads to erroneous conclusions[12]. Failure to follow the basic requirements for cross-cultural research design or data modelling may produce flawed research and achieve disappointing results[13]. The influence of segmentation variables can be determined with the assistance of a number of statistical techniques and it is usually best to seek the help of professional researchers.

- *It is most irresponsible to brief a research company and then to withdraw from the research process.* Often positioned as 'letting the boffins get on with it', such behaviour deprives the firm of an understanding of the research process and puts unreasonable pressure on the research company which can never know the product or market as well as the firm itself.

There is a great difference between avoiding interference with professional researchers and forcing the research house to take ownership of the segmentation analysis. Most good research houses actively encourage participation. Here are some questions to ask your marketing research associates:

1. *Did you perform univariate analysis and how did the variables inter-correlate?*

Once variables are identified and research has been conducted, determination of data distributions and inter-correlations can be a useful first step. Many statistical techniques, especially multivariate techniques, make assumptions about the data. For example, it is a common requirement that the data is normally distributed. Univariate analysis establishes the actual distribution of the data, as well as the very useful mean, mode, median, standard deviation and variance statistics.

(a) *Correlation can be very good.* Significant correlations between product choice and radio, newspaper and television consumption may reveal something about a higher-order phenomenon, such as something called 'need for information' or something about 'media dependency'[14].

(b) *Correlation can be bad.* High correlations of independent variables can reduce the predictive power of other dependent variables in some types of analysis, thereby increasing the possibility that a valuable data relationship will be obscured[15].

Ask to see statistics concerning the distribution of the data and data inter-correlations.

2. Are there any underlying structures in the data?

The ability to analyse so many variables these days can lead to paralysis and, as researchers attempt to understand which variables are the most important, they end up unable to make conclusions. To avoid this, many researchers attempt to reduce the dimensionality of the data using factor analysis or principal components analysis[16]. These techniques attempt to reveal common 'factors' underlying the data by exploring the nature of the inter-correlations of variables. When the data is correlated, a large number of variables can be reduced to a smaller number of factors that often reveal great meaning about segment characteristics. If no correlations occur in the data, these techniques do not produce much of interest.

Many marketing practitioners do not realise that factor analysis does not produce an exact number of factors. There are many techniques for deciding on a number of factors.

It is very important to know how much of the variance is 'explained' by the factors. Although the natural sciences often require factors to account for 90-95 per cent of the variance, the rule of thumb in marketing and social research is that the factors should account for at least 60 per cent of the variance. A solution accounting for over 75 per cent of the variance is considered quite good.

The correlation of the factors and the original variables (the factor loadings) is another important statistic. *Factor loadings* are the basis of determining what a factor represents, i.e. its inner essence. In general, factor loadings over .50 are considered practically significant[17].

- Ask the researchers why they chose to reduce variables, how much of the variance is accounted for by their factors, and which variables load on each factor. If you don't understand, ask them to explain until you do.

- Ask penetrating questions about cross-cultural issues. Satisfy yourself that the research has discovered universal concepts and that culture-specific factors have been taken into account.

SEGMENTING THE MARKET

Most segmentation analyses employ cluster analysis and many other multi-variate statistical techniques to partition respondents into homogeneous groups. Here are some questions to ask your marketing research associates:

1. Was cluster analysis used?

IOR markets can be segmented in many ways. Cluster analysis is a multivariate technique that is often used to group individuals, based upon their characteristics, such as responses to survey questions[18]. If the sample is representative and if the data is amenable to cluster analysis, the clusters which emerge from a study can be said to be representative of market segments.

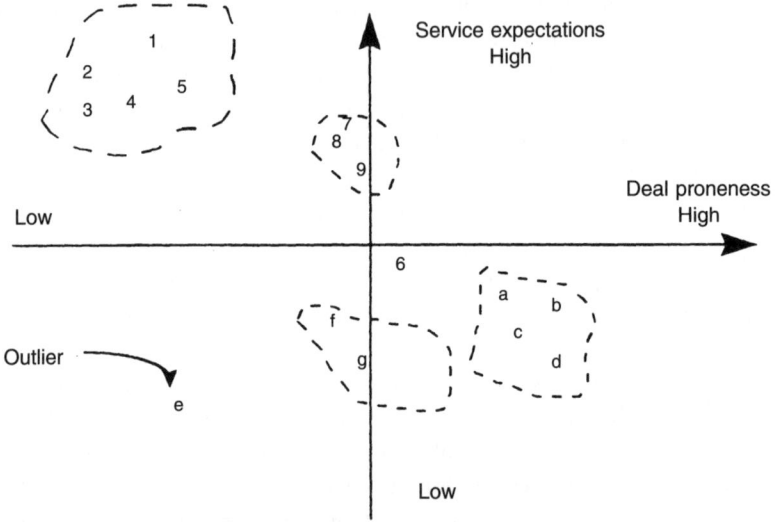

Figure 8.1 *Plotting respondents on two dimensions can suggest clusters*

The primary goal of cluster analysis is to partition a data set into two or more groups. It is used to explore segments and to confirm that they exist. Data can be non-metric or metric, and can consist of correlational measurements, distance measurements, and/or associational measurements. Outliers, those observations that appear to be almost random and which deviate from patterns in the data, can reduce the quality of the cluster analysis, and are often removed before final cluster analysis. In the case of Figure 8.1, respondent e is an outlier. Outliers may represent special consumer needs and should be explored fully before removal from the analysis.

As a user, you will want to know which clustering algorithm was used and why. There are two general types of algorithms. *Hierarchical algorithms* split the data into partitions and then partition each partition into successively smaller groups. This can be useful because researchers can look at the clusters at different levels of precision and determine which number of clusters best achieve the objectives of the research.

Compare the cluster analysis dendrogram in Figure 8.2 to the data in Figure 8.1. The first cluster, which includes respondents 1 to 5 has high service expectations and includes consumers who are less likely to buy a product simply because of a low price (deal proneness). If these were the only two dimensions tested, then this group might be called the 'demanding loyals'. The cluster analyst will conceptualise each market segment from the cluster analysis in this way.

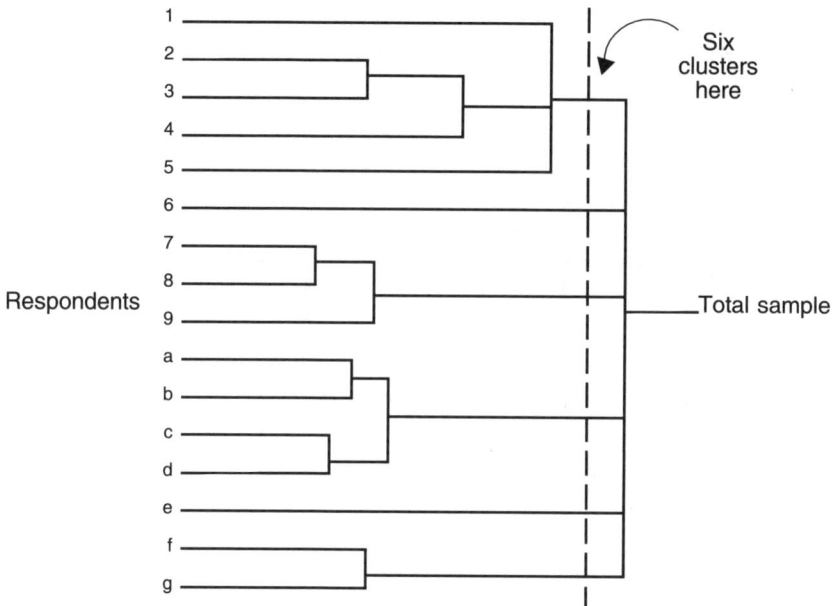

Figure 8.2 *A hierarchical cluster analysis dendrogram showing clusters*

Non-hierarchical algorithms present only a best solution for the fixed number of clusters chosen. Some segmentation procedures use hierarchical and non-hierarchical methods in tandem. Neither method is better and either may be best for a particular data set. Ask researchers if they tried both and ask to see both solutions.

2. *Was automatic interaction detection (AID or CHAID) or a related technique used?*

Automatic Interaction Detection (AID) is another technique for partitioning data amenable to parametric testing[19]. CHAID is a related technique (first proposed at the University of the Witwatersrand, Johannesburg) that is amenable to categorical data[20]. Classification and Regression Trees (CART) is another similar technique which is also amenable to categorical data[21].

The object of these techniques is to partition the data by looking for successive 'best splits'. For instance, in AID each split is determined by selecting a predictor variable and its categories and seeking to maximise the reduction in unexplained variation in the dependent variable.

The AID example in Figure 8.3 (below) illustrates a typical diagram output by these techniques. Each block reports the percentage of the sample and the average savings of the proposed segment. People under 35, with some university education and who report that their bank is not near their home, appear to be the biggest savers, although they are few in number. It is quite easy to visualise segments and propose strategies.

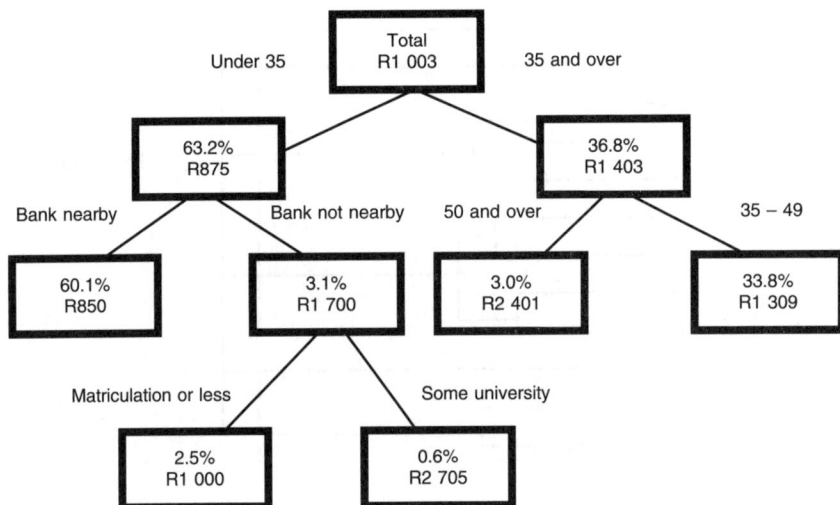

Figure 8.3 CHAID segmentation of a municipal bank market

PROFILING THE SEGMENTS

Once respondents are grouped into clusters, the clusters are profiled. Usually, this means running cross-tabulations for each cluster against the variables of interest. Where AID and CHAID are used to segment respondents, segment profiles are obvious (see Figure 8.3).

Researchers sometimes use discriminant analysis to verify the 'fit' of the clusters to the data. If this is done, be sure to ask if data was withheld from the original study or whether the discriminant analysis has been run on the same data as that used for the cluster analysis. If the latter is the case, disregard the results and ask them to split the sample so that a validation sample can be used (the discriminate analysis must show a good fit to the data — after all, the data was the basis of the cluster analysis).

Profiling the clusters brings the clusters to life and stimulates a market orientation. If possible, profile the profitability of each segment and compute the lifetime value of a typical segment member. Take the time to consider how each segment is likely to change over the next five years. Keep your notes in a scrapbook or database and refer to them often to compare how the market actually develops and your changing perceptions. This can be extremely valuable.

MARKET TARGETING

Segmenting the market can provide powerful information that often leads to superior sustainable customer solutions (SSCS). Market targeting is of critical importance. Returning to Figure 8.3 (page 108), a small bank may find that it can attract and serve the niche market comprised of younger and better educated people. A successful strategy might include direct marketing, personal banking assistants and product offers that include other investments such as stocks, bonds and venture capital participation. Thus, what appears to be a 0.6 per cent niche may well hold much more potential for total business. Another bank may find the higher volume but lower savings clients can be served best by providing no-frills service and convenient locations.

All enterprises have three choices for target marketing:

1. concentrated,
2. differentiated, and
3. undifferentiated.

1. BOE is an example of a firm practising *concentrated marketing* in South Africa. The bank targets professional people and corporate executives and offers a range of financial services. BOE does not operate retail bank locations, preferring to conduct banking through personal bankers on the clients' premises.
2. South Africa's Nedcor is a good example of a bank that practises *differentiated target marketing* by positioning three brands in the retail banking sector: Nedbank, Permanent Bank and Peoples' Bank. Nedbank further segments its customers so that, at the top of the pyramid, it courts higher income and influential clients with personal advisers who even deliver a chequebook to a customer when it is required by monitoring the numbers of cheques presented for payment. Nedbank's sister chain, the Permanent Bank, also services higher income customers through a reduced and redesigned branch network where the focus has shifted from transaction volumes to selling home loans and investments, and providing superior

service to fewer customers. Peoples' Bank is a no-frills bank targeted at lower-income clients requiring basic banking at a lower cost. Each Nedcor brand has its own reason for existence, a separate management team and separate retail locations. However, most areas of support are shared to obtain benefits of volume and specialisation. Nedcor has other specialised services targeted at the business community and even participates in cellular service provision.

The Standard Bank of South Africa practises a less differentiated form of target marketing, although E-Bank is a separate channel of delivery targeted at the same segment as Peoples' Bank. Standard differentiates with products designed for different segments, but serves all segments from the same locations.

3. The cellular telephone industry has expanded in most IOR countries using *undifferentiated target marketing* and allowing the price of services to segment the market. As cellular markets mature, more call tariffs, cellular handsets and accessories and value-added services appear, and target marketing strategies become more differentiated.

ARTIFICIAL NEURAL NETWORKS (ANN)

Artificial neural networks has become a trendy method for target marketing. The name tells much about the origin of the statistical technique — mathematical modelling of the human nervous system. ANN attempts to establish meaningful patterns and relationships in the data. Virtually any type of data can be fed into an ANN. The ANN sorts through the data and produces a model of the factors affecting the variable of interest, such as brand choice or sales. One unique aspect of ANN is that the models learn. The learning occurs as the model, which begins to find a solution with a random 'guess', successively compares additional generated solutions with sample data that has been withheld from the analysis. The model is repeatedly compared to real data and is adjusted in an iterative fashion until it is more 'finely tuned'.

ANN is an emerging set of analytic techniques which hold great promise. The researcher's expertise with ANN should be a critical recommendation when commissioning ANN analysis.

EVALUATING SEGMENT ATTRACTIVENESS

The rapidly changing nature of IOR markets and the transnational challenge of regional expansion that confronts many firms today, makes the regular review of market segmentation a required business practice. The advent of portable computer-based statistical packages has made the evaluation of alternative segmentation schemes immediate and relatively inexpensive, and the packages allow the inclusion of an almost unlimited number of variables.

So when has one achieved effective segmentation? What are the signs that segmentation needs to be reviewed? Here are some criteria (of equal relevance in business or consumer markets) that will help you to decide.

- *Homogeneity*: Segments should be composed of people with relative similarities that have been related to an important aspect of purchase or consumption derived from experiment and observation.

- *Measurability*: The characteristics of interest should be measurable. A significant part of this book has been devoted to measurable segmentation criteria.

- *Observability*: Staff responsible for implementing strategies − salespeople, marketing managers, credit approval, distribution − must be able to observe the segmentation criteria so that they can implement the proper strategy for the type of customer with whom they are in contact. Some very predictive criteria, such as personal values, are difficult to observe. Astute companies support staff interfacing with clients with systems that note customers' value types and preferences in customer records. An alternative approach teaches staff to relate values to more easily observed criteria, such as clothing or other personal possessions.

- *Accessibility*: Segments must be accessible for communication, interaction and distribution. Accessibility is increasing and changing as Internet and Intranet addressability become more widely accepted. However, many IOR consumers and companies are far removed from cyberspace and will remain so for some time.

SELECTING TARGET SEGMENTS

In any segmentation analysis, it's likely that more than one attractive segment will emerge. Managing the future and managing the globalisation of the enterprise are important influences in target market selection.

PLAN TO WIN FUTURE BATTLES WHEN CHOOSING TARGETS

The IOR is a fast-changing region in which competitive environments are certain to remain turbulent. These anticipated market conditions must be considered when contemplating target market strategies. The firm's resources must also be taken into consideration. The issues discussed later in the book (see Chapter 13) concerning resources, competencies and scenario planning, are material to such thinking.

What are our strengths and weaknesses? How will we monitor this segment for change? Where will we earn our profits? When? Which segments are expected to grow/decline? How will the costs of reaching each segment change in future years? Which segments are expected to be most profitable? Why?

Astute target market selection requires vigilance, flexibility and competitive foresight about two additional issues.

- First, as seen in the hierarchical cluster analysis example, some segments are closely related to other samples and sometimes super-segments exist that comprise the sum of many smaller related segments. A properly constructed offer to a super-segment may often retain great appeal to many of the sub-segments.

  Should firms always approach a super-segment? The decision is a trade-off between defensibility and economies of scale. A smaller niche may be easier to defend. However, being confined to a very small segment with similar requirements to other segments may place the firm at a competitive disadvantage to another firm appealing to a super-segment.

- Second, addressing a segment requires an investment in all elements of the marketing mix — in salespeople, distribution and the like[22]. Target marketing strategies should investigate economies of scope that leverage those resources across a wider potential customer base when criteria such as costs, performance, common market requirements or technology suggest such leverage is possible.

The key is to plan for the future when selecting target segments so that future growth and profitability are enhanced. Many enterprises plan segment-by-segment target marketing well in advance and enter related segments as they capture or reach critical mass in each segment.

IDENTIFYING INTERMARKET SEGMENTS

Critical mass is often difficult to achieve in poorer IOR nations for many products. For instance, although many people may wish they possessed these products, few can afford an automatic dishwasher or swimming pool in most IOR countries. The challenge is to define target markets that encompass groups of people with distinguishing homogeneous characteristics that transcend national boundaries. Intermarket segments are comprised of such people[23], i.e. people with similar values, consumption patterns, expectations and lifestyle. What makes intermarket segments so attractive? Although intermarket segments can be very small in one country, they may be very large in another — or they may be small in all countries, but very attractive when considered as a whole.

There is little doubt that Lim Jui Khiang sits in his Hong Kong office thinking about intermarket segments[24]. Adroit International concentrates on custom-designed interactive street kiosks that use sound and video to sell things, such as tickets to entertainment and sporting events. They even collect parking fines and take bank deposits. Adroit designed and manufactured electronic kiosks for Standard Chartered Bank in Singapore that allow customers to talk to bankers without visiting a branch. Singapore Airlines and Deutsche Bank use his multimedia training systems. Adroit is teaming up with companies such as NTT of Japan to provide tenant information systems for large apartment buildings, and has even taken on designing a website for Hewlett-Packard. Lim recently won a contract to develop interactive kiosks for Singapore's seven largest banks — beating IBM to win the business.

In each case, Lim is thinking of wider intermarket opportunities and has retained the multimedia rights to his products which he hopes to market overseas. Pie in the sky? Japan's investment giant Nomura Securities doesn't think so — it just purchased 20 per cent of Adroit.

PRODUCT POSITIONING

The best segmentation analysis is of little value unless it can be translated into relatively enduring and attractive product positioning. A product position is where your brand lives in the consumer's mind. Slogans such as 'Always Coca-Cola', 'We try harder' (Avis), 'Xerox, the Document Company' and 'Where do you want to go today?' (Microsoft), are designed to evoke immediate associations with a carefully designed product position.

IDENTIFY POSSIBLE POSITIONING CONCEPTS FOR EACH TARGET SEGMENT

A number of techniques can be used to develop compelling product positioning concepts[25]. The symbolic world, the meaning world, and the competitive environment can provide platforms for product positioning.

Symbolic world positioning concepts

- *Positioning by attribute or benefit*: The most frequently used positioning strategies seek to identify the brand with a particular set of attributes, benefits or features which can be physical or abstract, functional or psychosocial. Most IOR markets have examples of toothpaste brands that have been positioned either as cavity protection products or on a fresh breath platform. Motor-car spares shops often position on the depth or breadth of their inventory, or on speed of service.

- *Positioning by quality or price*: McDonalds positions on quality, service, cleanliness and value attributes. Friendliness to kids, as evidenced by the Ronald McDonalds clown, is also integral to the McDonalds brand positioning. The food is less expensive than other restaurants. However, McDonalds is not the lowest priced fast food in most IOR locations where the chain operates. Price can serve as an analogue for quality when consumers feel uncertain about other ways of evaluating brands. Low price-high quality strategies may not be successful in such cases. Quality and price positions are relative to product and product category.

Meaning world positioning concepts

- *Positioning by use*: Johnson's Baby Shampoo is positioned as a baby shampoo and as a gentle alternative for adults who shampoo frequently. Cellular telephones have been positioned on a convenience platform and as a tool to enhance security.

- *Positioning by usage occasion or class of user*: The products people use when they are in the public eye often differ in quality to the products they use at home. Outdoor sports aficionados may find special appeal in added-value benefits, such as insect repellent or moisturisers, when using a suntan lotion product in different situations, such as a fishing trip or a day at the beach[26].

Competitive environment positioning concepts

- *Positioning by product category*: A motor car which positions on a platform of 'the most luxurious car you can buy for the money' is positioning on the basis of product category (in this case, luxury cars). Popular music (rap, soul, rock), soft drinks (cola) and cellular telephones (tariff packages) are examples of other products which frequently position on product category membership. Product positioning concepts of this type often become comparative to other product category members.

GAP ANALYSIS: VISUALISING PRODUCT POSITIONS AND MARKET OPPORTUNITIES

Laddering[27], discussed earlier in this book, and the recently developed similar consumer-adaptive perceptual mapping techniques[28] can elicit much information about consumer belief systems. In the same way, structured in-depth interviews can provide useful data about both consumer and business markets.

Researchers often use perceptual maps to display competitive positioning information. Techniques such as multidimensional scaling and correspondence analysis can be very useful. Consider the map of shampoo brands in Figure 8.4 (page 115).

One must be careful about assuming that the correspondence of brands and perception represents an association, but a review of the original data shows that baby shampoos are generally perceived to be gentle and associated with a mother's love. Many brands cluster about fashionable and more 'adult' positioning concepts. Colgate Family Shampoo fights the store brand bulk shampoos on a value for money platform.

Gap analysis can refer to any of a number of techniques used to find appealing consumer offers which are relatively distant from competitive product offerings. Notice the absence of brands in the first quadrant of the map near clean and refreshing. Further analysis reveals that there are no brands closely associated with these perceptions – even though they are among the most important brand qualities to consumers. It appears that this may well be a significant opportunity for a new brand or for a repositioning of an existing brand. Dental care, personal deodorant, personal hygiene or other related personal care category brands with brands positioned on clean and refreshing platforms may well find a brand extension into this shampoo market opportunity too appealing to resist!

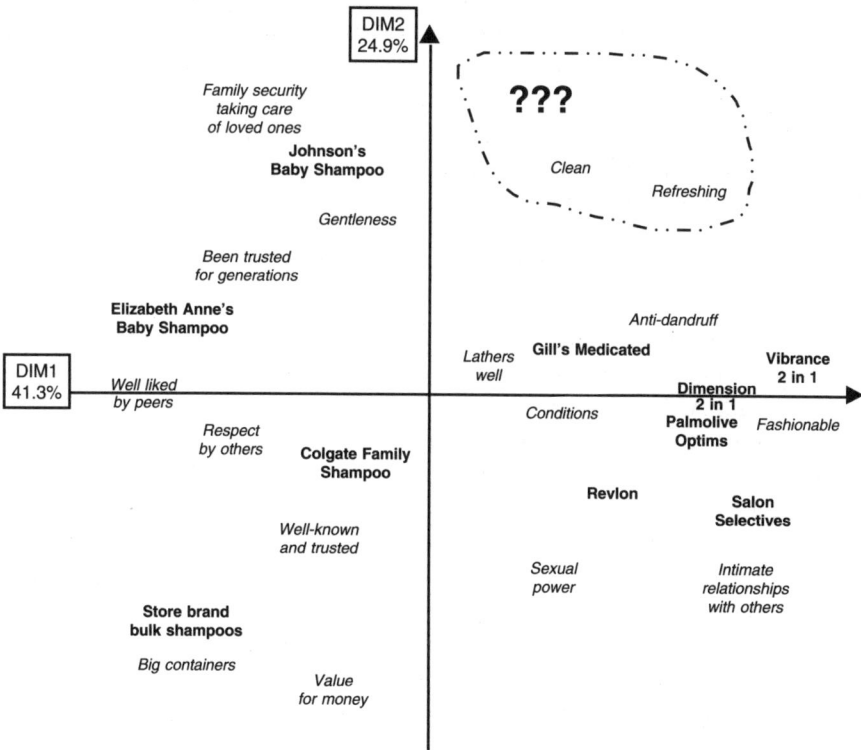

Figure 8.4 *Shampoo brands and brand perceptions (correspondence analysis of fictional data)*

IDENTIFY APPROPRIATE MARKETING MIX STRATEGIES FOR EACH TARGET SEGMENT

The success of marketing strategy depends on an appropriate mix of product, price, distribution and promotion strategies that result in a compelling offer to the target market. It is not enough to ensure higher relative prices for better quality products. These elements must seamlessly integrate at a micro-level to become part of a holistic product offer that 'feels like my kind of product' to members of the target market. Cultural fit is an important part of this equation.

Cultural fit

The IOR is marked by incredible diversity, especially of culture, access to resources and wealth. This diversity can be an impediment to regional brand success if it is not managed carefully.

Consider the case of Ego deodorant, a male deodorant range that ran an advertising campaign in South Africa in the mid-1980s. The television advertisement humorously promised prospective Ego users that they would become attractive to members of the opposite sex. A somewhat unattractive male was shown prior to using Ego and then after use. After using Ego, he became so attractive that he acquired a harem of beautiful women who were seen to pull him into their tent with obvious delight!

The launch was successful but it became apparent that black males were not stimulated to try the brand and research was conducted to find out why. The results suggested that many black men did not like the idea of using a product that so weakened them that women could overpower them. The advertisement was modified to show women admiring, but not overpowering the man, and black males began trying the brand in larger numbers. Today, Ego remains a popular South African brand.

Many IOR consumers hold orthodox religious beliefs opposed to the portrayal of the sexual motive, as is so often done in Western societies. Although a positioning of sexual power might be very tempting, it should be considered in the light of globalised communication and the perceptions of potential consumers in more conservative religious cultures. An appeal to status (keeping up or bettering your neighbours), individual rights (some cultures place more importance on group rights than individual rights), or excessive informality (considered rude in some cultures) can obscure a brand's positioning or make it unattractive.

Education can be another important factor. It has become quite common to launch concentrated cleaning product variants in products as 'micro' variants. Many IOR consumers, especially the lowest strata, shop often and carry items for long distances. Small pack sizes hold special appeal and could be a significant competitive advantage. However, many of these consumers are illiterate and may mistake micro variants for small pack sizes of normal strength products. The risk, of course, is that these price-sensitive consumers will not understand why such a small pack costs so much more than normal and may conclude that there has been a major price increase. Clever use of pack graphics is one way to overcome this problem.

Achieving cultural fit can be especially difficult. However, most major advertising agencies and research houses with international affiliations can provide assistance.

RESOURCES, COMPETENCIES AND OTHER CONSIDERATIONS

Choosing a product positioning requires careful basic analysis of the company's ability to deliver the resources and competencies necessary to execute the positioning strategy. Much of the balance of this book addresses the process of determining what is desired and what is possible.

Summary

The identification of profitable groups begins with market segmentation. Cross-cultural issues impact on identifying segmentation variables, on determining the nature and scope of the variables' influence on purchase and consumption, and on segmenting the market. Segment profiles reveal the inner essence of the research concerning the segments. Profiles assist in the evaluation of segment attractiveness and the identification of intermarket segments. A consideration of the organisation's resources and competencies is also required to select target markets. Product positioning concepts should be chosen for each target segment, bearing in mind the globalisation of communication and the influence of particularly strong beliefs about religion and morality in many IOR cultures. Appropriate marketing mix strategies are then developed and agreed with other stakeholders.

The next chapters address a wide range of tools that are useful for managing the competitive environment.

ENDNOTES

1 See Kotler (1991).
2 Most marketing textbooks cover the topic of market segmentation in depth. Some well-known articles include (consumer markets) Assael & Roscoe Jr. (1976); Wind (1978) (business to business markets); Bonoma & Shapiro (1983); Hlavacek & Ames (1986); Wind & Cardozo (1974) (international markets); Day, Fox & Huszagh (1988); Hassan & Blackwell (1994); Weber (1974); Wind & Douglas (1972).
3 See Wind (1978: 319-320).
4 For an international perspective on focus groups, see McDonald (1994).
5 McCort & Malhotra (1993), is an excellent review of cross-cultural marketing issues.
6 The HRAF originated at Yale University in 1937 under the direction of George Peter Murdock. The file consists of two major sourcebooks: Murdock (1975), provides an inventory and classification scheme for world cultures that will have a familiar feel to managers who have used the Standard Industrial Classification (SIC) codes. Each of eight major geographic regions is further broken down into cultures, societies and tribes. Murdock (1971).

7 The library may be accessed at the following Internet address: http://www.cowan.edu.au:80/library/iorr/home.htm.
8 Brislin (1986), is a well-written and detailed practical guide to this process. See also Samiee & Jeong (1994), for a critique of advertising research methodologies in a cross-cultural context.
9 Brislin (1986), addresses the practical application of the translation process.
10 I am quite fond of two well-written marketing research textbooks: Dillon, Madden & Firtle (1994) and Malhotra (1993). These books include practical and theoretical information about all aspects of marketing research.
11 Market orientation has become a very important research topic. See Jaworski & Kohli (1992-93); Kohli & Jaworski (1990).
12 Although there is no substitute for a basic understanding of algebra and matrix mathematics, becoming a skilled user often requires only an understanding of basic data assumptions and of the interpretation of the output from a statistical procedure. There are a number of very accessible texts for understanding statistical analysis in marketing and business. Aczel (1989); Keller, Warrack & Bartel (1988) and McCall (1986), are typical of this type of book. Morris (1989), is a very practical and simple introduction to business analysis.
13 When research is conducted across cultures (or when working with small sample sizes), nonparametric statistical techniques are often required. Siegel & Castellan (1988), is the most widely accepted reference. Greenacre (1993), is a very accessible book that opens the world of perceptual mapping to those with data violating the assumptions of parametric techniques. Research design is a complex process, but a number of texts can lead one through the major issues. Keppel (1991) and Kerlinger (1986), best benefit readers with an algebraic background, but are accessible to others willing to dig for the answers. Brislin, Lonner & Thorndike (1973); Lonner & Berry (1986) provide an excellent introduction to the issues of cross-cultural research. No company conducting inter-regional research in the IOR should be unfamiliar with cross-cultural research issues.
14 DeFleur & Ball-Rokeach (1989), propose a theory of communication based on media dependency theory that is compatible with the Belief System Model of Consumer Behaviour that I propose in this book. See Chapter 11.
15 See Hair Jr., Anderson, Tatham & Black (1995: 92-96).
16 Stewart (1981) continues to be an excellent review of proper and improper use of this technique.
17 Hair Jr. et al.(1995: 384-386), report that factor loadings become significant statistically at the sample sizes in parentheses following each factor loading: .30 (350), .40 (250), .50 (120), .60 (85), .70 (60), .75 (50).
18 For an excellent review of cluster analysis in marketing, see Punj & Stewart (1983).
19 See Armstrong & Andress (1970), for a discussion of AID.
20 See Kass (1980).
21 See California Statistical Software (1985).
22 See Kotler (1991: 284).
23 Hassan & Samli (1994).
24 See Curry (1996: 63).
25 Moore & Pessemier (1993), provides an excellent reference to the process of product positioning.
26 See Dickson (1982).
27 Reynolds & Gutman (1988).
28 Steenkamp & van Tripp (1996), discuss the validity of these new techniques.

9 Industry Analysis

Understanding and taking charge of your industry

Why do certain firms competing in particular industries regularly earn profits while other firms competing in what appear to be similar industries barely survive? Why do some industries become noted for fierce competitive rivalries and relatively unimpressive returns on investment? Tracing a finished product back to its constituent parts, which firms are keeping the final product competitive in the marketplace? How? Are they being rewarded adequately for their contribution? Does the value added by your company make you indispensable?

INDUSTRY ANALYSIS

Industry analysis includes a body of analytic techniques that examine how the characteristics of an industry impact on the nature of competition and the potential for profits. Using an analogy based in agriculture, industry analysis concerns the soil and the nature of the field.

- What nutrients exist and how will they nurture this crop?

- How are industry participants using those resources?

- Will the weather benefit this crop or other crops in nearby fields?

- How do the fertilizer merchant, the farmer, the co-operative, and all the other participants contribute to this crop and how are they rewarded?

This chapter explores current thinking about taking charge of the enterprise and its future by analysing and managing the structural characteristics of an industry. It explores the nature of rivalry, the process whereby value is added, the determination of industry boundaries, industry and market attractiveness, and important tools for determining strategic response.

INDUSTRY STRUCTURE

The industrial economics perspective has had a particularly important influence on industry analysis research, especially the work of Harvard's Michael Porter. Porter proposed two models which have been particularly influential: 'the Five Forces Model' and the 'Value Chain'.

THE FIVE FORCES INFLUENCING INDUSTRY STRUCTURE

According to Porter, industry structure is influenced by five forces[1]:

1. The threat of new entrants.
2. The threat of substitutes.
3. The bargaining power of buyers.
4. The bargaining power of suppliers.
5. The industry competitors and the intensity of their rivalry.

These five forces offer a convenient way to organise a firm's thinking about industry structure.

The threat of new entrants

The threat of new entrants can limit profitability and influence the intensity of rivalry in an industry and in closely related industries. Computer software giants are often alleged to use premature new product announcements as threats of market entry. Of course, the complexity of software development requires some flexibility in deadlines and much co-ordination with many outside firms, and allegations may often be unfounded. Nevertheless, there is little doubt that many firms attempt to limit profits in substitute product areas by threatening imminent market entry.

Strong marketing is built best when *entry barriers* are high[2]. Table 9.1 includes some common barriers to market entry.

Absolute cost advantages	Access to distribution, especially exclusive access	Access to inputs, especially exclusive access
Developed and differentiated brand image	Scale economies	Economies of scope
Threat of retaliation	Government policy	High capital investment requirements
High switching costs	Proprietary learning curve cost advantages	Proprietary product and process design cost advantages
Proprietary product and process patents	Substantial brand equity	

Table 9.1 *Some common barriers to market entry*

Exit barriers can be economic, strategic, cultural or emotional. These barriers keep firms competing in an industry when it might make more sense to exit. For instance, a common and insidious exit barrier is the perception that an unprofitable product or service remains core to the business because 'it's part of our heritage'. Aggressive firms acknowledge and manage exit barriers in an industry.

EXIT BARRIER	REASON
DEDICATED OR SPECIALISED ASSETS	Assets have little or no value except for the specialised use. Buyers likely to be current competitors. Costs of breaking down the assets or relocating can often exceed the value. Management perceives inadequate returns as preferential to write-off.
DEDICATED FINANCIAL COST OF EXIT	Devotion of corporate support services, such as legal or financial staff, to negotiate divestment with stakeholders. Requirements for severance pay, provision of services or spare parts through third parties, government fees, etc.
INTER-RELATEDNESS	The business may be part of a chain of related businesses and its loss may diminish the effectiveness or synergy of the whole.
CONFIDENCE OF FINANCIAL MARKET	Exit may diminish the attractiveness of the firm in the eyes of capital markets or potential acquisitors.
HORIZONTAL INTEGRATION	Exit may influence costs across a range of horizontally integrated businesses or open the related businesses to a substantially stronger competitor.
VERTICAL INTEGRATION	Exit may influence downstream vertically integrated products or processes.
INFORMATION	Discontinuing participation in an industry may isolate the firm from the information provided which benefits other products or businesses in the greater business.
MANAGERIAL AND EMOTIONAL BARRIERS	Exiting can be perceived to be a blemish on a career. Aggressive firms may feel a stigma of giving up. Managers having a tough time in other businesses may perceive the firm's resolve to be softening and feel their own position is becoming untenable.
GOVERNMENT AND SOCIAL BARRIERS	It is almost impossible to close down a business in some countries due to laws meant to protect employment and local communities. Firms with a strong dedication to employee security may feel a similar barrier.
ASSET DISPOSAL MECHANISMS	Selling off the assets for less than their book value may allow the new owners to compete at a greater advantage over other firms. Government subsidies have a similar effect.

Table 9.2 *Some common exit barriers*

The threat of substitutes

Think of your product or service as a bundle of benefits, and the firms competing in an industry as a bundle of competencies. Firms providing substitutes deliver all or a substantial part of the benefits required by the end-user. The threat of substitutes is often greatest from firms not competing in the industry, but with access to all or a major part of the competencies required for effective competition. The manufacturers of shampoos must certainly keep an eye on other liquid toiletries manufacturers. Pity the telephone company that must keep an eye on cellular telephone networks, television broadcasters, satellite television providers and cable companies.

Of course, substitute providers may or may not have access to many of the competencies provided by an industry. Miniature golf and video arcades are in direct competition for consumers' leisure money, despite being very different businesses at face value.

The customer often initiates the threat of substitutes, especially when switching costs are low. It is important to remember that a purchase is an exchange of three kinds of resources: *time, money* and *cognitive processing* (thought). Customers often flock to substitutes that appear to be more expensive but actually require less time or thought. Thus, the relative price performance of substitutes must be considered across all three resource dimensions.

Some industries are characterised by customers who are prone to switching behaviour and substitution.

The bargaining power of buyers

Firms practising strong marketing adapt strategies in response to the changing power of buyers and suppliers[3]. The bargaining power of buyers is a significant influence on rivalry. Buyer perceptions of price-sensitivity and bargaining leverage can be useful predictors of when buyers are likely to exert power. Buyers are more price sensitive when a product is a major contributor to overall input costs, when overall firm strategies call for cost reductions and when a product has little influence on end-user perceptions of quality. When buyers are price sensitive, they are more likely to exert buying leverage. Buyers also exert buying leverage when they perceive low switching costs or high importance of purchases to the supplier, as signalled by supplier sales performance or a perception that the buyer constitutes a significant portion of supplier sales.

The bargaining power of suppliers

In theory, a sale happens when the buyer and supplier receive benefit from a sale, but many marketers confess that, in the IOR, power often seems to rest with 'the person with the cash'. This is because suppliers often fail to recognise when they are most powerful.

Suppliers have more power when the buyer perceives the supplier to be important, such as when the product is an integral part of the final product or performs an important function for the end-user. When buyers perceive alternatives to be unattractive, such as when switching costs are high or substitute products have a limited presence, supplier power receives another boost. Suppliers who differentiate and find unique brand positions benefit from more power. Perhaps one of the strongest sources of supplier power is the threat of competing with the buyer through forward integration. However, this can backfire if the buyer backward integrates and competes with the supplier.

Industry competitors and rivalry

When I graduated from Ohio State, I was fortunate to land a job at Glicks' Furniture Rental in Columbus working for David Dowds, then the Chairman of the Furniture Rental Association of America. I was even more fortunate to be trained by Sam Abramson. Sam learned business the hard way, day-by-day he taught me many business truths that continue to be a primary influence on the way I think about business.

One of the first things I learned from Sam was to monitor the actions of competitors and to understand how those actions affected profits. Referring to corporate politics within one of our accounts at the time, Sam said: 'Steve, remember that "what don't feed outside, feeds inside."' He meant that the company's failure to develop creative strategies for growth had caused its staff to begin targeting each other for invective rather than targeting customers for sales. Industries are the same. When industries grow slowly, conditions often spawn internal politics instead of strong marketing.

No firm should choose to participate over the longer term in an industry characterised by immature and unsophisticated competition that constantly drains profits away. Sustained slow growth is not the only sign of rivalry that may lead to undesirable competition. Low entry barriers, easy substitution and high exit barriers are other signs. Buyer power and supplier power are important rivalry determinants. Industries characterised by inconsequential product differentiation, undeveloped brand identities and real brand equity and lack of competitor diversity may also experience higher rivalry.

Financial analysis can yield other important information about rivalry. Industries characterised by intermittent over-capacity, high fixed costs and capital investment and declining productivity are susceptible to undesirable rivalry. In manufacturing, and other businesses where finished production can be stored, high storage costs may suggest higher rivalry.

How many of these characteristics describe your industry? What can you do about it[4]?

THE VALUE CHAIN

Competition takes place horizontally and vertically within an industry structure[5]. Every enterprise can be thought of as a bundle of activities[6]. Things are designed, manufactured, sold, delivered and accounts are serviced.

According to Porter's Value Chain model, these primary activities include inbound logistics, operations, outbound logistics, marketing and sales and after-sales service. Porter suggests that these primary activities are supported by the activities produced by investments in human resource management, technology development, infrastructure and procurement of assets and skills. The value chains of each participant in a distribution channel interlink to create a supply channel value chain from raw material to final end-user.

The value chain model may serve as a useful tool in analysing many industries. However, the value chain need not always consist of the primary activities and support activities identified by Porter. As shown in Figure 9.1, an internet service provider may feel more comfortable identifying primary activities (bandwith sourcing and management, content sourcing and management, operations management and control systems, distribution of content and customer acquisition and retention) and support activities (human resources, communications, information and subscriber planning, management and infrastructure) that are more consistent with the world-view and managerial responsibilities of managers.

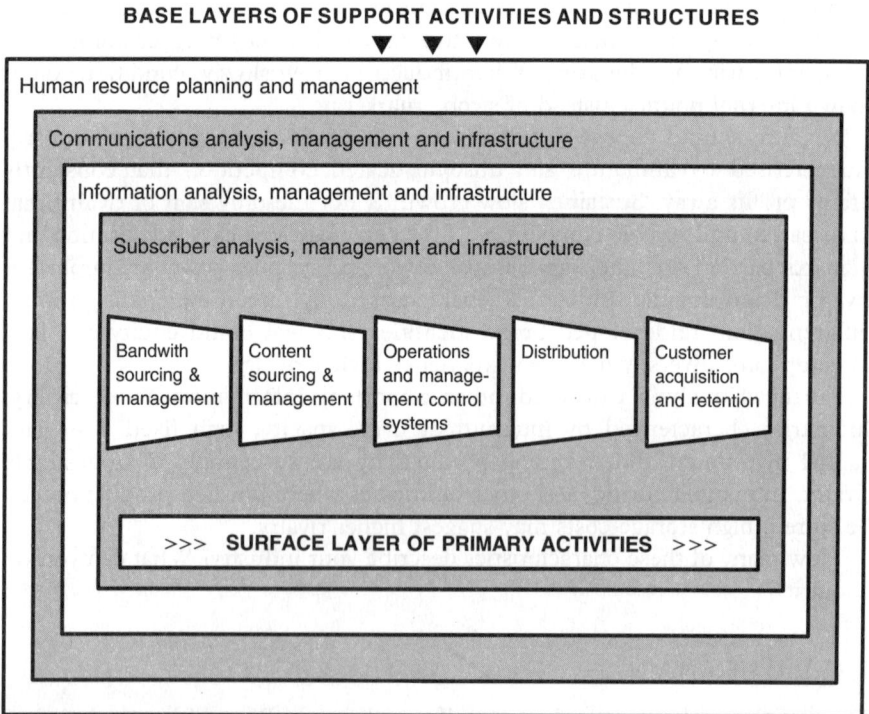

BASE LAYERS OF SUPPORT ACTIVITIES AND STRUCTURES

▼ ▼ ▼

Human resource planning and management

Communications analysis, management and infrastructure

Information analysis, management and infrastructure

Subscriber analysis, management and infrastructure

| Bandwith sourcing & management | Content sourcing & management | Operations and management control systems | Distribution | Customer acquisition and retention |

>>> **SURFACE LAYER OF PRIMARY ACTIVITIES** >>>

Figure 9.1 An internet service provider's value chain

However you conceptualise it, the value chain concept is very useful when contemplating how the firm (and its competitors) operationalise strategies and construct competitive advantage.

'You only gotta manage two costs!'

Your local health and fitness gym provides a useful example of the value chain. Health and fitness gyms are service providers and all service providers live and die by their performance on two characteristics: the cost of maintaining a customer and the cost of acquiring a new customer. While other statistics may be useful, these two statistics should be ever-present in the mind of gyms practising strong marketing. All other costs can be thought of as components of these two costs.

Key Success Factors (KSFs)

What are the key success factors (KSFs) that underlie the management of these two cost areas? The value chain provides a platform for such analysis. The intersection of each primary activity (e.g. Operations) with each support activity of a gym illustrates the usefulness of value chain analysis for this purpose. Consider how each intersection reveals possible core competencies:

- *infrastructure* (the provision of attractive training facilities and changing rooms);

- *human resources (HR) management* (the provision of highly-skilled consultants familiar with the training needs of different client groups such as executives, or athletes participating in different sports);

- *technology development* (the provision of proper training equipment and systems that monitor clients' body fat, heart rate, blood pressure and other fitness indicators); and

- *procurement* (rental space, health food, cleaning supplies, training wear).

In the same way, inbound logistics benefit from careful planning of procurement (the purchase of equipment and shopfittings), technology development (procurement information systems), human resource management (having a skilled team to project manage new gym openings) and infrastructure (office facilities from which to work). When core competencies are essential to success in a market, they are known as KSFs.

Value chain analysis is conducted in this way. It is not enough to identify key success factors with the value chain, or any other tool. The interplay between and within the various support activities and primary activities in an industry must be understood holistically[7]. There can be no substitute for this level of complete understanding.

Porter suggests shaping the size of the various components of a value chain model in line with financial statistics, such as the proportion of fixed assets devoted to each block of his model (which differs from the one presented in Figure 9.1). However, the most important outcome of value chain analysis is the identification of core competencies that provide the KSFs required for superior sustainable customer solutions (SSCSs).

I find it more useful to create a grid such as that in Figure 9.2. In each block of the grid, the firm should write the distinctive competencies, special efforts and critical resources that it commits to that have an impact on creating SSCSs. Similarly, a grid can be completed for each competitor, substitute and possible new entrant.

	Bandwith sourcing and management	Content sourcing and management	Operations management and control systems	Distribution	Customer acquisition and retention
Bandwith sourcing and management					
Content sourcing and management					
Operations management and control systems					
Distribution					
Customer acquisition and retention					
Subscriber analysis, management and information					
Information analysis, management and information					
Communications analysis, management and information					
Human resources management analysis and management					

Figure 9.2 A value chain grid

The discussion of supply channel value chains continues later in this chapter. Value chain should be analysed within the context of stages of market emergence.

STAGE OF MARKET EMERGENCE: REVISITING THE PRODUCT LIFECYCLE

Products can be thought of in many ways, for example:

- as a *brand* (Nike, Reebok),
- as a *product form* (running shoes), and
- as a *product category* (athletic footwear)[8].

Various product forms emerge in response to environmental factors in a market, such as culture, wealth or accessibility to international media. In the IOR, it is important to understand the stage of market emergence associated with the product. A very useful tool in this regard is the product lifecycle.

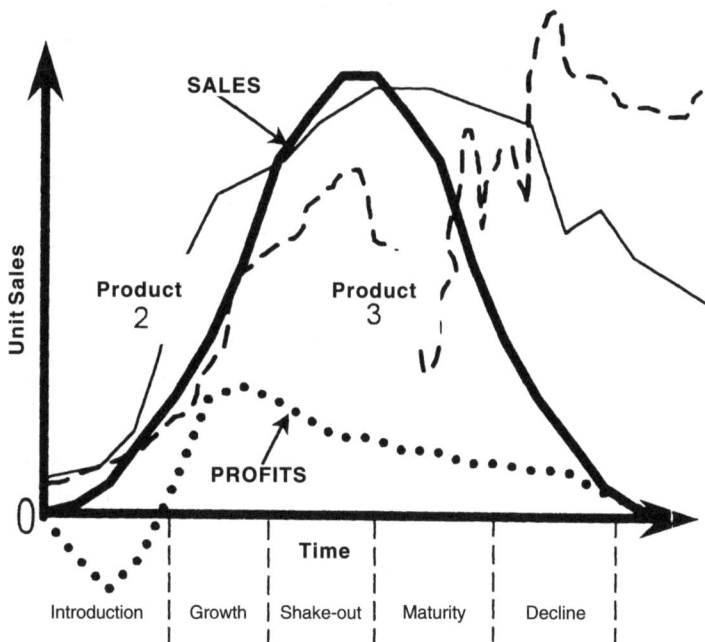

Figure 9.3 *The ideal product lifecycle and associated profit curve with two less normalised sales lifecycles*

The product lifecycle has received much attention since the 1970s and is included in most marketing textbooks, despite its lack of application in business[9]. The lack of application may be due to the amount of data that is required for its use, or perhaps the lack of data to which results in a specific industry can be compared[10]. Traditional lifecycle models feature a bell-shaped normal curve as shown in Figure 9.3 above, although other curves are likely to better describe the lifecycle in a specific industry (represented here by product 2 and product 3 curves, but many more have been identified)[11].

The four phases of the traditional lifecycle include *introduction, growth, maturity* and *decline*[12]. An additional stage is sometimes added to denote the shake-out period that often coincides with reduced profitability that signals the end of the growth phase. Customers who become users during each are divided into four categories: *innovators, early adopters,* the *middle majority* and *laggards.*

Marketing mix strategies have been linked to product lifecycle stages[13].

- When sales are low and customers few during the *introduction* phase, then offering a basic product at cost-plus pricing, building distribution selectively and promoting to early adopters and dealers with an emphasis on sales promotion to encourage trial, seems to be a most effective strategy.

- During the *growth phase*, product strategies begin exploring added-value extensions, penetration pricing emerges, intensive distribution is built, advertising concentrates on educating and building awareness and interest in the mass market, and sales promotion declines as heavy consumer demand requires less stimulus at the point-of-sale.

- By *maturity*, the marketing competencies required for success have changed. Marketers must be able to enhance products and added-value components, carefully manage competitive pricing, manage intensive distribution outlet strategies, and design compelling promotions that demonstrate differences and benefits while emphasising brand switching sales promotions.

- Product diversity *declines* in maturity. Prices also tumble and distribution contracts. Sales promotion and advertising focus on retention of hard-core loyals.

The product lifecycle is probably not a useful tool for analysing an individual product or brand sales. However, it is very useful for analysis of sales at product form and product category level analysis. It is an especially useful tool for analysing the stage of market emergence across different market segments or regions.

It is important to understand the industry from the perspective of the value chain. Are the competencies that emerged from the value chain analysis consistent with the requirements of the product lifecycle stage? Which competencies will be required in the immediate future — when the next stage of the product lifecycle emerges? When will that be?

THE BUSINESS PROFILE MATRIX: PRODUCT LIFECYCLE AND COMPETITIVE POSITION

Each stage of the product lifecycle may require certain competencies in a particular industry. For instance, mobile telecommunications companies launching in the IOR are likely to require executives capable of managing the chaos produced by rapid growth and market expansion. Food companies might require brand skills plus strong cost controls.

The firm's ability to compete in a particular sub-regional market will depend in part on its ability to demonstrate or acquire the appropriate competencies relevant to the stage of market emergence in that sub-regional market. Plotting the firm's relative competitive position in a sub-regional market (dominant, stronger than others, parity competitor, weaker than others, unable to compete) against product lifecycle stages can be revealing. Hofer and Schendel[14] suggested the product-market evolution matrix nearly 20 years ago. They plotted product-market evolution stages (development, growth, shake-out, maturity, saturation, decline) against competitive positions (strong, average, weak).

What I propose is different because it is a tool for sub-regional analysis that employs the product lifecycle and more reliable positions of analysis for competitive position. (I find many managers have difficulty establishing whether the firm is strong or weak on a particular characteristic, but I find most can say immediately whether they are stronger or weaker than a known competitor). So, on one axis plot the product lifestyle, and on the second axis plot your ability to compete.

The validity of the business profile matrix depends on your ability to define critical elements that determine your ability to compete[15]. Overall costs, product quality, knowledgeable salespeople or any number of characteristics can emerge as important keys to success at different stages of the product lifecycle. Determining the position on the matrix is relatively easy once you have determined a weighted measure of competitiveness, and the position in the product lifecycle. Assign a point value to each response (Dominant = 5 points, Stronger than others = 4 points, etc.) and average the point value across all the characteristics you have selected. You may wish to give certain characteristics more weight in your analysis.

MULTI-MARKET PLANNING

IOR firms must contemplate IOR strategies regardless of whether they intend to conduct business within a narrow sub-region or an individual country, or whether they intend to operate outside their countries, or at the more ambitious scale of global marketing. Global marketing is no longer a topic for tomorrow, it is part of conducting business today.

Firms that plan to rise to the IOR challenge have to acknowledge the unique diversity of IOR countries and the various stages of market emergence around the IOR. This suggests that analyses such as industry structure modelling, value chains or product lifecycles should be conducted at three levels: individual nation, IOR region and worldwide.

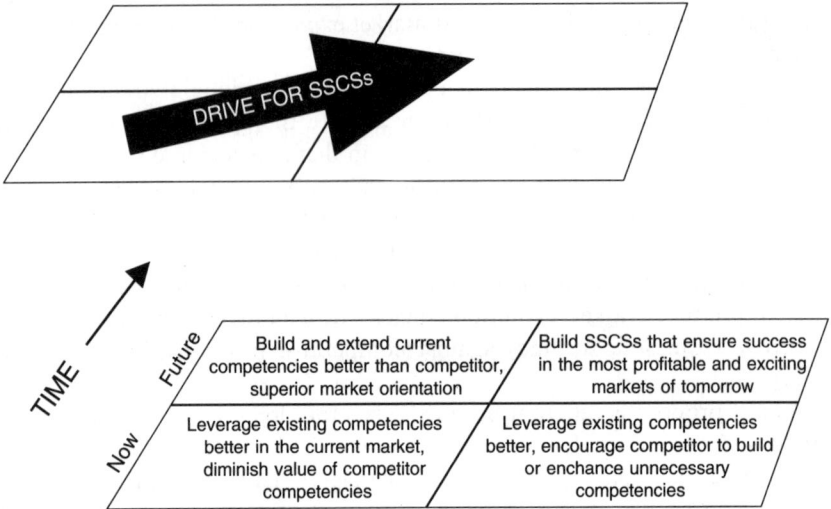

Figure 9.4 *Managing core competence over time*

INDUSTRY BOUNDARIES

Another important consideration in industry analysis concerns industry boundaries. Figure 6.2 (page 69) described the traditional view of industry boundaries but, to the untrained eye, industry boundaries are disappearing in many industries. Consider financial services and, more specifically, retail banking. Many retailers offer credit card services, often using private label cards. Offering these services builds a host of core competencies required in financial services, such as credit approval, transaction processing, credit and behavioural scoring, credit collection and related activities. Is it any wonder that Marks and Spencer, the UK retailer of clothing and food, now offers an extensive range of financial services which includes insurance and investment products, or that Pick 'n Pay has decided to offer a few savings products?

Boundaries disappear only when one conceptualises the enterprise as bricks and mortar. The enterprise is not bricks and mortar – it's people, ideas and core competencies[16]. Core competencies define the actual boundaries of industries in the fast-changing, contemporary environment.

Boundary analysis answers the question: 'Who competes in this industry and who might compete in it tomorrow?' In order to conduct boundary analysis, it is vitally important to do the following:

1. Qualify and quantify the core competencies – the KSFs – required to compete effectively in an industry.

2. Then classify not only traditional industry participants but also participants in other industries according to possession or their ability to acquire those competencies.

3. Finally, contemplate the competencies that might shape tomorrow's market and lead to superior sustainable customer solutions (SSCSs).

Summary

Understanding industry structure is more complex than a simple census of firms said to be competing in an industry. As industry boundaries blur, new competitors will appear from nowhere to challenge competitors who have not understood the new reality – that competencies rather than infrastructure determine modern industry boundaries.

The structure of an industry determines much of the profitability of its players. Threats of substitutes and new entrants, and the power of buyers and suppliers stimulate rivalry and ultimate profits. Astute firms realise this and take steps to enter and manage industries so that profitability is possible.

It is not enough to identify KSFs. The core competencies required for success must be identified, understood in a holistic sense and managed. Every manager in a firm should know the firm's position in the value chain today and where the firm wants to be tomorrow.

Much of the ability to succeed in capturing that vision of tomorrow rests on competitiveness. The next chapter explores tools for understanding and managing competitiveness.

ENDNOTES

1 Porter (1979; 1980).
2 For more discussion on entry and exit barriers, see Abell & Hammond (1979), Aaker (1988) and Porter (1980).
3 Porter (1980) remains an excellent source for understanding the relative power of buyers and suppliers.
4 Leenders & Blenkhorn (1988), and Poirier & Houser (1993), propose a process for managing sourcing and making it a more integral part of the marketing process. The effect of the business partnering approach they espouse is joint channel management.
5 A very practical discussion of these two types of competition appears in Chapter 6 of Abell (1993).
6 See the discussion in Porter (1985), especially pages 33-61.
7 See the discussion in Chapter 3 of Ohmae (1982).
8 See Kotler (1991), especially page 350.
9 Rink & Swan(1979) is an excellent review of lifecycle research.
10 See Jain (1993: 256-258).
11 Kotler (1991).
12 Tellis & Crawford (1981) suggest another useful approach that includes five stages: divergence, development, differentiation, stabilisation and demise.

13 This discussion draws on Kotler (1991), especially page 365. Porter (1980), and Ohmae (1982), include detailed strategies for all phases of the product lifecycle. See also Enis, La Grace & Press (1977).

14 Hofer & Schendel (1978).

15 Hamper & Baugh (1990), propose a survey and scoring procedure that may be appropriate in many industries.

16 Quinn (1992) has proposed this idea in a most elegant way.

10 Competitor Analysis

Understanding and managing competitors

WORLD-VIEW: MANAGING THE FUTURE

How many great firms, once thought to be in positions of unchallenged dominance in their industries, have suffered massive reversals because of failing to manage the future? How many jobs have been lost when companies focused their business on customers rooted in the dying industries of yesterday, and failed to see the merit of smaller customers in the fast-growing industries of tomorrow?

The answer to these questions is the same — 'too many'. Proper analysis of the competitive environment is a basic step in building strong marketing that creates the future. At the heart of competitor analysis lie two questions: 'How do companies succeed in this industry today?' and 'How will companies succeed in the future?[1]'

MOMENTUM: THE INABILITY TO ESCAPE THE PAST

Success seems to be a significant precursor to failure these days. Unparalleled achievement leads to an intoxicating feeling of contentment and satisfaction that is often mistaken for 'knowing the business' or 'industry leadership'.

The icy winds of momentum blow hardest in the bright lights of extensive public recognition. The disappearance of any meaningful difference between the vision of the future and the perception of today should be a signal to every manager that crisis is at hand. Satisfied management teams lose the will to change, the will to become better and the will to get closer to customers. They become over-confident. They become ripe for plunder.

Momentum builds over an extended period as the firm liquidates the fruits of yesterday's strong marketing for short-term profits today. Astute managers know that press accolades concerning how well their company or a competitor's company is performing are a wake-up call that momentum may be setting in.

THE HANDICAP OF ABUNDANT RESOURCES

If one looks at the most successful countries, it becomes obvious that an abundance of resources may be a barrier to success. Consider Singapore, which started with so little in the way of resources that it was forced to import even its drinking water. Consider Switzerland, a resource-poor nation in the midst of plenty. However, both countries exhibit value systems that place great importance on achievement, cleanliness, hard work, order and other values that can be linked immediately to their successes. Now consider the multitude of poorer countries in Africa that are blessed with an over-abundance of resources. Could an abundance of resources be a barrier to national competitiveness?

Corporate resources may also be a barrier to long-term competitiveness. Success and achievement attract investment, and investment provides an abundance of resources. Abundant resources taint perceptions of reality at all levels of the enterprise, especially at lower levels where they are most easily wasted. When self-delusion sets in, resources begin to substitute for creativity and are seen as far more important than in fact they are to corporate well-being.

The firm becomes unable to escape its own momentum and a twilight zone descends to imprison the company in its past.

INERTIA: THE INABILITY TO CREATE THE FUTURE

Success can have another debilitating effect on strong marketing[2]. 'Industry leadership' and 'knowing the business' can lead to well-entrenched business methods, procedures and protocols. Almost invisibly embedded in the optimised business designs and processes (often acquired at high cost and sources of great pride in the firm), are rules that emerge to take on the appearance of fact.

All firms develop these rules — these theories of the business[3] — that guide decision-making. Rules become corporate legends that can be quite intoxicating because they impart such a heroic aura to the firm and its senior management. This can be especially true in firms where an individual (often the founder) becomes 'larger than life', or where authoritarianism is deeply rooted. Real leaders constantly recreate the business to fit the changing world and they get everyone involved in the job.

Have you ever heard anyone say 'We (or Brand X) tried that in 1989, it doesn't work — we give Brand Y another year before they discover their mistake.' *What if your competitors solved the problems you could not solve and are on the way to real competitive advantage?*

Or, 'We have led this industry since its inception. Our managing director, Mr A. N. Other, is the world authority in the field.' *Yesterday's success is not today's* — what significant innovations are you working on today?

Or, 'We invested over R40 million to build this plant, that's a significant entry barrier for Brand X.' *It may also be a millstone around your neck if Brand X can find a way to meet or exceed your product benefits without the investment.*

Players living by old rules are vulnerable to new rules. There is no future in living by rules made in the past. Winning companies put processes and procedures in place that are designed to adapt to the changing business environment.

ANALYSING YOUR COMPETITORS' WORLD-VIEW BEGINS WITH COMPREHENSIVE COMPETITOR INFORMATION

Firms slide easily into the clutches of inertia and momentum over a relatively long period. How can you measure the competition's (and your own) momentum and inertia? What about other elements of world-view, such as projections of the future direction of the industry?

There are laws in every country concerning commercial information — laws to which every firm should strictly adhere. However, a recurring theme in this book suggests that all firms should *source, compile* and regularly *analyse* information about their competitors, suppliers, buyers, stakeholders and themselves. Everyone in the enterprise must be responsible for sourcing such information and the person responsible for compiling and analysing such information should be considered to have a major responsibility.

Every firm should realise that unethical information collection is unnecessary, in any case, when everyone pulls together to collect and pool information.

It is not good enough to collect information a few weeks ahead of an important decision or to scour information sources in a mad frenzy only when required. Information collected over time and catalogued according to well-documented procedures provides the greatest value. Only collecting information in this way allows regular reports be sensitive to small changes that often presage major sweeping strategic changes in the marketplace.

Few firms do a very good job of impressing the value of information collection on individuals at all levels of the enterprise. I cannot recount how many times I have sat in meetings with clients and heard someone say, 'But I knew they were going to do that last year', while senior management looked on in amazement. This is bound to happen in a turbulent competitive environment but it does not need to happen if a marketing intelligence system is established and well managed.

Clearly, ethical information gathering should be incentivised and managed from the highest levels of the company. Figure 10.1 (page 136) depicts the elements of a comprehensive marketing intelligence system. Monthly profiles of important players should be generated for senior management review.

INFORMATION SOURCES

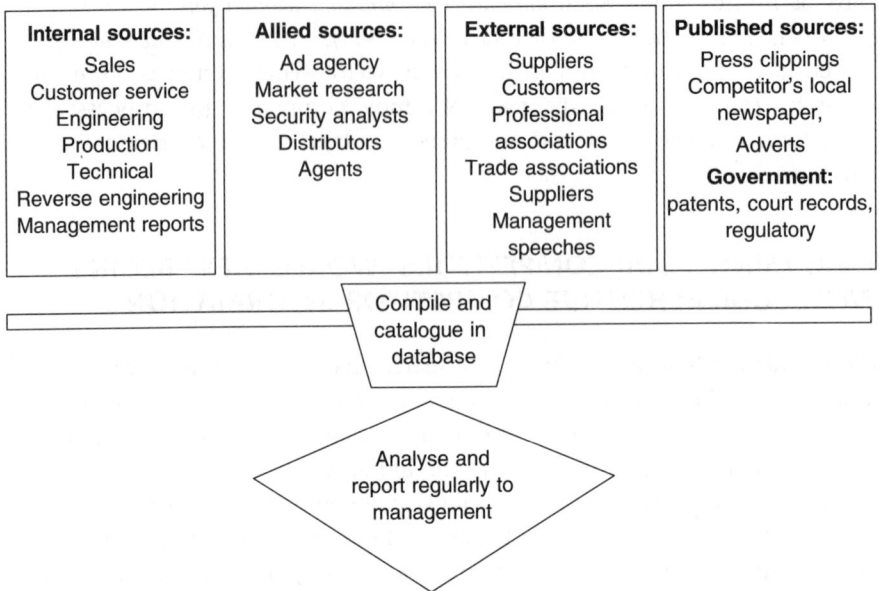

Internal sources:	Allied sources:	External sources:	Published sources:
Sales	Ad agency	Suppliers	Press clippings
Customer service	Market research	Customers	Competitor's local
Engineering	Security analysts	Professional	newspaper,
Production	Distributors	associations	Adverts
Technical	Agents	Trade associations	**Government:**
Reverse engineering		Suppliers	patents, court records,
Management reports		Management	regulatory
		speeches	

Compile and catalogue in database

Analyse and report regularly to management

Figure 10.1 *The marketing intelligence system*

LISTENING TO MARKET SIGNALS

Market signals provide information about competitors' strategies, motives, goals, objectives and performance[4]. Obviously, many firms use signals to mislead their competitors, but even a misleading signal can tell the astute observer of a competitor much about its motives.

Many signals are indirect. For example, the import of certain electronic components can be a valuable indirect signal to a manufacturer of radio equipment. Or, an employment advertisement may signal commencement of operations by a new division concerned with launching a new product. If you fail to monitor all your competitors' communications, prepare to be surprised with bad news.

DIRECT SIGNALS

A direct signal often concerns the nature of competition and can be made before or after an action is taken. Pre-empting competitors, threatening action, testing competitor will and resolve, communicating perceptions about the nature of competition in the industry, minimising competitive response (or over-response) to an action, avoiding simultaneous actions or communicating with investors and the financial community — these are some of the reasons why firms send direct signals.

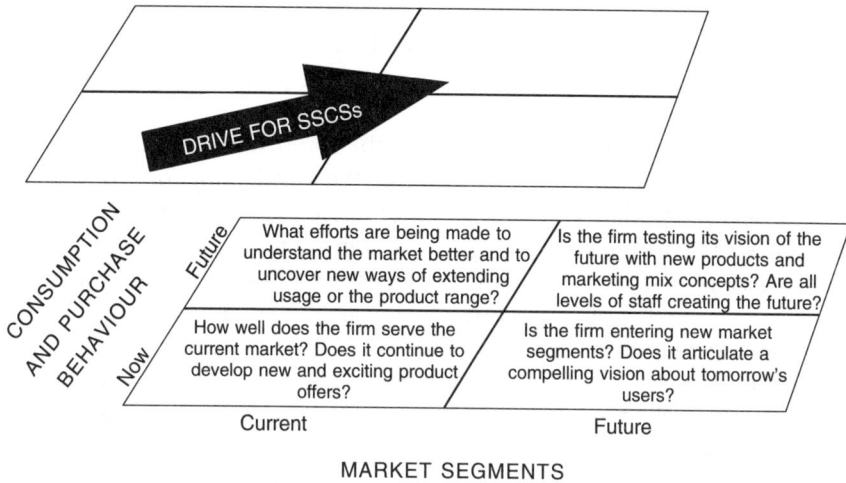

Figure 10.2 *Some critical thoughts about signs of inertia and momentum in a competitor press release*

Signals about the industry often reveal much about the firm's perceptions of the nature of competition. Comments that 'the industry is pricing itself into extinction', or that 'many firms will not continue to operate much longer at the current prices', may reveal sentiments about the need for price discipline or that the producer is struggling to make profits at correct prices. Comments that 'this industry had better understand that its image will not be enhanced by sloppy service' may signal that the company considers sloppy service by some competitors to be limiting industry sales potential, or that the company feels it has a service advantage and aggressive marketing is imminent.

The introduction of a fighting brand or the acquisition of a competitive brand, which can be used to compete on price or some other characteristic on a short-term basis without damaging the main brand, should be construed as a major signal of intent.

Listen carefully to direct signals, even those that appear to have little value, but do not allow them to become the sole basis for understanding competitors. For instance, competitors often release statements about the nature of competition in an industry. If a competitor complains about low-cut pricing, observe their actions over future months. Are they consistent with public pronouncements and other statements? If a competitor describes the industry structure, does their understanding match yours? Do they show signs of managing the future? Figure 10.2 illustrates some questions one must ask when encountering even seemingly innocuous information about a competitor.

INDIRECT SIGNALS

Indirect signals can be especially revealing. However, one also must be careful about reading too much into indirect signals that position the competitor as unsophisticated or non-competitive.

One of America's top retailers reviewed the competitive situation during its annual shareholders' meeting. Every year, the retailer mentioned the fast-growing Wal-Mart while adding a verbal footnote that Wal-Mart competed in rural areas and small towns and was not a direct competitor. Even when Wal-Mart surpassed this chain after more than ten years of such announcements, the chief executive could only mutter that Wal-Mart was entering the cities and the chain was watching them closely to understand their success!

There is little doubt in my mind that Sam Walton's cultivated and carefully managed 'good old boy' image had much to do with the leading retailer's delayed reaction to Wal-Mart. Wal-Mart constantly gave the impression of being quite satisfied to be a small-town niche player, well suited to rural markets. Building large stores in peri-urban and rural locations allowed Wal-Mart to block competition and to establish low-cost structures across the chain. Any firm entering the small-town locations would quickly find that it could not achieve significant profits from dividing such a small pool.

Walton realised that cities were expanding and, years later, many of his outlets were now in the best suburban locations simply as a result of urban growth. Moreover, building out of town in many directions allowed Wal-Mart to establish regional warehouses in central urban locations. Building urban outlets was a logical progression, probably well planned some 20 years previously.

By the time other major retailers wanted to compete more directly with Wal-Mart, Walton had already achieved a 7 per cent to 9 per cent advantage in operating costs over most major retail chains, making it unlikely that Wal-Mart's competitors could compete successfully on price.

WORLD-VIEW CONSISTS OF UNWRITTEN RULES AND ASSUMPTIONS

Measuring world-view is about measuring the unwritten rules and assumptions that guide a competitor's actions. Firms that can anticipate the thoughts that guide competitor activity are more likely to anticipate the actual activity when it occurs — and to have a proper strategic response at hand. Here are some things to consider which may reveal much about competitors' assumptions:

- *Mission and objectives.*

  Read your competitors' annual reports and other documents. What do they say about the future? What percentage of the sentences dwell on the past (their traditions, their heritage, etc.) and what percentage dwell on the future? Are the mission and objectives realistic and achievable? On what key success factors will the competitor rely in order to achieve this vision?

- *Satisfaction.*

  How have they performed against their objectives? Do they seem satisfied? Would you be satisfied? Why? Who is most dissatisfied and why?

- *Motives and drives.*

  What motives and drives are evident? How are senior managers remunerated? Is remuneration likely to focus their attention on the longer-term management of the business or on short-term results? Do they want to become an industry leader? A profitable company? A cost leader?

- *Current strategy.*

  What is the competitor's current strategy? Is it likely to succeed? Is it consistent with its mission and objectives? How does it compare to yours?

- *Future objectives.*

  Do they enunciate a plan for the future? Is there a vision of the future that appears to be an animating force in the company, or does the company make statements to impress shareholders and the investment community with little real understanding or intention to follow them through?

- *Markets served.*

  What market segments does the company serve well? Which segments contribute the bulk of its sales, costs and profits? Which would it defend most or least vociferously? Does it understand developing nation markets, and are its products and campaigns transferable there[5]? Does it understand how to design distribution channels to reach IOR sub-regional markets[6]?

- *Globalisation.*

  Is the firm thinking globally? What is it doing to globalise its sources of demand, sources of supply and methods of effective management?

- *Resources.*

  What is the firm's cash position? What economic value has it added or lost? How much free cash flow does it generate[7]? What does a review of previous years' financial results say about financial trends? What about key people? Who has joined them? Who has left? Why? Have they made any progress in becoming faster, more flexible or better in any significant way that required an investment in people, plant or ideas? Why? What resources appear to be fat muscle and what appear to be lean muscle?

- *Management style and intra-organisational conflict.*

  What is the competitor's management style? Do people who leave them speak of them with fondness or acrimony? Are they authoritarian and, if so, is that appropriate to the business? Do they encourage creativity and entrepreneurship? Do they stifle dissent? How do they handle failure? Does the competitor seem to be able to manage internal conflict at a level that remains functional, without engendering dysfunctional conflict[8]? Are diverse opinions valued or do they become a means of classifying dissident elements for exclusion?

- *Empowerment profile.*

  What is the constitution of the staff? Which elements of the national population are under-represented or over-represented at various levels in the organisation? Does the firm actively encourage diversity? How? Do historically disadvantaged (black South Africans, Indian Untouchables, physically challenged, gays, etc.) feel they have an equal opportunity for advancement? Are the holidays of religious minorities acknowledged, and can staff observing those holidays trade for work on other religious holidays they do not observe?

- *Response profile.*

  Does this firm over-react or under-react to environmental pressure? How does it respond to competition or to outside threats? How is it responding to environmental trends?

- *Transnational product roll-out strategies.*

  How is this firm likely to roll-out products internationally? Does it use small countries with developed markets as test markets, or does it use predictable clusters of countries[9]? Does it launch sequentially, i.e. one country then another, or concurrently (in all or many countries at once)?

- *Country of origin effects.*

  Country of origin can have a halo effect (i.e. when one characteristic affects judgement of other criteria) on brand image[10]. For instance, consumers in the opposing sides of a war may not wish to buy each other's products for generations. The former communist countries will struggle to overcome poor quality product perceptions for decades. What elements of country of origin are imparted to this product in the various sub-regional markets of interest?

MEASURING THE STRENGTH OF COMPETITIVE BRANDS

Two of the more exciting developments in marketing during recent years have been the prolific research stream into brands and relationship marketing. Both of these concepts can have a major impact on competitive strategy.

BRAND EQUITY

Chapter 4 introduced the concept of brand equity. Proper analysis of purchase and consumption behaviour reveals much information about competitive brands. Research methods such as laddering tie the major components of *brand image* (symbolic world associations and meaning world associations) to brands and lifestyle.

Ideal product analysis, often using a multidimensional scaling technique, is one way to measure the appeal of brand images. In ideal product analysis, consumers are asked to evaluate brands on a number of salient dimensions that capture the essence of brands or potential brands competing in the market. They also evaluate an imagined 'ideal product' on those same dimensions.

Figure 10.3 (page 142) appeared earlier in Chapter 8. Now a point appears that represents the ideal brand evaluations of a sample representing a market segment comprised of young girls between the ages of 11 and 15 who are active in gymnastics. The analysis suggests that these consumers are attracted to brands that they can associate with the values of family security, taking care of loved ones, trusted for generations, gentleness and well-liked by peers. This particular map suggests those brands may be Elizabeth Anne's and Johnson's Baby Shampoo, subject to a closer examination of the actual data. The gap associated with the values of clean and refreshing probably does not hold much value to this particular segment but may be very compelling to another segment.

Market simulation is another important method of gauging the competitive strength of current and future product. Market simulation requires knowledge of the value of various combinations of product characteristics to the consumer, and of trade-offs between those combinations. Conjoint analysis is the method used most often to provide this information[11]. Conjoint analysis asks consumers to evaluate combinations of two or more brand characteristics at a time across the range of measured characteristics. A typical conjoint analysis using this trade-off procedure might ask consumers to indicate preferences for combinations of product features, advantages and benefits (i.e. three flavours and four aromas, three flavours and three serving sizes, etc.). The full profile procedure presents consumers with a complete set of product characteristics on a card or survey document (i.e. chicken flavour, mild aroma and 100 gm serving), and then asks consumers to rate the various choices.

The results of the conjoint analysis tell researchers the utility of various combinations of benefits and provide answers to questions such as, 'Would consumers be willing to pay three cents more for a stronger aroma?' Researchers use what they learn from conjoint analysis to model the performance of current and new products in the marketplace.

By providing information about symbolic world and meaning world associations, ideal product analysis and conjoint analysis are effective tools for measuring two of Aaker's five brand equity constructs[12]: *brand associations* and *perceived quality*.

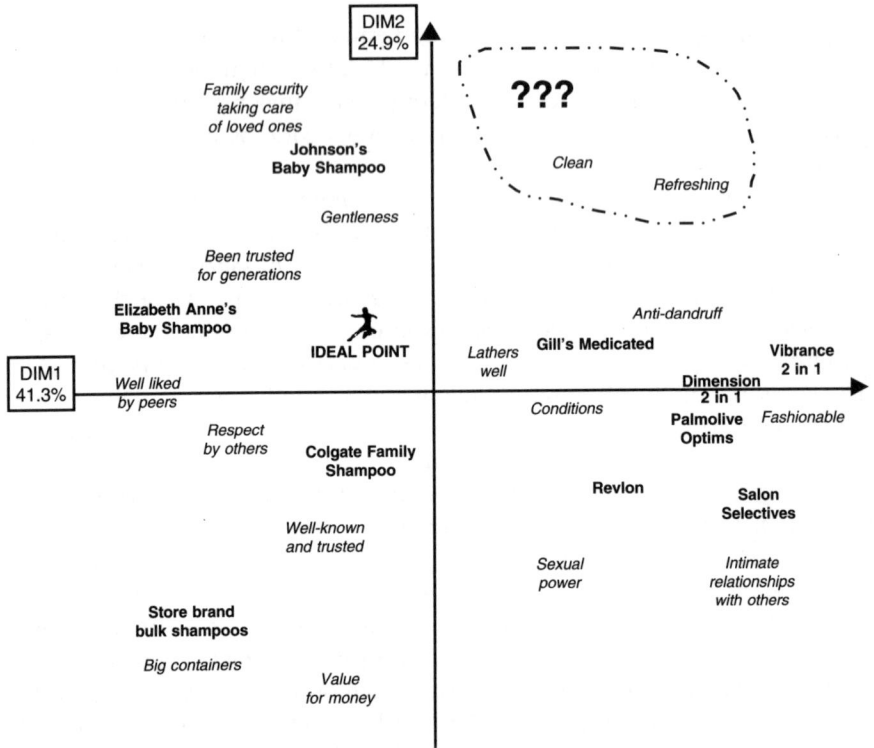

Figure 10.3 *An ideal point plotted on a correspondence analysis map*

Brand loyalty is usually quantified by measuring the price premium consumers are willing to pay for a brand. Some other useful techniques include: measurement of purchase and consumption behaviour (repurchase, brands used, share of usage, usage occasions); measurement of affect toward the brand (liking, satisfaction, commitment); and personification of the relationship with the brand ('Emily, what would cause you to like that person more?').

Unaided and aided brand awareness are measured by asking consumers to indicate the brands they can recall in a product category, and then asking them to note from a list which brands they recognise. The unaided list generally approximates the consumer's consideration set (see Chapter 5).

Other proprietary assets include competitive advantages such as patents, trademarks and special distribution channel or information advantages which require a simple census by key managers.

BUYER-SELLER RELATIONSHIP

Perhaps the most telling questions of competitor analysis concern the relationship between the firm and the market. Relationship management is definitely the hot topic in marketing[13]. Business relationships with customers can and should be measured and understood on many levels (see Table 10.1).

In business markets, relationships exist on many levels. Firms should seek potential supplier partners that impart relatively little operating risk to the business and relatively more added value to the firm's products. It seems logical that firms with more suppliers would negotiate better prices and thus maximise profits. However, PIMS (Profit Impact of Market Strategy) research has shown that the most profitable companies concentrated between 25 per cent and 50 per cent of purchases with three suppliers[14].

Commitment by customer	Trust in company	Co-operation	Mutual goals
Interdependence, unbalanced power	Satisfaction with performance	Comparison level of the alternatives	Adaptation
Non-retrievable investments	Shared technology	Structural bonds	Social bonds
Shared ownership of data	Common directors	Common investors	

Table 10.1 Some selected dimensions of buyer-seller relationships in business markets[15]

Improved profitability is only one influence cutting contemporary supplier lists. The move to the ISO 9000 standard, the institution of Just in Time (JIT) ordering systems, the increase in business partnering and sharing of information in distribution channels, the pressure to improve quality and reduce costs – all of these contribute to shortened supplier lists. Such trends require constant monitoring, measurement and understanding by the firm, concerning itself and its competitors.

Business relationships, however, are conducted on more formalised bases that can have a limiting influence on the complex nature and content of the relationship. Relationships between consumers and businesses exist on very different levels and include dimensions that are even more complex.

The nature of the relationship between consumers and brands is the basis of brand equity. It includes the brand as person, the brand as friend, the brand as symbol. Individual differences and environmental influences, the components of the belief system, the constituent aspects of the symbolic world, the emotional forces and the summation of the meaning world – all materially influence the nature of consumer relationships with brands. The content of consumer relationships with brands can include these associations to the brand and other constructs such as those in Table 10.2.

THE NEW MARKETING

Trust	Brand credibility	Brand identity	Loyalty
Novelty	Future positive re-inforcement	Perceived value pro-position	Benefits of choice reduction
Performance on past promises	Conditions favouring consumer inertia	Type of bond: financial, social or structural	Generalised response to situation (conditioning)
Satisfaction with past performance	Commitment		

Table 10.2 Some other dimensions of buyer-seller relationships in business markets[16]

FINANCIAL ANALYSIS

Financial analysis of competitors should be exhaustive. The object is to understand the influence of various strategies on competitors and to understand how competitor strategies will influence the firm. The formulae for the ratios in the following table appear in most financial management textbooks. Monitoring these ratios over time can reveal very useful information about a competitor's strategies and their ability for strategic response.

RATIO TYPE	USEFUL FINANCIAL RATIOS
PROFITABILITY	Gross profit margin, operating profit margin, return on capital employed, net profit margin, return on investment, return on equity
LIQUIDITY	Current ratio, quick ratio (acid test)
ACTIVITY	Average collection period, average payment period, inventory turnover, asset turnover, fixed asset turnover, weighted average cost of capital
DEBT	Debt to assets, long-term debt to equity, debt to capital, short-term liabilities to total debt, times interest earned
MARKET	Market value added, economic value added, earnings per share, dividend payout, dividend yield, price/earnings ratio, book value per share, price to book value

Table 10.3 Some useful financial ratios

Summary

Without diminishing the importance of financial analysis, this chapter has introduced a wide range of qualitative and quantitative issues for the consideration of managers responsible for analysing the competitive environment.

144

The battle to build organisations where everyone challenges the status quo constantly but where conflict does not disrupt unity is never-ending. Even the best firms can succumb to inertia and momentum — the two insidious destroyers of market value. Astute strategists realise that the most successful firms can be challenged when these forces set in.

Perceptive strategists listen to the verbal and non-verbal content of competitor signals. They put systems into place to monitor channels where indirect signals are likely to be intercepted. They listen to what has been said and to what has not been said.

Their own unwritten rules and assumptions about the market influence competitors. Strong marketers mine these theories of the business for information to predict strategic response by a competitor to the environment and to the firm.

Strong marketers build brand equity as well as sustained and constantly renewed customer relationships. Their understanding of building and enhancing brand image and of positioning strategies is one of their characteristic strengths.

Finally, the necessity to compile, manage and distribute information about competitors and stakeholders is ignored at one's peril. Information is everyone's responsibility and the individual managing the marketing information system should be considered a senior player on the team. Financial analysis of competitors should be conducted and archived regularly.

Building strong marketing requires a fine sense of the competition and the market. The skills imparted here are critical to managing the competitive environment.

ENDNOTES

1 Fombrun (1992), especially Chapter 3; Hamel & Prahalad (1994), especially Chapter 4.
2 Bonoma (1981).
3 Drucker (1994).
4 Porter (1980), includes an excellent discussion of market signals. See pages 75-87.
5 Shimp, Samiee & Madden (1993).
6 See Rosenbloom (1991); Samiee & Walters (1990); Sharma & Dominguez (1992).
7 Joel Stern and his associates have done much to change perceptions about financial analysis. See Stewart III (1991), for a review of EVA and free cash flow thinking.
8 See Menon, Bharadwaj & Howell (1996).
9 Herbig & Kramer (1991), advocate a cluster approach.
10 Shimp et al. (1993).
11 See Dillon, Madden & Firtle (1994: 570-580); Malhotra (1993: 684-697).
12 Aaker (1991).
13 Cravens (1995), offers a number of articles that sum up current research trends.
14 See Buzzell & Gale (1987: 62-3).
15 Extended from Wilson (1995: 337).
16 Extended from Berry (1995); Bitner (1995); Sheth & Parvatiyar (1995); Wilson (1995: 337).

11 Competitive Techniques

A bag of tools for marketing analysis

Lovelle Henderson's responsibility is typical of many general managers in the IOR. Henderson is the country manager for Experian (formerly CCN Group Limited), a leading British financial and credit information management multinational. Henderson oversees two Strategic Business Units (SBUs), Experian Scorex and Experian's credit bureau. Another local company has franchised Experian's Mosaic brand name from Europe.

Experian arose from the 1997 $1.8 billion merger between the CNN Group and what was the TRW credit bureau in the USA. The merger propelled the new Experian into world leadership and brought the world's largest relational database under Experian's control. Henderson knows that the merger will cause adjustments in the Nottingham, UK head office, and will make it important to manage her interaction with superiors more intensively.

Experian Scorex offers the only ISO 9000 accredited credit-scoring systems in the world, supplemented by a host of automated processing and credit management software products. The nature of these products brings the firm into direct competition with other international scoring system providers and with other software providers. The nature of the automated systems is such that it removes the burden of credit authority and monitoring from the Information Technology (IT) department and allows credit managers to manage credit with incredible flexibility. Marketing departments champion products such as Experian's because the products allow companies to respond quickly to competitive activity while maintaining tight controls.

Experian's credit bureau is growing fast and expects to be the market leader before the year 2000. Experian is building intelligence into its bureau at a rapid rate and competes directly with the highly respected D&B (Dun and Bradstreet)-affiliated Information Trust Corporation credit bureau.

Financial services, retail and telecommunications companies are major users, and Henderson's extensive experience in South African banking helps her to monitor the progress and fast growth of the business. Without co-ordination, both SBUs could propose different solutions to a potential client by linking various divisional products and services — thereby confusing and alienating the potential client. Henderson must also master a comprehensive knowledge of a wide range of competitors and understand the impact of their behaviour on the business.

This chapter introduces tools useful to managers of product portfolios such as the portfolio that Henderson manages for Experian in Southern Africa.

Many companies are finding IOR marketing complexity to be on the increase as never before. The competitive set expands every time globalisation persuades an outsider such as Experian to enter regional markets, whether directly or through mergers. More competitors often produce more pressure to achieve a low cost position. *When management headcount reductions become a cost-savings tool, management attention is diluted across a wider range of products.* Today, it's not unusual for IOR executives to manage more than five products or brands.

Competitive multinationals such as Experian can swamp local competitors or radically decentralised multinationals by bringing the weight of global resources to bear on a local market. However, IOR countries are often low priorities to globalised multinationals because of the relatively small size of the local market, and such pressure is not evident.

This chapter expands the focus on individual products and brands to a bag of tools including techniques that can be employed usefully in the analysis of multi-product or multi-brand portfolios. The techniques included in this chapter model certain aspects of the environment and the firm in order to focus attention on important strategic issues.

Managers who use these techniques should be aware that all models have limitations when used as part of the process of crafting strategy. The discussion concerning each technique is meant to focus management attention on the benefits and limitations of each technique, thereby increasing the likelihood that the technique will be used in a fashion that delivers the most value to strategic planning.

SOME GENERAL LIMITATIONS OF MODELS

All models and competitive analysis techniques are subject to a range of general limitations. These include:

- *Artificial simplicity*: The competitive environment is but one of many environments in which the enterprise conducts business. Models over-simplify the environment, generally reducing all analysis to an understanding of a few characteristics. Other characteristics and events can impact on the enterprise in unexpected ways that remain unexplained when a limited set of characteristics acts as proxy for all influences on marketing success.

- *Inapplicability*: There is no guarantee that a particular model will be applicable to a particular situation or industry. Models may explain the performance of one product very well while performing very badly when used to understand another product in a related industry.

- *History*: Models assume that trends in the past will continue into the future. This can be a major limitation in today's fast-changing environment.

- *Superficiality*: Models present snapshot pictures of a point in time that may obscure issues or contributing progressions of events underlying the current state of affairs. It may be tempting to accept the snapshot as reality while rejecting the complexity of the actual environment.

Used properly, models can improve any manager's understanding of the market. The general problems above are avoided by using each tool to answer the appropriate questions for which it was designed, by using the proper scales of measurement for each concept, and by keeping a keen sense that all models have limitations. No model will outperform the comprehensive understanding of a manager who has developed the empathy for the brand and market required for strong marketing. Yet, most exceptional managers rely on models to understand the environment, the enterprise and its stakeholders.

SWOT (STRENGTHS, WEAKNESSES, OPPORTUNITIES & THREATS) ANALYSIS

The analysis of strengths, weaknesses, opportunities and threats (SWOT analysis) is a popular analysis technique. SWOT analysis consists of

1. external environment analysis (opportunities and threats), and
2. internal environment analysis (strengths and weaknesses).

Once both internal and external analyses have been completed, it is useful to bring the information together in a SWOT analysis. Managers must avoid the temptation to do so prematurely as this is likely to lead to a muddled analysis where strengths and opportunities, and weaknesses and threats become confused in some minds. For this reason, SWOT analysis is more fully discussed on page 153.

EXTERNAL ENVIRONMENT ANALYSIS: THE OPPORTUNITIES AND THREATS GRID

Opportunities and threats exist outside the firm and impact on methods of effective management, sources of demand and sources of supply.

Trend and impact	Supporting evidence	Conflicting evidence	Timing	Probability and priority	Responsible executive and actions
One million new mobile-paging subscribers will enter the market in 1998. Impact: Will encourage new competition unless we take immediate steps.	Market penetration for paging increased from 0.5 % to 1.0 % (857,142) during the planning period and non-linear regression analysis of the previous five years points to a market penetration of 2.1 % (1.8 million) by the end of the 1998 financial year. Normalised churn scores predict that about 100,000 subscribers would leave the market during the period. Sales for the first three months of the financial year support this notion. This compares with a range of penetration of 2.7 % to 2.9 % in Country A, Country B and Country C, the closest comparable countries. Market penetration has lagged a combined index of these three countries by 3.73 years.	Ken Mpondo believes the industry will be ill-equipped to handle the incoming subscribers and notes that no paging company has installed application processing systems.	Ongoing projection from current year. To be evaluated and reported to senior management committee on a monthly basis.	75 % Priority ❶	Ken Mpondo Sue Chatz 1. Report monthly ↻ 2. Investigate application processing systems and report to committee by 1-03-98.

Table 11.1 The opportunities and threats grid (Note: all names used in this table are fictitious)

Basic concepts

- A marketing opportunity exists when the company identifies an attractive arena in which company marketing activities can create a competitive advantage.

- A threat exists when an external trend, development or competitor will erode the company's position unless purposeful marketing activity is undertaken[1].

Procedure

1. The first step of external environment analysis is the identification of important environmental trends[2]. Any external trend or factor, whether from the purchase and consumption environment or the competitive environment, should be included in the analysis if it offers the potential to impact on the ability to create a competitive advantage or to erode the company's position. These trends must be cast as specific assumptions about likely trends that imply marketing action during the planning period or in the longer term.

   Consider these fictitious examples that might apply for a mobile communications company in either India, South Africa or Thailand this year.

   Trend: One million new mobile paging subscribers will enter the market in 1998.

   Trend: In response to service bottlenecks last year, approximately 40 per cent first-time subscribers will evaluate offers from other service providers.

   Trend: Mobile subscribers will become more cost conscious during the period, limiting price increases to less than the rate of inflation in the Consumer Price Index.

2. The second step is to test the validity of each assumption. What evidence supports the assumption? What evidence exists concerning the timing and magnitude of the trend? It is not enough to make statements; substantiating evidence must be presented that supports each trend. If the management team disagrees, then this should be noted and evidence to support alternate points of view should be noted.

3. The third step involves assessing the short-term and longer-term impact of the identified trends and prioritising the trends for management action and surveillance. Table 11.1 (page 149) includes a completed opportunity and threat grid for the first identified trend. Note that this particular trend has a high probability and has been marked for monthly reporting to management. Should evidence change, it will be up to the responsible managers to bring this to the attention of management for a change in planning.

If you are in doubt about typical environmental trends, re-scan the earlier chapters of this book and note each environmental aspect. Think about how each aspect has changed in recent years and how you expect it to change in the future. Most companies would go on to develop a far more extensive list of trends and events than previously considered for marketing planning. Firms with many opportunities and few threats have been characterised as ideal, those with many opportunities and threats as speculative, and those with few opportunities and many threats as troubled[3].

Assumptions

- The model assumes that management is aware of all opportunities and threats and is capable of evaluating their nature.

- There is an implicit assumption that past events and trends influence the future and, therefore, that management can evaluate the future probability of trends.

Common application problems

- Managers may have difficulties recognising trends and events and identifying relevant evidence. These problems may be more pronounced in fast-changing markets and enterprises. It may be some time before management teams become comfortable with agreeing on the probability and timing of identified trends.

- The process of identifying and managing opportunities and threats may require more management resources, especially time, than are available.

- Organisational dynamics being what they are, some managers may be suspicious when others are given responsibility for trend monitoring. This is especially true when others might advance a personal or sub-group political agenda by distorting trend information. In such cases, it is wise to appoint a committee to interpret and manage trend monitoring.

INTERNAL ENVIRONMENT ANALYSIS: THE STRENGTHS AND WEAKNESSES GRID

Strengths and weaknesses reside within the enterprise and concern methods of effective management, sources of supply and sources of demand[4]. The value chain model (page 123) is a convenient starting place for the analysis.

Basic concepts

- Strengths and weaknesses are flip sides of a coin. One company's strength is a competitor's weakness.
- Strengths are what the enterprise does well and include the distinctive competencies that underlie the primary and support activities of the firm and a superior understanding of sources of supply and demand. *There is no greater strength than market empathy.*
- Weaknesses are constraints that limit the firm's ability to take a specific action. *There is no greater weakness than the lack of market empathy.*

Procedure

Surprisingly little has been written about the process of identifying, qualifying and quantifying strengths and weaknesses[5]. Tools, such as Kotler's Marketing Effectiveness Rating Instrument or Marketing Audit or the Services Marketing Audit framework advocated by Berry and his associates[6], may help a firm to identify strengths and weaknesses. Some typical strengths and weaknesses appear in Table 11.2 (page 154)[7].

The process for internal environment analysis is the same as the process for external environment analysis. Strengths and weaknesses are identified from the past and projected into the future. Each identified strength or weakness is then evaluated for validity in the expected conditions of the planning period. The impact of the strength or weakness is then qualified and its impact is quantified on an agreed scale. I prefer quantifying each strength or weakness on a scale of 0-100 per cent so that the scale is comparable to the external environment estimation of probability.

Assumptions

These are very similar to external environment analysis.

- The model assumes that management is aware of all strengths and weaknesses and is capable of evaluating their impact on the firm.
- The analysis requires management to predict the future with reasonable accuracy and to assess the impact of strengths and weaknesses in that future environment.

Common application problems

- Managers may have difficulties in identifying strengths and weaknesses. These problems may be more pronounced in companies where momentum and inertia have been entrenched.

- Lower level managers may feel uncomfortable noting organisational weaknesses that reflect poorly on their superiors. Using techniques such as the *jury of executive opinion* — where each individual's perceptions of strengths and weaknesses are polled blindly and the total results are shared with each individual (without disclosing any individual's personal perceptions) — can be helpful. A second blind poll is then conducted and the total results are shared with the group. Each individual then enters group discussions with an awareness of how widely shared his or her viewpoint is among the group. Senior executives must be careful not to probe to see who had a minority opinion if an individual decides not to bring up a point for discussion. This defeats the purpose of the exercise.

- The process of identifying and managing strengths and weaknesses may require more management resources, especially management time, than is available. Management teams must be comfortable with each other for the best analysis to emerge from the procedure.

- Organisational dynamics also impact on internal environmental analysis. Senior management must be careful to build consensus and involve affected parties in the ongoing management of strengths and weaknesses.

- Firms are encouraged to concentrate on high importance and low performance areas[8]. Resources devoted to areas where performance is high but importance is low should be evaluated for possible reassignment.

- Low performance in low importance areas should be disregarded while other remedies are being implemented. However, this should be monitored to ensure that it does not grow in importance while the company disregards it.

SWOT ANALYSIS

I have found it useful over the years to produce an opportunity and threat matrix as shown in Figure 11.1 (page 155), instead of the traditional SWOT four quadrant chart. Note that the most serious priority is Priority 1 and the area of the circle that denotes the point shows the seriousness of the impact of each opportunity or threat.

Using this methodology, a table is constructed in very little time, showing the strengths and weaknesses that may have an impact on the firm's ability to achieve its strategic objectives concerning each opportunity or threat.

VALUING EXPERIENCE AND LEARNING: SCALE AND EXPERIENCE EFFECTS

Two techniques suitable for single products or portfolios follow: the *experience curve* and *stratification analysis*.

Issue and impact	Supporting evidence	Conflicting evidence	Timing	Performance score and importance	Responsible executive and actions
We have superior brand equity Impact: Allows us to achieve higher margins and insulates us from some forms of competition. May lead us to become complacent.	Our brand is first in unaided awareness, first in aided awareness, is considered the tried and trusted brand by 6 out of 10 potential subscribers (more than double the #2 brand) and commands a 7.2 % price premium over the nearest brand. Source: Independent research conducted in December 1997.	Although market penetration for paging increased by 100% during the period, our sales grew only 92%. Service quality has suffered during periods when the subscriber base ramped up too quickly. Brand X was recently shown to deliver better service in an independent study published in the *Sunday News*.	Ongoing projection from current year. To be evaluated and reported to senior management committee on a quarterly basis.	85 % Priority ❶	Linda van der Merwe Bill Smit 1. Report quarterly ↻ 2. Investigate Brand X and report to committee by 1-6-98

Table 11.2 The strengths and weaknesses grid (Note: all names used in this table are fictitious).

OPPORTUNITIES AND THREATS

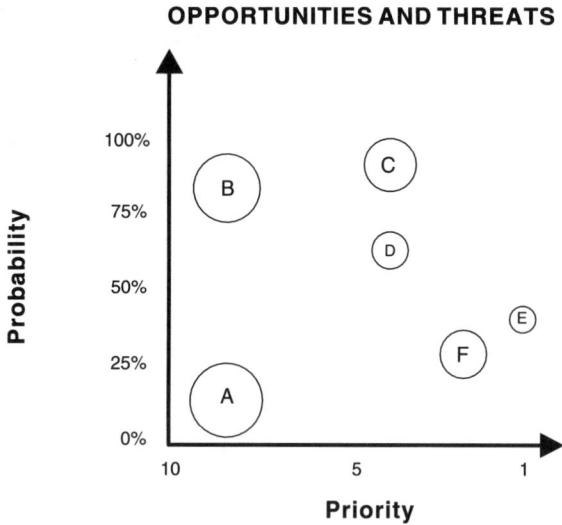

Figure 11.1 *An opportunity and threat matrix*

EXPERIENCE CURVE

Scale

During the 1970s, the Strategic Planning Institute began to publicise Profit Impact of Market Strategy (PIMS)[9] findings regarding market share and profitability[10]. Scale economies are a well-documented phenomenon. Large-scale plants cost less to build and operate and require fewer staff for comparable output units. Advertising and research costs per store drop dramatically when comparing a 100-outlet chain to a 10-outlet chain. Volume discounts are a prime example.

Experience

The experience effect captured much attention. The Boston Consulting Group and others were reporting that costs fell regularly and predictably with each doubling of cumulative production (cumulative production means starting at zero and adding every year's production to a cumulative figure)[11]. The plot of costs against cumulative production became known as the experience curve. The experience curve is used most often to plot changes in cost that might accrue from more aggressive marketing, such as market share expansion strategies.

DOMAIN	CONSUMER MARKETS	BUSINESS MARKETS
PURCHASE AND CONSUMPTION ISSUES	Superior knowledge of environmental characteristics, individual influences, needs, search behaviour, information processing, alternative evaluation behaviour, purchase behaviour, determination of satisfaction, divestment or post-consumption alternative evaluation.	Superior knowledge of environmental characteristics, individual influences, needs, search behaviour, buying centre roles and influences, information processing, formation of individual and organisational preferences, purchase behaviour, determinants of satisfaction, divestment or post-consumption alternative evaluation.
SUPPORT ACTIVITIES	Advantages derived from: infrastructure, human resources, technology, information and procurement	Advantages derived from: infrastructure, human resources, technology, information and procurement.
PRIMARY ACTIVITIES	Advantages derived from inbound logistics, operations, production outbound logistics, marketing and sales management, service.	Advantages derived from inbound logistics, operations, production outbound logistics, marketing and sales management, service.
PRODUCT	Superior design, brand equity, brand loyalty (not inertia), dominant market share, more efficient production methods, brand associated with quality and integrity.	Superior design, brand equity, brand loyalty (not inertia), dominant market share, more efficient production methods, brand associated with quality and integrity.
PROMOTION	Superior relationship management, effective sales promotion and advertising competence, competent salesforce, superior merchandising, high awareness, trial and usage, ambitious new product programme supported by management.	Superior relationship management, competent salesforce, effective sales promotion and advertising competence, high awareness, trial and usage, ambitious new product programme supported by management.
PRICING	Superior inventory management, advanced trading skills, keen knowledge of buyer utility, advanced behavioural modelling skills.	Superior inventory management, advanced trading skills, keen knowledge of buyer utility.
DISTRIBUTION	Superior distribution, channel support for brand, well-defined service procedures, appropriate customer targeting.	Superior distribution, channel support for brand, well-defined service procedures, appropriate customer targeting.
FINANCIAL MUSCLE	Access to: adequate capital, low-cost capital and advanced financial management techniques, applications processing and behavioural scoring systems.	Access to: adequate capital, low-cost capital and advanced financial management techniques.
MANAGEMENT	Experienced management, senior management in place more than ten years, visionary and capable leaders, flexibility/adaptation, entrepreneurial flair.	Experienced management, senior management in place more than ten years, visionary and capable leaders, flexibility/adaptation, entrepreneurial flair.

Table 11.3 Selected strengths and weaknesses

Concepts

Figure 11.2 below is a 90 per cent experience curve, called that because total added-value costs, i.e. marketing, sales, distribution, administration and all other non-production costs reduce to 90 per cent of the previous period each time production doubles. From a different perspective, the same phenomenon suggests a learning effect that decreases costs by 10 per cent every time production doubles. Plotting the average price against cumulative production (the dotted line in Figure 11.2), usually shows that margins are best in the growth phase of the product lifecycle.

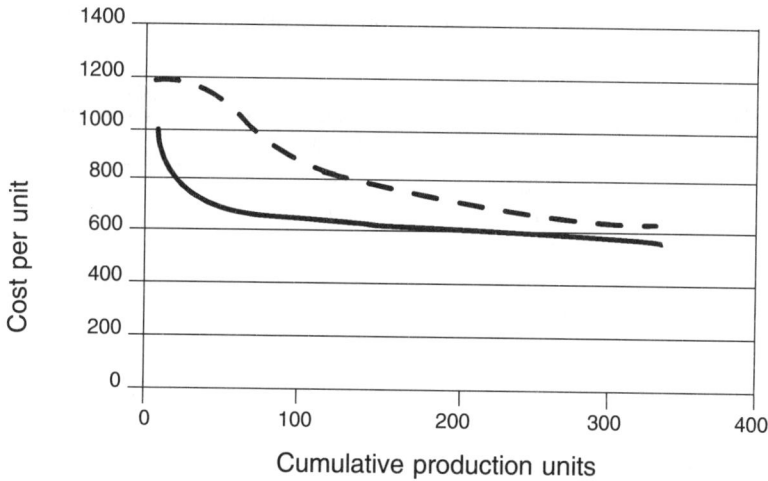

Figure 11.2 A 90 per cent experience curve showing unit costs

Experience curve analysis answers the question, 'How should we expect our costs and the costs of our competitors to change over time?' The answer to this question points to likely trends in industry pricing.

From where should you expect the learning effect to emerge? From what areas should you attempt to accelerate it? Experience accrues from labour efficiency, work specialisation and method improvements, new or improved production processes, better-performing production equipment, more efficient allocation of the resource mix, product standardisation and product redesign[12]. Shared experience occurs when two or more products share the same support activity assets or processes.

Procedure

First, production and deflated average unit costs must be established. This requires pooling cost and production data for at least a five-year period, and for longer, if possible. Cost data should be adjusted for inflation so that constant currency (for instance, 1990 SA Rand) is used throughout the analysis.

Next, the experience curve formula should be applied[13]:

$$C_q = C_n \left(\frac{q}{n} \right)^{-b}$$

where:

Cq = the cost of unit q adjusted for inflation

Cn = the cost of unit n adjusted for inflation

q = the experience (cumulative production) to date

n = the experience (cumulative production) in an earlier period

b = a constant that depends on the learning rate (see Table 11.4)

Experience curve	Value of b	Experience curve	Value of b
100 %	.0000	80 %	.3219
97.5 %	.0365	75 %	.4157
95 %	.0764	70 %	.5146
92.5 %	.1126	65 %	.6216
90 %	.1522	60 %	.7369
85 %	.2347	50 %	1.0000

Table 11.4 Selected values of the exponent b for experience curve calculation[14]

Finally, various curves should be fit to actual data to see which most closely represents the experience effect. Various strategies to manage experience and learning can then emerge from the analysis.

Assumptions

- The experience curve has great appeal as a planning vehicle for future costs. However, there are many cases where planners naively cut prices in the hope that higher market share and lower cost structures would follow naturally. Such naive applications of experience curve logic have often lead to sobering outcomes that convince many strategists to consider experience curve limitations carefully[15].

- The experience curve is not an invariable law of business. Its existence must be proven through analysis.

- It is difficult to define market boundaries in some industries. The experience curve may show differing levels of accuracy when different industry boundaries are applied.

- Experience curve logic assumes the accurate assignment of costs. Exceeding budgeted costs can have severe consequences in some organisations. As a result, costs often get assigned to available budgets, regardless of what policies senior management may impose in trying to define added-value costs. Choice of a unit of analysis to act as proxy for total costs may be difficult in some industries.

- The experience curve assumes that the future is similar to the past. As such, it ignores economic cycles and national factors, such as protectionism or a change of government, which can impact on industries in a discontinuous way.

- The behaviour of costs may change over time and minor costs may become more influential on total costs. Costs change as other factors such as share, scale and scope of operations change.

- The experience curve assumes that all costs reduce in a predictable way, mainly as a result of learning. The role of discontinuous events is ignored. Thus, radical innovations and reactions to events such as the Arab oil embargo and the trade difficulties of the late 1970s and early 1980s are ignored. Significant currency fluctuations are another case in point.

- The experience curve may focus too much attention on costs and too little on innovation. In essence, efficiency is emphasised at the expense of effectiveness. This can be very harmful in markets where demanding customers consider product and process improvements to be more desirable than lower prices.

- The curve does not take competitive response into account. This is a particular problem when the firm embarks on a strategy to increase market share.

Common application problems

- Total value-added costs may be too small a component of total costs to influence an experience curve.

- The company may not have the resources to build the support activities needed to meet the required production levels for a particular cost reduction.

- Even managers with the best intentions may be unable to allocate costs correctly across shared resources or across widely dispersed organisational structures.

STRATIFICATION ANALYSIS

Stratification analysis is a simple technique used for operationalising Pareto's well-known 80-20 rule. The analysis usually focuses attention on the source of sales, profits or costs which may be of interest.

Stratification analysis may be conducted on one variable using a one-way table, or on many variables using a multi-way table.

Basic concepts

Sales, costs, profits or any product-market related concepts that management may wish to understand in relative terms.

Procedure

Product	Sales turnover	Gross profits
Acme Air Widget	9 964	1 127
Acme Widget Supreme	12 226	6 749
Gizmo Air-conditioned Widget	17 694	12 220
Dealer brand widgets	1 256	858
Export widgets	22 698	9 992
Acme Dynamo Widget with Wonder-Edge	446	188

Table 11.5 *The fictitious Acme Widgets Company's widget range*

Step one: Gather the appropriate data together. Table 11.5 includes the raw sales and gross profits data for the Acme Widgets Company.

Step two: Compute the percentage each product contributes to the total of the variable. (Export widgets account for 30.6 per cent of total widget sales turnover.)

Step three: Rank the data by its percentage contribution to the total. (Export widgets are the largest contributor to sales turnover and they come first.)

Step four: Plot each product on a bi-plot where the bi-plot dimensions are the cumulative proportion of the *variable of interest* (sales in this case), and the *percentage of total products* (if there are ten products, each additional product adds 10 per cent; if there are five products, each adds 20 per cent). Note that the plot uses the cumulative proportion of the total of the variable of interest. Export widgets account for 30.6 per cent of total sales turnover, and export widgets plus Gizmo Air-conditioned Widgets account for 68.2 per cent of total sales turnover. Draw a curve through the points as in Figure 11.3.

Stratification analysis yields the most benefit when a multi-way table is used. Figure 11.4 (page 162) shows a two-way stratification analysis of sales and gross profit margin. On average, each of six products should account for 16.67 per cent of sales and gross profit.

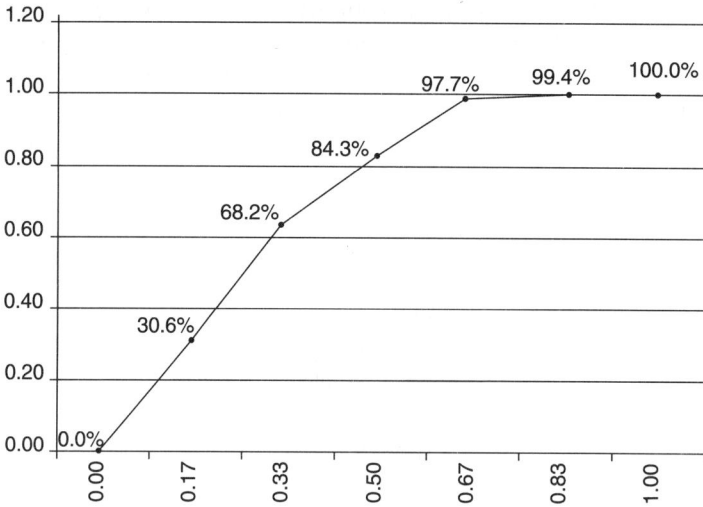

Figure 11.3 *A stratification analysis of Acme sales turnover data*

In what will be a recurring theme in other matrix techniques, the area of the circle representing each product shows the nominal value of sales. Although Acme Air Widgets accounts for a larger proportion of sales than an average brand, its profit contribution is below average. This suggests further investigation. The two smaller products should be investigated to see how many resources they demand. These products may be candidates for new strategies (divestment? invest to grow?).

Assumptions

- Assumes that the variable of interest is important to understanding the firm's objectives. This is not always true. For example, sales and profit contribution may not be important if the products are niche market segment leaders.
- The value of the analysis is subject to the quality of the data. Incorrect allocations of costs seriously prejudice the analysis.

Common application problems

- With the best of intentions, managers often misallocate costs and sales. This is a most significant problem where budgets are 'cast in iron' and no tolerance is accepted for variations.
- The model may be overly simplistic and may direct management attention to areas that are not problems. For example, dealer brand widgets may not

contribute as much to sales or profits but, without them, Acme's distribution coverage would be substantially reduced. Acme Dynamo Widget with Wonder-Edge is a new product launched this year and sales would be expected to be lower than an average product.

- It can be difficult to agree on standardised factors for the analysis between brands in firms managing product portfolios.

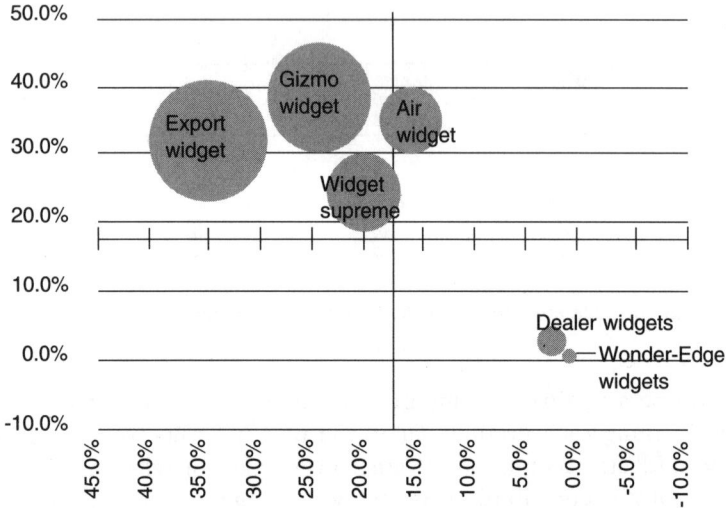

Figure 11.4 *A two-way stratification analysis of Acme sales and gross profit from Table 11.5*

Summary

This chapter explored four major techniques for environmental analysis. The basic concepts, procedure, underlying assumptions and common application problems were discussed for each technique.

The *opportunities and threats grid* presented a formalised way to manage exploration of the external environment. *The strengths and weaknesses grid* was shown to provide similar discipline for internal environment analysis. A new SWOT analysis methodology was suggested which avoids the temptation to mix internal and external issues in a SWOT analysis until both issues are investigated separately.

A method for operationalising and forecasting the value of *experience and learning* was suggested, and one-way and multi-way approaches to *stratification analysis* were discussed.

The next chapter discusses more competitive techniques that can be applied to product portfolios.

ENDNOTES

1 Both of these definitions are adapted from Kotler (1991: 48-49).
2 Day (1990). Kotler (1991). This section relies on Day (1990: 68-69) and Kotler (1991: 48-49) from which it was adapted slightly. Both are books that I believe should be on every marketer's bookshelf.
3 Kotler (1991: 50).
4 I am indebted to Professors Roger Blackwell of The Ohio State University and Salah Hassan of Georgetown University for this insight, gained from an unpublished collaboration: Blackwell, Burgess & Hassan (1992).
5 The procedure advocated here relies on Day (1990); Jain (1993); Kotler (1991); Kotler, Gregor & Rogers III (1977); Kotler, Gregor & Rogers III (1989); Stevenson (1976).
6 Berry, Conant & Parasuraman (1991: 255-268). Kotler (1991).
7 This list has been adapted from Kotler (1991), and Jain (1993).
8 Kotler (1991: 51).
9 The Strategic Planning Institute's corporate database of market conditions, competitive position and financial and operating performance. By mid-1986, Buzzell and Gale reported on data for four years or more, concerning more than 2 600 SBUs. Buzzell & Gale (1987: 34-35).
10 For example, Buzzell, Gale & Sultan (1975).
11 Abell & Hammond (1979: 107).
12 See Abell (1993: 148-154).
13 Abell & Hammond (1979: 108).
14 Robinson (1986).
15 Experience curve problems culled from Abell & Hammond (1979); Mintzberg (1994); Ohmae (1982); Robinson (1986).

12 Portfolio Analysis Techniques

Matrix techniques for analysing product portfolios

During the 1970s and 1980s, strategic planners began experimenting with a number of analytic techniques. Most of these techniques consisted of bi-polar matrices upon which products were plotted and many were stimulated by research concerning scale and experience effects. Planners at the Boston Consulting Group (BCG), General Electric, the Strategic Planning Institute and other think tanks produced many techniques, but the BCG Growth-Share Matrix and the Business Screen have probably received the most attention over the years.

Despite their flaws, many firms find portfolio techniques give very valuable insight. One study showed that about 75 per cent of diversified firms widely use portfolio planning models[1]. This chapter introduces a range of techniques appropriate to product portfolio analysis.

THE GROWTH-SHARE MATRIX

Popularised in the early 1970s[2], the growth-share matrix is a display of the bi-polar relationship between market growth and market share. A typical plot appears in Figure 12.1 (page 165).

Basic concepts

- Relative market share is measured according to the following formula: (Business unit share divided by the leading competitor's share).

- Market growth is measured according to the following formula: [(Current annual sales minus previous annual sales) divided by previous annual sales].

Procedure

Some conventions apply in usage of the matrix. The value of annual sales in local currency is represented by the size of the circle representing each product. You will achieve best results if the area of the circle is proportional to sales. Avoid the temptation to use the diameter of the circle as a proxy for sales, the resulting circles do not seem to relate to the difference in sales. Microsoft Excel 97 has this function built in.

Market growth is plotted on a normal scale in percentage points and is adjusted for inflation. Relative market share is generally measured using a log scale (which has the effect of providing maximal differentiation of lower share performers) as shown in Figure 12.1. However, some practitioners feel the log scale is unnecessary, and use an interval scale for the dimension.

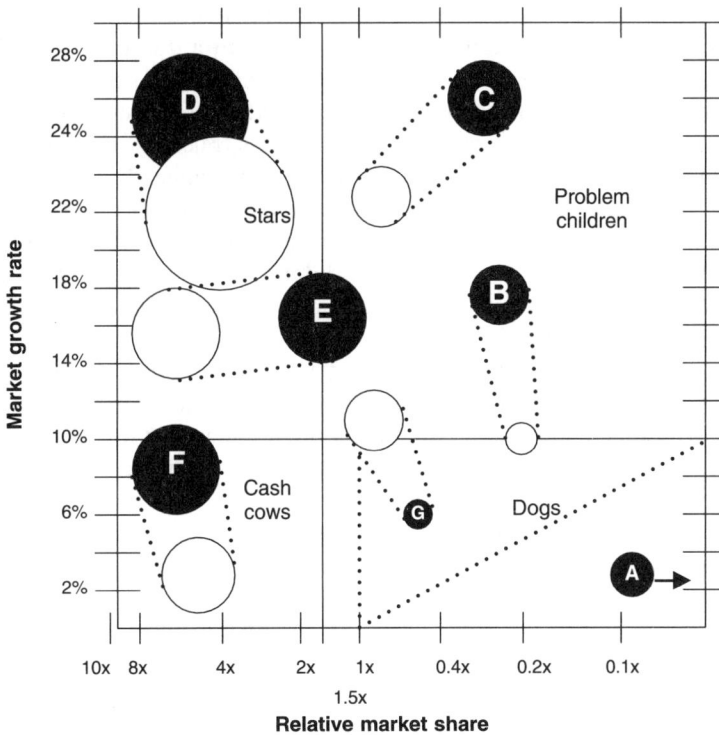

Figure 12.1 *A growth-share matrix*[3]

Four types of products are classified on the grid. A line drawn from the point where relative market share equals one and one-half times the share of the leading competitor, and one drawn where market growth exceeds 10 per cent, separates these classes. The separation of market growth at the 10 per cent is somewhat arbitrary. Since the line serves as a proxy for dividing products in the growth phase from other products[4], many planners adjust accordingly. The positions of the products in Figure 12.1 are plotted for the immediate period (black) and for the forecast period (white).

Products D and E are *stars*. Stars are high growth, high share products which may or may not be self-funding. Should these products maintain market share, they have a high probability of becoming significant cash generators. However, a star may well be a cash user in the short- and medium-term.

Product F is a *cash cow*. The forecast appears to call for cash generated by F to be invested elsewhere, resulting in a loss of market share. Cash cows generally generate cash that can be used to fund other products, especially stars. These products have large shares of slower growing, more mature markets. Many companies can trace the payment of interest, dividends, R&D and corporate overheads to cash generated by cash cows. Many cash cows have strong brand equity. The slow growth of the market signals to potential newcomers that every customer must be won from a dominant brand, a very sobering prospect that tends to decrease the likelihood of new market entries.

Problem children (C and B) are low-share products competing in fast growth markets. Product C is forecast to follow a success trajectory moving to average share and within range for growth to star performance. Risk is high with a product such as C. Product B is forecast to follow a disaster sequence from problem child to dog (the other disaster sequence is from star to problem child). Product B may well be a candidate for divestment if it is a late introduction that never reached the critical mass necessary to become competitive and to gain distribution.

Many problem children such as B may be late introductions into a product category and the 'snapshot on the grid' may represent no more than an early picture of ultimate success. Yet pioneers often encounter lower entry barriers and higher returns − suggesting that a late entrant may have a much rougher time moving toward stellar performance[5]. The problem child's symptomatic low market share probably indicates a required change in the marketing mix. Problem children generally suck up resources: people, time and management attention.

Products A and G are *dogs*. Dogs are low-share products in slow growth markets. They do not generate much cash, but do not require much either. Dogs can be cash traps but generally require only the investment of their modest cash flow and, sometimes, modest additional capital. Product A is being harvested. No real effort is put behind the brand and no cash is invested. Eventually it will be liquidated, but it may be very profitable in the short-term so long as it does not demand resource investment.

Product G is a bit of an *anomaly*. The market growth rate is increasing from 7.5 per cent to 12 per cent. Management has decided to invest in order to grow relative market share from 0.5x to 1x. Normally, this would suggest a tough fight and probably be a high-risk strategy. In this particular case, the company knows that a management buy-out has shifted a competitor's attention to other products, and that the competitive product's service levels have dropped dramatically. Distribution is being gained with little effort and almost no investment, as production capacity is free to handle the growth.

The typical large IOR company has products scattered across the matrix, and a typical product may appear in various positions on the grid when its relative share and market growth rates are compared across regional markets in isolation.

Strategic implications

- As a first priority, portfolio managers should secure the position of cash cows while avoiding the temptation to reinvest in them excessively[6].

- Cash generated by cash cows should first be used to support stars that are not self-sustaining. Once these needs are met, promising problem children should be supported.

- Any problem child that cannot be funded should be divested.

- Dogs may be candidates for astute market re-segmentation. Dominance of a niche can turn a dog into a cash cow with careful management. Otherwise, the dog should be managed for liquidity and divested when appropriate.

- Firms must be careful to balance product portfolios. A cash cow may finance many problem children and dogs for a period but, over the longer term, such a portfolio offers higher risk than most firms would desire. The economic value added by such unbalanced portfolios may be negligible.

Assumptions

These strategic recommendations have been criticised for their simplicity and lack of predictiveness in certain cases[7]. The following issues have been noted about the assumptions underlying the growth-share matrix.

- It may be impossible to determine market share or growth accurately.

- Market share and growth are assumed to correlate with cash flow. In reality, the relationship may be weak or non-existent.

- Market boundaries are assumed to be fixed. Many industries, such as financial services, are undergoing massive changes in market boundaries. Do retailers and telecommunications firms act as banks? Consider the similarities and you decide.

- Inflation and foreign exchange are assumed to be steady influences. In many IOR markets, both of these can fluctuate wildly over the span of a decade.

- Growth and cash flow are assumed to be the primary objectives of the firm's strategy. Tax avoidance, equity generation and expansion through acquisitions may be over-riding strategic objectives.

- Growth and share are assumed to occur on a single level. Multi-level, transnational and transregional issues may remain hidden in the analysis.

Common application problems

Defining market boundaries can be difficult. There is a strong temptation to define the market in either a flattering way or in a way consistent with the firm's traditional world-view that misses the essence of market dynamics. Even rather innocent distortions can have a significant impact on the analysis, and finding the right level of aggregation can be difficult.

When market share, boundaries and growth can be determined accurately, managers may distort market boundaries intentionally to mislead senior management. Although senior managers may sense intentionally misleading market boundary definitions ('We became market leaders in the fast-growing Tuesday evening convenience outlet, chocolate with nuts ice cream-on-a-stick market during the period . . .'), they may not be close enough to the business to suggest more accurate definitions. In such cases, a wise strategy is to ask to see a number of portfolio analysis techniques at various levels of market aggregation.

Simplistic interpretation can lead to impractical strategic response. One study of 87 enterprises with dog products classified the management of 40 per cent of the products as ineffective (ROI < 5 per cent). Dog products managed with high quality medium-price strategies, and careful support and investment, often gave adequate returns[8].

THE BUSINESS SCREEN: ATTRACTIVENESS AND COMPETITIVE POSITION

General Electric and Shell emerged as hotbeds of strategic planning in the 1970s and 1980s[9].

GE and the well-respected McKinsey consulting firm promoted a business assessment matrix that popularised the interaction of industry attractiveness and competitive position as a determinant of marketing strategy. With the inclusion of market share (as an aspect of competitive position), and market growth (as an aspect of industry attractiveness), many strategic planners felt the tool offered a next step in complexity from the growth-share matrix. At about the same time, Shell's Directional Policy Matrix, a very similar analytic tool, was developed. Shell's matrix examined the interaction of competitive capabilities and prospects for sector profitability. These two tools became very popular and continue to be featured in most strategy texts.

Over the years, I have used a hybrid approach that explores the nature of the interaction between market attractiveness and competitive position[10].

Basic concepts

- Competitive position is defined by the firm's strengths and weaknesses as measured by internal environment analysis (see page 148).

- Market attractiveness is defined by examining the firm's opportunities and threats as measured by internal environment analysis. Commonly used factors include aggregate market indicators (market size, market growth, stage in product life cycle, sales cyclicity, seasonality, resource requirements, historic profit margins, required competencies, etc.); environmental indicators (technological, regulatory, cultural, etc.); and industry factors (competitive intensity, value chain relationships, etc.).

- Although more elegant strategies have been proposed for the business screen[11], three generic strategies emerge from the analysis (see Figure 12.2). The white blocks denote blocks where the firm is strong and the market is attractive. Protecting the position, investing to build and building selectively can be effective strategies in these types of product-markets. Managing selectively, building selectively or refocusing the business are logical strategies for the grey blocks in the matrix. In these blocks, the combination of market attractiveness and competitive position is not compelling at

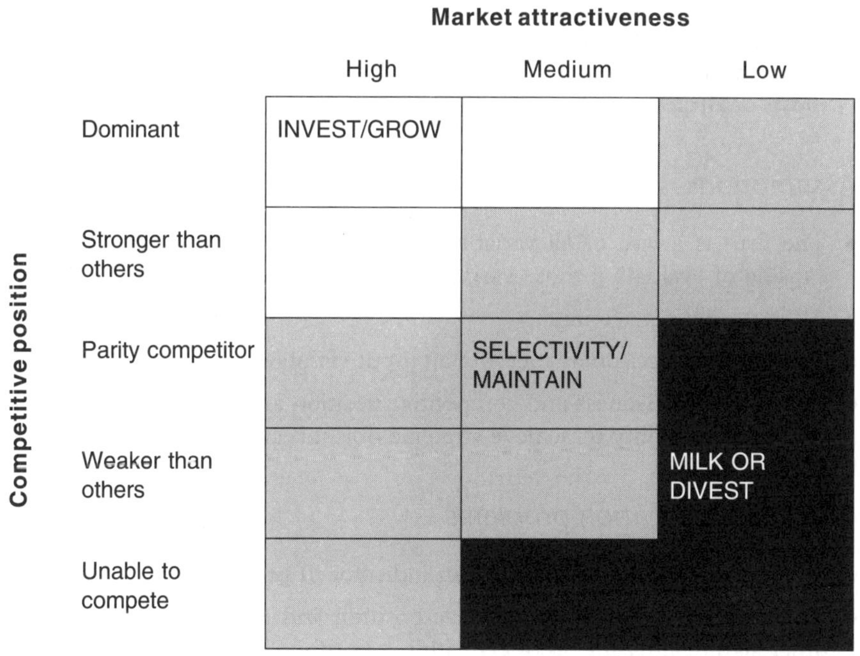

Figure 12.2 Strategies suggested by the business screen.

present, but may be if the right strategies are pursued. The black blocks of the matrix denote unsatisfactory situations where harvest, divestment or milking the brand is suggested. These strategies are generic and require much investigation at the coalface prior to acceptance by the management team.

Procedure

- *Step one:* Internal and external environmental analysis should be conducted as a first step. See Chapter 11 for a discussion of these analytic techniques. If you have conducted internal environment analysis, use the factors identified on the strengths and weaknesses grid. Similarly, the opportunities and threads grid that emerges from external environment analysis can be the basis of key external factors. It is important to reconsider forecasts for external factors and notations of the desired position for strength and weakness to ensure that these remain current.

- *Step two:* Evaluate the firm's position on each variable. Competitive position can be evaluated on the five-point scale proposed in Chapter 9 (where dominant = 5 points, stronger than others = 4 points, and so on through the remainder of the scale-parity competitor, weaker than others, unable to compete). Market attractiveness can be measured on a five-point scale (where highly attractive = 5 points, more attractive than most = 4 points, and so on through the remainder of the scale-parity market, less attractive than most, unattractive).

Assumptions

- The firm is aware of all variables underlying market attractiveness and is capable of evaluating those variables in the context of the firm's needs.
- All input data is accurate.
- The firm can accurately measure all input variables on an appropriate scale.
- Industry attractiveness and competitive position are important determinants of the firm's ability to achieve strategic objectives.

Common application problems

- Market growth rate may not be an indicator of profitability.
- The trade-off between competitive position and market attractiveness may differ significantly for products within a portfolio.
- The strength of the link between the various characteristics and overall market attractiveness (or competitive position) may differ for individual

products. Framed differently, the weights of the variables may differ from product to product, thereby producing a misleading picture when viewed in the aggregate.

- Management may be too inexperienced with a product or too far removed from daily events in a particular industry to make valid judgements about either dimension.

- Any of the problems noted for external environment and internal environment analysis (see page 148).

COMPETITIVE ADVANTAGE MATRICES

Growing interest in competitive advantage in the early 1980s popularised two matrices. The Boston Consulting Group's (BCG's) New Portfolio Matrix contrasts the size of advantage with the number of approaches to achieve advantage. The KSF-Positional Advantage Matrix contrasts differences among competitors concerning a key success factor with the influence of the source of advantage (suggested by a KSF) on positional advantages in the market.

BCG'S NEW PORTFOLIO MATRIX

Many of the ways in which competitive advantage can be gained, such as understanding purchase and consumption behaviour better, have been discussed in this book. Clearly, resource and environmental constraints limit the range of strategies available to the firm, and the advantage created by a strategy will be of a unique magnitude. These two strategic facts form the basis of a simple matrix to guide creative strategy development (see Figure 12.3 on page 172).

Basic concepts

The matrix in Figure 12.3 suggests four pure types of industries. Each industry type suggests strategies that might be most efficient. The key to the analysis is to understand what these differences imply in a specific product-market.

- *Fragmented industries*: Size of advantage is small and there are many approaches to competitive advantage. Market share is often less important. Finding a profitable niche may be the best strategy.

- *Specialisation industries*: Size of advantage is large, approaches to competitive advantage are many. Focus and superior brand image may be more important than size. Winners own dominant shares in a niche. Losers attempt to spread.

- *Volume industries*: Size of advantage is large, approaches to competitive advantage are many. Market share is often very important. May require

SIZE OF ADVANTAGE

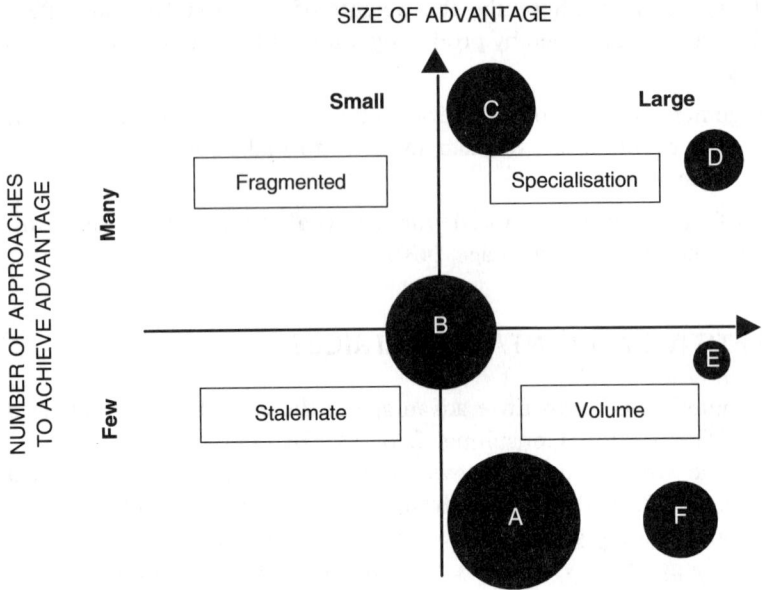

Figure 12.3 *BCG's New Portfolio Matrix[12]*

intensive capital investment. Low costs are imperative. Process management is also important.

- *Stalemate industries*: Size of advantage is small, approaches to competitive advantage are few. Market share is often less important.

Procedure

The industries in which products compete are evaluated on the two scales. The number of approaches to achieve advantage can be audited with the help of the strengths and weaknesses that emerged from the internal environment analysis (see page 148). The jury of opinion method is one process for judging the size of advantage.

Industries transit the matrix over time, given certain strategies by participants in the arena. McDonalds' (Product A) emergence from the fragmented American restaurant industry is a key example of a focus strategy that transited from *fragmented* industry to *specialisation* and then to *volume*. No doubt, McDonald's is ever mindful of the struggle to avoid moving into *stalemate*[13].

Product B would be a concern to management because the matrix suggests so many options. The successful strategy will hinge on the ability of the firm to find a key success factor that delivers a large competitive advantage. If the firm can find one, then specialisation and volume are available for consideration. If not, the firm seems destined to find a profitable niche in a fragmented industry, to manage costs intensively in a stalemate industry, or to divest.

Assumptions

- Assumes that approaches to advantage will be successful during the planning period, or that the firm is capable of predicting which advantages will be successful during the planning period (and has predicted the future correctly).

- Assumes that the firm is aware of all approaches to achieve advantage and can accurately measure the size of an advantage.

- Makes the assumption that firms can pursue strategies that are appropriate to their environment (such as avoiding tying up resources in fragmented and stalemated industries). Appropriate strategies may not always be clear or available to the firm due to constraints.

- Firms are most successful when significant advantages are achieved in specialisation and volume industries.

- Volume firms should be aware of actions that could cause the industry to slide towards stalemate. Specialisation firms should be similarly advised of actions that could cause a slide to a fragmented industry classification. Both should have strategies in place to avoid such a slide.

- Industries are not assumed to be fixed but rather changing over time.

Common application problems

- Inability to foresee conditions in the market during the planning period: 'caught by surprise by change'.

- Lack of awareness of avenues to advantage or difficulty measuring the size of advantage.

- Inability to pursue appropriate strategies due to inadequate resources or inadequate competency pool.

- Inadequate size to influence industry shifts towards fragmentation or stalemate.

THE KSF-POSITIONAL ADVANTAGE MATRIX

This matrix[14] brings together three dimensions discussed earlier in this book: brand positioning, key success factor (KSF) attributes and relative competitive position.

Basic concepts

- Relative competitive position on a key success factor reflects management opinion, as drawn from objective data, concerning the relative position of a firm on a KSF attribute. Measured on a two-point nominal scale: *we are better, they are better*.

- Influence of the KSF attribute on positional advantage reflects management opinion of the strength of a KSF on success in an industry as measured by a two-point nominal scale: strong and weak. Management must determine a relevant method for establishing measurements on the scale for the analysis. Where data permits, statistical estimates may be made. Otherwise, required investment, estimated sales derived as a result of the difference in competitive advantage, or another proxy may be used, depending on the objectives of the analysis. The strong/weak dimension separates the top and bottom grids.

- The size of difference in competitive position is measured on a two-point nominal scale: small and large. This scale is measured using management opinion formed after careful analysis of available objective data.

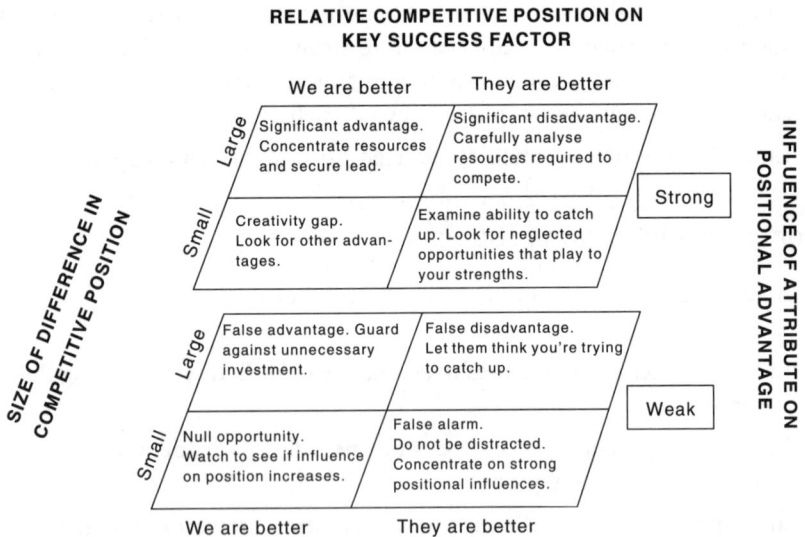

RELATIVE COMPETITIVE POSITION ON KEY SUCCESS FACTOR

Figure 12.4 The KSF-positional advantage matrix

Procedure

The position on each axis must be determined first. Again, a jury of executive opinion may be useful in reducing strongly felt extreme individual opinions prior to a meeting. Where consensus will be reached on scale values, KSF attributes can be culled from the strengths and weaknesses that emerged from the internal environment analysis. Table 11.3 (page 156) is a good starting place if internal environment analysis has not been conducted.

Industry positions can be plotted over a number of years and markets, and for a number of KSFs on the same grid. Changes over time and differences between markets may be very useful places for more investigation.

Many multi-dimensional analytic techniques (e.g., multiple regression, logistic regression or correspondence analysis) could be used to explore the nature of relative differences in competitive position or the relative influence of an attribute on positional advantage, where data permits. The strengths and weaknesses grid is a very powerful tool to use as a basis for this analysis because it rests on the evidence that management has at hand and objectifies the discussion (see Table 11.3).

Classifying key success factors on these very simple bi-polar scales (i.e., strong-weak, small-large, better-worse), focuses management discussions quickly and brings a group to a consistent and realistic world-view.

Assumptions

- Assumes management is aware of all KSFs and can measure the firm's relative position versus competitors and the influence of each KSF on positional advantage.

- Assumes that successful approaches to advantage will be successful during the planning period, or that the firm is capable of predicting which advantages will be successful during the planning period (and has predicted the future correctly).

- Makes the assumption that firms can pursue strategies that are appropriate to their position on the grid. Appropriate strategies may not always be clear or available to the firm due to constraints.

- Assumes that industries change over time and that the past is some indication of the future.

Common application problems

- Lack of awareness of all KSFs.

- Inability to measure accurately and/or to agree on relative competitive position, size of differences in competitive positions or influence of attributes on positional advantage.

- Caught by surprise by change. Failure to account for unforeseen innovation or discontinuous changes in KSF importance during the planning period.

- The inability to pursue appropriate strategies due to inadequate resources or inadequate competency pool.

OTHER MATRICES

By now you will have captured the essence of matrix analysis, the positive and negative aspects of the technique and the typical data requirements. The value of any matrix technique to crafting strategy in a particular industry will vary due to many factors. Here is a brief discussion of some additional matrices you may wish to consider.

COST OF A NEW CUSTOMER – COST OF MAINTAINING A CUSTOMER

Two costs should dominate the thinking of marketing people: 'What does a new customer cost?' and 'What does it cost to maintain an existing customer?'.

Of course, any such analysis is dependent upon output from an accurate activity-based costing system (see page 189)[15]. However, constructing a matrix of these two dimensions can focus management's attention on very important relationship marketing concepts, such as lifetime value (see page 252).

Once products are plotted on the two dimensions, consider the placements in light of the product lifecycle. How do these costs compare for growth phase products? What strategies are in place to reduce these costs? What strategies are in place to keep customers from leaving? How appropriate are the firm's marketing spends in light of these costs?

MARKET GROWTH – BUSINESS GROWTH

The Boston Consulting Group's Growth Gain Matrix has received much attention[16]. The matrix contrasts market and business growth. The market growth rate appears on the vertical axis and the business growth rate on the horizontal axis.

Problem children will generally appear on the matrix at a point outside the maximum sustainable growth rate determined by the following formula:

$$G = \frac{D}{E} * (r-i)\,p + rp$$

where:

G	=	the maximum sustainable long-term asset growth rate
D/E	=	the debt/equity ratio
r	=	the after-tax return on assets (adjusted for inflation)
p	=	proportion of earnings retained (or 1-dividend payout ratio)
i	=	current after-tax cost of debt

Those gaining market share will appear on the far right of the matrix, just below a diagonal line drawn where market and business growths are equal. Problem children losing share will appear on the extreme top left of the matrix, indicating product growth far below market growth in a fast-growing market. Cash cows and stars appear near the diagonal line. Products losing share will appear above the diagonal line and those gaining share below it. Dogs and cash cows will tend toward the market growth rate axis above the diagonal line.

A vertical line drawn at the maximum sustainable growth rate (from the horizontal business growth rate axis) will intersect the diagonal line at a point that should be considered the centre of the matrix. Too many products to the right of this line suggest that the firm will require funding in order to continue funding growth. That is, if the weighted growth rate of the products exceeds the maximum sustainable growth rate, the firm should be planning to gain external funding to fund the growth.

CAPITAL INTENSITY – PROFIT IMPACT OF MARKET STRATEGY (PIMS)

PIMS findings tied profitability to capital intensity long ago[17]. Try constructing matrices exploring the interaction of working capital and fixed capital with other variables, such as productivity, number of employees, return on sales, etc.

MARKET DOMINANCE – CAPITAL INTENSITY

It may be helpful to understand capital intensity in the sense of whether or not it buys market dominance. Plot market dominance on one axis and capital intensity on the other. If capital intensity is required in order to build economies of scale or scope that deliver a sustainable competitive advantage and a profitable business, what's wrong with capital intensity in such a case?

GROWTH – RETURN MATRIX

Contrasting growth and profitability can focus attention on investments in managerial ego. It's fun to run a star product, but unprofitable growth or negative cash flow can kill the company. Remember that cancer is an undisciplined growth that kills and the annals of corporate history are filled with examples of enterprises that waited too long before seeing the doctor.

BUSINESS PROCESS ANALYSIS

Business re-engineering has become very popular as the rate of change has increased. However, the topic is not new to marketing. Two matrices may help to understand the relation between business process and marketing strategy.

BUSINESS PROCESS – PRODUCT LIFECYCLE GRID

Hayes and Wheelwright were among the first to recognise that business processes transit lifecycles that can be linked to product lifecycles. Consider for a moment that standardisation is likely to increase as sales volumes increase and the product lifecycle moves toward maturity. Because processes and volumes are often related, business processes vary as product lifecycles mature. For instance, consider how often the shake-out stage leads to more capital intensity and, consequently, more standardisation and less flexibility as pressure on cost mounts.

Construct a matrix where the horizontal axis is the product lifecycle. On the vertical axis, place the business process cycle, moving from processes that are consistent with low volume-low standardisation markets to processes that are consistent with high volume-high standardisation. For instance, many below-the-line (promotional) agencies use artists to render rough artwork for client pitches. As these agencies move to greater size, they typically install computer capabilities and their account executives work with computer artists to generate rough artwork quickly that brings various promotional ideas to life. While the new technology may be limited to the clipart images available to the software and may lack creativity, it allows account executives to render many rough ideas quickly and at much lower cost than before. All businesses proceed through such process transitions – this trend is not limited to large manufacturing firms.

When you draw the matrix, consider those businesses where the business process and the product lifecycle are 'out of sync'. Has the market matured while you have clung to out-of-date processes? Have you invested in processes ahead of growth that has never come? This grid can do much to focus management attention on important process decisions.

BUSINESS PROCESS – COMPETITIVE POSITION GRID

It is likely that the analysis of business process and product lifecycle will lead to the question of further investments. Marketing people always want investments in 'new and better' things. But what will such investments deliver? How can you formalise the decision?

The next chapter will discuss the Strategic Profit Model as a way to understand investment logic. However, you can construct a very simple matrix that will help you make the decision. The matrix answers the key question, 'What will this investment do for our competitiveness in this market?'

To construct the matrix, plot the business processes and competitive position at present, and then plot the new business processes and competitive position as they will be after the proposed investment. This simple analysis can yield much insight into the quality of previous investment decisions when viewed in light of the present and expected competitive environment.

Summary

This chapter considered the positive and negative aspects of a number of matrices designed to measure aspects of product portfolios. Matrices are not substitutes for good business thinking and no matrix should determine strategy. Rather, matrices are models that guide strategic thinking so that strategies can be crafted carefully and the probability of success can be maximised.

Once a management team becomes familiar with a number of matrices, they often experiment with matrices of their own design. These will frequently provide additional insights and should be encouraged by management. Widespread knowledge of the firm's position on a few significant matrices often leads to consensus in world-view, and to commitment to strategy implementation.

However valuable matrices may be in creating strategic insight, one thing must always be remembered: managers run businesses, not matrices. Never allow simplicity to obscure the complexity of the marketplace, and never offer simple solutions when complex issues are required.

Once firms have understood competition, it becomes necessary to understand the resources the firm can bring to bear to satisfy competition and beat competition. The next section of the book explains managing resources.

ENDNOTES

1 Haspeslagh (1982).
2 Abell & Hammond (1979: 174) contend that the portfolio concept originated with the Boston Consulting Group in the early 1970s; see Henderson (1973).
3 Adapted with permission from *Perspectives*. The experience curve – reviewed IV. The growth-share matrix of the product portfolio. © The Boston Consulting Group, Inc., 1973.
4 Abell & Hammond (1979: 176).
5 Porter (1980: 232-234) discusses antecedents and consequences of being first (pioneering).
6 This section relies extensively on Jain (1993). However, most strategic marketing texts make similar recommendations.
7 For example, Bettis & Hall (1983); Christensen, Cooper & DeKluyver (1982).
8 See Byars (1991); Woo & Cooper (1980).
9 This section relies on Abell & Hammond (1979); Kotler (1991); McDonald (1996); Robinson (1986).
10 See Day (1986: 204-205); Kotler (1991: 41-44); and McDonald (1996: 93-96) for discussion about market attractiveness and competitive position matrices.
11 See Day (1986: 204).
12 Adapted with permission from *Perspectives*. Strategies in the 1980s. © The Boston Consulting Group, Inc., 1981.
13 Jain (1993: 283-284).
14 To my knowledge, this matrix is original to this text. Burns (1986), suggested a similar model based on attribute importance. Day (1990: 136-138) suggested a similar matrix, but measured the influence of each source of advantage on positional advantage. Although I have not seen it elsewhere, I believe this simple tool often contributes significantly to the

understanding of competitive advantage in an industry.

15 If you are unfamiliar with activity-based costing, the topic is covered in many accounting texts these days. Glad & Becker (1994), is a personal favourite that is devoted to the topic and includes linkages between activity-based costing and competitive strategy.

16 Abell & Hammond (1979), and Robinson (1986), describe this matrix in more detail.

17 See Buzzell & Gale (1987), Chapter 7.

PART THREE

Managing
Resources

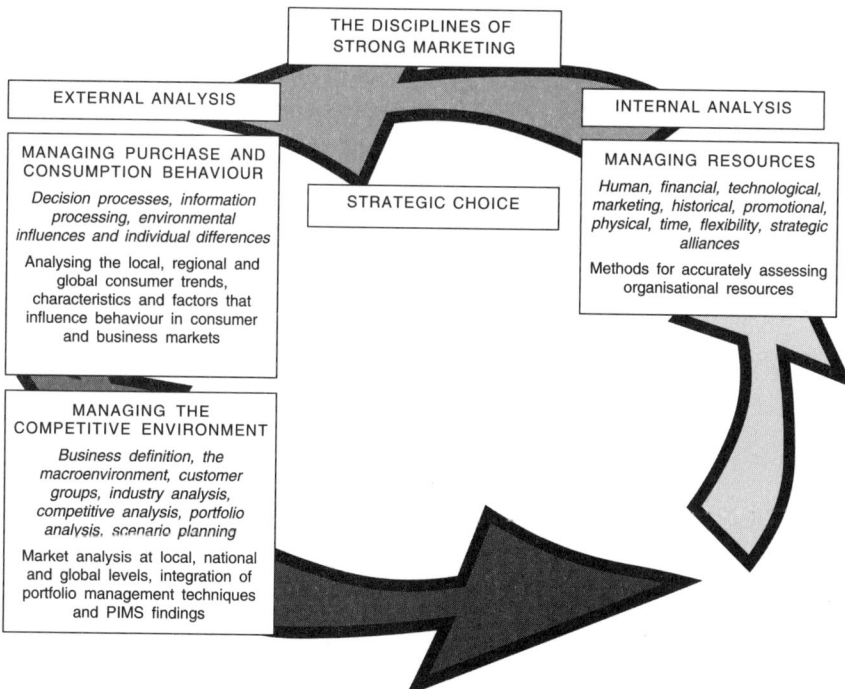

THE DISCIPLINES OF
STRONG MARKETING

EXTERNAL ANALYSIS

INTERNAL ANALYSIS

MANAGING PURCHASE AND
CONSUMPTION BEHAVIOUR

*Decision processes, information
processing, environmental
influences and individual differences*

Analysing the local, regional and
global consumer trends,
characteristics and factors that
influence behaviour in consumer
and business markets

STRATEGIC CHOICE

MANAGING RESOURCES

*Human, financial, technological,
marketing, historical, promotional,
physical, time, flexibility, strategic
alliances*

Methods for accurately assessing
organisational resources

MANAGING THE
COMPETITIVE ENVIRONMENT

*Business definition, the
macroenvironment, customer
groups, industry analysis,
competitive analysis, portfolio
analysis, scenario planning*

Market analysis at local, national
and global levels, integration of
portfolio management techniques
and PIMS findings

13 | Astute Resource Management

Getting the most out of what you've got in the digital economy

Cadbury-Schweppes (South Africa) Limited's 1996 year-end results give shareholders much reason to celebrate. Sales turnover climbed 17.8 per cent, earnings per share increased by 24.2 per cent, and profit before tax skyrocketed by 32.2 per cent. Not bad for a business participating in mature food industries such as carbonated soft drinks, drink concentrates, packaged desserts, baking aids and jams.

The board applauded marketing's contribution to performance by noting market share gains in the confectionery business, Schweppes' growing market and growing market share in carbonated soft drinks, and cleverly timed new product introductions by business units. However, resource management appears to be another Cadbury-Schweppes strength. Margins were enhanced significantly despite cost pressures in many businesses. Financing costs were well down. One can easily imagine that operations required management to use more information technologies than ever before and that the ambitious targets challenged staff members to do more in less time.

Consider the resources managed by Cadbury-Schweppes – finances, people, values, time and information. Building strong marketing requires more intensive resource management than ever before. This may be even truer in the IOR where resource constraints are often more severe due to low economic development and fast market growth.

Previous chapters focused on the management of external influences of firm success. Purchase and consumption environment management skills build strong marketing by growing markets, capturing more market share and increasing profit margins. Competitive environment management skills build strong marketing by providing an understanding of how environmental factors assist and retard growth, and how competitors attempt to thrive in that climate.

Proper management of purchase and consumption and competition is not enough to guarantee strong marketing. Knowing the market's problems has little value if the company does not possess the competencies to provide solutions. Identifying strategies most likely to bring success in a competitive environment is no guarantee that the firm possesses the resources required to pursue those strategies. Abundant resources may only reinforce inertia and momentum. Beginning with this chapter, focus shifts to internal issues.

Resource management skills build strong marketing by shaping management's perception of the firm's capabilities and competencies. Armed with resources and understanding, an enterprise can align itself with the market in a way that increases its chances of success in the competitive environment. Resource management is so important that each of the major resource groups has spawned a discipline devoted to its management (e.g. financial management, human resource management, information technology management).

This chapter explores the impact of financial, human resource and cultural resource management on the planning and implementation of strong marketing strategies.

FINANCIAL RESOURCE MANAGEMENT

Firms that fail to manage financial resources competently suffer sobering and often fatal consequences. Yet, many marketing people find financial management concepts to be baffling. Whether this can be traced to the organisation of marketing education as a separate discipline, or to some other factor, it is clear that many IOR marketing people lack adequate financial management skills[1].

No marketing strategy should be proposed unless the impact of the strategy on financial performance is understood. Marketers who lack adequate financial skills can find influencing company policy to be a most frustrating task. This section briefly exposes some of the financial management skills required for strong marketing.

Strong marketing requires prudent financial analysis, planning, implementation and control. Specific, measurable, achievable, related and time-bound (SMART) financial goals must be communicated throughout the enterprise to the people responsible for their achievement. The great diversity in literacy, numeracy and business education at various levels of the organisation can make this very difficult in IOR countries. This suggests the need for financial planning tools that are sophisticated enough for planning by financial specialists, as well as being accessible to marketing specialists and other non-financial staff.

THE STRATEGIC PROFIT MODEL

The strategic profit or DuPont model[2] became very popular during the 1960s and 1970s as a tool for financial planning and communication. Some firms and industries have developed very intricate models that include many detailed levels and industry-specific ratios. For instance, I remember using a strategic profit model (based on a National Home Furnishings Association model) that included more than ten levels of ratios when I was a sales and marketing manager at Glick's Furniture Rental in Ohio during the 1970s.

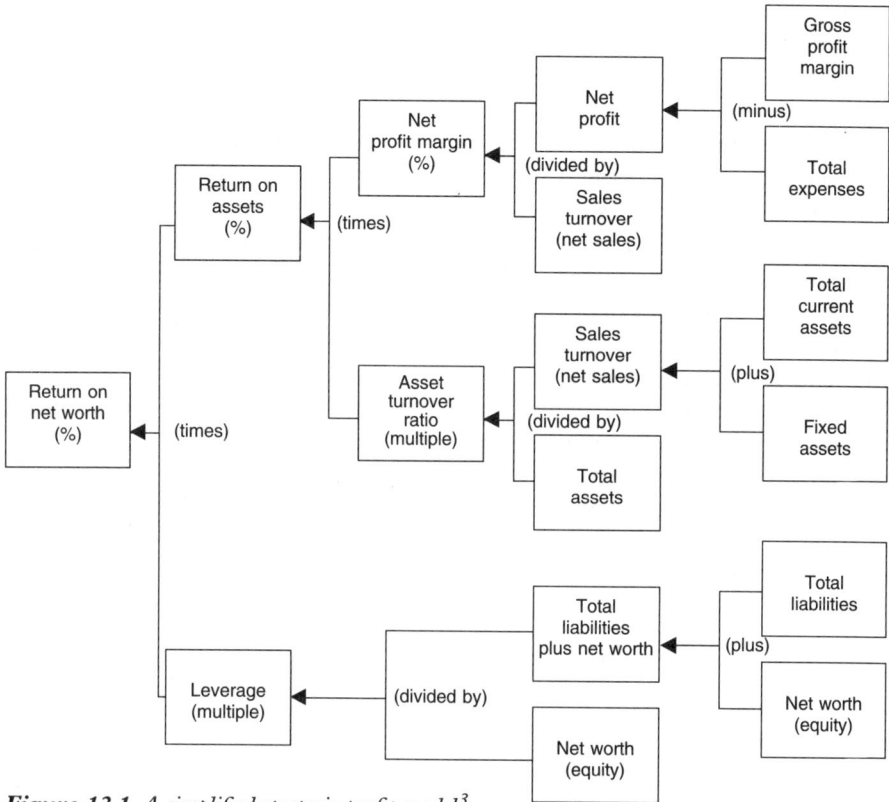

Figure 13.1 A simplified strategic profit model[3]

The graphic representation of the inter-relationships of key financial ratios is a major advantage of the strategic profit model. The model can provide detailed analysis of any financial ratio of interest leading to return on net worth or to provide a subset of information to a particular audience, such as a region or functional department.

Thus, the strategic profit model offers the advantage of unified communication across the enterprise, and becomes a powerful tool of focus. Those responsible for planning or implementing plans, can see the impact of a strategy at a glance, so long as the information provided is accurate.

The simplicity of the tool means that associates at every level of an organisation can grasp the financial implications of proposed strategies or performance with relative ease. Even labourers with educational disadvantages can grasp the significance of changes in key financial ratios after a short training exercise. Companies that insist on sharing complete financial results with all staff, such as Wal-Mart[4], will find the strategic profit model to be a useful planning and communications tool.

The advent of Direct Product Profitability (DPP) was a logical progression from the strategic profit model. DPP applies strategic profit model thinking to the allocation of shelf space, the assortment of brands stocked, and other merchandising strategies at retail, although the model is considered quite outdated by the accounting profession.

Return on investment (ROI) and return on net worth (RONW) have been used in Figure 13.1 (page 186), even though they have been criticised as inadequate tools for measuring the real rate of return on a company's assets since the mid-1960s[5]. This is because the calculation of return on investment uses accounting net income rather than cash flow, and uses accounting depreciation in the tally of net income and asset value. Accounting depreciation generally differs to real depreciation, thereby perverting the related inputs to ROI and RONW analysis.

Discounted cash flow analysis is an alternative method for investment analysis and capital investment planning.

Nonetheless, many firms still feel that ROI and RONW are important tools for developing effective marketing strategies and are probably likely to continue to do so for the foreseeable future – especially with the advent of activity-based costing, which is discussed later in this chapter.

ECONOMIC VALUE-ADDED

Economic value-added (EVA®) is another concept attracting great interest at present. EVA is a registered trademark of Stern Stewart and Company, a management consulting organisation[6].

First proposed by the American academic Joel Stern in the 1960s, EVA is winning an increasing number of fans in the corporate world. Many of the top companies adding shareholder value, including world champion Coca-Cola, use this management planning tool. Proponents suggest that sales, profit, return on equity, cash flow, dividends and other indicators of market value, are far inferior to the concept of economic value-added.

The argument proponents make in favour of economic value-added is, essentially, that Stern and his followers believe that contemporary accounting methods have become far removed from financial reality, and that such reporting methods cause managers to contemplate actions which may destroy rather than enhance the value of companies. They point out numerous traditional accounting practices that they believe distort the true performance of an enterprise. Instead, they argue that a firm's market value is determined by *free cash flow* i.e. the cash generated by a company's operations (net operating cash flow) less gross additions to fixed assets and incremental working capital (i.e. less net investments). Those who believe that the role of marketing is to enhance the value of the firm may find much utility in adopting EVA as a management planning tool.

Economic value-added is derived according to the following formula:

$$EVA = [r-c] \times capital$$

where:

r = the rate of return, calculated by dividing net operating profit by capital

c = the weighted average cost of capital, calculated as the opportunity cost equal to the total rate of return that a company's investors might hope to achieve (or by comparison with some other hurdle rate)

The weighted average cost of capital is usually computed according to the following formula:

k_a = $p_1k_1+p_2k_2+\ldots p_nk_n$, where k_a is the weighted average cost of capital, p_x is the proportion of the firm's total capital which comes from source n (i.e. equity or a specific type of debt) and k_x is the average cost of capital from source n[7]

capital = represents the totality of cash ever put into the organisation, measured by adding common equity and debt.

It is important to understand that EVA proponents suggest rather complex adjustment of traditional accounting information in order to provide financial information amenable to EVA analysis[8].

EXPECTED VALUE ANALYSIS

Expected value analysis, often used in conjunction with decision trees, presents the strong marketer with another useful financial planning and communication tool.

Constructing a decision tree is very simple. Consider the problem facing Eugene Ntombeni. Market research has determined that the Operation SuperWidget first year profit opportunity is estimated to be R2 000 000. The decision tree in Figure 13.2 (page 188) captures two elements of Eugene's decision process. Should Eugene develop the new nozzle technology or outsource it?

If the company commences development, it has a 75 per cent chance of developing the nozzle successfully. If the nozzle is successfully developed, the company can expect to earn R560 000 less the R100 000 development cost. This is calculated by taking (R900,000 × 0.40) + (R400,000 × 0.50) + (R0 × 0.10). If the company fails, it will lose R100 000. The company has a 75 per cent chance of success and a 25 per cent chance of failure. Thus, Eugene can expect a return of R320 000 if the company pursues in-house development.

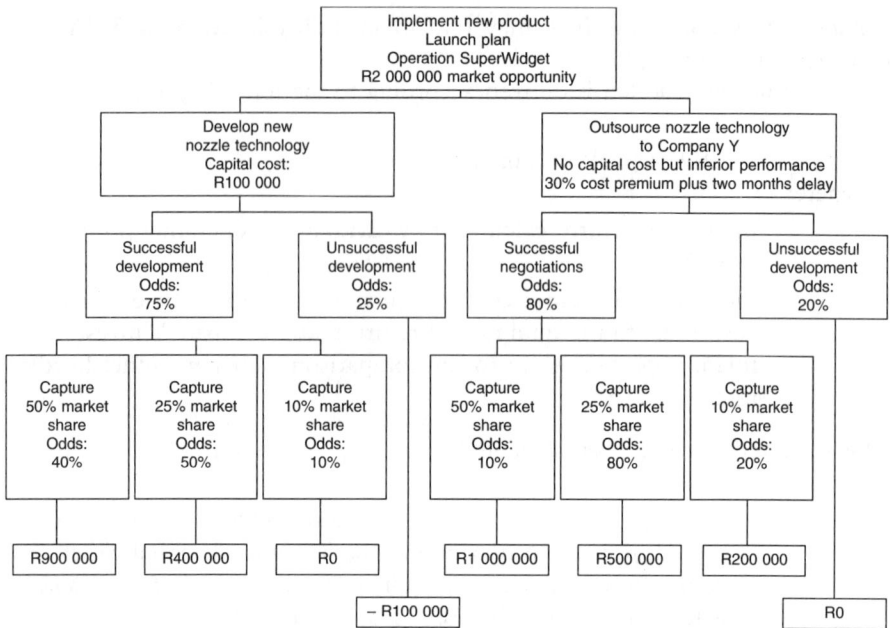

Figure 13.2 A simplified decision tree

If the company outsources, it avoids the R100 000 development cost, but it also foregoes the advantage of a unique product feature which research indicates will boost market share significantly. The expected value of this node is R368 000, less the 30 per cent cost premium the firm must pay for the outsourced nozzle.

Eugene must now consult his sales and cost projections carefully. At the point where the discounted cumulative cost of the 30 per cent cost premium for the outsourced nozzle exceeds R48 000, Eugene will be wiser to pursue in-house development.

Of course, the weakness of expected value analysis is the assignment of probabilities and estimation of outcomes in the model. The jury of opinion technique may help analysts to arrive at better estimates, but the analysis is no better than management's ability to forecast probabilities and expected payoffs accurately for each decision tree branch. For this reason, management should always explore and agree the assumptions of a particular expected value analysis prior to discussing the results.

ACTIVITY BASED COSTING AND MANAGEMENT

Many modern IOR economies bear little resemblance to the labour-intensive, production-led economies of earlier in this century. Others have changed little, or have even, perhaps, changed for the worse. How strange it is that so many companies continue to use similar accounting systems across the IOR that are based largely on concepts developed between 100 and 500 years ago!

Clearly, we have developed significant capabilities to store and analyse cost and performance information during the past decade that did not exist previously. In addition, earlier discussion in this book noted the increasing support for the disaggregation of service-based components of manufacturing, and a general increase in the contribution of services to the overall economy. These developments have led to a significant trend towards activity-based costing and management systems in the accounting profession, but remain unknown to many marketing professionals[9].

Activity-based costing (ABC) more closely aligns costs to resource usage. This is accomplished by assigning resources to activities and then linking activities to cost objects using predetermined and well-reasoned bills of activities that mirror true costs as accurately as possible.

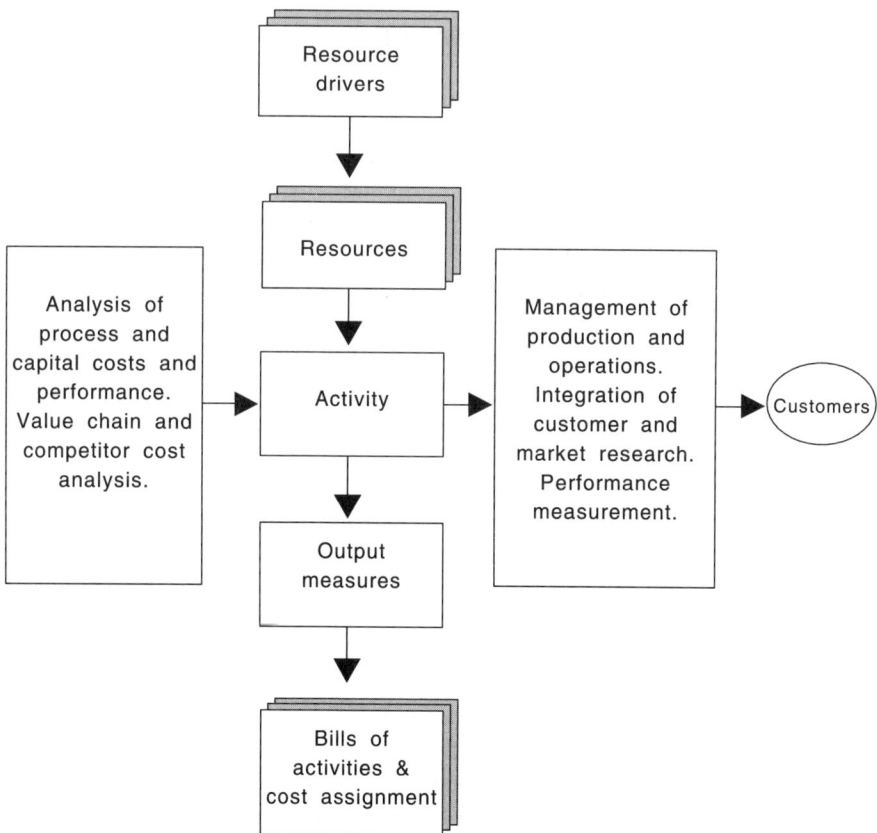

Figure 13.3 *The major components of the activity-based management (ABM) system[10]*

A well-defined methodology establishes the nature of costs and links costs to Porter's Value Chain (see Chapter 9), thereby giving activity-based management (ABM) systems a theoretical link to that well-accepted business strategy paradigm (see Chapter 10). In ABC, the traditional conceptualisation of overhead costs is replaced by the assignment of traced costs to Porter's supporting activities in the proportion of usage of those resources. Capital costs are also traced directly to activities and customers. A small amount of non-traceable costs (generally less than 5 per cent of the total) is assigned across the business in proportion with resource usage.

ABC is the fundamental information source for activity-based management systems. Because costs are linked to cost objects, continual improvement strategies and business and process re-engineering can be more accurately established. The benefit delivered to the strategy process is very high. ABC and ABM are essential in today's fast-paced marketplace, where accurate information is a necessity.

HUMAN RESOURCE MANAGEMENT

How many companies have failed simply because they lacked the right people? Of all resources, people are the most difficult but most rewarding to manage. If you are to win, you must do it with the right people.

'YOU WIN WITH PEOPLE'

When I was a boy I idolised one of the most colourful and most successful college football coaches in history, Coach Wayne Woodrow 'Woody' Hayes. My memory of Woody is always of a man on fire, marching up and down the sidelines in a short-sleeved shirt with snow blowing during an Ohio State-Michigan game. His intensity and desire to win continue to shape my attitudes toward competition.

Hayes coached the Ohio State Buckeyes to two national championships and numerous near misses. During the 1960s and 1970s, the Buckeyes dominated college football as no other team in history. Hayes was a gregarious and demanding man with a number of colourful sayings that captured the essence of his beliefs. None was better known than his often-repeated exhortation that 'You win with people!'

Noting that people usually have left your life by the time you are capable of paying them back for their help, Hayes advocated 'paying forward', and he made a habit of doing so continually. He rarely accepted personal praise without immediately deflecting it to a team member.

When this gridiron warrior died a few years ago, he was eulogised for his achievements, fiery temperament, demanding nature and ethical behaviour. More touching were the hundreds of tributes paid by the poor or disadvantaged who Hayes had helped and sworn to secrecy[11]. Woody inspired an intense loyalty from his players, assistant coaches and fans that should be an inspiration to corporate leaders.

Woody Hayes knew pressure. He coached in a city of just less than a million football-mad fans. Yet, Ohio Stadium's almost 100 000 seats have filled for every game since the 1950s, and seats are allotted on a lottery basis (one game only per alumni). Ohio State fans expect excellence. OSU produced Jesse Owens, Jack Nicklaus and a slew of Olympic champions, professional athletes and national championship winners across the range of college sports. However, the pressure of coaching strong marketing in the IOR would challenge even Woody. The most pressure comes from change.

THE EMERGING DIGITAL ECONOMY

Change, complexity and uncertainty characterise the emergence of the digital economy in the IOR. Everything seems to be changing in IOR markets these days – markets, politics, socioeconomics, values and just about anything else you can imagine. Who would have dreamed that South Africa would emerge peacefully as one of the most politically-correct nations during this decade?

The winds of change may have swept Africa during the 1960s, but the winds of democratisation are sweeping the entire IOR during the current decade. People have seen the lifestyles of the industrialised nations and they want prosperity. At the same time, they want to maintain their national and cultural identities. Many IOR sub-regions rank among the fastest growing per capita wealth generators in the world. The fact that many of these same countries have some of the fastest-growing populations draws attention to the incredible growth that is taking place.

One kind of growth (e.g. exports, GDP, population, crime, etc.) often influences growth in another. For instance, economic growth can initiate social adjustments. Social adjustments, in turn, may trigger a range of psychological adjustments, and these may be the genesis of changing economic performance in an economy. Consider the role of family conflict, a frequent outcome of social adjustment.

The trends underlying globalisation and the emergence of a digital economy have been well documented by Tapscott[12]. It is easier than ever to acquire high technology and many IOR countries are attempting to leapfrog into information-intensive and other modern enterprises. Governments which believe they can avoid these trends fool only themselves. Kicking and screaming, we are being led to a world government of some kind. This has important implications for education, labour laws, the employment of children and a myriad other issues.

TAPSCOTT'S TWELVE THEMES OF THE DIGITAL ECONOMY

Twelve themes have been noted as characteristic of the emerging digital economy.

1. The rapid explosion and accessibility of knowledge.
2. The easy storage and communication of knowledge as a result of digitisation.
3. The new technologies that enable virtual and simulated worlds to be explored to solve business problems and seek innovation.
4. The breaking down of large organisations into molecular bodies.
5. The integration and internetworking of the new molecular business units.
6. The decreasing need for intermediates.
7. The convergence of communication, content and computing.
8. The rapid increases in product innovation.
9. The increasing participation in production by consumers.
10. The trend towards immediacy in all aspects of business.
11. The globalisation of markets.
12. A growing feeling of discordance sweeping the planet.

All of these themes are relevant to the IOR but many are felt more severely because of the massive change in the region[12]. The cumulative effect of these trends is to increase the uncertainty of IOR markets and to alter the effectiveness of organisational structures.

ORGANISATIONAL STRUCTURES

Traditionally, organisations are considered most effective when they are at a state of steady equilibrium, producing regular and predictable patterns of behaviour and results, demonstrating great internal harmony and exemplary adaptation to the external environment[14]. Increasing questioning of this notion marked the early part of the 90s. As a result, popular and academic researchers began to explore the nature of chaos[15]. Today, it's accepted that some element of organisational chaos is required for a firm to succeed. The matrix and Theory Z[16] organisational structure types are widely used in organisations experimenting with chaos.

THE MATRIX ORGANISATIONAL STRUCTURE

Marketers will immediately recognise the matrix organisation for the product manager style of organisational structure was popularised by Proctor & Gamble, Johnson & Johnson and others. In its original form, the organisational structure charged the product manager with responsibility for all aspects of the product – including production, operations and finance. It was clearly a difficult stretch in the contemporary business environment. The addition of stronger functional management aspects over the years have changed the product management model and most product managers have little control over non-marketing functions today.

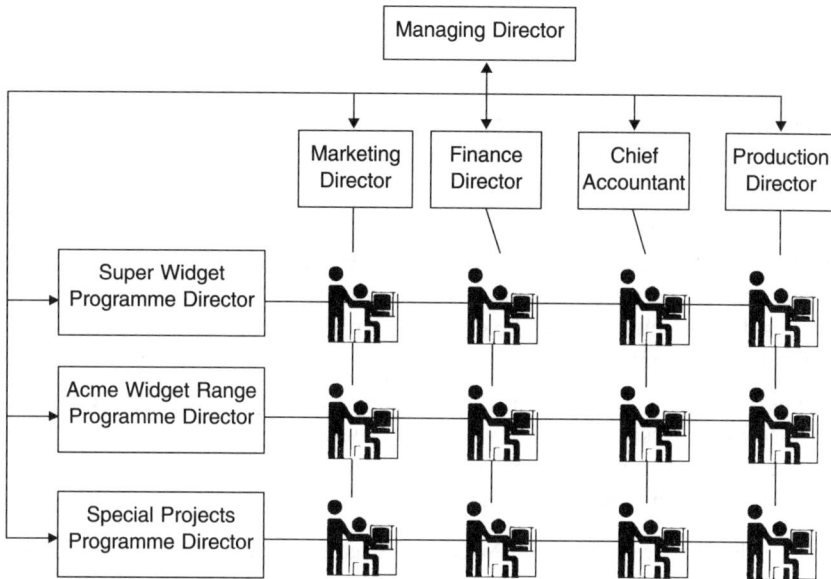

Figure 13.4 *A traditional matrix organisation*

The matrix organisation can act as a launching pad for strong marketing[17]. For example, managers can be placed in charge of managing all products developed for certain segments. Matrix organisations are ideally suited for fast-changing and uncertain business environments. More importantly, the matrix organisation offers high integration leading to improved communication, more thorough information sharing, and increased face-to-face interaction. Matrix organisations offer functional management and specialist career paths, the possibility to share resources, and the capability to enact decisions closer to the business.

The downside of matrix structures is that the amount of time spent in meetings can become excessive and democracy can be taken to the extreme of anarchy. Too much democracy can lead to inaction and organisational paralysis. Role confusion and the problems associated with serving two masters also can emerge. Management must be aware of excessive politics in a matrix organisation and be prepared to take action to stop it. Many of the problems of matrix structures can be overcome by blending consensualised ('Japanese') and individualised ('American') approaches to business.

ROLES PEOPLE PLAY

Marketing also must be sensitive to the roles played by various members of the organisation. Mismatches between people and positions can lead to job dissatisfaction that severely limits marketing success[18].

- *Line executives* are responsible for the day-to-day activities of the company – either creating the product or providing it to the customer. *Staff personnel* are specialists whose job it is to advise, but not command, the line managers. Accounting, R&D and human resources are typical staff personnel areas.

- People with titles such as product or project manager are, typically, *integrating role players*. These individuals must smooth the way between the various departments so that the company's objectives do not become hostage to interdepartmental conflict.

- *Boundary role players* represent the company to the outside world. They liase with stakeholders, especially with customers. Most sales and marketing people play *boundary-spanning roles*, becoming (or generating the material that becomes) the face of the company to outsiders.

Strong marketing strategies acknowledge the nature of demands and limitations placed upon people playing each role. For instance, boundary roles such as sales often create internal conflict for people playing those roles. Consider the sales person torn between loyalty to customers and the firm. Assigning integrating tasks within the organisation to a person playing a boundary role seems likely to cause tremendous conflict leading to a less than desirable outcome.

ORGANISATIONAL LIFESTAGES

Building strong marketing also requires a keen understanding of the seasons of an organisation's life. Greiner made a significant contribution when he identified five stages in the evolution of organisations[19].

The notion that firms pass through crises at the end of each lifestage is central Greiner's theory. Table 13.1 details the major components of Greiner's theory of organisational evolution. Alternative theories suggest that organisations go through incremental change and experience much smaller setbacks along the way. Both strategies suggest that building strong marketing successfully (i.e. growing the firm) will lead to organisational issues that should be addressed in the strategic marketing plan.

GROWTH THROUGH	CRISIS
CREATIVITY – Early growth comes from the actions of a small tight-knit group of players working in a very personal and informal way.	LEADERSHIP – Formal management practices must be instituted.
DIRECTION – The setting up of formalised systems spawns centralised control.	AUTONOMY – Control must shift to lower levels in the hierarchy.
DELEGATION: – Decentralisation then proceeds to characterise management.	CONTROL – A crisis of control then emerges that requires the installation of supporting systems for co-operation and communication.
CO-ORDINATION – The new systems encourage growth until administration becomes a burden.	RED-TAPE – Head office and divisions become increasingly separated.
COLLABORATION – Red-tape can only be overcome by increased interpersonal collaboration and control. Effective control is accomplished by intercultural sharing rather than formal controls.	? – Greiner thought that this stage might lead to a stage of psychological saturation when all would become tired of teamwork. He also thought further stages of multi-organisational growth might emerge from future research.

Table 13.1 Greiner's stages of company evolution[20]

The concept of self-empowered may well be worth considering in organisations where collaboration has emerged. Although the concept has been given the most attention in production and operations environments, it is applicable to marketing and sales as well.[21]

UNDERSTANDING WHO IS REALLY IMPORTANT

Shortly after I graduated from Ohio State, I accepted a job offer from Glick's Furniture Rental in Columbus. Glick's Rental was a two-store chain back then but was soon to become the tenth largest furniture rental company in America, under the leadership of David Dowds. Every new manager spent the first day in the firm with Dowds in a quirky little office he shared with Blair Williams, the Columbus regional manager.

Dowds, in his mid-thirties, spent the day sharing his thoughts as he worked. I was quite surprised to be spending the day with the President of the Furniture Rental Association of America. Nevertheless, I was feeling a little bored after three hours of sitting, when Dowds indicated I should follow him to the showroom.

When we entered the showroom, Sam Abramson was presenting to a customer and Dowds indicated that we should listen to his presentation. Sam was the best salesperson I ever met, and I remember his presentation to this day. He listened, probed and worked to understand exactly what the customer needed. Although Sam made a big impression on me, something Dowds did made an even bigger impression.

Glick's built the first showcase outlets in America and the rental outlets followed the same fully accessorised room grouping merchandising plan. As Sam and the customer moved from one room to another, the customer stopped to stub out a cigarette. Large NO SMOKING signs were posted but had been ignored by the customer. As the customer turned the corner, Dowds scooped up the ashtray and took it to be cleaned – returning it a few moments later. I asked Dowds why he didn't just ask me to empty it, and his answer remains with me to this day:

'I suppose that I am trying to demonstrate something to you. I want you to understand our values. We make our living right here in this showroom. No one, not you or me, is above emptying an ashtray, replacing an accessory or straightening a seat cushion in order to make this showroom look its best. That's one of the most important jobs in this company.'

Dowds beat Tom Peters[22] – who advanced the notions of the upside-down organisation chart, and managing by wandering around – by about five years in understanding that management was one of the least important functions in the company.

Glick's had no employees, they had *associates*. Calling people associates was more than a semantic exercise. Glick's considered associates to be family, and management took a sincere interest in how associates felt. When my car was damaged beyond repair by a snowplow in a blizzard, Robert Glick loaned me his own car and then arranged a huge discount on a car at Ricart Ford.

Banc One, The Limited and Worthington Steel, often mentioned by Peters and others for their outstanding accomplishments, were other Columbus firms who had associates in their employ but no employees.

LEADERSHIP

Dowds was an effective leader and he understood the value of formal and informal communication to leadership. When I wrote my first memorandum, it was a big day for me. It was my first opportunity to use those thirteen-letter words I learned at Ohio State. Dowds almost immediately asked to see me and proceeded to show me a copy of another memo. I had to admit that the other memo was written better and complimented him on it. Dowds made his point when he indicated that a warehouseman, who had not graduated from high school, had written the memo. I remember that lesson as well.

- Always communicate with people in the language they use.

- Keep it short and simple. Don't use words that might make people feel inferior.

- Use communication to lead and motivate. People that work for you like to think that you're better than they are but they don't like to think that you think you're better than they are.

- Remember that what you don't say is often more important than what you do say.

Some of the strong marketing skills every manager requires today are:

- Respect for the individual.
- Attention to detail.
- Constant mentoring.

LEADERSHIP IS NOT . . . TOXIC EXECUTIVE POWER

Before defining leadership, it seems appropriate to define what it is not. The toxic executive is not a leader[23]. In General Electric's 1991 Annual Report letter to shareholders, Jack Welch noted that the company had been soul-searching about executive effectiveness. Noting two manager characteristics – alignment with the company values, and achievement of financial commitments – Welch noted that the future at GE was easy to predict for those who could claim both, and for those who could claim neither. He noted that those who failed to achieve forecasts but who shared company values should be given another chance elsewhere in the organisation.

Welch was scathing about managers who did not share GE's values but who had been tolerated for years because of the attainment of financial results. He noted that these 'autocrats, big shots and tyrants' created long-term failure by coercing performance from individuals, rather than earning it. He indicated his wish to remove these individuals from GE.

Toxic executives abuse personal trust, practice dishonesty, conduct only dominant personal relationships, withhold praise, steal credit, assign blame, interrupt and dominate meetings, play favourites, destroy teams, create rivalry, avoid mentoring, criticise peers, find fault, abuse power and practice illogical decision making. They are a cancer that should be removed from any organisation.

Toxic executives destroy strong marketing, and they do so faster than ten capable executives can build it.

LEADERSHIP IS . . . POWER WELL-EARNED

The new marketing requires strong leadership. Leadership is about power[24]. Power goes beyond the traditional boundaries of authority, control over reward and punishment, appealing personal characteristics and expertise. Mao-Tse Tung was wrong. Power does not come from the threat of violence or punishment (the barrel of a gun). Power accrues to managers that earn it from their staff every day, bit-by-bit.

Power comes from personal energy and physical stamina, focus, sensitivity to others, flexibility, the ability to tolerate conflict, submerging one's own ego and getting along.

The rapid change in the economy and people's attitude to work is encouraging leaders to experiment with new forms of marketing organisations.[25] Leaders revel in organisational structures that fit today's complex and changing business environment. Strong marketers understand the nature of leadership and the approach to management that is required today.

Every problem should be seen as an opportunity to foster leadership. How managers respond to problems and involve staff is indicative of leadership.

Research suggests that demanding leaders who push high production performance need to show high concern for those reporting to them[26]. The *balance between concern for people and concern for production* is an important leadership dimension. Effective leaders find a balance between the two concerns that fits the overall organisational requirements. Other research suggests that leadership style should change in response to the nature of problem at hand, depending on the rationality of the problem, the information at hand, the problem structure, the impact of staff support on implementation, the shared benefits of a solution, and the likelihood of conflict about preferred solutions[27]. Obviously, these issues require careful attention from human resource professionals in many organisations and tactics will differ from organisation to organisation.

MOTIVATION BY UNITY OF PURPOSE AND HAVING FUN!

W. Edwards Deming has probably done more to demonstrate the value of unity of purpose than anyone in the past 50 years. An American, Deming had made his mark in statistical quality control before World War II, but found his services in low demand in the gung-ho post-war economy. The Japanese saw the value of what he espoused and adopted him. Today, he remains a legendary national hero in Japan.

Deming's 12 points became Japan's anthem for world leadership[26]. Essentially, the 12 points included:

- Creating constancy of purpose for product and service improvement, getting everyone involved and driving out fear of participation.

- Seeking constant improvement, dropping numerical quotas and ceasing dependence on mass inspection.

- Letting the workers develop the slogans and breaking down the barriers that keep them from associating freely across disciplines.

- Avoiding price as a sole determinant of supplier selection.

WHAT'S YOUR CREDO?

Johnson & Johnson developed the concept of social responsibility. Enshrined in its credo are immutable laws concerning the company's responsibility to the public and the community, the health care professions, the employees and, finally, the shareholders. If that sounds like a recipe for poor financial returns but feel-good platitudes, think again. J&J managers challenge their credo sentence-by-sentence every year – if they can't believe in any aspect of the credo, it gets removed. Can you think of a better way to foster unity of purpose? J&J ranks as one of the most admired and most profitable companies year after year, and as one of the all-time leading creators of shareholder value. That's one of the paradoxes of building strong marketing – *shareholders put last come first!*

The latest Johnson & Johnson Credo reads as follows:

We believe our first responsibility is to the doctors, nurses and patients, to mothers and fathers and all others who use our products and services. In meeting their needs everything we do must be of high quality. We must constantly strive to reduce our costs in order to maintain reasonable prices. Customer's orders must be serviced promptly and accurately. Our suppliers and distributors must have an opportunity to make a fair profit.

We are responsible to our employees, the men and women who work with us throughout the world. Everyone must be considered as an individual. We must respect their dignity and recognise their merit. They must have a sense of security in their jobs. Compensation must be fair and adequate, and working conditions clean, orderly and safe. We must be mindful of ways to help our employees fulfil their family responsibilities. Employees must feel free to make suggestions and complaints. There must be equal opportunity for employment, development and advancement for those qualified. We must provide competent management, and their actions must be just and ethical.

We are responsible to the communities in which we live and work and to the world community as well. We must be good citizens support good works and charities and bear our fair share of taxes. We must encourage civic improvements and better health and education. We must maintain in good order the property we are privileged to use, protecting the environment and natural resources.

Our final responsibility is to our stockholders. Business must make a sound profit. We must experiment with new ideas. Research must be carried on, innovative programs developed and mistakes paid for. New equipment must be purchased, new facilities provided and new products launched. Reserves must be created to provide for adverse times. When we operate according to these principles, the stockholders should realise a fair return[29].

Wal-Mart's Sam Walton also knew how to foster unity of purpose and have a good time[30]. Walton insisted that every employee have access to detailed financials for the company and their outlet so that everyone knew the company's goals and their part in achieving them. He visited each of his over 800 outlets annually and his comments to staff demonstrated his in-depth knowledge of the outlet's operational situation. Many staff members treasured Sam's remembering of their name or his enthusiastic rendition of the Wal-Mart cheer. When it looked like the company would not achieve its goals one year, Walton promised to do a hula dance on Wall Street if the goals were met (and did it when the goals were exceeded).

The Limited grew from a tiny one-store operation in a suburban Columbus shopping centre (the same centre where the very first automated teller machine was installed by Banc One) to become the world's largest retailer of women's clothing within the span of two decades. Les Wexner understands that work should be fun and rewarding. He holds his annual awards ceremony for the top 100 store managers in Colorado during peak skiing season. In addition to distributing videotapes of the awards ceremony to every branch, The Limited publishes *Applause, Applause,* an in-house magazine that identifies top achievers by photo and name.

Vodacom and MTN, South Africa's two cellular telephone network operators also know something about motivation and leadership. Both networks have offered generous awards to employees and to service provider employees who go the extra mile to provide good customer service or achieve ambitious sales goals.

VALUING DIVERSITY

Diversity is a most important human resource asset and should be nurtured and protected[31]. More importantly, diversity is a strength that should be leveraged. Companies where people from minority groups do not feel comfortable are probably trying to build strong marketing with quite a handicap. Management often achieves tremendous insight into market dynamics when it can tap differences in culture, race, religion, physical ability, sexual orientation or social class. Companies that fail to *value* diversity (you will note that I did not say manage but value diversity) are like motor cars running on low octane fuel – they may get there but they don't win any races.

The other night, I watched as a child on television asked Nelson Mandela why he had not applied the lessons of Islam to solve South Africa's crime problem. I was not surprised when Mandela began to recite crime statistics from the Islamic countries and recounted how Muhammad had encouraged his followers to give a small percentage of their wealth every year for the assistance of the poor. He then noted that the government was borrowing from Islam and the other religions and identified some areas where South African cultural differences would limit the effectiveness of Islamic law.

I am certain that Mandela could have initiated a similar discourse about Christianity, Judaism, Buddhism, Hinduism or the Bahá'i Faith with equal clarity. Such are the requirements of this man's job, forging one of the world's most culturally diverse and divided nations into one of the world's social miracles.

CORPORATE CULTURE

Although it is ignored frequently, the legacy of a firm can become a major resource. General Johnson (Johnson & Johnson), Sam Walton, Conrad Hilton, Colonel Harland Sanders (Kentucky Fried Chicken) Henry Ford, Alfred Sloan and other company founders often become legendary heroic figures that embody a company's history and values.

Companies must always be careful to manage the company within the constraints of such values or communicate why such values are not relevant in a particular situation. I remember a situation at J&J where we had had a particularly rough time with new agency staff concerning the conceptualisation and production of a television advertisement. After having spent nearly R200 000, the agency presented an advertisement that clearly did not embody the warmth and tenderness associated with Johnson's baby products. The advertisement was not bad, nor was it particularly good.

Many managers would have used the advertisement because of the investment. How does it look to spend R200 000 on nothing? Yet the advertisement clearly would not have pulled heartstrings as well as the existing advertisement did. Most companies would have shifted the responsibility for the advertisement to the ad agency, but the agency had 'hit' every campaign for 20 years and was going through tremendous temporary upheaval after the departure of senior executives.

Managing Director Clive Schreuder was extremely disappointed, as we all were, but took less than two minutes to decide to shelve the advertisement and to continue showing the existing advertisement. No witchhunt for a guilty party followed the decision. Schreuder attributed his decision to 'managing for the longer-term', a value espoused constantly by General Johnson some 50 years before. Schreuder has gone on to hold other international posts for J&J.

SUMMARY

This chapter focused on resource management skills. Such skills build strong marketing by shaping management's perception of the firm's capabilities and competencies.

Strong marketing requires prudent financial analysis, planning, implementation and control. Financial management systems in many IOR companies are incapable of providing the kind of accurate information needed to make decisions in the new digital economy. Economic value-added (EVA) is one approach to improved financial planning that is gathering much support. The activity-based costing (ABC) and management systems (ABM) approach provides the best opportunity for accurate costing information for marketing planning and appraisal.

A new kind of leader is required today. Sensitivity, caring and the ability to listen are as important as drive, motivation and communication. Success today is not so much adapting to the environment as it is creating it.

Managing human resources requires a fundamental shift in attitude in many firms. Recognising and valuing diversity, understanding the nature and limitations of the roles people play, choosing appropriate organisational structures, placing as much emphasis on manager alignment with company values as is placed on financial results – these are some of the differences noted in successful organisations.

Time, information and relationships are also important resources and they are the focus of the next section of this book.

ENDNOTES

1 A number of excellent financial texts can help remedy such a deficiency. Keown, Scott, & Petty (1996), is an example of the many excellent comprehensive introductory financial texts now available. Atrill (1996), may be a friendlier introduction to those who feel challenged by financial management concepts.

2 Called the DuPont model because it was developed and popularised by DuPont.

3 Adapted by permission of John Wiley & Sons, Inc. from Retailing Management by Davidson et.al. (Fourth Ed.) ©1975 John Wiley & Sons, Inc.

4 See the personal profile on Sam Walton in Bateman & Zeithaml (1990: 579).

5 See Schall & Haley (1988). The proponents of EVA have been among the most vociferous critics of ROI.

6 Stewart (1991), has become the guidebook for executives pursuing the EVA idea. The South African office of Stern Stewart and Company is in Johannesburg and can be reached on (011) 883-5894.

7 Schall & Heley (1988), Chapter 7.

8 Readers seeking more information should consult Stewart (1991).

9 Glad & Becker (1994), explores the major concepts of ABC and ABM systems. The book is well written, succinct and very practically oriented.

10 Adapted from Glad & Becker (1994).

11 See Hornung (1991).

12 Tapscott (1996).

13 Nadler & Nadler (1990), is an excellent resource material on human resource development issues. Chapter 25 and Chapter 26 focus on IOR nations.

14 Stacey (1993), Chapter 4, includes a very accessible introduction to research concerning chaos and organisational structure. Maynard Jr. & Mehrtens (1993), and Ray & Rinzler (1993), address the issues of organisations in the emerging business environment.

15 Tom Peters was most prolific and his 1992 work probably contains the most comment about chaos and organisational structure. For the more academic and mathematically inclined, Stacey (1991), includes some appealing arguments about chaos.

16 Many firms in the IOR may find it beneficial to pursue hybrid organisational strategies, similar to the Theory Z management style advocated by Ouchi, in order to overcome these problems. See Ouchi (1981); Ouchi & Jaeger (1978).

17 Davis & Lawrence (1978); Kolodny (1981), review the pros and cons of matrix organisations.
18 See Dawis (1992).
19 Greiner. (1972: 37-46).
20 Greiner (1972).
21 If you are unfamiliar with the concept of self-empowered teams, Wellins, Byham, & Wilson (1991), is an excellent introductory text with a practical slant.
22 Peters & Austin (1985).
23 This discussion draws on Reed (1993).
24 Readers interested in leadership and power will find Kotter (1988); Kotter (1990); Kotter & Heskett (1992) and Pfeffer (1992), to be of interest. Schein (1992), is another well-respected contribution. I can recall a specific lesson at Glick's concerning every individual attribute Pfeffer identifies as a source of power.
25 Achrol (1991).
26 Blake & Mouton (1964).
27 Vroom & Yetton (1973).
28 See Walton (1986) for a practical application of Deming's method.
29 Reproduced with kind permission from Johnson & Johnson.
30 See Bateman & Zeithaml (1990, page: 579).
31 A great many books have been written about managing diversity. One of my favourites is Thomas Jr. (1991).

PART FOUR

Managing Interaction

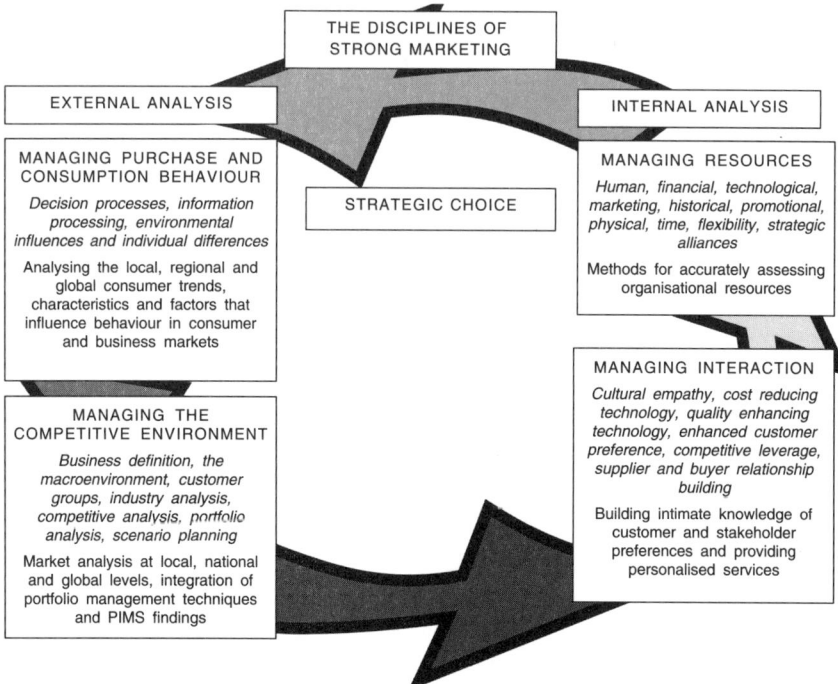

THE DISCIPLINES OF
STRONG MARKETING

EXTERNAL ANALYSIS

INTERNAL ANALYSIS

MANAGING PURCHASE AND CONSUMPTION BEHAVIOUR

Decision processes, information processing, environmental influences and individual differences

Analysing the local, regional and global consumer trends, characteristics and factors that influence behaviour in consumer and business markets

STRATEGIC CHOICE

MANAGING RESOURCES

Human, financial, technological, marketing, historical, promotional, physical, time, flexibility, strategic alliances

Methods for accurately assessing organisational resources

MANAGING THE COMPETITIVE ENVIRONMENT

Business definition, the macroenvironment, customer groups, industry analysis, competitive analysis, portfolio analysis, scenario planning

Market analysis at local, national and global levels, integration of portfolio management techniques and PIMS findings

MANAGING INTERACTION

Cultural empathy, cost reducing technology, quality enhancing technology, enhanced customer preference, competitive leverage, supplier and buyer relationship building

Building intimate knowledge of customer and stakeholder preferences and providing personalised services

14 Managing Strategic Alliances

Working with customers, suppliers, government and competitors for profits

He did not have a university degree. He did not have exceptional management experience. He was a student engineer at STC where he served the South African post office, and he had the vision and burning passion to build South Africa's first high-tech company. His inability to acquire equity in the foreign-owned STC operation found him starting his own company in a small factory. Many people thought he would lose as he fought against international giants to establish his own business. But Venter went on from these humble beginnings to build the largest technology company in Africa.

Dr Bill Venter's incredible success story illustrates the compelling role alliances can play in building strong marketing. Hearing that STC had concluded an agreement for its sale, Venter flew to New York and camped outside the door of the legendary Harold Geneen for days until Geneen agreed to see him for fifteen minutes. The meeting stretched to hours and Venter managed to convince Geneen to sell control of the company to him, based on his vision for the company and the outstanding profitability of his own company.

Over the years, Venter has brought together one of the world's most impressive arrays of strategic alliances. Altron's Altech, Powertech and Fintech subsidiaries maintain strategic alliances with suppliers of capital, technology and information that include top names from ABB, Alcatel and AT&T to Xerox.

When asked for comment, Venter makes a strong case for strategic alliances in developing nations. He believes that local partners open markets for industrialised nation products while gaining access to the latest technology without 'recreating the wheel'. Most compelling, alliances build high-technology competencies and careers in the developing world while focusing research and development budgets on adapting technologies to regional requirements and on implementing original research in other areas. Altron allocates 4.5 per cent of total sales to technology development. The figure swells to nearly 10 per cent when licence technology fees are added.

Such investments often bring rich returns. For instance, overseas alliance partners have licensed technologies developed by Altron for use in products sold around the world. Thus, companies from industrialised nations gain more from alliances with the developing world than from additional sales. Venter is justifiably proud of Altron's increasing export sales which won the President's Export Award a few years ago.

Strong marketers realise that IOR economies are often too small to allow world-class technology developments. They also realise that IOR companies often lack the competencies or resources required to respond to the fast pace of change. They realise something Venter came to understand back in the 1960s: there is logic in building strategic alliances.

THE LOGIC OF STRATEGIC ALLIANCE BUILDING

There is some confusion regarding the definition of strategic alliances. A merger is not a strategic alliance, nor is an acquisition, because both arrangements take a player out of the market. Franchising, licensing, cross-licensing and arm's length buy/sell contracts are also not strategic alliances. Although firms may have the same intent when entering these types of agreements as many firms have when entering strategic alliances, Yoshino & Rangan (1995) argue that such agreements are often entered under the pressure of foreign law. They note that Unilever, Colgate Palmolive, Suzuki, Pepsi-Cola and DuPont forced partners to give them managing control when Indian legislation made this possible. Although Altron has entered many joint ventures, they remain strategic alliances in my mind because the relationships meet the conditions mentioned below. Strategic alliances meet three conditions simultaneously[1]:

- The two or more firms that unite to pursue a set of agreed upon goals remain independent subsequent to the formation of the alliance.

- The partner firms share the benefits of the alliance and performance of the assigned tasks – perhaps the most distinctive characteristic of alliances and the one that makes them so difficult to manage.

- The partner firms contribute on a continuing basis in one or more key strategic areas, e.g. technology, products, and so forth.

Typical strategic alliance agreements include:

- Non-traditional contracts – joint R&D, joint product development, long-term sourcing agreements, joint manufacturing, joint marketing, shared distribution and service, standards setting and research consortia.

- Equity agreements that do not result in market entry – minority equity investments and equity swaps.

- Equity agreements that result in market entry but not in a subsidiary of a MNC — 50/50 joint ventures, unequal equity joint ventures.

Strategic alliances are symptomatic of the emerging view that organisations consist of the core business, an extended enterprise that includes suppliers, distributors, customers and all other stakeholders[2]. There are convincing arguments about the nature of competition and co-operation that suggest a major re-think is in order in many companies.

Consider the reaction in your boardroom if someone suggested licensing your technology to a competitor in order to keep the firm on its toes. Yet, that is exactly what one well-respected team of researchers suggests[3].

Firms enter alliances to learn, to gain or protect core competencies, to respond faster or more flexibly, and to increase added-value capabilities. Some recent examples illustrate why firms enter strategic alliances.

VALUE-CHAIN AND SUPPLY-CHAIN MANAGEMENT

Strategic alliances create opportunities for supplier-buyer relationships that support and enhance continual improvement programmes. Alliances of this type often emerge as firms attempt to achieve a low-cost strategy or to improve products or service. Many firms enter alliances in order to manage the value chain better.

Consider the alliance between Digital and Microsoft[4]. Digital CEO, Robert Palmer, believes his firm's strategic alliance with Microsoft will 'offer exciting and unprecedented implications for our customers and for the computer industry. We are convinced that the next wave of enterprise computing will primarily be client/server and heavily involve group solutions, with Microsoft Windows playing a major role.' Microsoft obviously gains a window of its own into the world of client/server technology — not a particular strength of Microsoft at present. How much is that worth? Microsoft's investment to train Digital engineers to use its product will cost about $100 million.

Buyers are not always the proposing party for value-chain management alliances. Consider Tandem Computers' alliance with Microsoft featuring Tandem's mission-critical computing platform with Microsoft's Windows NT operating system[5]. The alliance not only provides a vehicle for promoting the usage of Windows NT, but also exposes Microsoft to previously unreachable distribution such as petrol station/convenience store markets.

Microsoft's alliance with the American Institute of Certified Public Accountants is another example of such an alliance[6]. Microsoft will train CPAs to provide technology and business systems consulting services. Undoubtedly, CPAs will develop a level of confidence in Microsoft products during the training, suggesting ready recommendation in the future.

RESPONSE TO THE CHANGING MARKETING ENVIRONMENT

Many companies enter alliances in response to the changing marketing environment. Sometimes the requirement for an alliance emerges in answer to a new market opportunity.

The recent alliance between Hewlett-Packard and Verifone focuses on the emerging requirement for secure Internet payment facilities[7]. HP and Verifone will participate jointly in VISA/MasterCard SET worldwide trials, and develop joint security-enhanced Internet payment production solutions for financial institutions and retailers. 3 Com's alliance with Acer is a similar response to the increased requirement for external internetworking connectivity[8].

Some alliances emerge when non-competitors share customers and find themselves working together to solve customer problems. Compaq's enterprise storage management alliance with Computer Associates' Cheyenne division includes joint market research, strategic planning, product development, market development, service and support[9]. The genesis of the alliance is Computer Associates' leading position as a supplier of mission critical software and Compaq's position as a leading supplier of client/servers to over one million customers. The alliance expanded an already successful OEM (Original Equipment Manufacturer) arrangement. The alliance between Document Sciences (a leading provider of document automation solutions) and JetForm (a leader in enterprise-wide forms solutions), is another example of this type of alliance. The alliance results in the provision of integrated document and forms solutions.

The convergence of computing, communication and content also creates alliance opportunities. Thirty per cent of the respondents to a recent Cambridge Work Group survey indicated that convergence would alter their approach to alliances[10]. Respondents noted the need to break through market barriers, decrease time to market and gain access to new technologies. Eighty-one per cent of software company executives and 78 per cent of communications executives cited the need to improve marketing, sales and distribution as reasons for alliances.

JetForm's global presence demonstrates another alliance stimulant: globalisation. Exporting strategies must manage interdependencies of scale across the various markets. Establishing an international affiliate requires the management of operational cross-market dependencies as core management skill requirements. Network-based strategies require management capable of exploiting scale, operational and scope dependencies. This complexity may be beyond the competence or resources of some firms, resulting in a need for an alliance.

BEING FIRST, BEING FASTER

The advantages of being the first mover were noted previously in this book[11]. Being first can be very important. Strategic alliances often offer the advantage of much faster market entry. Often strategic alliances occur in response to a first-mover strategy, as competitors jockey for position and attempt to respond to the new threat.

Time has become an important competitive weapon[12]. Improving speed of service has become necessary for survival in many industries.

PRIVATISATION AND DE-REGULATION

Privatisation and de-regulation also lead to strategic alliances. South Africa's sale of a 30 per cent stake in Telkom to American and Malaysian telephone network providers will result in the transfer of technology and capital. SBC, the American partner in the venture, is no stranger to South Africa and participates as an equity partner in MTN, one of two GSM çellular network providers.

Privatisation and de-regulation can be explosive political issues and strategic alliances require great finesse.

RESPONSE TO CHANGING POLITICAL ENVIRONMENTS

Strategic alliances also allow firms to respond to changing political require-ments and government objectives, such as increased trade with other signatories of the international trade agreements. For instance, IOR governments often have specific development goals that may require access to new technologies not available in a particular national economy.

Empowerment of the historically-disadvantaged may be the response to changing political environments that received the most attention. South African black-owned businesses have achieved equity in major groups as a result. The development of local ownership is an analogue taking place in many other IOR economies. Although it is certain that much of this activity has taken place because of government influence, such programmes can result in improved local market focus and can capture the synergy of a company's diversity better.

THE PROCESS OF CRAFTING STRATEGIES FOR ALLIANCES

Alliances are a vehicle for achieving firm objectives. They are not an end, but a means to achieving goals. Alliances require careful management by the partners. Strong marketers realise that this often begins long before negotiations of alliance structure commence. The process of crafting strategies for alliances involves six steps.

STEP 1: ALL PARTIES INDEPENDENTLY COMMIT TO INVESTIGATE AN ALLIANCE STRATEGY

The first step of a successful alliance begins when the firms decide on an alliance strategy[13]. Many alliances fail when firms make the mistake of rushing a potential alliance partner. Once the perceived advantages of the alliance have been communicated, wise negotiators give the other firm adequate time to reach internal consensus and commitment to the decision. American firms often report confusion when awaiting a decision by potential Japanese customers or alliance partners because the two nations have such different styles of decision making.

It is foolish to begin negotiations with talk about alliance structure, and wise negotiators realise this. How can the firms negotiate when they have not agreed what skills each brings to the party? Why negotiate something that might fall apart due to the lack of consensus? If all parties have agreed that an alliance is in their interest, the parties have a better chance of success in negotiating alliance structure, and the alliance has a better chance of succeeding.

STEP 2: PERFORM VALUE-CHAIN ANALYSIS

Pre-work should include most forms of analysis examined in the first two sections of this book. Without intimate knowledge of purchase and consumption behaviour and the competitive environment issues, few firms will be able to negotiate a mutually advantageous agreement.

In essence, all alliance negotiations focus on value-chain issues. The value chain should be dissected so that the value of each activity is understood and the competencies and resources required can be inventoried. This requires careful analysis when international operations are among the resources of either player.

STEP 3: RECONFIGURE THE VALUE CHAIN

The next step involves reconfiguring the value chain to leverage resources and competencies of the partners maximally. Reconfiguring the value chain often requires much thought about the centralisation or distribution of alliance activities. Requirements for operational and management information should be identified and inventoried.

It is very important for the senior management team to agree to the type of alliance required. Reflecting on the potential for conflict and the extent to which organisations must interact can be especially productive in arriving at a joint perception[14]:

- *High potential for conflict* and *low levels of organisational interaction* suggest a **pre-competitive alliance,** and the potential for future competition must influence firm thinking.

- When the *potential for conflict is high* and the extent of *organisational interaction is low,* a **competitive alliance** is suggested, and firms must take extreme care to protect core competencies and control partner access to knowledge and learning.

- *Low conflict potential* and *low interaction* are **pro-competitive**. Most of the alliance examples above fall into this type of alliance. While it may seem quite inviting to play open cards in such relationships, one must always remember that the nature of an alliance can change, and that a pro-competitive alliance today can be a competitive alliance five years down the road.

- When *organisational interaction is high* but the *potential for conflict is low*, a **non-competitive alliance** exists. Johnson & Johnson South Africa's alliance with Debs-Vogue during the 1980s was of this type. Although both made disposable feminine-hygiene and infant-care products, the nature of the market focus of each was different enough to preclude direct competition.

STEP 4: CONSIDER THE CONSEQUENCES OF A FAILED ALLIANCE

Alliances sometimes fail even with the best support of senior management. This is a strong threat when managers fail to gain the co-operation of middle management and boundary role players in the firm, when alliances join previous competitors or firms competing in other fields.

Consider the position of a firm entering an alliance that required it to shut down manufacturing operations. A junior manager innocently discovered that the alliance partner had been negotiating in bad faith (thanks to a document mistakenly left behind after a negotiating session). The document revealed that the intended partner believed the confidentiality and non-competition agreement it had negotiated offered sufficient loopholes to take a chance. Further, the intended partner's attorneys had given assurances that the matter would not come to court for two years. The managing director who told me this tale back in the mid-1980s confided that he believed the company would have lasted just six months had the agreement gone through.

Companies should always have fallback positions in the case of problems with an alliance and should be particularly careful during the first year.

STEP 5: NEGOTIATE A STRUCTURAL FRAMEWORK
FOR THE ALLIANCE

The structural framework for the alliance may be negotiated only after prior steps are complete. There is no support in the literature for the notion that certain types of organisational structures apply to certain types of organisational motivations and objectives. Alliance partners will want to ensure that proposed structures are relevant to the scale, scope and objectives of the alliance, and appropriate to the resources and competencies available to the alliance. Porter's five forces model (see page 120, Chapter 9) may be very useful in assisting management to form accurate perceptions of their negotiating position.

There is much room for innovation in structuring alliances, and parties should investigate many alternatives. Whatever the structure that emerges, it must be appropriate not only to the opportunity but also to interaction with the partners' organisational structures. This may necessitate changes in the organisational structure of one or more of the alliance partners.

STEP 6: ONGOING MANAGEMENT AND EVALUATION

Objectives and goals are dynamic and constantly require re-evaluation in the face of a changing environment. Firms should review the performance of the alliance in terms of achieving the firm's objectives in the context of these changing influences. It is also important to evaluate the changing goals and objectives of alliance partners, and of the alliance partner's other alliance partners. Such analysis will provide early warning of changing perceptions of alliance partners and allow the firm to address these concerns proactively.

Some key points about alliance management:

- Enshrine important points in an agreement. Understand and frame the adaptive behaviour required by both partners in that agreement. Make sure the agreement is vetted by a competent and experienced business lawyer well-versed in the laws of the country that will apply to the agreement[15].

- It is vitally important that high-quality people be attracted to the alliance and that clear lines of accountability and responsibility are established[16].

- It is necessary to school management to understand that collaborative alliances with competitors are another form of competition. Associates at all levels must understand the implications for trading information and co-operating with partners[17].

- Management should not worry about overly harmonious relations. Some degree of conflict probably indicates that both parties are getting maximal benefit from the relationship.

- Management of alliances often requires shrewd political manoeuvring and complex strategies to steer an alliance partner systematically toward a desired position, or to engender a co-optive relationship[18].

- Differences in time perspectives should be identified and methods of responding to those differences should be established[19].

- Train associates at all levels to emphasise alliance partner similarities in objectives, in firm and management characteristics and in organisational cultures[20].

- IOR alliances often cross borders. Ensure that the laws of the country and the agreement protect your intellectual rights. Ensure that you can withdraw your intellectual and other resources immediately in the case of a default or major breach of the agreement by a partner.

It makes good sense to write a clause into the agreement that the offending firm will pay the legal expenses of the complaining firm if prima facie evidence of a violation of intellectual rights occurs.

- Ensure that associates of the alliance and both partners are sworn to confidentiality. Make alliance partners responsible for policing and prosecuting any associate who is in or leaves their employ if that associate violates the confidentiality agreement. It may also be wise to spell out what might constitute grounds for beginning an investigation and for prosecution, and in which courts legal disputes will be settled.

- Follow the advice of Bill Venter. Always leave something on the table for the other firm. Make the alliance work for both firms by ensuring everyone benefits. Don't forget to incentivise the managers responsible for the alliance and for interactions with the alliance.

ALLIANCES AS NETWORKS

Value-chain and strategic alliance management are aspects of a growing trend towards viewing competition as a multi-firm construct, that is, as networks of firms competing one with another. Strategic alliances are encouraging firms to produce levels of quality, efficiency and effectiveness that were never possible in firm-to-firm competition. The leap in thinking to the inclusion of value-chain members in competitive networks is a logical outcome of successful strategic alliances.

Dramatic success and failure has characterised this new building of strategic networks. One recent study of 200 independent motor-car retailers suggests that trust and relationship commitment are key mediating variables[21]. The study suggests that shared values are a positive influence on both trust and relationship commitment. Communication (+) and opportunism (-) influence the degree of trust in a marketing network. Commitment to the relationship varies positively with higher relationship benefits and higher termination costs.

Summary

- Strategic alliances are a special type of agreement to co-operate with another firm in which both firms share the responsibilities and rewards of the alliance.

- Alliances are an important aspect of managing interaction. Strategic alliances are a natural outcome of many trends in the contemporary marketing environment, such as the increasing need for co-ordinated management of the value chain, the need to respond to changing market characteristics, the need to be first or to move faster, and a response to de-regulation and privatisation.

- The survival of many firms may depend on the ability to manage strategic alliances. Firms must craft alliance strategies, as is the case with any strategy. A six-step procedure is suggested for firms wishing to investigate the attractiveness of strategic alliances.

The next chapter focuses on a different aspect of managing interaction: interaction with customers and the emergence of the new digital marketing concept.

ENDNOTES

1   Yoshino & Rangan (1995).
2   See the argument in Moore (1996: 25-29).
3   Brandenburger & Nalebuff (1996: 104-109).
4   Based on McCloy (1995).
5   Based on M2 Presswire (1996c).
6   M2 Presswire (1996b).
7   Excerpted from Cambridge Work-Group (1996c).
8   Cambridge Work-Group (1996a).
9   M2 Presswire (1996a).
10 Cambridge Work-Group (1996d).
11 See Hamel & Prahalad (1985) for a discussion of first-mover strategies.
12 See Stalk (1988).
13 This section is loosely based on Yoshino & Rangan (1995).
14 See Yoshino & Rangan (1995: 17-21).
15 McCall & Warrington (1989) is an excellent source concerning the issues of cross-cultural and transnational alliance agreements.
16 Godfrey & Bleackley (1988).
17 Hamel, Doz & Prahalad (1989).
18 Dixit & Nalebuff (1991) is an excellent primer on step-by-step strategy formulation. Garguiolo (1993) suggests that players should not rely solely on perceptions of alliance partner dependence on resources, but should rather attempt to gain leverage by first building a co-optive relationship with the alliance partner.
19 See Ganitsky, Rangan & Watzke (1991).
20 Harrigan's 1988 landmark study of 895 strategic alliances competing in 23 industries during the period of 1924-1985 suggests the importance of such similarities on alliance success.
21 Hunt & Morgan (1994).

15 Managing Customer Interactions

New ways of managing one-on-one interactions

We are witnessing nothing less than the birth of a new marketing era. The new marketing is holistic, cross-functional and intensive. At its heart lie new interactive communication, information and computing technologies enabling dramatic improvements in identifying, recruiting, understanding, serving and retaining customers. The new marketing requires the mastery of skills most marketers would not have considered to be marketing skills previously. Long-term survival depends on understanding the new interactive technologies well enough to master strong marketing – a fact altering the struggle for supremacy in industries and boardrooms around the world.

Consider how bankers around the world are managing customer interactions to shape competitive success. Distance banking has become a reality. South Africa's Nedbank leveraged its close relationship with Microsoft to be among the first in the world to launch secure Internet banking. Across the world, Huntington Bank has opened 15 fully automated branches in Columbus. The new Huntington Access Branches are 24-hour, full-service banking centres without tellers. Two-way video kiosks, linked to main office by an ISDN line, allow customers needing additional assistance to discuss their problems with a human teller they can see and hear. The branches allow a full range of services, including loan applications[1].

Client security is a growing concern and many banks are experimenting with voice recognition systems, instead of the typical personal identity number (PIN) entry. The success of this system will open the door to many exciting innovations in customised service, and expand distance banking service possibilities. Reacting to a developing nation environment, Standard Bank deployed Diebold automated teller machines (ATMs) that identify customers by analysing thumbprints. The ATM displays the customer's photo as the transaction begins, ensuring that even illiterate customers feel secure about transactions. The new ATMs print bank-guaranteed cheques – a plus in South Africa where many people do not operate cheque accounts.

VISA will soon begin its worldwide test market of smartcard technology in South Africa. Smartcards decrease the time required for transaction approval, increase security, allow users to block certain types of transactions (such as cash withdrawals), enable loyalty programmes and incorporate certain fraud protection algorithms linked to user behaviour patterns. Many card issuers may even choose to give approval for certain types of transactions based on reading usage information and credit limit information from the card.

Consumers demand more privacy in banking transactions. Back in the USA, BankBoston has installed screen filters that keep people behind you from seeing your ATM transaction. Long wings that jut out from the side of the ATM, and coloured tiles that demarcate the user's personal space, are other innovations to increase user privacy. The new ATMs provide a full range of services, including the issue of cheques and postage stamps.

Banc One and Fifth Third pioneered mini-branches inside American supermarkets earlier in this decade. Bangladesh pioneered the extension of micro-credit. Now retailers are leveraging point-of-sale presence to capture financial services business for themselves. South Africa's Pick 'n Pay have established a financial services business that operates from their supermarkets. The UK's Marks and Spencer offer a range of financial services that include life assurance and investment products. What other financial services products can we expect to emerge in South African retail outlets?

MANAGING THE DETAILS OF CUSTOMER INTERACTIONS

The new marketing requires firms to manage interaction more intensively than ever. Like banks, competitors in many industries are moving to capture the synergy of interactions in order to build strong marketing. Firms are mining data gleaned during point-of-sale interactions to gain intimate knowledge of consumer needs, and to discover new business opportunities outside traditional business boundaries.

Consumers' expectations for relationship quality are increasing because of the emergence of the new marketing. As consumers place more weight on relationship quality, enterprises must become more adept at identifying profitable customers, building appropriate relationships and providing flexible, adaptable and accessible interactions at the lowest cost and in the shortest time.

The new environment compels firms to manage the details of customer service more intensively, with fewer people and lower costs — requiring new levels of multifunctional teamwork and technical literacy.

Perhaps the most surprising aspect of the new reality is how slowly companies have adopted it. Companies cannot ignore interactive marketing opportunities in the educated, economically active consumer segments. They dare not ignore the application of new technologies to mass-marketing in the broader market. The new realities not only make customer relationship management possible, but necessary for survival.

BE CAREFUL OF 'NANOSECOND NINETIES' SNAKE OIL

The term 'snake oil' comes from the American Wild West where charlatans sold snake oil as a cure for all ills. Hapless buyers soon discovered the product was useless as a medicinal aid. Every uncharted territory draws its share of snake oil merchants and the cyberhighway has been no exception. Companies must beware of those who obscure the true nature of the new environment by making new technologies and the new intimacy of consumer relationships seem intimidating or unreasonably difficult to achieve. They are wrong. Armed with proper knowledge of the process of strong marketing, most companies can begin practising strong marketing from existing resources. New technologies open the door to new levels of empowerment that unleash individual productivity, improve performance and cut costs.

A few gurus have suggested that the rapid pace of change precludes thorough marketing analysis (such as proposed in this book). They are wrong — very wrong — and companies following them put their survival at risk.

Fast change does not preclude analysis — it points to automating it, building in decision systems and artificial intelligence, widening access to it, and providing it in real time.

- Associates need database support systems to be effective.

- They need more, not less, analysis.

- They need to know which options are likely to be most attractive to a particular prospect or client. Flexibility and adaptability degenerate into unprofitable anarchy unless people know what they should be doing and why they should be doing it.

- Support structures must give staff an insight into what they see and hear during customer interactions and guide them in choosing appropriate and profitable responses.

Empowerment is not an abdication of management responsibility. In strong marketing, an appropriate information and technology infrastructure directs, channels and supports empowerment. Designing and providing such a supportive infrastructure may be the greatest challenge of strong marketing. Relational intimacy is more than 'touchy-feely' relationships. It requires automatic delivery of current, detailed information, when and where it's needed.

If you think your existing systems are adequate, then consider this. Customers have learned to expect companies to 'remember' more about them during interactions. After all, *customer relationships are relationships*. Would your lover be more pleased if you remembered birthdays and anniversaries or if you asked regularly whether today was the day? So what do customers think when your associates probe a set of customer preferences during every interaction? Are they thankful that you asked or surprised you don't care enough to remember? How do they feel when you fail to offer something they really need? Have you ever needlessly lost a customer simply because no one offered the service the customer wanted, although it was available?

In 1980, J&J representatives could access monthly sales for the last three years of the 100 gm baby-powder pack size in every outlet in South Africa, and get information about a possible order. It's no wonder J&J so dominated distribution channels.

THE EMPHASIS ON INTERACTION IN STRONG MARKETING

The new marketing is more than a new toolkit. It emerged as international and industrial marketers became increasingly dissatisfied with the traditional view of marketing that was rooted in the four themes of product, price, place and promotion. Marketing theorists responded by expanding the original four Ps to include people, process, physical evidence, public relations and the like. While moving the debate forward, these attempts failed to address many shortcomings of the traditional marketing concept such as managing ongoing customer relationships, managing network marketing or overcoming international barriers to trade[2]. In essence, managing interactions took on a central role in marketing management.

The new marketing is a shift in emphasis rooted in the American school of relationship marketing, and the European school of interactive marketing. It challenges strategists to think of marketing as a more holistic interdisciplinary set of activities and relationships. It includes product, price, place and promotion strategies, but expands the marketing discipline to include five non-traditional themes rooted in interaction management. This chapter explores these five themes.

- *Marketing as interactive, relational network management*

  Traditional views of marketing strategy and competition have largely ignored value chains. Competition occurs between transcorporate networks, not companies. These relational networks exist within, without and between organisational boundaries, and require careful, co-ordinated management by network participants. Strong marketing is the integrating element and the lifeblood of network marketing management. *Everyone in the network must think of the people that they serve as customers,* whether these people are internal or external customers or strategic alliance partners. Everyone in the network depends on many relationships outside their immediate control. Network relationships should be thought of as network assets.

- *Marketing as cross-functional activity management*

  Marketing is a group of cross-functional activities performed by people throughout the network and the enterprise, and it always has been. Don't the promises and performances of associates in marketing, sales, accounts, operations, customer services, distribution, credit and every other department, constitute the currency of success in most important marketing activities? Interactive relationship marketing and new technologies require everyone to play a role in delivering and managing subsets of the total range of marketing activities. *As in an orchestra, strong marketing can be coached and shaped by the conductor and senior players, but the music must ultimately be played by all.*

- *Marketing as information management*

  The power of the database alone would revolutionise marketing. New database technologies enhance interaction management, enable firms to apply predictive models to customer data and improve market orientation. *If the traditional marketing concept moved the enterprise from a shotgun approach to a rifle, strong marketing has moved the enterprise from the rifle to the laser.* Information management technology increasingly enables firms to conceptualise and interact with one-to-one market segments.

- *Marketing as acquisition and retention management*

  After decades of research supporting the notion that *it is more profitable to retain customers than to attract new ones*, strong marketing has awoken firms to action. This is not only a reaction to slow growth markets. Strong marketers increasingly plan activities and budget for customer retention with the same attention traditionally given to advertising, promotions and public relations. The costs of acquiring and retaining customers are increasingly becoming key operating statistics subject to intensive management and reporting.

- *Marketing as transaction and relationship management*

  Focusing on interactive relationships does not suggest that every customer wants a long-term relationship or that every relationship is the same. *Relationships must be appropriate to the long-term interests of the customer.* Strong marketing also focuses on the nature, content and cost of transactions, and recognises that transactional approaches to marketing remain appropriate in some product markets.

MARKETING AS INTERACTIVE, RELATIONAL NETWORK MANAGEMENT

Throughout the value chain, companies enter relationships in various markets – with recruitment markets, internal staff, suppliers, venture capitalists, customers and others. The notion of network marketing was introduced in the previous chapter as a natural progression of value-chain management. Relationships exist with other value-chain members and with outsiders. Relationships may be among the most important network assets.

RELATIONSHIP TYPES

By definition, buyer and seller interactions are value-chain interactions. It should be remembered that the strategic alliance is a special kind of value-chain relationship. The buyer and seller relationships of strategic alliances and value-chain analysis have been explored in previous chapters. It bears noting that buyer and seller have responsibilities in their relationship. It is curious that so many firms are such unskilled buyers, acting only to reduce prices in buying interactions despite the evidence that companies are more profitable when they cultivate good relationships with fewer suppliers[3]. A buyer market and supplier market interaction occurs in every exchange. These two primary types of relationships probably receive the most management attention and are the basis of most marketing plans.

Firms also conduct relationships with recruitment markets, internal markets, referral markets and influence markets, and can conduct multiple relationships with other companies. For instance, a firm might conduct supplier, buyer and referral relationships with another firm. Understanding how a counterpart interacts with other firms in similar relationships can be a powerful indicator of appropriate relationship strategies.

- *Recruitment relationships*

  Finding people with the skills that are required in the new interactive relationship environment is not easy. The need for highly skilled people is increasing the importance of relationships conducted with recruitment markets. Employment agencies, corporate head-hunters and other recruitment firms have become much more professional and specialised as the recruitment market has globalised. Many firms find it necessary to conduct successful relationships with different recruiters who focus on specialised management, financial staff, marketing and sales or information technology needs.

  Communication and promotion often dominate the recruitment relationship marketing mix. Many firms find it is more important to create literature and recruitment materials of a high standard these days. Recruitment materials that describe only the business, financial results and company's vision are not adequate in many markets. It is vitally important that recruiting materials also communicate dimensions of the corporate culture that are related more directly to longer-term successful associate relationships.

- *Internal relationships*

  Internal markets consist of managers and associates within the firm. Strong marketing often causes people to become more passionate about their work. Associates in boundary roles can experience much conflict as they communicate both the needs of customers and network marketing partners internally, and the interests of their own company outside the firm. This conflict can be most acute in firms adopting strong marketing after long periods of sales or production orientations. This points to one role of internal marketing: communicating corporate vision and strategies to reduce internal conflict.

  Internal marketing strategies are generally the domain of human resource (HR) managers who act in concert with senior management. Internal marketing requires carefully thought out segmentation of the workforce and the development of a marketing mix[4]. The HR manager's products consist of services (such as assessment or conflict resolution), and courses and programmes for human development. The location and delivery of these courses and services requires careful planning for each target segment. Although much of the communication with internal clients is conducted verbally, it must still be carefully planned and executed to be consistent with the target segment. Negotiating transfer pricing and budget allocation are also important internal marketing competencies required by the HR manager.

- *Referral relationships*

  Companies in diverse industries such as the medical professions, furniture rental, law and life assurance, rely extensively on referrals for their business. Referral markets are not limited to customers but *consist of everyone who is in a position to refer others to the firm.* Marketers have always been interested in word-of-mouth advertising. It may be the most effective form of communication and it's almost free. Yet very few companies ask satisfied clients for referrals.

  Successful referral relationship marketing programmes require careful planning and pre-testing. Intuit became a world leader in personal financial software because users referred others to Intuit's Quicken. The company is so focused on referrals that associates refer to customers as apostles. However, when the firm attempted to formalise the referral process, they met stiff resistance. First, customers criticised a plan to pay them for referrals, asking that the money be spent instead on future product and customer support improvements. Then customers resented a discount coupon promotion, asking why Intuit was giving new customers better prices than existing customers had paid when the product was already reasonably priced.

  Relationship gurus, Cross and Smith[5], believe that successful referrals:

- Follow through on promises made in referral promotional offers. Proper follow-through includes sensitivity to the individual's privacy and the risk taken by referring your firm. Don't hard-sell referred prospects!
- Establish attractive incentives and test them prior to offering the promotion in the marketplace.
- Make it easy to refer your company. Provide easy to complete response devices, pay the cost of response and let everyone know how and where to respond.

Firms that fail to leverage successful service relationships to expand the customer base ignore a potent form of marketing.

- *Influence relationships*
  The popular financial press suggests that many IOR countries are liberalising competition. The trend affects a wide range of industries and many chief executives spend the majority of their time with regulatory, financial, political and other influence markets. It is particularly important to understand how other influence relationships affect and influence the relationship counterpart. This is especially true concerning governmental, regulatory and parastatal bodies. Influence markets require as much careful attention and planning as other markets. Influence relationships are also conducted with non-governmental bodies. Venture-capital and institutional investors are important influence markets. So, too, is the financial press. Influence markets tend to be very specific to industries.

RELATIONAL STAGES

Stages of commitment and loyalty to the firm characterise the interactive relationship between customers and the firm. These stages have been classified in various ways, and two popular examples appear in Table 15.1. In both examples, customers begin with limited knowledge of the company, make an initial purchase, form an interactive relationship during additional purchases, begin to feel a sense of community with the company, and become advocates and partners. These stages of relationships have obvious and important implications for marketing strategy.

- *No relationship exists – the parties are unaware of each other*
  At this stage of the relationship, the analytic process advocated by strong marketing can be the most important competency to the firm. Only through competent analysis can the firm identify the skills and resources it requires but lacks, and begin the process of finding other firms that possess them. Research and communication skills are very important because they fuel the analytic process.
  In consumer markets, the ability to identify members of target segments is of the utmost importance at this stage.

RELATIONSHIP MARKETING LADDER OF CUSTOMER LOYALTY	CROSS AND SMITH'S DEGREES OF CUSTOMER BONDING
Prospect	Awareness
Customer	Identity
Client	Relationship
Supporter	Community
Advocate	Advocacy
Partner	

Table 15.1 *Two frameworks of stages in relationship building*[6]

- *The parties become aware of each other*

  Empathy may be the most important skill at this relational stage. Firms, like people, enter relationships with a vision of achieving some benefit. The ability to understand what benefits another firm might seek and to 'wear' that firm's world-view can be of critical importance. At this stage, the 'aware' firm must approach the other firm. Communication and negotiation skills often become very important.

  In consumer markets, the firms must also have great empathy with the target segment. This implies an ability to understand every important element of the belief system, including the influences on symbolic world associations and the holistic association with the meaning world.

- *A first interaction occurs (a business agreement or contact of some kind)*

  Empathy, communication and negotiation skills remain important when two parties interact for the first time. During interaction, the parties attempt to confirm or disconfirm prior expectations, and to establish an advantageous position in the relationship (see Chapter 5 for a review of cognitive consistency theories). It is important that at least one of the parties has sensitivity and empathy for the other's position. Otherwise, the chances are that this will be the last meeting. Symbolic gestures during the first interaction often have an important influence on the nature of the ongoing relationship and the relative positions of power each party will wield in the relationship[7]. Concerning consumers, a first purchase activates the processes of post-purchase evaluation and subsequent decision processes.

- *A repeat interaction occurs (another business agreement or contact of some kind)*

  The processes begun in an initial interaction continue in the second. Each party must continue to develop empathy for the other. The nature of the relationship will begin to be sorted out. Who will do what? How do you do business?

Reinforcement becomes most important and each party must exceed the other's expectations. Concerning value-chain relationships, it is important to note that I have not indicated that one must give the other party everything they want. Relationship building is a process of give and take. All parties come into that process with opinions about what is possible, what is probable and what is not negotiable. If one listens to the other — not only to what they say, but to what they do not say — it will become easier and easier to sketch these various opinions and to look past what the other party says in the thrust of negotiations.

- *Regular interaction occurs and a sense of commitment and loyalty develops as the parties begin to know and rely on one another*

As regular interaction occurs, operations and delivery systems become more important. Strong marketers embrace technology that informs them about their performance and the performance of the other party. Management must know immediately when something does not go right. Something will always go wrong and the mark of a great company is how it recovers when something goes wrong[8]. Both parties must also be alert to the changing requirements of the other. Communication, flexibility and adaptability are vitally important.

Legality is not a framework for conducting a successful long-term relationship. This does not mean that one should abandon legal agreements. Frame agreements fairly and reduce them to writing in most cases. Nevertheless, no relationship will continue if one party feels unfairly treated and resentment can develop as conditions change over time. Astute relationship builders realise this and redraft agreements from time to time to mirror changing conditions.

Speaking of his long relationship with Mark McCormack (renowned sports agent and author), golfing great Arnold Palmer recently told CNN's Larry King that he and McCormack had not signed a legal agreement but had negotiated in a spirit of fairness with one another for nearly 40 years[9]. Palmer noted that the relationship had not always been smooth but that it had operated based on a handshake in the 1950s. Both made millions.

- *The parties develop a smooth working relationship and advocacy develops*

The greatest compliment one can pay another is to refer someone to them for business. Referrals are great ways to get new business. However, referrals place two relationships at risk, the new relationship and the relationship with the referring party.

Operational and delivery systems remain critically important. Customer records should note the party that referred a customer. If something goes wrong early in the relationship, the referring party should be made aware of the problem and what the firm plans to do about it — so long as this does not violate the privacy of the new relationship. Automated applications processing and behavioural scoring systems can aid in the smooth processing of applications.

One of the most common problems occurs when someone referred to the company has a bad credit rating. This is embarrassing for everyone involved. Never reveal details of another's credit rating to a referring party, even under threat of losing the original relationship. It pays to say something like, 'We have a good relationship and you know how we conduct our business. We have the utmost respect for the privacy of our customers and applicants. I can only tell you that we were unable to approve Mr Jones' credit application although we tried very hard to do so.' You may also wish to indicate that the company would consider a suitable co-signer. This gives the referring party the opportunity to offer to stand surety and usually becomes the end of the discussion. Beware, fraud rings often set up what look like legitimate accounts and operate them for substantial periods before pulling a scam under the name of a customer that they have 'referred'.

MARKETING AS CROSS-FUNCTIONAL ACTIVITY MANAGEMENT

The new marketing requires that firms institutionalise the belief that marketing is a set of cross-functional activities. Perhaps the most serious problem with marketing concepts of the past has been in management and organisation of marketing strategies. Marketing people have traditionally been responsible for the planning and success of all marketing mix activities. Nevertheless, marketing people have had little responsibility in actual performances that determine the success or failure of these plans. The best advertising, pricing and distribution strategies will come to naught if a restaurant gives poor service and serves inconsistent food quality.

Institutionalising marketing as a set of cross-functional activities begins with identifying marketing activities performed throughout the company for internal and external customers. Each department of the company should identify their customers and report the customers' expectations as written performance standards, such as:

- Customers expect to receive cooked breakfast meals within five minutes of ordering.

- Customers expect their plates to be heated to between 40° and 45° Celsius.

External customers' expectations should be validated with research or, where the customer base is small, in direct interviews. Internal customer expectations can be determined in focus groups, by questionnaire or in team-building sessions. It is important that internal and value-chain partners understand and agree to the expectations placed on them by each department.

The next step is to establish procedures for measuring performance against established agreed standards, and for measuring the communication of these results to interested parties. Banc One discovered a very effective way to communicate performance against standards throughout the company. The bank regularly publishes performance results and posts these where associates can see them in each branch. The reports list the worst-performing branch or department at the top of each list, then continue in order to the best-performing at the bottom of the list. Apparently, few branches or departments stay at the top of the list for very long.

There is a disturbing tendency in many companies to bring promotional campaigns to the market with extreme speed these days, without consulting the associates responsible for the marketing activities necessary for the promotion's success. Many promotions fail as a result. Even when security considerations preclude advising staff of the exact details of a promotional offer, management must ensure that adequate resources are available throughout the firm to deliver on the promotional promise.

The process of identifying marketing performances and setting standards makes everyone aware of their role in the success or failure of the company. Everyone in the company must feel represented in the process and free to contribute to it. Some companies rotate associates between internal suppliers and internal customers so that each department can understand the procedures of the other and thereby anticipate problems better. It is important to gain agreement from all interested parties concerning performance standards. Many companies measure departmental expectations and communicate these to other parties before holding a meeting to agree on standards and responsibilities.

MARKETING AS INFORMATION MANAGEMENT

The new marketing embraces information management. Perhaps the most telling characteristic of the new marketing paradigm is the incorporation of information that allows relational intimacy and intensive cost management. How else could firms achieve the relational intimacy required by customers today, while keeping staff costs down and achieving competitive scale and scope? Thus, many firms employ automated systems to do most of the analysis and reporting. The new marketing requires that firms become competent in three broad information tasks: information acquisition, information storage and retrieval, and information analysis.

INFORMATION ACQUISITION: THE STEADY FLOW OF PROSPECTS

In consumer markets, information management plays a central role in identification of prospects and the management of marketing to them. Direct one-to-one marketing efforts depend on a steady flow of new prospects —

usually obtained through access to lists of names and addresses held by external parties.

Lists are rented and purchased. Government lists, such as population census, motor vehicle, telephone, radio and television licence lists and similar files can be reasonably accurate and large. Private lists, such as retailers, sports clubs, internet service providers, conference companies and insurance companies, also make names available to others. However, many such lists have extremely low response rates, especially if the lists are well marketed to direct marketers. It's an old marketing truth that the more offers someone receives, the more likely they are to fail to respond to a new offer. There is usually an agreement that companies will not pay for names already on their databases (duplicates or dupes) or for names with incorrect addresses (nixies). Many list providers pay a premium for nixies so they can improve the quality of their lists.

- *List choice*

    With so many available lists of names, marketers must choose lists that include high proportions of people from the target market. Lists that include extensive information are the most useful. Marketers choosing lists would be wise to remember the rules concerning when attitudes are most likely to predict behaviour. That is, (a) action, (b) target, (c) timing, and (d) context.

    (a) Lists that indicate *related behaviours and interests* will yield greater response rates. A direct marketing effort for a new fishing rod will yield better results when the prospects come from a fishing magazine subscriber list instead of a sports magazine subscriber list. Both sources will probably outperform the motor vehicle registry. Account holders at major outdoor enthusiasts' shops may outperform all the lists.

    (b) Lists should identify prospects capable of the *target behaviour*. If the major outdoor enthusiasts' shop is known as a great value fishing-rod retailer, the list may perform poorly because the target behaviour (fishing-rod purchase) has already taken place. However, if the offer is unique and the prospects are financially able, then the offer may be well received.

    (c) Direct marketing should take place at a *suitable time*. Direct marketers telephoning homes in the early evening plague the United States. I have been in homes in recent years that received as many as five calls in an evening. Timing also refers to time of month (when consumers have money), time of year (important for seasonal products), and to the age of the information (the more current the better).

    (d) The context in which the behaviour has been commissioned is also important. Astute marketers look for behaviours that indicate changes in characteristics related to purchase and consumption. For instance, events such as a marriage, birth, divorce or death in the family are powerful indicators of lifestage changes that may indicate consumption patterns. In fact, sending a life offer during a prospect's birthday week can increase the likelihood of response by as much as 600 per cent[10].

- *List targeting*

Confronted with a list of names, the marketer must question how many of these names represent real opportunities for relationships. For many companies, this is a budget issue. Which 250 000 of these four million names should I approach? This question is answered increasingly by using decision logic provided by (a) scoring systems, and (b) geographical information systems.

(a) Scoring systems

Credit scoring systems became popular in the 1960s as tools used primarily to determine credit risk. Credit bureaux launched customised credit bureau risk scores in the mid-1970s. However, at the time, credit bureaux held only collections and bad debt data. During the mid-1980s, companies began to pool monthly reports of all customers' performances on credit bureaux, including positive payment profile data. This facilitated scoring models dedicated to debt collection success, success in litigation, first year credit card revenue, holistic credit bureau scores, and a host of risk indicators. A hot, new area is modelling the behaviour of people who fail to qualify for credit using existing credit scores.

Marketers have really only begun to benefit from scoring during the past five years. Perhaps the most widespread use of scoring in marketing has been in the modelling of response by direct marketers, especially banks and credit card issuers[11]. Response models allow the marketer to pull names from the list that are most likely to respond to a particular offer (provided that the profile used to select respondents predicts likely purchase behaviour and that the list is accurate). Lifetime value and attrition analyses are also important in marketing. Modelling and scoring systems are explored in detail later in this chapter.

(b) Geographical information systems (GIS)

Scoring systems often include geographical information and may be delivered as part of a GIS. Neighbourhoods may also be characterised by relative homogeneity concerning lifestyle, culture, demographics or lifestage that relate strongly to purchase and consumption behaviour. The length of time people have been in residence can provide purchase and consumption information as well. Geographical information systems consist of a database that includes a geographical location co-ordinate (called a geo-code) for each member, and a query and edit capability that allows the information to be combined, manipulated and analysed. The advent of desktop mapping systems incorporating off-the-shelf GIS software has made GIS available to smaller firms.

Geo-coded files open the world to many kinds of analysis. Retailers and their suppliers can model target markets and explore the performance of individual outlets in comparison to performance indicated by target market populations within a catchment area. Distribution planning and truck routing are two popular applications. Banks can calculate actual branch profitability. Target marketing, however, remains the largest application. Possibly because of their involvement in real-estate financing, banks have been among the biggest adopters of GIS. The UK's National Westminster can locate over 98 per cent of its customers geographically[12]. CCN, Claritas, Equifax and CACI are among the large GIS and related services providers in the world.

Geo-coding depends on accurate cadastral (land and title information) data. Although available in South Africa (but of inferior quality compared to American and European data), this is not the case in many Asian countries. For instance, China, Thailand and Indonesia have only some three per cent of land parcels mapped[13]. As the cost of data and processing continues to drop and information continues to rise, users should prepare to move fast with technological developments. Some companies are already exploring the use of multimedia maps to view time-series data and other multidimensional GIS information and graphic sequences[14], for example, the pattern of diffusion in new product sales, or the changing spread of an agent's sales.

NEW TOOLS OF THE TRADE

Marketers also sometimes use response campaigns in the mass media and other traditional media to encourage consumers interested in products or related items to communicate with the company. Behavioural and geodemographic information from existing customer files for other products is another very valuable prospect source. Strong marketing utilises a range of new interactive tools to manage information[15]. Unlike traditional media, the new tools offer two-way communication – thereby facilitating information gathering and distribution.

- *The Internet and the World Wide Web*

  Once limited to defence and academic use, the Internet has exploded during the past two years as a marketing tool offering instant global access for products and customers. The Internet and the World Wide Web (Web) have become synonymous. However, the Web is only one aspect of the Internet — e-mail, newsgroups and file transfer sites are other important Internet marketing tools.

  The Web is a system for exploring the Internet. Users generally access the Internet via some form of on-line communication, such as a modem, the company mainframe computer or a dedicated data line. A browser is a software package that formats Internet information for viewing. Browsers present the Web as a collection of digital text, pictures, sound and movies

(Netscape and Microsoft Internet Explorer are two popular browsers). Websites generally consist of a page or a series of pages of information that people can browse through. Many sites allow only passive viewing, but the trend is toward interactive sites allowing people to order and receive customised information. Web radio is becoming popular and many radio stations have begun broadcasting on the Web. Content includes news and music but American sports events seem to be the most popular. The first Web TV stations were launched recently but offer only limited content.

Promotional activity on the Web is growing. It has become common to use the Internet for customer service, product information and other marketing activities. However, to interact on the Internet, people have to be on-line and at the right web-site. Software that allows users to capture data while off-line for later downloading is a recent development[16]. These Web VCRs are a logical response to the expanding content of the Web. A number of companies are rushing to launch software that allows web-sites to identify users and send them the information they would like to receive.

Pointcast offers a Windows screen-saver that automatically accesses the Internet to download news, sports scores, stock prices and other data of interest to the user[17].

The breadth and depth of information contained on the Internet is fascinating. There are thousands of Internet newsgroups devoted to science, sport, medicine, and almost any other interests you can imagine. These newsgroups can provide information about lead user preferences and opportunities to communicate with users.

Many Internet service providers or content providers track the way that consumers use their services by recording what services users access at their site. Some companies deposit a small data file on a users' computer hard drive (called a cookie) indicating what information was accessed at their site, and allowing web pages to customise information that users see on the next visit.

Privacy has become a major Internet issue. Some sites sell user information onward to other providers in the same way that magazine publishers sell subscriber lists. Many users feel that planting cookies on their hard drives or selling information about them violates their individual right to privacy. About two-thirds of Americans recently polled in the Equifax/ Harris Consumer Privacy Survey said companies should not be able to track usage for marketing purposes[18].

Using the Internet as a marketing tool requires careful planning. One should verify that target market members have access to the Internet, and that identification, recruitment and interaction strategies are practical. Firms that report disappointing results from the Internet generally err in one of these critical activities. Internet access is the major consideration. The Equifax/Harris poll found that, although 60 per cent of Americans use computers, only 20 per cent use the Internet and on-line services. Even among these users, a large proportion uses the Internet only for business and rarely visits new sites. International data is unavailable but most experts would agree that the Americans have the most widespread access to the Web, and that the Internet is accessible to less than five per cent of the population in most IOR countries. However, those with access may constitute a major share of many markets and be more likely to be opinion leaders. Sites must feature the right products and the right content. It is also important to set realistic objectives. Extended problem-solving products seem to be the most likely candidates for the Internet. An information site for a limited problem-solving product may get very little traffic. Most people wouldn't order a motor car over the Internet, but they may well participate in a motor car club such as Saturn's successful club in the USA.

Marketers should also be aware that experts forecast the Internet will experience capacity problems as it grows, albeit for temporary periods. The recent crash of America On-Line, America's largest Internet service provider, has given colleagues around the world a grave portrait of what may happen should capacity be outstripped[19].

- *Bulletin board services (BBS)*

Bulletin board services were the forerunners of the Internet. Users dial into a BBS with a modem to access information and receive computer files and software. In general, BBS sites are not networked — when users dial a BBS they are limited to accessing that site. The Internet can be a very expensive medium to deliver on-line information to small customer bases. BBS is a less costly alternative offering much of the functionality of the Internet. This suggests a surge in growth for BBS providers. BBS providers increasingly provide access via the Internet. Many firms offer private BBS services. File Transfer Protocol (FTP) sites on the Internet often provide similar services to BBS. FTP is a protocol that specifies the structure of the file so that computers can communicate. There are other protocols, but file transfers over the Internet conform to FTP. BBS communications are open to a wider range of protocols, but communications software packages facilitate the co-ordination of protocols on the sending and receiving computer.

- *Magnetic stripe cards and smartcards*

Magnetic stripe cards, such as your credit card or ATM card, have become important marketing tools for identifying customers in loyalty programmes. Information on customer identity, account and customer type can be included to alert staff to the customer's name and personal preferences at the point-of-sale.

Smartcards perform a similar function, but contain computer chips with much larger storage capacity than magnetic stripe cards. Information on customer preferences, purchases and other items can be stored and downloaded from smartcard memory. Smartcards are turning up every-where: as Subscriber Identity Module (SIM) cards in GSM cellular telephones, as pre-paid telephone cards, as club membership cards and as credit cards. Collecting promotional cards has become a fast-growing hobby.

Smartcard technology presents exciting possibilities. Retailers can record SKU (stock control units) level data on smartcards, and offer customised promotions or advertisements at the point-of-sale. Credit cards can log purchases and account balances making immediate point-of-sale credit approval possible. Loyalty programmes and promotions can be targeted at segments using smartcard technology.

Telephone calling cards are becoming a promotional communication vehicle in many countries. Companies purchase pre-paid calling cards in bulk and send them to finely-tuned prospect lists. The cards can be printed with the company logo, a picture of a product or a commercial message. A typical promotion offers ten or 15 minutes of calling time to anywhere in the country. Using the calling card the first time initiates an interactive commercial message for the company, such as 'Thanks for using the Acme satellite television calling card. While we are activating your free call time, we'd like to share some important news about satellite television rentals. If you would like more information about Acme satellite television at any time, press 1 and you will receive additional free time while you are connected to an Acme customer-care associate.'

- *Multimedia*

  Advertisers have always dreamed of blending audio, visual and interactive elements in adverts. Today this has become a reality, and the Internet and CD-ROM (and floppy disks for very short messages) have become vehicles for interactive multimedia messages. The range of multimedia vehicles continually expands. The growing popularity of digital cellular telephony is spurring cellular fax-on-demand. Digital videodisk technology may be the next great opportunity, if penetration improves. These technologies can be inexpensive and highly effective.

- *Information on demand*

  A wide range of more simple media continues to offer attractive marketing opportunities. Electronic mail (e-mail) is becoming necessary and will soon replace most forms of normal post in many market segments. The growing penetration of Internet telephone software promises to put audio-visual e-mail on the agenda very soon. The popularity of electronic diaries and contact management systems suggests that on-line personal assistants will soon become an important marketing resource.

  Automated calling and voicemail systems can greatly streamline customer services, improve access to a wider range of services, ensure service quality and reduce costs. Faxes can now be received via e-mail, a conventional fax machine, and even your cell phone, putting you in immediate touch with product or client service information. The ability to offer real-time data processing and continuous on-line access via the Internet or dial-up access has expanded this to a new realm of 'just-in-time' data provision.

- *Membership schemes*

  Companies have found customer clubs to be an effective way to learn about customer preferences and to provide added-value services. Many companies offer clubs and other membership schemes as subscription services to large client bases. Edgar's Club members are offered a chance to win big money every month, and the South African clothing retailer donates a similar prize to the educational institution of the winner's choice. The scheme has put millions of rands on Edgar's bottom line, and has greatly aided many communities. Nedbank has positioned a number of affinity schemes so that every financial transaction by a customer benefits an environmental, sports or other interest group of the customer's choice.

- *Narrowcast technologies*

  New narrowcast technologies are providing interactive multimedia information to specific groups using a spectrum of delivery vehicles. The provision of on-line share price movements to stockbrokers is an example of how Voicemail, e-mail, the fax and automated calling services are being used to deliver content to interest groups. New interactive voice-recognition technology promises to widen the interactivity of such schemes.

- *External databases*

  Internet service providers, credit bureaux and other on-line services are amassing incredibly comprehensive databases. Typical information includes product use, interests, credit, demographic or lifestage information. Providers often enhance databases with geographical information, credit scores or generic market segmentation information. Users generally access external databases via the Internet, BBS, or through some form of on-line connectivity. Timing varies and users access external databases when evaluating direct marketing campaigns, processing customer applications, on an ad-hoc basis, or as part of applications processing software.

  External information can be very valuable and it is not cheap. The price of information generally depends on its recency, comprehensiveness, relevance and accuracy (in addition to normal market forces). Batch processing is the least expensive processing alternative.

  External data should be viewed with caution. This is especially true of the market segmentation information offered by many providers. Although they are often backed with colourful presentations and claims of international successes, there is no guarantee that a generic scheme will perform well in an industry, as noted in Chapter 8. Marketers should be cautious and avoid adopting these generic segmentation schemes without extensive validation and comparison to existing in-house or industry-specific schemes.

  Credit bureaux are among the most active marketers of external database information. Credit bureau information is generally limited to the credit-active population, but it can be of exceptionally good quality. It is very current because it is updated by users monthly. The purchase of credit bureaux information typically requires that the firm provide the same level information about its own credit database on a monthly basis. Credit bureaux often provide aggregate credit information to non-providers, usually at postcode or suburb level.

Credit bureaux information is increasingly coming under threat from privacy legislation around the world. Nearly two-thirds of Americans now strongly favour legislation to regulate the use of consumer information, and a bill to limit access to medical information, currently in the US Congress, is expected to be passed soon[20]. Credit bureaux exceed privacy legislation requirements in most countries, and limit marketing access to sensitive information in most cases. Programmes exist that can eliminate poor credit risks from proposed mailing lists, but the use of credit information for building lists or marketing purposes is strictly prohibited by most credit bureaux. Credit bureaux information should be acquired, disclosed and used in ways that respect privacy.

- *Interactive real-time market research*
  Digital surveys and on-line analysis programmes have extended traditional capabilities to offer instant market research and results. Sample composition is often suspect and results should be viewed with caution. These technologies should probably be viewed as a tool to facilitate customer complaints rather than as a marketing research tool.

INFORMATION STORAGE AND RETRIEVAL: DATABASE FUNDAMENTALS

Oracle, Hewlett-Packard and EMC^2 recently surveyed 200 South African IT (Information Technology) executives about data warehousing plans[21]. Over 60 per cent of respondents reported that their firm was already implementing or planning to implement a 'data warehouse' in the short-term. Many of these data warehouses will be used for marketing purposes and many will be so poorly designed as to be inadequate for marketing purposes. A complete introduction to database processing is beyond the scope of this book, but the material discusses the major issues affecting strong marketing[22].

Systems analysis and design, and database processing are complex and highly specialist topics that most marketers know little about. Databases are collections of information about things of interest in the business, such as customer particulars, orders or accounting records. Databases facilitate the co-ordination and organisation of information. Most marketers are familiar with spreadsheets and the notion that data can be held in tables. Although spreadsheets have increasing functionality, they are not databases. Database management systems (DBMSs) are self-contained, self-describing and offer a wide range of functionality not available in spreadsheet software. Figure 15.1 below indicates the relationship between various elements of a typical database management system.

Database processing has emerged from the older information processing model called file processing. File processing was characterised by separate application programme-dependent systems that included both the application and data. One file processing system was generally incompatible with other file processing systems; these systems were also hard to change and wasteful of computer processing resources. One particularly wasteful characteristic of file processing was the duplication of data from one system to another. Data duplication increases the cost of data processing by increasing the storage required, the amount of processing memory required, and the amount of processing time. Many legacy systems feature file processing[23].

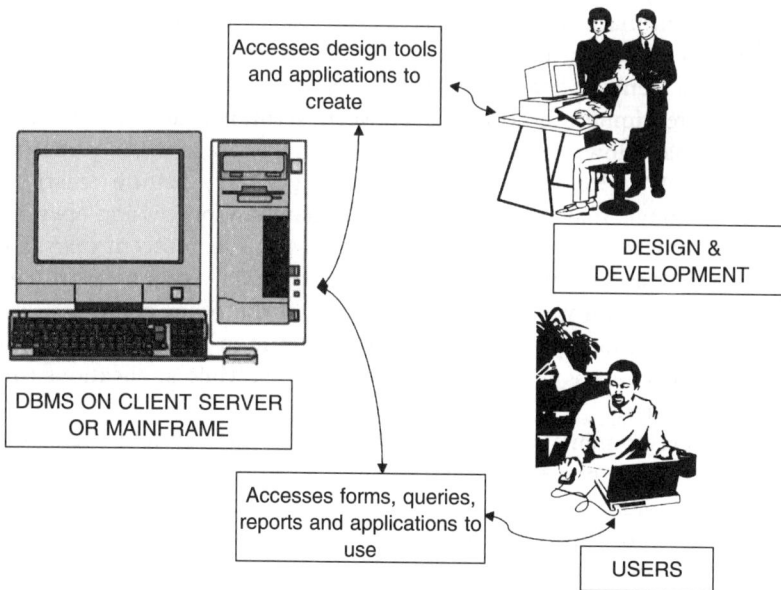

Figure 15.1 *A database management system*[24]

Database management systems (DBMSs) are a major advance on the file processing model. As Figure 15.1 above shows, DBMS consist of data files held on a server or mainframe, a database management engine software programme featuring design tools and processing functionality, and development and user interfaces. Application and developer databases include metadata. Metadata is used to store the structure and format of tables, forms, queries, reports and other application components. A data dictionary typically allows developers to manage and track the data accessed by all applications.

It is important to understand some basic database terminology. The DBMS holds data in tables. A form is an organised way for viewing and entering data on screen. Forms may include decision logic or other rules to ensure valid data entry. Developers and users use queries to view, change and analyse data in various ways. Queries specify the tables from which data is to be returned and set the rules by which individual cases in each table are included. Queries are often the source of records for forms and reports. Developers and system managers query the data dictionary when a change, such as in the percentage of value-added tax or employee tax, has the potential to affect many applications. Reports present data in a printed format. The DBMS gives developers and users control over the size and appearance of everything on a report. A macro is a set of one or more actions that perform particular operations, such as printing a report or selecting a subset of the total data. Macros help automate common tasks.

Various system architectures support multi-user database processing. Teleprocessing systems feature a large computer, usually a mainframe, and many access terminals. The terminals act only as access points for data entry and display, and all processing is conducted on the central processing unit (CPU) of the central computer (usually a mainframe). Resource-sharing systems feature limited networking between terminals and other network components that allows sharing of large computer storage disks, printers and other peripherals[25]. Resource-sharing systems generally feature smart terminals. The terminals may or may not conduct database processing operations. Client server systems have achieved the greatest attention in recent years. Client server database architecture features a client server computer (usually a microcomputer) performing services on behalf of the other computers in the network (usually also microcomputers). It is common to see system designs where the client server is responsible for the DBMS, while applications run on the client machines.

Current developments are shaping new distributed system architectures featuring distributed processing or databases. Distributed processing leads to systems where more can be done at once, to greater independence and availability and more flexible system design. Distributed processing is more difficult to control, more expensive, more complex and exposes the firm to higher security risks. Distributed database architecture allows some or all of the databases to be housed on different machines. Databases may be duplicated and synchronised in real-time or at various times during the day. Distributing databases improves performance and processing while driving down communication time and costs. Distributed database systems are also easily scaled (scaling refers to adding or subtracting components of a system in response to changing requirements), can be more reliable and can be tailored more easily to user requirements. Distributing databases can have negative influences on network traffic and can result in higher cabling costs. Some IT experts feel that distributed systems are too new and require further development before they are truly accepted as reliable — as with any IT solution, many factors determine the attractiveness of distributed systems.

Finally, data communications are an integral part of any system. Some systems feature dial up access via modem (as most people do when calling an Internet service provider on their home personal computer). Higher volume users often require dedicated telephone data lines that can range from 9600K to much larger size, depending on the particular application. Larger lines cost more. A more recent innovation is the Integrated Services Digital Network (ISDN) line. The ISDN line is a 2MB communications line consisting of what are essentially 'virtual lines' in the telephone exchange. The most exciting aspect of ISDN is that the virtual lines can be changed to almost any desirable configuration of voice or data lines (including video), as in the case of the Huntington Bank Access Branches discussed at the beginning of the chapter.

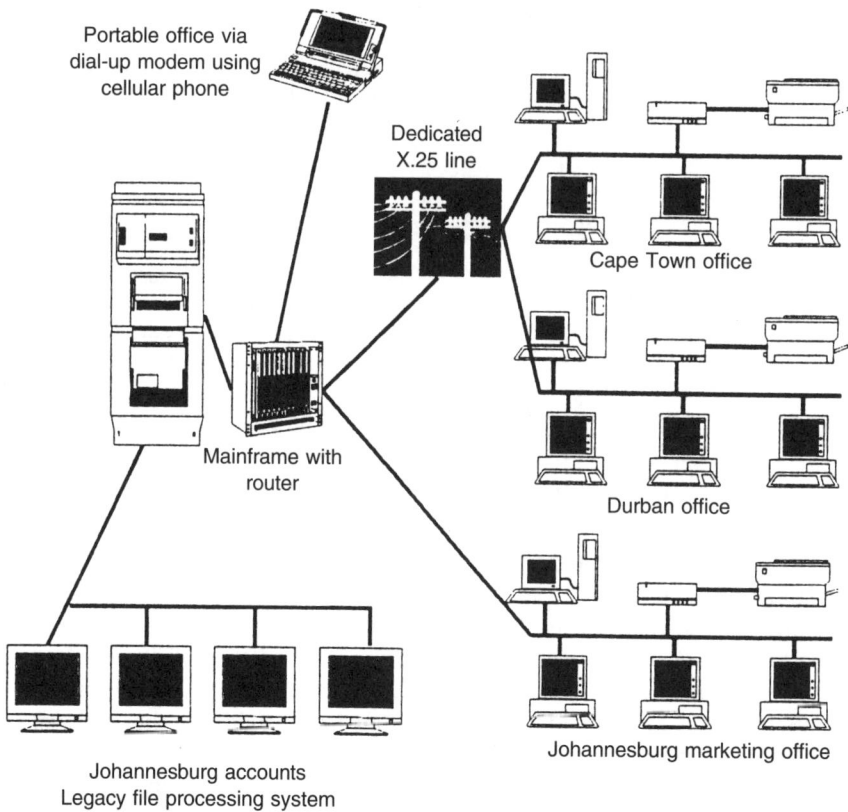

Figure 15.2 A simple network for a company with offices in three locations

INFORMATION ANALYSIS: WHAT KIND OF DATABASE DO YOU NEED?

Database structure has a major impact on the usefulness of a database for marketing. Marketing databases tend to be structured according to two popular models: structured and relational database models.

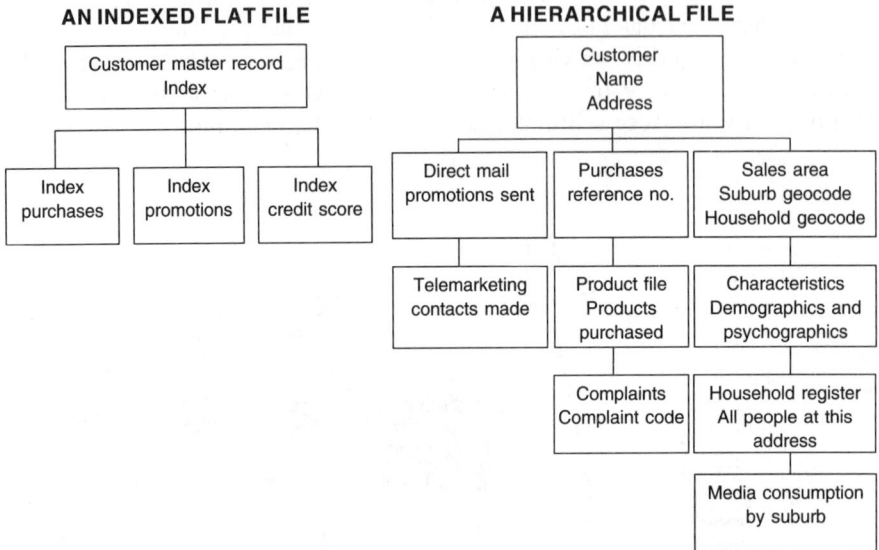

AN INDEXED FLAT FILE

```
        ┌─────────────────────────┐
        │  Customer master record │
        │         Index           │
        └─────────────────────────┘
      ┌──────────┬──────────┬──────────┐
┌──────────┐ ┌──────────┐ ┌──────────┐
│  Index   │ │  Index   │ │  Index   │
│ purchases│ │promotions│ │credit score│
└──────────┘ └──────────┘ └──────────┘
```

A HIERARCHICAL FILE

```
                ┌──────────────┐
                │  Customer    │
                │    Name      │
                │   Address    │
                └──────────────┘
    ┌───────────────┬──────────────┬──────────────┐
┌──────────────┐ ┌──────────────┐ ┌──────────────────┐
│ Direct mail  │ │  Purchases   │ │   Sales area     │
│promotions sent│ │reference no.│ │ Suburb geocode   │
└──────────────┘ └──────────────┘ │Household geocode │
                                   └──────────────────┘
┌──────────────┐ ┌──────────────┐ ┌──────────────────┐
│Telemarketing │ │ Product file │ │ Characteristics  │
│contacts made │ │  Products    │ │ Demographics and │
└──────────────┘ │  purchased   │ │  psychographics  │
                 └──────────────┘ └──────────────────┘
                 ┌──────────────┐ ┌──────────────────┐
                 │  Complaints  │ │Household register│
                 │Complaint code│ │All people at this│
                 └──────────────┘ │    address       │
                                  └──────────────────┘
                                  ┌──────────────────┐
                                  │Media consumption │
                                  │   by suburb      │
                                  └──────────────────┘
```

Figure 15.3 *Two types of structured files*

Structured databases include flat file, indexed flat file and hierarchical structures. All these structures have been in use since the 1960s and are viewed as old-fashioned by many. IBM DL/1 is the only surviving hierarchical database application for mainframe use. Flat files have a number of problems for marketing use and the indexed flat file and hierarchical structures are the only two real options available.

In indexed flat files, information is collected in a number of strings. Each string includes an index field that matches an index field in other strings. A typical marketing application might consist of a customer master string including customer details, a direct marketing history string indicating communications directed to each customer, and an order history string with historical purchasing information.

Hierarchical files store information in trees. In order to access information, a database must access each node of the tree and advance on to the succeeding nodes. A typical marketing application might store information in a tree similar to Figure 15.3 (above).

In a relational database (i.e data relationships, not human relationships), data is stored in a number of separate tables. Figure 15.4 shows four tables from a marketing database used by a company selling on the Internet: CUSTOMER, CYBERCODE, ORDER and PRODUCT. The company uses a cybercode similar to a geocode to determine a customer's cyberspace location, and a stand-alone application provides a customer segmentation description based on cybercode, purchase behaviour and other characteristics. You will note that each object contains a relationship to at least one other object. In this way, the entire database can be queried to include any combination of fields from the various objects.

CUSTOMER

Customer	Name	Address	City	Postal code	Telephone	**CYBERCODE**	**ORDER**

CYBERCODE

Cybercode number	Segment description	Estimated annual purchases	**CUSTOMER**

ORDER

Order number	Date	**CUSTOMER**	Quantity	**PRODUCT**	Extended price

PRODUCT

Product code	Unit	Description	Case packing	Unit price

Figure 15.4 *Four tables from a relational database*

A relational database is usually structured according to the rules of normalisation. Every normalised relation has a single theme, and the normalisation process removes relationships from the database that may be subject to modification anomalies. There are six normal forms. Normalisation results in a database that is structured to reduce its size and eliminate duplication. In practice, some data duplication remains in every database.

Although the choice of database seems quite straightforward in these days when hierarchical databases are considered so old-fashioned, it is not. The relational database holds all information in atomised form. In other words, no information can be held in summary counts. In Figure 15.4 above, CUSTOMER may contain relationships with many CYBERCODE or ORDER tables. Selecting customers for marketing action may result in many hours of processing (days in the larger databases), as the computer reads records one-by-one to assemble a query that selects customers from certain segments with a certain minimum annual purchase budget, who have not yet bought a certain product, and who live in a geographic area with parcel delivery. A limitation in many processing applications, the structure of the hierarchical database is often of the same shape or pattern as marketing data. Customers live in households or work in companies, they make repeat purchases and they share cyberspace addresses.

The *hierarchical model* is superior when data relationships form a natural order, when variables of interest do not change much over time, and when accessing individual records, detailed fine-tuning and conserving computer processing resources are important[26]. The *relational model* is superior when it is important to examine single- and multiple-data relationships, when conserving computer storage is important, when data access must be flexible and when development speed is important.

WORKING WITH YOUR *IT* DEPARTMENT

With this very basic introduction, we proceed to discuss some procedural issues that marketing should understand about databases. What marketers want from a database is quite simple – access to customer information so that they can identify profitable groups and profitable products, select individuals for direct marketing, manage promotional campaigns, test concepts and perform other marketing activities. Most marketing people wish this could all be accomplished without any involvement in database processing issues. It cannot. IT people are not marketing people or mind-readers, and they do not always understand what information marketing requires or what they will do with it when they get it.

It is not necessary to know your exact hardware and software requirements in order to enjoy a productive working relationship with your IT department. It is important to think clearly about what you hope to accomplish from the system, now and in the future. You should quantify the data you require, the people who need access, how many people could need access at any one time and the time of day access would be required, and have a comprehensive understanding of any applications software you might require once you have the data (such as a statistics package or campaign management software).

Unfortunately, many companies do not enjoy productive relationships between IT and marketing people. No doubt, this is a problem caused by both departments and by cultural differences. Nevertheless, the failure of marketing people to recognise the politics of information or the complexity of information technology management is a major factor under the control of marketing people.

The IT manager's primary concern is the day-to-day operation of mission-critical systems, such as accounting or production and operations management applications. Regardless of whether it should be so, few IT managers consider marketing database processing as the most important objective of the IT department. Although most IT managers realise the growing importance of information to marketing success, they don't necessarily know the implications for systems in the enterprise. Many marketing people are unfamiliar with the overall effect of development requests on IT resources. This lack of understanding often leads to requests for databases when a spreadsheet or a data query tool is needed. On the basis of a newspaper article or TV programme, marketing managers sometimes make very specific recommendations concerning software and hardware when they should, in fact, be setting out performance requirements that allow IT experts to make recommendations.

A major cultural difference often fuels distrust – marketers seek risk and IT managers seek to avoid it. To the IT manager, marketing managers often expect many team-days of code to be written overnight without any regard to the impact of the application development on the performance of mission-critical applications. The same marketing managers are the first to complain when the system crashes and sales cannot be entered before month-end. To the marketer, IT managers seem especially gifted at two things – knowing how things cannot be done (without having any idea about how things can be done) and conveniently remembering that they 'said this was going to happen a hundred times' when a system collapses (although no one else can remember). Both sides of the debate have a point.

However, marketing people have control over their own behaviour and can make great strides by learning more about IT. Until they do, many IT managers will view marketing application development requests as appeals for a blank cheque in terms of application development time, processing time, memory usage, storage and IT support. Proper knowledge will enable marketing people to brief IT competently so that system access, resource requirements and development time can be budgeted with confidence.

- *Some basic questions for prospective database users*

  Here's how to make sure you're doing the right things that allow your IT department to assist you properly. In consultation with all prospective users, consider the following points:

  1. *Know your subject.* Take the time to read good textbooks about database processing and strategic database marketing. Nothing beats preparation and knowledge.
  2. *Know your database users.* Don't rely on a few people to know everything about the system. Consult the people who will use the marketing database. Consult other departments who may want access to the marketing database.
  3. *Know the customers who will fill the database.* Who are their target markets and how will those markets change over the next few years? How many customers do they expect to have now and in the future? What customer characteristics do they want to keep in the database? Which characteristics are the most and least important? Will you market to individuals or households? Will you hold prospects and customers or just customers on the database? Exactly what fields do you wish to include in the database (always leave a buffer of files for future expansion)?

4. *Know what you expect the database to do.* How will you conduct analysis and campaign management? With what application software? Will you use the database to keep customer purchase histories? What other files will you use from existing databases?

5. *Know how to keep the database current.* Who will be responsible for updating addresses? How will information from accounts be added to the system? How will you track major lifestage events on the database, such as birthdays, marriages, divorces, etc.? What records are necessary for data updates and maintenance?

6. *Know how you want to manage privacy.* What procedures will you use to remove people from active mailing? If you access external data, how will you ensure that it is used as agreed? Is the source of data important to track?

7. *Know how to manage risk.* How will you avoid sending offers to bad debt risks? If you use a credit bureau, will you process credit on-line or in batch mode? Will the marketing database interface with an on-line applications processing and/or credit scorecard system? If credit or behavioural scoring will be used, will these be calculated on-line with each access or off-line in batch mode?

8. *Know how to manage security.* Who will have access to the system? How will managers deny access to discharged employees? Will a firewall be set-up to keep unauthorised people out of the system? How many levels of security are necessary (users would have access to only the functions they require, not to management reports)? What are your requirements for a disaster recovery programme (if the database went down, what would you require in order to begin functioning again)? Where will off-site backups be stored? Will users' keystrokes be stored for future investigations?

9. *Know how to manage usage and reporting.* What regular reports are required? Who will request ad-hoc reports and queries? What type of query functionality do you require? What type of selection procedure would you follow in a normal campaign or query? How many records would be selected then? How often will this be done?

10. *Know the other output required.* What format is required for postal mailings? Will telephone selections be downloaded to an automatic telephone calling system or some other call management system? What outside fulfilment companies are you likely to use and in what format do they require information?

The answers to these questions will prepare you to discuss your basic requirements with the IT department or to participate in management team discussions about database issues.

MARKETING AS ACQUISITION AND RETENTION MANAGEMENT

Another major shift in marketing thinking concerns the emphasis on customer retention. Spurred by the slow-growing markets of the industrialised nations, marketers have finally heeded the wealth of research suggesting that it is more profitable to retain customers than to acquire new ones.

THINKING IN TERMS OF SHARE OF CUSTOMER

The emphasis on retention and the new information technologies have fuelled interest in understanding the company's share of an individual's total spending in addition to the company's share of the market. This shift in thinking has major implications for marketing management.

In practice, share of customer can be difficult to estimate and manage. Governmental sources of individual income are generally unavailable for marketing purposes. However, census statistics are often released for aggregate suburban or postcode level data, and modelling can reveal important patterns at individual level when this aggregated data is appended to customer files. Small area income and consumption models are very useful in this regard. Individual income estimation models usually model the individual against a small area model, or incorporate small area mean income as a factor.

Companies managing share of customer generally report progress according to market segment, sales area and other aggregate characteristics. A host of multivariate statistical tests can be employed to determine the reasons for various shifts in customer share and the efficiency of marketing campaigns.

- *Mining economies of scope*

  In addition to his many accomplishments, Bill Gates may be the world's best miner. Building on his successful Microsoft DOS operating system, Gates has systematically mined economies of scope to gain leadership in a host of application software areas. Thinking in terms of share of customer guides thinking to explore economies of scope. These are economies available to multi-product firms. Scope economies generally occur in the support activities of the value chain, but can be mined in primary activities such as outbound logistics and after-sales service.

  Strong marketers can mine economies of scope best because ongoing analysis provides them with superior knowledge about target market purchase and consumption behaviour, and the firm's competencies and resources. They are then empowered to provide additional products either directly or in association with other firms.

MANAGING CUSTOMER ACQUISITION

Companies that acquire the right customers build a customer base worth keeping, and make many marketing mix and customer retention strategies possible. The market has no pity on firms that manage customer acquisition programmes badly; even when they get everything else right. Once profitable groups of customers have been defined, successful interactive relationship marketing hinges on identifying profitable individual customers for marketing action. This requires access to information about individuals within the firm's communication and distribution reach, careful thinking about customer purchase and consumption behaviour (especially concerning the individual characteristics and environmental influences most likely to lead to profitable customer relationships), activity-based costing and a DBMS. It often also means installing infrastructural support incorporating the decision logic and automated processing advances that are revolutionising the nature of customer acquisition.

Increasing promotional costs and decreasing response have fuelled much interest in statistical modelling approaches. It is important to note that modelling can apply to groups of customers as well as to individual customers. This means that new modelling approaches will change the face of marketing in every product category, including fast-moving consumer goods.

- *Data warehousing*

  The new marketing requires intensive customer information management — a job ideally suited to data warehouse technology. A data warehouse is a separate database that contains a regularly downloaded subset of the operational database that is often enriched by data not held in the operational database. What is the major benefit of data warehousing? Secure access to information by those who need it, in a format they can understand and use without jeopardising the operational systems of the enterprise.

  The rationale for a data warehouse is simple: to provide information in a format that associates can understand and use, enabling those associates to make informed decisions and perform better. Most data warehouses contain automated analysis routines, flexible security and usage features limiting data access by each associate, and easy-to-use and understand on-screen instructions that take users through the various procedures. Once a data warehouse is installed properly, there is no need for any associate to wait for reports or to use information in a format that does not meet one's exact requirements.

  Data warehouses are already widely in use. First Union Bank, America's sixth largest bank, has data warehousing projects on the go for refinancing, knowledge-based marketing and service or call centre management. The Bank of Scotland, an early data warehousing convert that is internationally recognised for excellent productivity and returns, has extensive scoring and predictive modelling tools operating within a data warehouse environment. La Caixa, the second largest bank in Spain, has a 500GB data warehouse up and running, and currently has over 100 projects underway to provide users with new capabilities. Similar trends are evident in industries such as telecommunications, managed health care, hospitals, retailers, fast-moving consumer goods, pharmaceuticals, and many more.

Data warehouses have become the 'intelligence warehouses' of the millennium. Most companies download copies of relevant data to a data warehouse on a daily or weekly basis, depending on their requirements, but these are usually not on a real-time basis. Data warehouses often become the source for even smaller data marts that serve more focused information needs. In practice, IT departments may provide a data warehouse for a particular company, region or brand. Marketing and finance divisions may then have their own dedicated data marts that hold even smaller subsets of the data for very specific usage.

There are very good reasons for adopting data warehousing. First, it is profitable. SPL indicates in a 1996 survey conducted by computer industry analyst IDC, that firms implementing data warehouses achieved an average 401 per cent return on their data warehouse investment. Only 2 per cent reported no return when implementing a data warehouse.

Second, data warehousing drives better marketing and finance decision making in a pressured marketplace. As Table 15.2 below shows, many factors stimulate a decision to adopt data warehousing technology.

DRIVER	AMERICAN FIRMS REPORTING
Customer service	35%
Competitive pressure	29%
Market segmentation	26%
Customer profit analysis	26%
Risk analysis	23%
Organisational profit analysis	20%
Product profit analysis	19%
Direct mail	15%
Telemarketing	10%
Products and services	10%

Table 15.2 *Reasons for data warehousing adoption*[27]

Data warehousing and data mining are new and fast-changing areas that promise great advantage to strong marketers who can master the technology. Nevertheless, they require specialised competencies and marketers are right to feel a bit overwhelmed by the new technologies.

CIBC, Canada's second-largest bank, formed a sales and relationship marketing group to focus the bank on consumer-centred marketing and to change the way the bank did business. The group failed when it tried to build an in-house system providing vertical solutions, and it is true that most IT managers probably struggle to keep up with developments. Fortunately South African firms, such as Dimension Data and Persetel Q Data, have impressive capabilities in this regard and a host of smaller firms provide competent service concerning aspects of data warehouse application and business process design.

Understanding data warehousing begins with the data inputs. These can include operational data, external data from GIS, credit bureaux and marketing services companies and distributed data. One of the hottest data sources is call centre data. Through this, firms such as Chariots Systems Engineering, the Merchants Group (UK) and Siebel (USA) are generating new thinking about the role of sales and services staff and the usefulness of the data they generate. Software products, such as Prism and Sàgent, are used to manage the data warehouse or data mart and automate the flow of data into the data warehouse. New analysis tools by firms such as MicroStrategy, SAS and SPSS, allow users to view the data at various summary levels (so-called 'drilling down' and 'drilling up'), to sort and view subsets (slicing and dicing) and to perform data modelling, data mining and other forms of more comprehensive analysis. Query tools, such as Business Objects and Esperant, allow users to query the data and to perform data mining and rapid simple analyses and cross-tabulations often. Output from the data warehouse can be set to notify users when certain conditions occur, such as out-of-stock or rapid currency devaluation. Such output can be generated to a user's screen, a written report, a facsimile machine, an e-mail address and even a voice mail box or pager.

- *Data mining*

Data mining is the term given to the new statistical modelling approaches for understanding databases. Data mining is used to identify the individuals (or groupings of individuals in entities such as suburbs) where the greatest potential for profitable business lies, to predict consumer behaviour, to identify customers likely to defect, to cross-sell and upgrade customers based on past purchases, and to manage risk and profitability.

RESPONSE ANALYSIS: FINDING PROFITABLE CUSTOMERS

Response models are a special family of data-mining models used to identify individuals to whom marketing activities can be directed profitably.

Basic concepts

Response analysis has been used most frequently to determine the probability of response to and profitability of direct mail offers to individuals. This association to direct response marketing is unnecessarily limiting. Response analysis may be used wherever the likelihood of response to any marketing activity is of interest; whether the behaviour of interest is product purchase, a request for further information or consumption of an intangible (such as viewing a television programme).

Procedure

Response analysis requires five steps.

- *Step one: Identify consumer characteristics* that are statistically associated with the behaviour of interest (i.e. response to an advertisement or purchase of a new product).
- *Step two: Determine the probability of response* associated with every individual or group in the analysis, based on their characteristics.
- *Step three: Determine the cost of the marketing activity* for each individual or group using activity-based costing principles.
- *Step four: Identify individuals or groups where the return on promotion is positive or exceeds a certain hurdle rate*[28]. Ranking the individuals or groups and then partitioning the database into useful sizes is one way that modellers traditionally do this in practice.
- *Step five: Implement* the marketing activity of interest, record progress and measure results.

Assumptions

- Assumes that the firm is aware of *consumer characteristics predictive of purchase* and can accurately append the characteristics to the individuals or groups of interest in the database.
- Assumes that the firm is aware *of all consumer characteristics associated with response* (if the technique is to be most efficient).
- Makes the assumption that firms can *pursue strategies that are appropriate to their environment* (such as a direct mail shot to individuals where postal delivery is not made). Appropriate strategies may not always be clear or available to the firm due to constraints.
- Consumer characteristics are assumed to be fixed (or to change very slowly) and current.
- Assumes the *analyst is competent* with the application of the range of multivariate statistical techniques generally used in response analysis, that the data is scaled appropriately and the database is amenable to the required queries.

Common application problems

It is very difficult to find databases that include a wide range of descriptive characteristics useful in response model building. For example, elements of the belief system, such as values, have traditionally not been held on consumer files. In order to overcome this deficiency, modellers may consult external databases. This can be a limitation if the external database lacks accuracy, currency or comprehensiveness.

Segmentation schemes, such as those based on suburbs or neighbourhoods, may be very appealing. Nevertheless, they often lack reliability and validity and should be carefully evaluated.

MANAGING CUSTOMER RETENTION

Statistical modelling also impacts on customer retention programmes. Attrition analysis focuses on identifying customers who are likely to defect so that marketing activities can focus on keeping the customer. Attrition analysis also identifies unprofitable customers and highlights the reasons for their unprofitability. Marketing activities are directed at unprofitable customers to switch them to more profitable relationships or, where necessary, to discontinue the relationship.

Blasphemy! The customer is not always right

Speaking about 'firing' customers may seem to be blasphemy, but it becomes necessary on certain occasions. A South African newspaper consumer rights column recently reported on a complaint about an armed response security company. The complainant noted that he had activated his alarm and that the security company had taken more than 20 minutes to respond. On investigation, the security company noted that the complainant regularly activated his alarm in order to test the response time of the security company, as often as once a week. The security company replied that it had often discussed the excessive tests and the false alarms with the client to explain that his behaviour taxed its resources and placed other clients at risk. Another security company reported that less than one per cent of its customer base behaved similarly to the complainant.

Companies should never ignore such customers. Further investigation could result in a new product development featuring a frequent call service or a self-validating alarm system. However, while such products are feasible, most security companies would agree that such a customer would never be satisfied — or profitable. Thus, there comes a time when marketers must indicate the limits of customer service to certain customers and diplomatically 'fire' others. Increasingly, marketers are learning that not every customer is the right customer and not every customer is right.

Basic concepts

Attrition models (also called 'churn' models) are a special family of data mining models used to identify individuals with an unacceptably high probability of defection. Specialised models identify customers likely to defect as a result of dissatisfaction, bad debt and other reasons. Specialised marketing activities may be directed to profitable customers with a high likelihood of defection.

Procedure

Attrition analysis requires six steps.

- *Step one:* Identify consumer characteristics that are *statistically associated with defection* (i.e. response to an advertisement or purchase of a new product). These normally include behaviours, such as account payments, that are summary statistics from the accounting database.

- *Step two:* Determine the *probability of defection* associated with every individual or group in the analysis, based on their characteristics.

- *Step three:* Determine the *direct cost of servicing* each individual or group identified as likely to defect, using activity-based costing principles.

- *Step four:* Determine the *cost of the marketing activity* required to stop these individuals or groups from defecting, using activity-based costing principles.

- *Step five:* Identify individuals or groups where the return on the marketing activity to *stop defection* is positive or exceeds a certain hurdle rate. Ranking the individuals or groups and then partitioning the database into useful sizes is one way that modellers traditionally do this in practice.

- *Step six: Implement* the retention marketing activity of interest, *record* progress and *measure* results.

Assumptions

- Assumes that the firm is aware of consumer characteristics and behaviours that *predict defection*, and can accurately append the characteristics to the individuals or groups of interest in the database.

- Assumes that the firm is aware of all consumer characteristics and behaviours *associated with defection* (if the technique is to be most efficient).

- Makes the assumption that firms can pursue strategies that will *halt defection* profitably (in many cases, it is too late – consumers accept the incentive but defect soon afterwards anyway). Appropriate strategies may not always be clear or available to the firm due to constraints.

- Assumes the *analyst is competent* with the application of the range of multivariate statistical techniques that are generally used in retention analysis, that the data is scaled appropriately and that the database is amenable to the required queries.

Common application problems

Although it is common to find numerous statistics concerning financial contributors to defection, such as bad payment, it is not common to find reliable information about non-financial contributory factors, such as number or type of complaint. Identifying and quantifying these factors is the greatest challenge of retention analysis.

CUSTOMER LIFETIME VALUE

The lifetime value of a customer should be the criterion for all marketing action in the interactive marketing environment.

Basic concepts

Customer lifetime value is measured in many ways. Perhaps the most useful analysis (at individual and small group level) is at gross margin or contribution profit margin level. Direct marketers have traditionally estimated response, attrition and costs based on experience (rather than response or attrition analysis or activity-based costing). The adoption of data mining is improving lifetime value analysis. Lifetime value is sometimes calculated for a specific multi-year promotion in isolation from any other revenue and cost streams.

Procedure

Response analysis requires four steps.

- *Step one: Identify the possible revenue streams* that can be associated with a customer or customer group. Estimate the actual revenue to be received from each customer or group.
- *Step two: Identify the possible cost streams* that can be associated with servicing a customer or customer group. Estimate the actual costs to be attributed to each customer or group.
- *Step three: Construct a profit and loss statement* to gross margin or contribution margin for each customer or customer group.
- *Step four: Implement* lifetime value marketing, record progress and measure results.

Assumptions

- The assumptions of response analysis and attrition analysis apply. Where these analyses are not performed, it is assumed that the estimates based on experience are reasonable estimates of the overall population of customers.

- Assumes that the cost of managing individual or group profitability is not prohibitive.

Common application problems

The lack of reliable activity-based costing, response analysis and attrition analysis impinges on the quality of lifetime value analysis. Nevertheless, lifetime value analysis is a process. Once it has been performed, the results can be incorporated in the process and the analysis greatly improved.

MANAGING CUSTOMER PROFITABILITY

The lifetime value analysis approach opens the door to micro-management of profitability. Chapter 8 presented many techniques for identifying profitable customer groups. The same range of multivariate statistical techniques can be applied to marketing databases to understand acquisition, retention and the profitability of database segments, or to shed light on lifetime value differences between various segments.

Consider the CHAID analysis (a fictitious example) of a cable television subscriber base in Figure 15.5 (page 254). Input data might have included total revenue, advertising costs, customer service and support costs, and an estimate of the impact of hours of viewership on advertising revenue. Subscribers who fail to watch television impact on the viewership figures for the cable station. Viewership determines advertising revenues and a simple model might compare subscribers against a normal target viewing time or an average across the base. In this example, new subscribers are more profitable than old subscribers (a historical fact due to penetration in the market during the early days). New accounts paying on debit order are among the most profitable due to low costs of collection and the time value of their regular payments. The most profitable customers are established, view for more than five hours per week and call customer care less than once per month. The cable television company has a few clear-cut objectives: intensify efforts to attract new subscribers, raise the proportion of customers paying by debit order and increase the hours of viewership.

It is important to note what an eclectic and innovative approach database analysis can yield – highlighting the importance of thinking out future data requirements when setting up a database. It also suggests the importance of accurate revenue and cost information at individual customer level.

MARKETING AS TRANSACTION AND RELATIONSHIP MANAGEMENT

The final shift in thinking concerns marketing as transaction and relationship management. Much has already been said about relationship management in

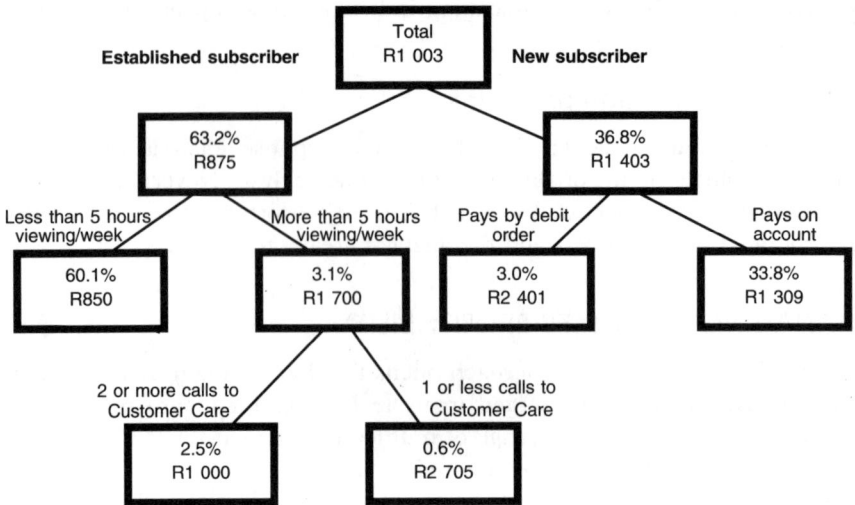

Figure 15.5 *CHAID segmentation of a cable television subscriber base*

this chapter. Although many marketing gurus these days speak of transactional marketing as a thing of the past, it remains vitally important to manage the speed and cost of transactions and to incorporate decision logic where this increases market focus and lowers risk.

All customers do not want ongoing relationships. For these customers, the flexibility, adaptability, cost and speed of transactions may well determine brand choice. New performance criteria, such as fastest processing time, lowest cost per transaction or easiest to use, are being heard more often than ever before. Two new tools are impacting on how firms pursue these new competitive positionings.

APPLICATION AND ORDER PROCESSING SYSTEMS

Automated processing has become a very important requirement for large-scale customer organisations in service industries. One recent automated processing innovation that impacts on strong marketing is the application processing system. Application processing systems (also called order processing systems in some industries) are software programmes that can reside on a mainframe, server or portable computer. They generally perform the following functions:

- Provide a formatted input screen for application entry that will accept an application only when certain items are completed and when those items fall within a valid range.

- Automatic date and time stamping for the application entry and all subsequent events.

- Automatic recording of any human interaction during each event.

- Automatic contact to on-line credit-referencing bureaux while application details are being inputted by a clerk.

- Automatic selection and application of appropriate credit scorecard or scorecards, customer price lists and tariff plans, and distribution and logistics infrastructure.

- Automatic acceptance or rejection of a credit application, based on pre-programmed decision rules. Referral when decision rules indicate that management desires a human decision.

- Automatic account opening in accounting database, and despatch of delivery invoices and packing slips to appropriate company departments.

- Automatic printing of credit disapproval notice with reason codes.

- Provide on-line management of all applications, including a look-up function so that authorised staff may enquire about the progress of any application at any time.

- Provide security that allows flexible assignment of access privileges by the system operator and senior managers. Record all security accesses.

- Provide marketing and financial management with functionality to change decision rules, including credit or behavioural scorecards if desired by management. No necessity for IT department intervention.

The advent of application processing and order processing systems has important advantages that impact on strong marketing:

- The firm can respond to market requirements and competitive activities instantly. Consider a cellular phone company that wishes to respond to a competitor's free phone offer. Credit score hurdles can be raised or lowered within the span of an hour without IT department intervention.

- Customer requests for information about a credit application can be reported in real time with significant detail.

- One person can do the work of many. In the time most clerks take to enter a credit application, a credit check has been done, all internal accounting files have been updated and all internal parties have been notified of required activities by the system.

- Fraud is a major concern in the new marketing. Application processing systems quantify and qualify credit approval. This removes low-level clerks from the actual approval process. Fraud syndicates frequently entice lower-level employees to participate in fraud. Any attempt to circumvent the credit approval process or to break security is automatically recorded and reported.

There is little doubt that application processing systems will revolutionise financial services, life assurance, telecommunications, direct marketing and other firms where applications and orders require extensive processing when received. Firms that fail to incorporate these systems will find themselves at a cost and customer service disadvantage.

Credit and behavioural scoring

As credit bureaux have evolved, they have included more and better information about consumers. The advent of comprehensive positive payment profiles has fuelled much more comprehensive models of credit and behaviour. Credit scoring began as an almost random assignment of point values to accounts by credit managers, based on their experience (i.e. +5 points for home ownership and -25 points for a court judgement against the applicant). Today, credit scoring experts build scorecards for specific industries and for specific market segments.

Scorecard builders use proprietary combinations of statistical analysis techniques, including logistic regression, log-linear modelling, AID, CHAID and ANN. It is common for a scorecard builder to request historical information about a large sample of good accounts, bad accounts and rejected applications in order to build a scorecard.

Credit scorecards increase profitability in two ways: by protecting the company from bad debt and by recognising when borderline cases are likely to be good payers. The inclusion of geodemographic and psychographic information (often called behavioural scoring) in credit-scoring models has aided the performance of scorecards significantly.

SEVEN STEPS TO INTERACTIVE MARKETING

Building a strong interactive marketing function is not an event. It is a never-ending journey that requires careful planning and management. Every company is forced to choose a unique route determined by its environment, industry, missions and goals, value chain and organisational forces. This journey requires commitment and co-operation from the entire management team.

Every journey must begin with an end in mind, and this chapter has shed light on the final destination and some important signposts along the way. Here are seven basic steps to follow when beginning the journey to interactive marketing.

Step one: establish a starting point

Start with the end in mind but know where you are as you begin the journey. The better one determines a starting point, the better the journey can be planned. Your starting point is determined by the current state of your data, information technology and data-mining assets. Establishing a starting point often requires a formalised sales, costs and systems audit. The objective of such an audit varies by company, but generally includes an analysis of 1. sources of demand, 2. sources of supply, and 3. methods of effective management. Most firms starting this journey discover that they hold very little non-transactional information in electronic form. Even information that is held may be of inconsistent quality or unavailable for on-line manipulation and analysis by decision makers.

Most IT managers do not recognise the depth of information required for interactive marketing. The activities and analyses that you envision for the future should act as an inventory sheet for evaluating the current situation. Noting the gaps between the current situation and the future, you will want to investigate the various ways of acquiring the data you require. Working with the IT department, as suggested earlier in this chapter, you must quantify the capabilities of the current database management system and exactly what would be required to support your projected requirements. If you lack data-mining skills inside the firm, you must determine what it would take to develop those skills and compare the cost against outsourcing.

A word to the wise for DBMS champions: ensure that you can demonstrate the return on investment for every data and system enhancement that you require. Have a fallback position that you can defend.

Step two: gain commitment to organise for marketing

Organising for the new marketing does not necessarily require any specific organisational structure, but it does require the support of the total management team, especially the chief executive and the board of directors. Nonetheless, the organisational structure must facilitate cross-functional management of marketing activities and holistic organisational learning. Structure must be flexible enough to change with the needs of the market.

Success rests on a holistic, cross-functional audit of every activity that impacts on interaction in the firm. Every activity and its constituent tasks must be understood in terms of its purpose, objectives, standards and impact on marketing success. For example, what relational types and relational stages are the focus of this task? How does the task impact on customer satisfaction? Who performs this task? With what objectives and to what standards? Could the work be organised or managed differently to improve the customer's experience or lower costs? Would automated processing help?

The right answers to these and other questions will require participation and commitment, not only from senior managers but also from many associates lower in the organisation. It is important to remember that the final system will impact on many associates and that commitment is required at all levels of the company. Consult widely and often during the process. Make this everyone's idea.

Step three: agree on a DBMS design

Even the most detailed audit will often leave grey areas concerning the future system requirements. These must be negotiated with the various functional teams. If you have consulted widely and often, then you will know the positions of most players in the organisation towards interactive marketing. It is vitally important to negotiate a database structure that will allow the types of interactive marketing activities required. Do not fall into the trap of running referral market and influence market databases on stand-alone portable computers, as this prejudices interactive marketing analysis. For example, many firms think it is important to link referral sources to new and existing business. Consider all influences on the various elements of the value chain. The more holistically you approach managing interaction, the more competitive advantage you will gain.

It can be quite exciting to contemplate the benefits of holding more information about account holders, where only limited information has been available. Knowing a customer's demographic, psychographic and behavioural characteristics reveals important information for qualifying and quantifying customer needs. The implication for selling appropriate 'add-on' products and for developing new products is obvious. However, one should not mistake such capabilities as the destination.

- *Holding DBMS seminars*

  Seminars make a lot of sense. All interested parties offer input into the process and become 'early-owners' of the new systems. DBMS seminars should answer the question, 'What characteristics, influences and factors are likely to be linked with the purchase and consumption of our products?'

  Many effective leaders hold two seminars to decide what information will be kept on the new DBMS. A first seminar allows product management, sales management, the marketing research house and the advertising agency to agree what information would be available in an ideal world where costs are irrelevant. It is not unusual for 250 customer characteristics to emerge for future analysis in a first seminar. These should be prioritised and used as input for a second seminar where managers from other functional areas attend. The second seminar should focus the discussion on the return on investments in data and system enhancements. A typical company might decide to capture 100 characteristics from existing files and outside sources and to capture 25 additional characteristics over time for future use.

  The seminars may be the proper time to consider geography as a possible unit of analysis. In many product categories, the recent development of cheap and powerful GIS packages has encouraged marketers around the globe to explore the utility of geography as a relevant customer characteristic for analysis. Geography remains one of the most powerful links to individual differences, social influences and situational factors in the new South Africa. Maps offer an intuitively appealing way to explore customer relationships.

However, desktop mapping is only part of the GIS revolution and many firms using GIS actually spend little time looking at maps.

- *Design customer relationships into the DBMS*

  One reason for GIS is the practical problems encountered when agreeing on the basis for identifying customer relationships within the database. Consider John Smith and Bev Jones (fictitious names). They have lived together for ten years and bank with Acme, where they hold a total of six accounts in three branches. Would an Acme staff member be aware of the total amount of business at jeopardy if a dispute over service charges arises concerning a small cheque account of John's? Is the J Smith of 23 Commissioner Street the same as John Smith of P O Box 19768, Johannesburg 2000?

  Accounts are not relationships. Every DBMS should have a unique identifier, such as a national ID number, so that multiple accounts can be traced to single relationships. The DBMS must also require verifiable information. Even in South Africa, one of the few countries to have a consistent verifiable identity number, clerks fail to capture identity numbers unless forced to by database entry rules. Many IT managers at banks and credit bureaux can tell you about song titles and other random text entered into customer address fields. On-line electronic access to current customer information is a basic requirement by client services people, debt collection or marketing people who contact customers. If the firm desires a quality data platform for micro-managing customer value, attrition and profitability, then the IT team must provide the functionality to organise information about customer relationships and make it available to everyone in the organisation who needs it.

  GIS may be an alternative solution. Information in a GIS is organised by geocode. A geocode is a reference code that identifies the latitude and longitude of an address. If a geocode can be appended to every record in the database, records related to it can be linked for easy review.

Step four: identify market segments

Once customer relationships are identified and linked to some basis for identification and analysis, companies can begin to explore ways to identify customer types and profile the customer base.

There is a tendency these days to confuse profiling and segmentation. Segmentation answers the question, 'What characteristics distinguish different types of people within the defined market?' The exercise generally produces a handful of segments that serve as the basis for strategic planning and action throughout the firm. For instance, segmentation analysis may define a segment called *Financial Strugglers*, consisting of people with the lowest household income, education and average revenue of all segments. Financial Strugglers may have a high incidence of complaints about service fees – accounting for some 45 per cent of all such complaints. This may suggest considerable saving in customer care if future offers to this segment include service charges in the basic price. Another group, called *Experientials*, may have the highest incidence of slow payment, but be among the lowest overall bad debt risks. Enhanced data would reveal that Experientials travel frequently and that 78 per cent have flown during the past year. Promotions to Experientials should include easy, direct-debit payment methods. A frequent-flyer programme might be a great source for prospects.

One should never make the mistake of segmenting the database and assuming those segments represent the total market without substantial proof that this is so. Nonetheless, it is possible to segment the database and then to determine the presence of those segments in the total market if one begins with sufficient information about the total market, and can marry that information to the database with a high degree of reliability.

It should also be noted that variables which do not provide much help in segmentation can be very useful for other purposes. For instance, many of the lifestyle characteristics, such as hobbies and air flight behaviour, may aid communications or promotional strategies.

- *Generic segmentation schemes*

    As mentioned earlier, many external sources can provide a generic segmentation scheme. These 'one size fits all' segmentation schemes probably won't present an optimal segmentation scheme for a particular product. An optimal market segmentation solution often requires a unique blend of statistical techniques and analysis, dictated by the quality and quantity of the data available for analysis and the inter-relationships of the available consumer characteristics. Complicating the exercise further, market segments blur as passing time influences changing individual characteristics, social influences and situation factors. Many companies have been surprised to discover that traditional market segment definitions no longer have any link to consumer preferences or behaviour.

    Brief the analysts to 'stick to the fundamentals' when constructing market segments. Segments should be relatively homogeneous, of sufficient size for profitability, likely to respond to promotional and product appeals of certain types, reachable by communication and distribution, and identifiable when customers or prospects interact with staff. Encourage market analysts to be creative when they explore the relationships between individual character-istics, social influences and situational factors, and the purchase or consumption behaviours of interest. Demographics, psychographics, usage patterns, benefits and related behaviours may all provide maximally-descriptive segment definitions.

    'Off the shelf' generalised segmentation models may not always provide optimal segmentation solutions, but they can be desirable for many applications. For example, firms with budgetary constraints may find that generic schemes reduce analysis costs and the total cost of adding a segment code to the database – at the cost of precision, of course. Generalised segmentation models can also be available on-line when credit checks are done. Thus, a wider range of characteristics can be utilised to model credit risk as well.

The strong emphasis on market segmentation may seem to run against the conventional wisdom of 'markets of one' these days. It does not. The new technologies allow marketing activities to be directed to individuals based on individual differences, environmental influences and past behaviours (such as the response to previous offers). It would be great if a DBMS could recommend a strategic action for every interaction, on-demand and in real time. However, such a system is beyond the capabilities and resources of most companies. Working at the level of individuals may be impractical for many industries or for some kinds of interactions with customers.

Step five: profile the customer base

Segments must live in the hearts and minds of the firm. When a segment definition is appended to every customer's file, associates know at a glance the type of customer with whom they are interacting or with whom they plan to interact. This is true, regardless of the basis of segmentation. A fast-moving consumer goods marketer might decide to segment the market into geographic areas with relatively homogeneous characteristics related to purchase, or to segment on the basis of the product mix sold by distributing outlets. The basis of segmentation might be the relative importance of certain personal values – it does not matter, so long as associates have some way to access the segmentation classification of every customer before or during interaction.

The value of segmentation is highest when segments can be tied to individual records in the DBMS. Profiling determines the presence of the segments in the database, the characteristics of people within the database and how different segments behave. Establishing the profile of the existing base sets a benchmark for understanding customer acquisition and retention. Profiling customers by neighbourhood, lifestage and gender may reveal distinct profiles for certain product purchases and be helpful in formulating marketing strategies. Although most marketing teams would be happy to profile their customer base by such basic demographic characteristics, data cleaning and enhancement make it possible for analysts to provide much more meaningful analysis.

Step six: begin interactive relationship marketing

Profiling opens the door to interactive relationship marketing. At this point, the DBMS should become operational. It is important to focus early efforts on DBMS users. Having achieved buy-in during the wide consultation process, the major focus should shift to researching users in the earliest days of implementing the new systems. What is different than was expected? How would the system provide better results? What's difficult to use? What types of reports would users like to see that are not available? It is important to respond quickly to these internal marketing forces so that the system becomes an integral part of the company management practice.

Even if you have consulted widely and often during the DBMS design phase, do not be surprised to find requests for additional data fields and, to this end, your project management plan should allow resources to provide changes to include more data. However, you should also be aware that users often request more when encountering even the most well-designed DBMS. But users often fail to use the functionality at hand, and it is wise to probe this and to direct usage toward the functionality that has been delivered. So don't be overly concerned about small requests. You will find that the majority of requests will be for customised reports during the first few months and that you can deliver these very quickly.

Step seven: ongoing analysis and management

It is vitally important to see the DBMS as a never-ending journey. Weekly meetings should be held for the first three months after commissioning the new system to encourage feedback and plot new DBMS strategies. It is important to survey users regularly concerning their perceptions about the DBMS and future enhancements. Many executives find that a committee of the Board is useful for ongoing evaluation. Monthly meetings would seem to be most appropriate.

Summary

This chapter explored the nature and management of interaction in the new interactive, relational marketing environment. Strong marketers plan and manage relationships with many different types of markets. They also plan strategies for the stage of relationship they enjoy with each participant in those markets. Comprehensive management of interaction requires a holistic understanding of the relationships held by each participant in the value chain. These relationships are important network marketing assets.

The chapter also presented five new ways of thinking about marketing management. *Marketing as interactive relational network management* includes the management of relationships based on a comprehensive understanding of types and stages of relationships. *Marketing as a cross-functional activity* requires the identification of every activity performed in the acquisition and maintenance of customers, and the adoption of a marketing approach by every associate responsible for those activities – even if those activities are performed for internal customers. *Marketing as information management* requires the use of a range of new interactive marketing tools to acquire information about customers and prospects, and about new database technologies to store and manage that information. *Marketing as acquisition and retention management* requires a change of focus to share of customer and to customer retention management, as well as competency in statistical techniques to mine the marketing database management system. *Marketing as transaction and relationship management* requires competency in new technologies that automate transactions so that the company can achieve a low cost-per-transaction competitive position, and also the skills to understand customers who do not wish to conduct ongoing relationships with the company.

The next chapter details, in part, the organisational process of transition required to adopt interactive relationship marketing. More importantly, it ties all the previous sections together and shows how to implement strong marketing strategies.

ENDNOTES

1 See Guglielmo (1996).
2 Well reviewed by Peck (1995).
3 Buzzell & Gale(1987).
4 Collins & Payne (1991).
5 Cross & Smith (1995: 174-175).
6 See Cross & Smith (1995); Payne (1995).
7 See Pfeffer (1992).
8 I can think of no better book that describes the needs of this and subsequent phases of relationships than Berry (1995).
9 Cable News Network (1997).
10 Kelley & Sanderson (1996).
11 See Frank (1996).
12 See Morrall (1995).
13 Ashton (1996).
14 See Monmonier (1996).
15 Bishop (1996) is an accessible book that provides detailed information on the new tools and their use.
16 Wildstrom (1996a) reviews some recently launched software of this type.
17 See Wildstrom (1996b).
18 Heubusch (1997).
19 Coy, Hof & Judge (1996) review the problems associated with Internet usage and future projections.
20 Castelli (1996).
21 Bosch (1996).
22 If you want to know more than appears here, Kroenke (1995) is an excellent introduction to database theory and practise. Kendall & Kendall (1995) address most issues confronted when contemplating a new system or when evaluating a current system.
23 Adapted from Kroenke (1995: 27).
24 A legacy system is an existing computer system largely based on older technology. Many companies continue to use legacy systems that perform an originally-intended function well.
25 Networking consists of cables that connect system components and network software. Novell Netware and Microsoft NT are two popular networking software packages.
26 Jackson & Wang (1994).
27 Source: SPL Data Warehousing Division.

28 Return on promotion is calculated in many ways, but can be thought of as the contribution margin produced by a marketing activity (i.e. a new product, a sales promotion or a direct mail offer) minus the cost of sales. In practice, budgetary constraints generally preclude marketing programmes directed at the entire base of profitable customers and many firms establish a hurdle rate above the firm's cost of capital or some other nominal rate. The hurdle rate can be computed using the following formula: where ROI is the return on a promotional interaction, CM is the contribution margin and CO is the cost of acquiring an order.

PART FIVE

Managing Focus

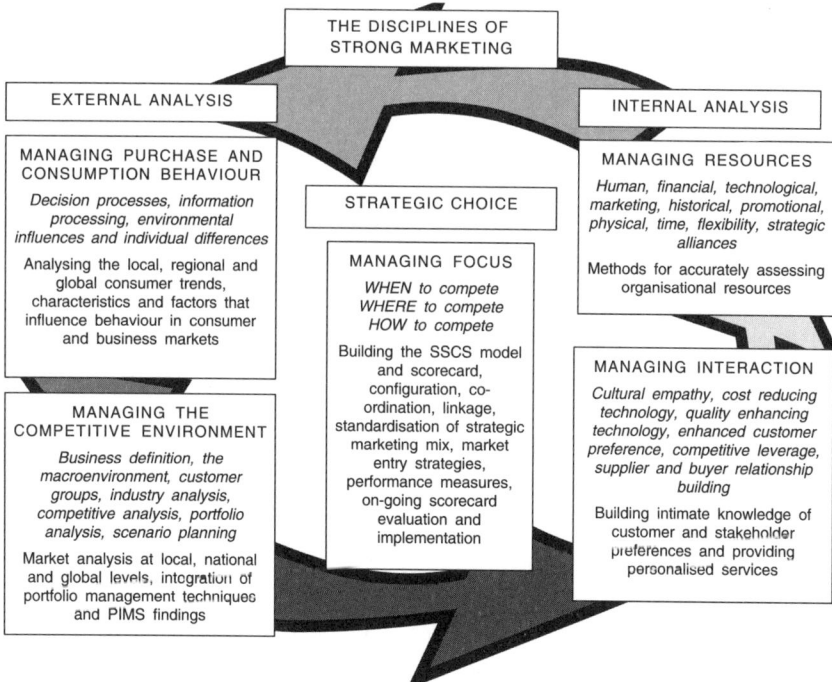

THE DISCIPLINES OF
STRONG MARKETING

EXTERNAL ANALYSIS

INTERNAL ANALYSIS

MANAGING PURCHASE AND CONSUMPTION BEHAVIOUR

Decision processes, information processing, environmental influences and individual differences

Analysing the local, regional and global consumer trends, characteristics and factors that influence behaviour in consumer and business markets

MANAGING THE COMPETITIVE ENVIRONMENT

Business definition, the macroenvironment, customer groups, industry analysis, competitive analysis, portfolio analysis, scenario planning

Market analysis at local, national and global levels, integration of portfolio management techniques and PIMS findings

STRATEGIC CHOICE

MANAGING FOCUS

WHEN to compete
WHERE to compete
HOW to compete

Building the SSCS model and scorecard, configuration, co-ordination, linkage, standardisation of strategic marketing mix, market entry strategies, performance measures, on-going scorecard evaluation and implementation

MANAGING RESOURCES

Human, financial, technological, marketing, historical, promotional, physical, time, flexibility, strategic alliances

Methods for accurately assessing organisational resources

MANAGING INTERACTION

Cultural empathy, cost reducing technology, quality enhancing technology, enhanced customer preference, competitive leverage, supplier and buyer relationship building

Building intimate knowledge of customer and stakeholder preferences and providing personalised services

16 Implementing Strong Marketing

The process of managing focus

Years ago, the late Tony Factor and I appeared on a TV programme to support the SA National Council for Child and Family Welfare. While we waited for the programme to begin, we chatted about retailing and business in general. I was surprised that the legendary South African discount retailer knew so much about my employer, Johnson & Johnson. When I asked Factor to what he attributed his years of success, he replied without hesitation 'Focus'. 'Think of your own company — babies, mothers, health care — J&J were there when you were born, they'll be there when you die. Always remember, it's the little lady in high heels that breaks floor tiles, not the 150 kg man.'

This book has proposed an analytic, cross-functional approach to marketing that spans the organisation. Purchase and consumption, competition, resources and interaction have been explored as important and inter-related disciplines of strong marketing. However, these disciplines cannot produce great things without the focus of 'the little lady in high heels'.

Many executives think of cutting the product line when the topic of conversation turns to focus, but the strong marketing discipline of managing focus involves much more. Strong marketing is continual analysis, delivery, detail management and learning. Managing focus brings these competencies to bear in the arena of choice. In fact, managing focus is the discipline that gives life to strong marketing by focusing attention and resources on the most appropriate opportunities. It is the skill of choosing when, where and how to compete, of defining the battlefield and of changing the nature of competition to favour one's own competencies and resources.

WHY FOCUS IS MORE IMPORTANT IN DEVELOPING NATIONS

Early visions of revenue and profit growth become bitter memories of lost shareholder value when companies lose focus. The belief that managerial excellence can overcome industry naivety is a frequent precursor of doom. The siren call can take the form of an unfocused diversification.

According to Jack Ries[1], IBM (Rolm), Coca-Cola (Columbia Pictures), Metropolitan Life (Century 21 Real Estate), Chrysler (Gulfstream Aerospace), Eastman Kodak (Sterling Drug), Dow Chemical (Marrion Merrill Dow) and Matsushita (MCA) are among the leading companies that learned sobering lessons when acquisitions (listed in brackets) failed to deliver promised synergies (all these companies divested within ten years). American Express, Sears, Xerox, Prudential Insurance and Westinghouse Electric are among the well-known companies that ventured into financial services and learned similar lessons.

Jack Ries compares highly diversified companies from developing countries that are attempting to break into global markets, to dinosaurs. According to Ries, the small size of developing nation economies does not make firms uncompetitive in global industries. It is the failure to focus and to build the specialised competencies and resources necessary to compete globally. By choosing diversification in home market industries over specialisation and global expansion, Ries argues that developing nation businesses create the conditions that make it hard to export and compete with larger, more established companies. Using the process explored in this chapter, South African firms can bring the full might of the new marketing to bear — locally and globally.

DECIDING WHERE TO BUILD THE NEW MARKETING

Strong marketing requires the right organisational structure in order to be most effective. Before beginning strong marketing, the senior executive team must choose an appropriate unit or units for building and managing strong marketing so that a project team can be appointed within each unit. Companies competing in one industry can often appoint one team to complete the required project team tasks. In more diversified or geographically-dispersed companies, the senior management team may find itself faced with some options to consider.

This book has explored and developed some concepts that are important to consider when choosing appropriate units for strong marketing.

- The basic assumption of the SBU model — that smaller structures focus better on marketplace opportunities and facilitate the achievement of overall goals and strategies — is well-accepted[2].

- Business entities are bundles of competencies acting in concert with other value-chain members[3](see Chapter 14). External factors, such as changing customer needs, blurring industry boundaries, strategic alliances and competitor moves, influence the competitiveness of the total bundle of competencies.

268

- In practice, ownership, administration, remuneration, government regulation and other issues often require the establishment or maintenance of separate business entities, although the various entities may have an overall common strategic purpose or common set of core competencies. Business entities, whether partnerships, separate companies, joint ventures or other forms, can be difficult to change once structured.

Strong marketing must be managed through and within these essentially artificial distinctions in the total business.

THE STRONG MARKETING UNIT (SMU)

Thus, senior management must consider the needs of the total business and the practicalities of established business entities when deciding where to build strong marketing in the organisation. For clarity, I will refer to the organisational building blocks of the new marketing as strong marketing units. SMUs may be an existing business entity, a part of a business entity, a committee or other formalised reporting body from many business entities or a combination of these. SMUs may be required at multiple levels of the organisation, depending on the scope of activities, the core competencies and the depth and breadth of the current product offerings of each company or strategic business unit (see Chapter 7).

Consider Liberty Life, one of South Africa's few multinationals. Liberty Life's commercial and retail property interests in the UK property market mirror significant interests in South Africa. Liberty's current structure suggests that strong marketing in the property businesses could be managed in the existing property SBUs (strategic business units) and, additionally, at country-level (through FIT (First International Trust) and Liberty Life Properties). Alternatively, Liberty might choose to manage strong marketing in the commercial and retail property SBUs, then at the commercial and retail property divisional levels, and then in an overall property corporation. Larger companies often identify many options for organising strong marketing, but Liberty will avoid defining SMUs too finely or too broadly. Defining SMUs too finely may limit vision and opportunities for scale or scope economies and result in duplicated assets, costs and activities. Defining SMUs too broadly may impair focus and allow the scope of the business to exceed organisational competencies — in other words, more diversified strategies are less successful (see Chapter 7).

ROOTING OUT DUPLICATION: THE 4Cs ANALYSIS

Exploring the nature of SBU linkages often reveals opportunities for integrated marketing, resource sharing and other factors that influence SMU definitions.

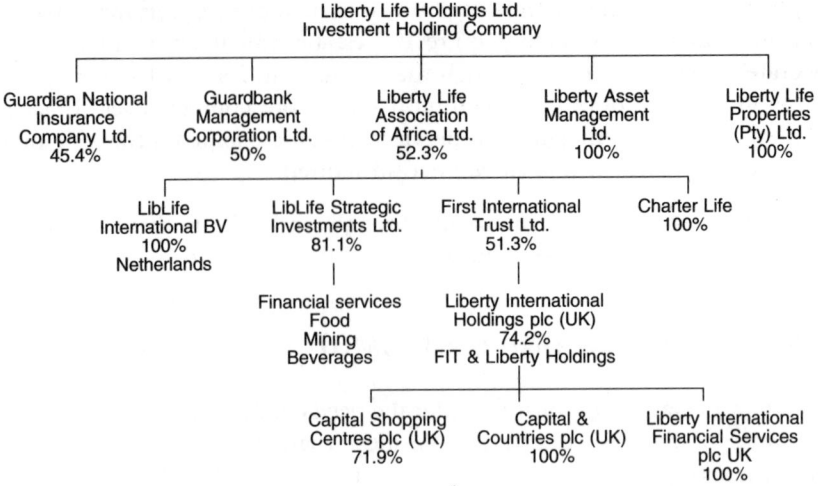

Figure 16.1 The Liberty Life Group companies[4]

The team must consider relevant aspects of purchase and consumption, competition, resources and interaction. Exploring the 4Cs (customers, competitors, communications and competencies) can highlight integration opportunities and duplication[5].

Not always obvious, duplication is a great destroyer of EVA (economic value-added, see Chapter 14), and opportunities to eliminate it should be pursued. For instance, although associates from three SBUs calling on the same customer would ring many bells, less obvious opportunities for group research may not. Duplication may suggest areas for SMU co-operation or focus attention on the creation of a higher order SMU that would include multiple business entities.

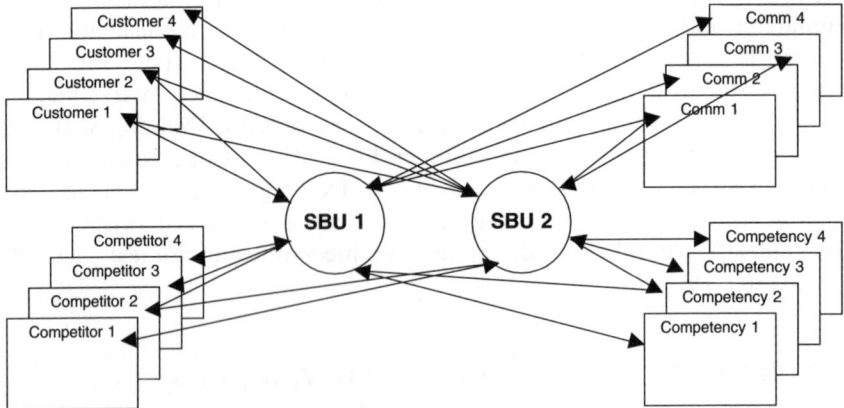

Figure 16.2 Identifying opportunities for SBU integration and co-operation using a 4Cs analysis

THINKING OF TOMORROW

From the outset, the senior management team must also be sensitive to possible changes within the organisation fostered by the new marketing. Globalisation is a common issue that requires consideration in current and future strategies. Industry-specific factors may also influence the choice of an appropriate level for managing strong marketing. The assumptions that underlie the SMU choice should be committed to writing for later evaluation as the process of building strong marketing unfolds.

Although a unique final structure will emerge in every company, some general guidelines are applicable:

- The SMUs will include a relatively distinct set of customers, competencies or competitors that are its major focus.

- Significant opportunities for integration and co-operation will be explored and exploited.

- The SMUs will facilitate the competent management of customers, competitors, competencies and communications that are the heart of strong marketing.

- Performance models and scorecards will be built at single or multiple levels of the enterprise, depending on whether these can lead to meaningful strategic management decisions at the corporate, divisional and operating company level.

- The SMUs will facilitate organisation-wide learning and continual renewal, including the redefinition of SMUs if necessary.

THE FIRST SEMINAR: BUILDING CONSENSUS

Calling senior managers from the various SMUs together for a seminar is the final preliminary step. The objective of the first seminar is to build consensus that a transformation to the new marketing is required, and to constitute the SMU project teams. The project teams should include the associates who will be responsible for managing the new marketing. It is important to include some associates responsible for performing day-to-day marketing tasks. Associates in these boundary roles can often analyse current levels of service provision, customer satisfaction and operating standards much faster than management. Outsiders, such as strategic alliance partners, advertising agencies and marketing research houses can play a role in the meeting.

The project teams must transcend departmental, divisional and hierarchical differences if strong marketing is to be built, and team-building sessions are an important part of the first seminar. Attendees from the various departments, divisions and hierarchical levels of the enterprise should be encouraged to share their perceptions of the company's marketing. No doubt, marketing will be perceived as a department — a set of pretty pictures cast in print and electronic media, or a group of 'sales guys' — to associates from other disciplines. In fact, many people performing important marketing tasks will probably not see themselves as marketing people. Many associates may feel defensive about a team of people looking at their work through a magnifying glass.

The project teams should leave the first seminar with a brief to collect facts, identify information gaps and conduct analyses for the report back in the second seminar. Teams must avoid the temptation to begin drawing conclusions and formulating strategy until the analytic process paints a reliable and holistic portrait of the SMU's current situation. The team should be assured that senior management wants to avoid an atmosphere of incrimination and personal faultfinding. The analysis will turn up things that could be improved (be very suspicious if it does not). Attendees must understand that they will be building strong marketing in the second phase of the programme, albeit under the guidance of senior management.

ESTABLISHING A STARTING POINT

Many teams will leave the first seminar impressed with the concept of the new marketing. They may be tempted to complete the analysis quickly by 'filling in the blanks' using information at hand and guided by the accepted 'truths' that guide the business today. Teams should be encouraged to realise that you need two things to plan a journey: a reliable map and knowledge of your present position. If you don't know where you are, you have no idea in which direction to proceed. If you do not have a map, you have no idea how far or in which direction to go. Thus, the project team must explore the battlefield and the SMU's current competitive situation. Teams that take shortcuts during this first phase of the strong marketing process short-change themselves for the entire process.

Some teams may complain about the depth of analysis required. These teams should be encouraged to proceed and assured that 'analysis paralysis' can be avoided — if the teams begin with existing or easily acquired information and then identify and prioritise additional information that will improve the analysis. The traditional audit is a useful first step (see Chapter 11). Once they begin the analysis, they will discover that most of the information is at hand. The teams will transit two broad streams of analysis.

Stream one: identify market segments

This book has addressed two main streams of analysis. The first stream develops a comprehensive understanding of purchase and consumption behaviour to identify market segments and their detailed preferences. At the end of this stream of analysis, the team should know the purchase and consumption preferences of each segment and understand the implications for action by the SMU. After the analysis is complete, the team should be able to complete a fact sheet such as Table 16.1 (page 274) from memory. Facts sheets are useful for summarising the analysis conducted in this stream. Figure 16.3 (page 275) shows how the various analyses of Part 1 of this book impact on segmentation of a market.

Team members should be encouraged to evaluate the SMU's previous activities and competitive activities critically. Many teams will have a pre-existing notion about segments and customer preferences, but the team must be careful to qualify such knowledge. Every firm could serve customers better and every competitor is doing some things right. Honesty is of critical importance.

The linkages between the stages of the decision process and meaning world associations, information processing, environmental influences and individual differences must be identified. If current information does not exist, the team must validate its previous knowledge about these linkages. It is wise to bring the marketing research house and advertising agency into this stream of analysis. The advertising agency probably conducts media analysis anyway, and can contribute useful knowledge about information processing and media consumption. One must be careful to consider what marketers say about themselves and what others say about marketers. Advertising agencies some-times disregard the latter and make the false assumption that consumers have internalised every communication element from competitive advertisements. The research house can contribute knowledge from past marketing research about the behaviour, preferences and product usage of various generalised classes of consumers. Involving these outside marketing partners has the additional benefit of helping to identify needed information, its priority and cost.

Stream two: environment, competition and resource analysis

A second stream of analysis develops a comprehensive understanding about how the SMUs and competitors are satisfying the needs of the various segments in the current environment and in the expected future environments. The analysis can proceed along a number of well-defined routes in which the completion of one analytic technique provides input into another technique. Figure 16.4 (page 276) highlights the links between the various analytic techniques. For example, macroenvironmental analysis provides input into the opportunity and threats grid and the opportunity and threats matrix. Experience curve analysis yields information useful in the determination of the product life cycles, the BCG Growth-Share matrix, and so on.

Resource analysis is conducted for the unit and its competitors in order to understand the competencies and resources required and currently at hand. It is very important to consider the importance of the revenue and profit streams created by business units to overall corporate objectives of the unit and its competitors by conducting stratification analysis. Thus, the team builds an

TARGET SEGMENT PORTRAIT: FEMALE EXECUTIVE HEAVY CELLPHONE USER		
Characteristics (over 75 per cent incidence): Company director of a firm employing more than 100 people, average R857 per month total subscription and airtime, the firm pays the bill, over 500 minutes airtime per month, HHI (household income) over R250 000 per year, aged 40-55, female, English- or Afrikaans-speaking, time pressured, easily frustrated by complex cellular handset commands, demands cognitive simplicity or calls customer care for assistance, requires itemised bill and will refuse direct debit, uses voice mail, primarily calls between 7am and 7pm, low off-peak usage, travels overseas twice per year for an average of two weeks, travels out of town at least three days each month, reads financial press, interested in fitness, flea markets and scuba diving, will not visit an outlet and demands personal visit by salesperson.		

Segment perceptions
How companies currently influence purchase and consumption

Need recognition	Very little communication targeted at value-added services. Communication about tariffs.
Search	Traditional media and sales. Heavy spend.
Pre-purchase alt evaluation	No meaningful differentiation at service provider level. Network differentiation on coverage is disappearing.
Purchase	Expansion of retail sector. Commoditisation. Packaged deals with emergency services and accessories. Handset discounting.
Post-purchase alt evaluation	Smaller service providers call clients.
Divestment	Some service providers take trade-ins for upgrades.
Satisfaction	Satisfaction research conducted by network operators.

Dominant meaning chains (personal effectiveness, power, convenience, security)

ATTRIBUTE	CONSEQUENCE	VALUES
Mobility	Can communicate anywhere	Personal effectiveness: convenience, productivity, security, control, power
Voice mail	Portable answering machine	Privacy, control, security
Network coverage	In-touch anywhere in the world	Personal effectiveness: convenience, productivity, security, control, power
Lightweight handset	Easy to carry and conceal	Convenience, ease of use, attractive

Major opportunities

Revenue growth: Increase use of value-added services
Value enhancement: Decrease calls to Customer Care Dept. and need for personal assistance. Employ SMS call-back facility to scroll step-by-step instructions for value-added services and common problems across handset screen by February 1999.

Table 16.1 *A fictitious segment fact sheet*

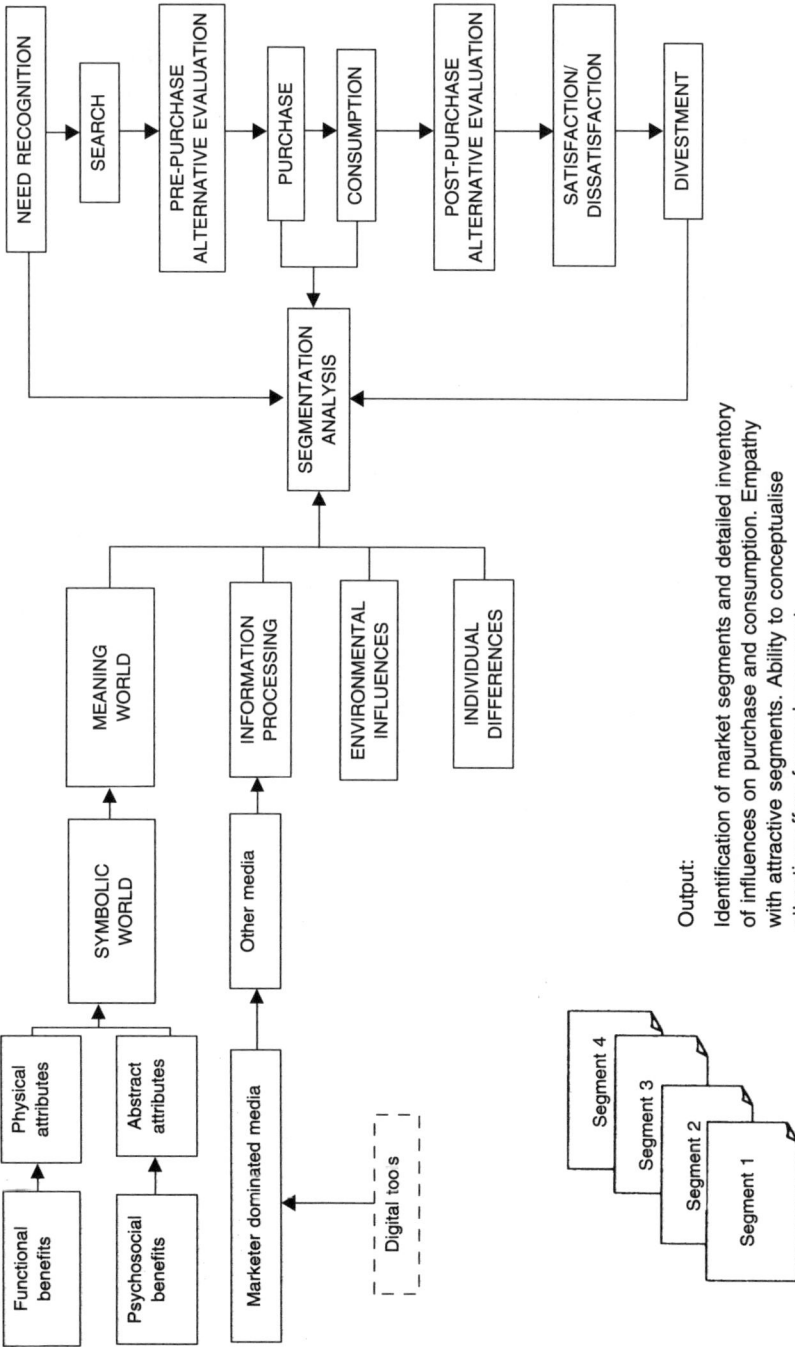

NEED RECOGNITION → SEARCH → PRE-PURCHASE ALTERNATIVE EVALUATION → PURCHASE → CONSUMPTION → POST-PURCHASE ALTERNATIVE EVALUATION → SATISFACTION/DISSATISFACTION → DIVESTMENT

SEGMENTATION ANALYSIS

MEANING WORLD
INFORMATION PROCESSING
ENVIRONMENTAL INFLUENCES
INDIVIDUAL DIFFERENCES

SYMBOLIC WORLD

Physical attributes
Abstract attributes

Functional benefits
Psychosocial benefits

Other media

Marketer dominated media

Digital tools

Output:
Identification of market segments and detailed inventory of influences on purchase and consumption. Empathy with attractive segments. Ability to conceptualise attractive offers for each segment.

Segment 4
Segment 3
Segment 2
Segment 1

Figure 16.3 The inter-relationship of stream one techniques leading to segment identification and understanding

275

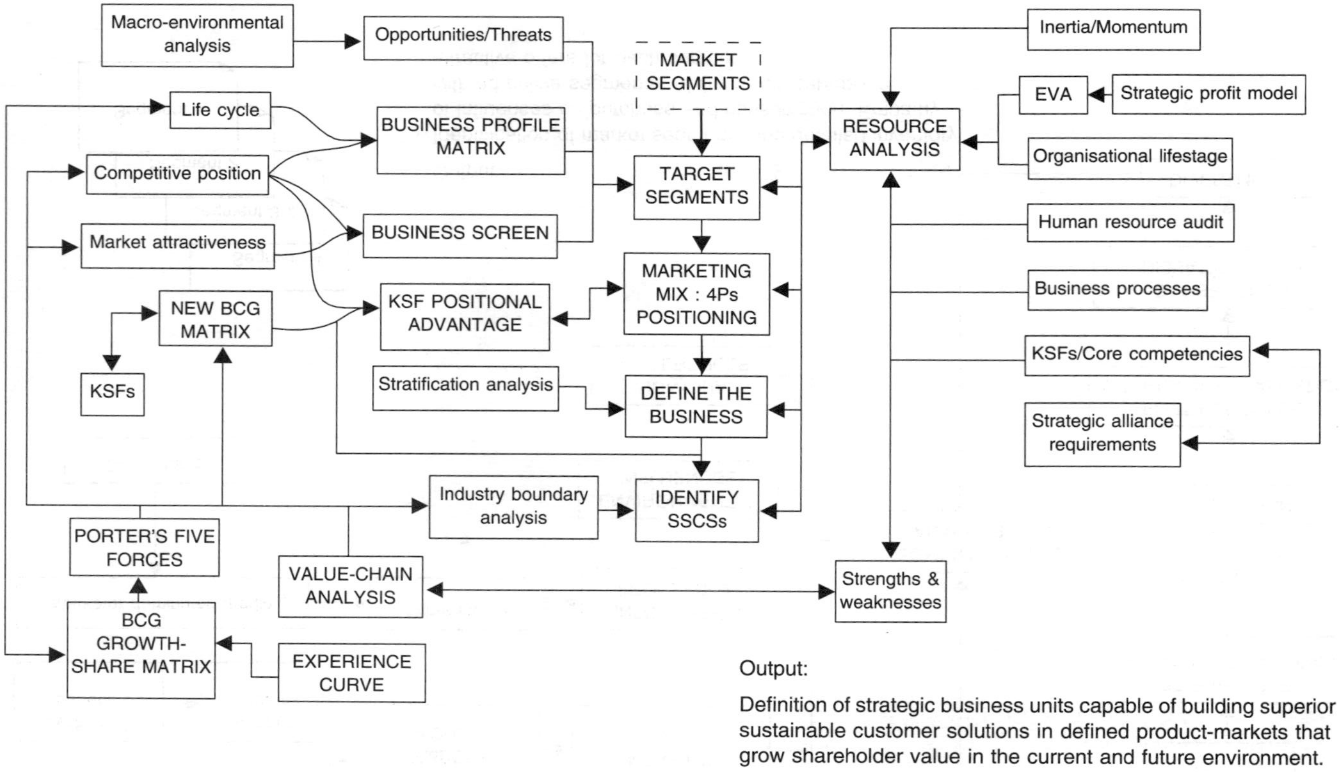

Figure 16.4 Stream two techniques for building knowledge of environmental and internal competitiveness

Output:

Definition of strategic business units capable of building superior sustainable customer solutions in defined product-markets that grow shareholder value in the current and future environment.

understanding of the target markets selected and served by the unit and its competitors, the positioning strategies at play and the strategies most likely to lead to superior sustainable customer solutions (SSCSs).

THE SECOND SEMINAR: BUILDING SYNTHESIS, LEVERAGE AND INSIGHT

On completing the analysis, the team should identify, quantify and qualify the gaps in its existing knowledge. Then, senior management should convene a second seminar so the results of the analysis, tentative objectives and measures and gaps in present knowledge can be presented. The second seminar is called to give the senior management team an opportunity to review the results of the analysis so that they can build synthesis, focus the SMU team on measurable objectives, maximise the leverage between the various groups and give the SMU project teams insight into the total group strong marketing effort. It is important to avoid the situation where individual SMUs maximise returns to the overall detriment of the enterprise. It is not necessary that SMU teams attend presentations by other SMUs, and the second seminar can be held on-site in the company's premises.

Those present should debate the vision and mission suggested by the analysis. After the SMU project teams present their findings and knowledge gaps, the senior management team may wish to withdraw to agree the way forward if there is sufficient lack of unity. Comprehensive analysis often creates opportunities for new strategic insights and the senior management team should be willing to test the assumptions that led to the creation of the SMU, to ensure that the assumptions remain valid. The senior management team should also consider opportunities for co-operation between the SMUs. The research required to plug knowledge gaps may be an ideal chance for the SMUs to co-operate and achieve scale economies.

Although the SMU project team will continue to develop objectives and measures as they build the SSCS model and scorecard, the most important output of this session is an agreed vision, mission and tentative list of objectives for the SMU. Once senior management is convinced the teams are ready, the SMU teams should construct the SSCS model and scorecard.

BUILDING THE SSCS MODEL & SCORECARD

The balanced scorecard approach has captured much attention in recent years[6]. The approach originated in the research arm of the well-respected KPMG auditing firm in response to dissatisfaction with the traditional financial accounting model. Kaplan and Norton were responsible for the pioneering year-long multi-company study that popularised balanced scorecards.

The Kaplan-Norton balanced scorecard approach translates the vision and mission statements of the enterprise into objectives and measures, using four perspectives: learning and growth, internal business processes, customers and financial. The scorecards and performance models of the new marketing approach advocated in this book are similar to the Kaplan-Norton balanced scorecard approach. For instance, both approaches utilise the objectives and measures approach popularised by activity-based costing and management[7]. No doubt, companies could come to the same conclusions using both approaches. Nevertheless, some conceptual and procedural differences between the models bear noting.

The new marketing model assumes that the five core disciplines of strong marketing are cross-functional. It assumes that companies focused on developing nation industries and consumers encounter more multicultural and faster-changing markets, requiring a more rigorous understanding of the behavioural aspects of purchase and consumption. It assumes that resources, especially experienced and competent management, are scarce in developing countries and that larger companies are highly diversified at the start of the strong marketing process. Thus, it assumes that the middle managers most responsible for achieving company goals must participate sooner in the process and that resources require more implicit modelling.

Contemporary executives spend much time managing the achievement of non-financial goals important to non-shareholder stakeholders, such as affirmative action or extension of services to the historically disadvantaged. The new marketing recognises that these results can be as important as financial results[8].

There is significant overlap in the internal business process/learning and the interaction/resources perspectives proposed by the two approaches. However, the strong marketing approach focuses management attention on the interaction processes that will determine winners in the new marketing environment. Perhaps the most striking difference between the models concerns the inclusion of competitors in the strong marketing model.

Building the SSCS Model

This section of the chapter details the processes required to build the SSCS model and scorecard for strong marketing.

The SSCS model graphically represents the interactions of the various strong marketing key success factors in each of the four disciplines that constitute the sustainable superior customer solutions. The model and scorecard are tools that institutionalise focus. Management will focus on the key success factors (KSFs), and the SSCS model and scorecard will become the basis for managing the business. Figure 16.5 shows an SSCS model for a financial services provider, such as a bank or insurance company.

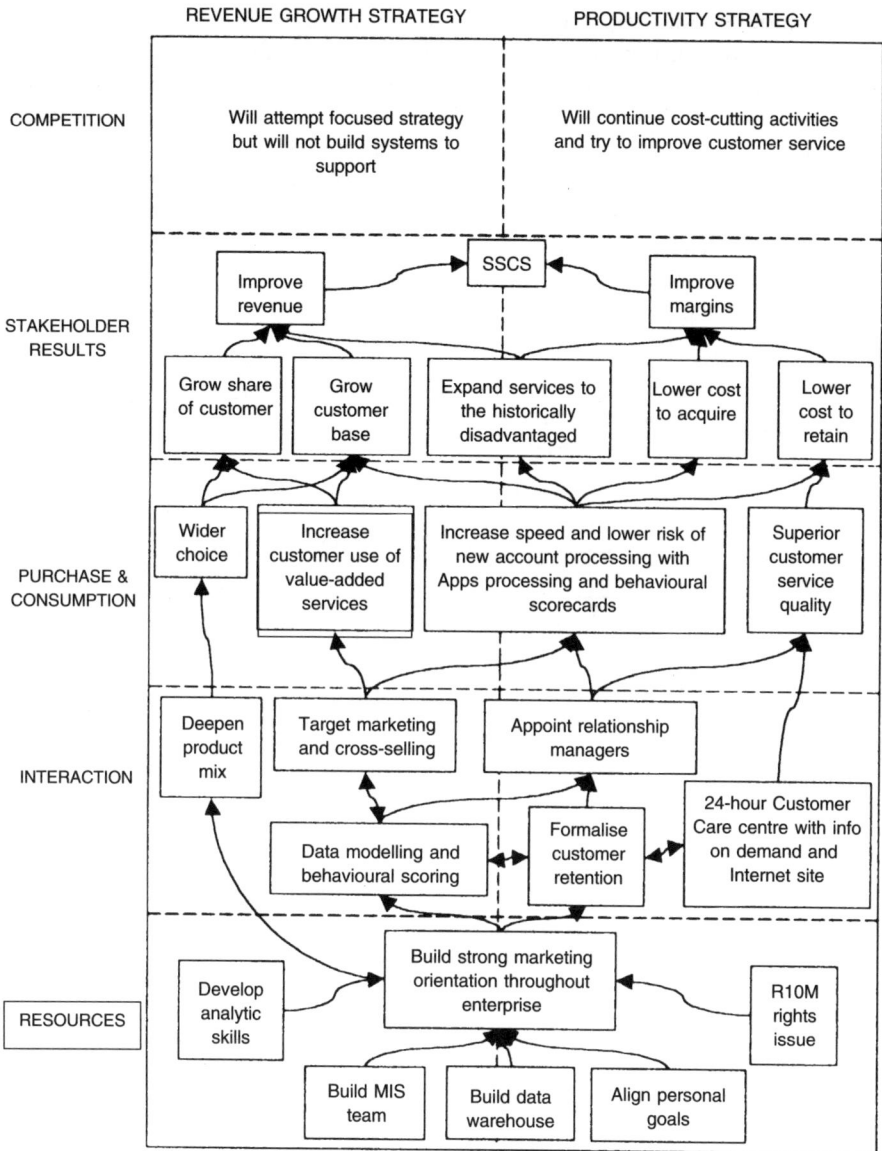

Figure 16.5 *An SSCS model for a financial service provider*

Note that the model consists of two general strategy streams: revenue growth and productivity. The model maps the inter-relationships of key success factors for the four main disciplines and a fifth region for stakeholder results along these two strategy streams. Some KSFs contribute to both strategy streams (e.g. increasing the speed of new account processing with applications processing or appointing account managers).

The model indicates that the financial services company has two main objectives: growing revenue and improving margins. The two major strategic objectives are supported by five key success factors: growing share of customer, growing the customer base, expanding services to the historically disadvantaged, lowering the cost to acquire a customer and lowering the cost to retain a customer. These, in turn, rest on offering new products, increasing the use of value-added services, responding quicker to customer applications for services, employing behavioural scoring to better understand the customer's actual needs and delivering superior service quality.

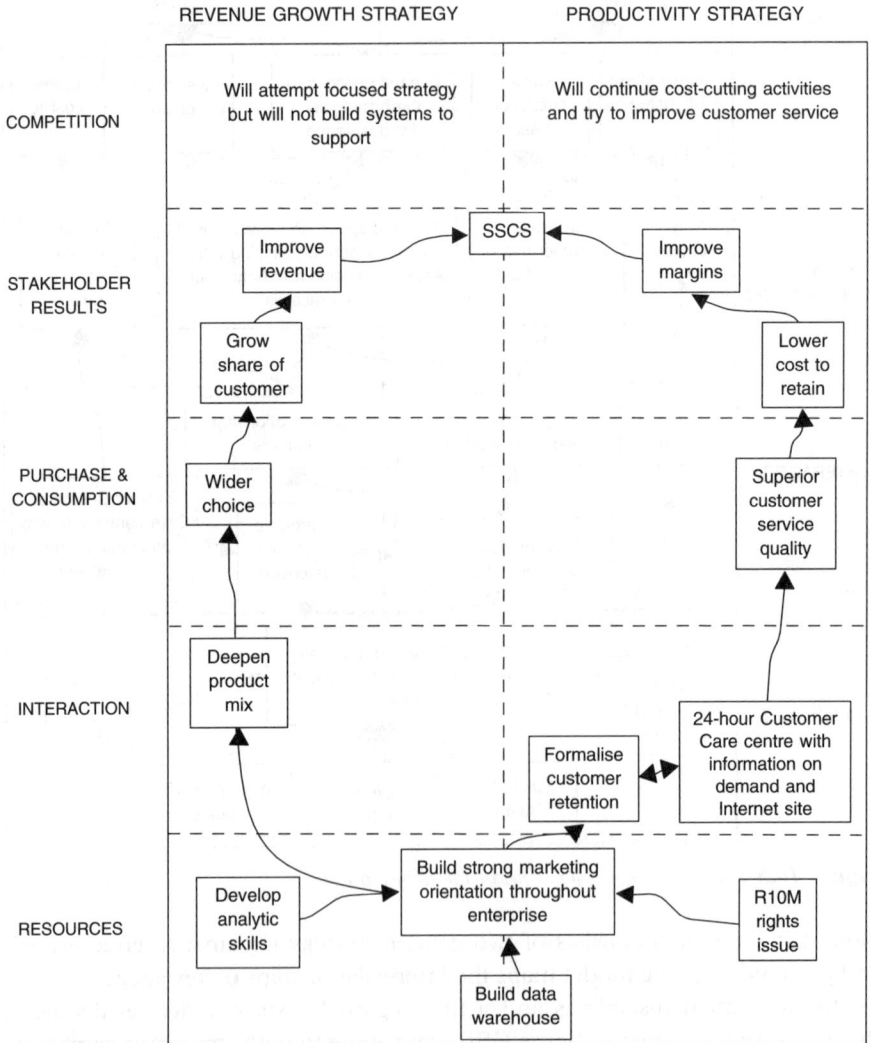

Figure 16.5(a) *Two streams of the SSCS model for a financial services problem (see figure 16.5)*

Even the simple diagram in Figure 16.5(a) may be confusing to some newcomers to the approach. Said differently, one way in which the company will achieve an SSCS is by improving revenue. Growing the share of customers is one way to improve revenue. Giving customers a wider choice is one way in which the company will grow its share of customers. Deepening the product mix gives customers a wider choice. Figure 16.5(a) isolates two streams of the model to make it easier to understand. Thus, the data warehouse leads to a strong marketing orientation, which leads to formalised customer retention programmes, and so on.

Asking penetrating questions as each stream is recorded often enriches the model by drawing attention to other requirements. How will the company build a database? (We need more people and approximately R3 million in development funding.) How will we develop analytical resources? (We need to hire additional MIS (management information systems) people and business analysts, and we need R2 million to fund the additional overheads.)

Key results and KSFs do not always positively influence other key results and KSFs in a model. In this example, expanding services to the historically disadvantaged is fraught with difficulties. Lack of market knowledge and prospect of increased risk leads the management team to believe expanding services will have a negative impact on margins during the year. Nevertheless, the expansion of services to the historically disadvantaged is an important aspect of good government relations and the company believes the market sector will eventually be profitable. Thus, the expansion of services is an investment in a future earnings stream.

The SSCS model highlights the importance to this company of building a data warehouse and beginning to model interaction. Data modelling enables attrition analysis for customer retention and identifies clients who deserve individualised attention from the relationship managers. Data modelling also enables cross-selling and target marketing programmes, and automated application processing and credit approval. In fact, the model shows that much of the company's success will rest on its ability to build and mine a data warehouse.

The SSCS model should include specific key success factors from the traditional marketing mix elements of product, price, distribution and promotion. Distribution and promotion strategies should appear in the interaction dimension of the model, while product and price strategies usually appear in the purchase and consumption dimension. The reference to deepening the product mix in the interaction dimension of the current model refers to the focus groups and dialogue activity stream, related to the product strategy of offering consumers a wider choice. The only price element (the time price) identified in this model is the faster application processing KSF. An actual scorecard would include specific strategies for all elements of the traditional marketing mix, including pricing strategies for interest rates or policy premiums.

KEY SUCCESS FACTOR	PERFORMANCE MEASUREMENT	GOALS & OBJ. CURRENT 1 YR TARGET 3 YR TARGET	SUPPORTING ACTIVITIES
RESULTS			
xxx	xxx	xxx	xxx
PURCHASE AND CONSUMPTION			
xxx	xxx	xxx	xxx
INTERACTION			
1. Data modelling	Attrition scorecard Lifetime value model	0, 1 ,3 scorecards 0, 1 ,3 scorecards	Appoint 2 business analysts with appropriate skills
2. Cross-selling	Response model Average number of products per client	0, 1, 3 scorecards 1.3, 1.7, 2.3 products	Appoint 2 business analysts with appropriate skills
3. Target marketing programme	Response model	0, 1, 3 scorecards	Appoint 2 business analysts with appropriate skills
4. Deepen product mix	Number of products	12, 16, 18 total products	4 focus groups per quarter Research budget
5. Appoint relationship managers	Number of associates hired in position. Coverage of top 10 per cent.	0, 64, 82 relationship managers nationally 0 per cent, 65 per cent, 100 per cent	Budget Training Identify top 10 per cent
6. Formalise customer retention	Number of closed accounts monthly Number of saved accounts monthly	2.2 per cent, 1.5 per cent, 1.0 per cent of total base 0.5 per cent, 1.0 per cent, 1.2 per cent of total base	Attrition scorecard Weekly retention report Retention budget
7. Customer care and info on demand	24-hour call centre Hits on WWW site or direct modem access	12, 24, 24 coverage 5 per cent, 20 per cent, 50 per cent of total traffic to website	New call centre software Interface to customer database to record interface Construct WWW site and modem access
RESOURCES			
xxx	xxx	xxx	xxx

Table 16.2 *The interaction KSFs for a financial services company*

Building the SSCS Scorecard

To build the SSCS model, the teams continue to develop and prioritise the KSFs according to the directives given by senior management in the second seminar, and to establish the links between the KSFs, purchase and consumption behaviour, interaction and resources. The final model is a graphical tool for communicating how each variable influences other variables.

The model does not indicate who is doing what, how they are doing it or when. This is the role of the SSCS scorecard. The team isolates performance measurements, objectives and goals for each variable. The KSFs, performance measures, goals and objectives and activities are then formalised in an SSCS scorecard. The scorecard becomes the basis for the SSCS model. Table 16.2 shows the Interaction KSFs from the SSCS model in Figure 16.5 (page 279).

An actual scorecard would be much more detailed, especially concerning the goals and objectives and activities. Always remember to set SMART goals: specific, measurable, achievable, related and time-bound.

I first learned about measurement from David Dowds at Glick's Furniture Rental in the late 1970s. Dowds put systems in place to measure the average number of pieces of furniture rented on a lease, whether room groupings or individual pieces were rented, for which rooms the furniture was rented, the proportion of the rental paid toward accessories, and the apartment communities where the renters resided. We also measured the productivity of our sales team by examining their performance on each of these criteria, and additionally measured their average dollar rental amount and proportion of customers served who actually signed a lease (closing ratio). The closing ratio and average rental were the most important indicators of sales performance. For every client who entered a store, the salespeople would record details of the rental or the reasons why the customer did not conclude a rental agreement. We measured the number of potential customers by placing electronic counters on the doors of each showroom. These statistics were reported to each sales associate in a private weekly meeting, and the key indicators were posted for the entire team to understand how we were progressing as a team. Laggards were not victimised. Everyone pitched in to help them with additional role playing and other assistance. The result was one of the highest average rentals in America. The average closing ratio exceeding 70 per cent in all outlets and 80 per cent in many.

The quality of performance of any activity can be captured by a few key measures. Dowds measured the productivity of our contract delivery fleet by measuring the number of deliveries per truck, the average number of pieces delivered per delivery, the average time per delivery and the average time between deliveries. Not only did it allow our warehouse manager to manage the contract delivery relationship, it allowed warehouse staff to advise customers about delivery times within an hour of the actual time (something most South African furniture retailers still cannot do today!). Dowds measured preferences for furniture styles and upholstered fabrics, carpet colours in apartment communities where the target market was most likely to reside, and the performance of the accounting staff, and even encouraged us to be aware of the effect of showroom lighting and accessories on sales performance.

Realising what Dowds was able to accomplish without the benefit of personal computers and how it focused everyone's attention on the important indicators of performance, I am constantly amazed at how little many managers know about their business. The purpose of an SSCS scorecard is to focus associates and management on measurable indicators of performance related to achieving the company's goals.

THE SSCS MODEL AND SCORECARD AS A BASIS OF INVESTMENT DECISION MAKING

The SSCS model and scorecard also act as a basis for ongoing investment decision making. Capital investment decisions are often based on expected cash flow, payback, internal rate of return, discounted cash flow or EVA. Many investments that appear to make sense from a financial point of view have the potential to dilute focus and ultimately destroy economic value. The SSCS model and scorecard concentrate management's attention on the effect of an investment on achieving the company's true goals, and on all the resources required to make an investment a success.

THE THIRD SEMINAR: AGREE ACTIVITY AND FINANCIAL PLANS

When the teams are ready to present highly detailed plans for final approval, the senior executives should convene a third seminar. The purpose of the third seminar is to agree on the SSCS model and scorecard. More specifically, the supporting activities and financial budgets should also be included. All senior managers and project team members should attend, as well as any middle management or key personnel responsible for KSFs or support activities.

The teams submit the financial plans to the financial management team at least two weeks before the seminar. This gives senior management the opportunity to consider the aggregate financial plans being presented at the seminar by all SMU teams before the meeting. The most senior manager in each SMU should present the plans. That individual and the SMU management team should sign off the plans before submission to the financial management team.

The inclusion of financial managers and the approval of budgets must be managed carefully. Kaplan and Norton note that they have encountered two types of financial executives[9]. The first views his or her role as a change agent and understands the limitations of the traditional financial model in the new environment. The second jealously guards the objectivity, auditability and integrity of the financial numbers currently being produced, and feels that softer, more qualitative measurements may dilute and even jeopardise the ability to control and measure financial performance to the current standards. Kaplan and Norton urge that the latter not be given major responsibility for developing or later managing the balanced scorecard. Although I recognise the value of the second type of financial manager in many enterprises, I would urge senior management to ensure that they do not allow this type of manager to dominate the approval of activity or financial plans at this important seminar.

The purpose of the third seminar is to cap the initial new marketing process and to send motivated teams to the final stage of implementing their plan on the battlefield. If the meetings degenerate into battles over numbers, much good work will be undone and the team will have the motivation of a damp squib. This does not mean that I advocate warm, fuzzy feelings over financial discipline. However, it is better to postpone the third seminar and to work out the numbers in separate meetings if the submissions to the financial managers look grossly out of line before the seminar. The activity plans and financial plans should be approved at the meeting by senior management.

The senior management objectives should be careful to evaluate the timing of activities. All should pay keen attention to the personal development plans that emerge as resource activities. The approval of the activity and financial plans should be a cause for celebration and the time is opportune for a team-building exercise. The participants will have worked extremely hard to achieve the detail management and focus required.

IMPLEMENTING THE PLAN AND INSTITUTIONALISING LEARNING

The SSCS model and scorecard focus the enterprise on doing the right things and on doing things right. It is important to maintain focus by institutionalising a process of continuous learning.

Most managers look forward to monthly or quarterly reviews with their superiors with the same anticipation as they do a visit to the dentist. Where victimisation, deceit and deception characterise the style of review meetings, very little happens that is productive. The new marketing cannot grow in such a company.

CHANGING THE FOCUS OF MANAGEMENT REVIEWS

Continuous learning changes the nature of the two kinds of meetings most companies have. Strategic management reviews begin to focus on reviewing strategic issues, attempting to understand unexpected outcomes, formulating solutions and identifying new strategic issues. A very small part of the meeting may be devoted to specific performance results. Operational management reviews still concentrate on short-term performance issues, but the issues covered widen to include all the key success factors. No doubt, many companies will find it difficult at first to widen the focus from financial performance and activities directly related to sales. However, as the SSCS model that the participants have constructed demonstrates, all objectives are inter-related and personal development and other soft goals require as much attention as financial performance.

SUPPORTING CONTINUOUS LEARNING

Many of the strategic renewal programmes advocated today, such as business process re-engineering, service quality or JIT (just in time) materials management, are embraced with the assumption that the business is flawed fundamentally, that it can be put right only after a major intervention, and that an instant cure can be expected. Many such programmes do produce immediate results. Unfortunately, these results often dissipate over time and leave the company in the same or worse condition than it was before the intervention. The SSCS model and scorecard facilitate continuous learning by focusing on the important things that must be done to achieve the company's goals.

In a company that practises strong marketing, as Glick's Furniture Rental did 20 years ago, everyone knows what to do and everyone can see when performance isn't leading to expected results. Instead of resorting to 'ass-kicking sessions', management can see at a glance if the problem is performance- or results-driven, and can focus on intervening to help the responsible associates fix the problem. This more mature response fosters a climate of mutual respect and achievement sadly missing from so many companies today.

FOCUS ISN'T PUTTING BLINKERS ON

Performance models and scorecards should be re-evaluated on a regular basis- at least twice yearly for the first three years. Managing focus doesn't require the management team to put on blinkers. South African and IOR markets are dynamic and fast-growing. This has encouraged many firms from the industrialised countries to enter regional markets and to shift the balance of competition. Firms can win the battle against these multinationals by practising the new marketing. Nobody wants to be on a senior management team of a company that does the analysis, builds the SSCS model and scorecard and still fails to achieve an SSCS advantage in the marketplace.

BE PROACTIVE AND GLOBALLY VIGILANT

The SSCS model is the firm's theory of the business, and effective long-standing market leaders constantly challenge their theory of the business.

- Did installing an automated application processing system lower costs and improve our processing times as much as we thought? How much?
- How did our competitors respond?
- How can we improve our performance?
- How are our competitors measuring performance?
- Are there any performance measures that we're missing?

Remember the lessons of Johnson & Johnson's counterattack against Nestlé: be globally vigilant. It is not enough to understand your own SSCS model. You must understand your opponents' SSCS models and the models operating in other regional and global markets. Every link in the model, every performance measure and every result must be challenged regularly by the team.

DO COMPETENT ANALYSIS AND LISTEN TO THE BOUNDARIES

The new marketing does not require every manager to become a statistician. There are many 'experts' selling half-baked solutions on the silicon highway these days. Some argue that things are changing so fast that companies have no time to plan or analyse markets. Some propose that middle management is no longer needed when companies organise themselves so that associates in boundary roles can inspire constant small changes by radically empowered staff in organisations.

There is little doubt that advances in information technology have made many middle management jobs obsolete, or that highly educated workers in developed countries are capable of much more as a result of that infrastructural support. Managers in South Africa and the IOR must be careful to understand the impact of education, computer literacy and other factors, before they accept that these specific global trends are impacting on the practice of business in our regional markets. For instance, if a global competitor is achieving significant competitive advantage in Europe due to the use of GIS (geographical information systems) to route delivery trucks, then the company should look at this in South Africa. The commercial rationale for incorporating GIS would include the quality of South African GIS (it is good) and the actual benefits that would accrue in terms of revenues and cost savings. This suggests more, not less, analysis, and analysis that is well within the means of any company.

Although there's plenty of empirical evidence suggesting that the centralised, paternalistic, authoritative control structures that characterise so many South African and IOR companies are no longer effective, I have yet to see one study where scientific proof supports the notion that chaos is desirable in any company[10]. I am also unaware of any leading firm of any size that does not work according to an organised plan based on competent market analysis. Associates in boundary roles must be heard, and their perceptions must help shape the analysis that is the basis of the SSCS model and scorecard. Associates must be empowered to speak when management needs to hear what other relationship partners want or need. Nevertheless, this does not mean that competent analysis and business control should be abandoned. Rather, analysis must be increased and automated, and results reported more frequently. Business control in an age of fraud is a primary concern that is not abandoned in the firm practising strong marketing.

USE THE SSCS MODEL AND SCORECARD

The SSCS model and scorecard are the basis of managing focus. In turn, managing focus is the enabling discipline of strong marketing. Every operational management review must consider the operating measures enshrined in the SSCS scorecard. Every strategic management review should consider the SSCS model and the impact of desirable strategic initiatives on it.

Summary

Firms that build the new marketing have the greatest chance for survival and prosperity in an age of rapid change and discontinuity. Building strong marketing is a process of continuous learning and renewal based on competent management of purchase and consumption, competition, resources and interaction. The SSCS model and scorecards that crystallise this knowledge are the basis for focusing the organisation to achieve superior sustainable customer solutions. There can be no greater advantage, no greater achievement in business and no greater chance for personal growth.

Kaplan and Norton note that the average firm can build a balanced scorecard within 16 weeks. This is a reasonable time to build strong marketing, if the firm has reasonable knowledge at hand. Twenty weeks is probably a more realistic horizon when firms begin with little hard information on hand.

ENDNOTES

1 Ries (1996).
2 See Hall (1978).
3 See Hamel & Prahalad (1994); Prahalad & Hamel (1990); Quinn (1992).
4 From Liberty Life's 1996 Annual Report.
5 I find it easier to refer to the main disciplines of strong marketing as 'the 4Cs' in the earliest stages of instilling strong marketing, mainly for pedagogical reasons. These are familiar terms to almost everyone, even if the terms are not exactly right.
6 Kaplan & Norton (1996). Kaplan & Norton (1992: 71-79). Maisel (1992: 47-52).

7 Kaplan & Norton (1996) call these objectives, measurements, targets and activities. Glad & Becker (1994) would call the same constructs key success factors, performance measures, goals and objectives and activities. I have used the latter terminology.

8 Kaplan & Norton (1996: 34-35) argue that their approach does as well, although they indicate that such goals were not originally intended as part of the model.

9 Kaplan & Norton (1992: 310-311).

10 Having chaired the cellular service providers association and served as managing director of the largest independent cellular service provider – a company that grew 2-3 per cent a day and achieved profitable trading in its first year – I speak from experience as well as from a theoretical perspective.

Appendix
The Indian Ocean Rim
(IOR)

Understanding the characteristics and trading patterns of IOR countries

The IOR region includes some of the world's fastest-growing economies. It begins at the confluence of the Indian and Atlantic Oceans near Cape Town and ends at Australia's southern coast. Led by its major trading nations – Singapore, United Arab Emirates, South Africa, Malaysia, Thailand, Indonesia and India – the IOR is emerging as one of the world's major trading regions.

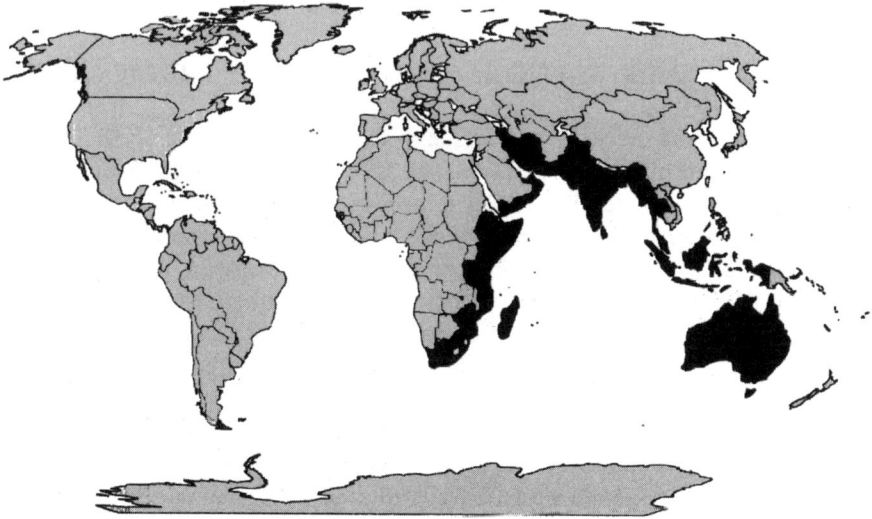

Figure A.1 *The IOR countries (shown in black)*

IOR regional characteristics differ greatly to those of the industrialised nations. Economies are smaller, poorer and less developed. Consumers are younger, less well educated and variously acculturated. Nevertheless, just as leading international strategists have begun to realise that industrialised nations ignore African markets 'at their own competitive peril'[1], there is a growing realisation that the IOR can become a substantial market for companies capable of looking past the stereotypical images of poverty to focus on the overwhelming opportunities of these fast-growing and largely untapped markets.

Although many IOR countries appear to be more globally competitive today, countries outside the region account for some 74 per cent of exports to IOR countries and buy 80 per cent of regional exports[2]. The pattern of trade with the industrialised nations, established in colonial times, continues today and is characterised by a significant portion of raw commodity exports and finished goods imports. This suggests a bounty for companies that focus on the substantial opportunities for growth through regional trade of finished goods and services. If IOR enterprises could capture just another 10 per cent of total trade, regional trade would increase significantly with knock-on effects to regional employment, living standards, currency values and political stability.

The IOR is awakening to this opportunity and regional governments have formed an Indian Ocean Rim Initiative (IORI) to explore co-operation. Despite the signing of two agreements, many believe that the IORI is making slow progress. It's true to say that little concrete and meaningful regional co-operation is taking place. The combined effect of urgent action on the part of individual IOR firms could be the catalyst that kick-starts the achievement of this massive opportunity.

NATIONAL CLASSIFICATION: AN INTEGRATIVE FRAMEWORK

So, how does one begin to understand the diversity of the IOR so that opportunities and marketing plans can be approached in a systematic way? A good first step is to identify similar countries in the region so that country groups can be prioritised and identified for expansion. It is tempting to begin by looking for countries in close geographic proximity. After all, geographic proximity is a strong influence on economic development and transnational similarities, as Porter has argued for more industrialised regions[3]. However, recent research tells us that integrative frameworks should embrace more than geographic proximity (or per capita GNP for that matter)[4]. Consider the vast differences between Singapore and Indonesia as illustrated in Figure A.2 (page 293), although only about 20 kilometres separate them across the Singapore Strait. Malaysia and South Africa have similar levels of human development, despite Malaysia's higher per capita GNP.

The central premise of *The New Marketing* is that the contemporary marketing environment requires higher levels of individual and corporate analytic competencies if firms are to build lasting competitiveness. Many companies don't have people with market research and planning skills, so they often 'buy' or 'rent' these skills by hiring consultants. Companies that get the maximum return from consultants before final payment is made, make sure the consultants have the specific skills and experience required and that their letter of appointment specifies which people in the company must be trained by the consultants to understand and use the research report or market analysis.

This appendix presents two alternative classification schemes (of the type consultants often provide) for IOR markets with populations of over one million people and for which reliable statistics are available:

1. The first scheme classifies IOR countries according to trading patterns and using International Monetary Fund trade statistics.

2. The second method classifies markets based on traditional country classification variables.

Methodological approaches to industry-specific classification schemes are also discussed, and the reader should feel more competent to discuss such analyses after reading this appendix.

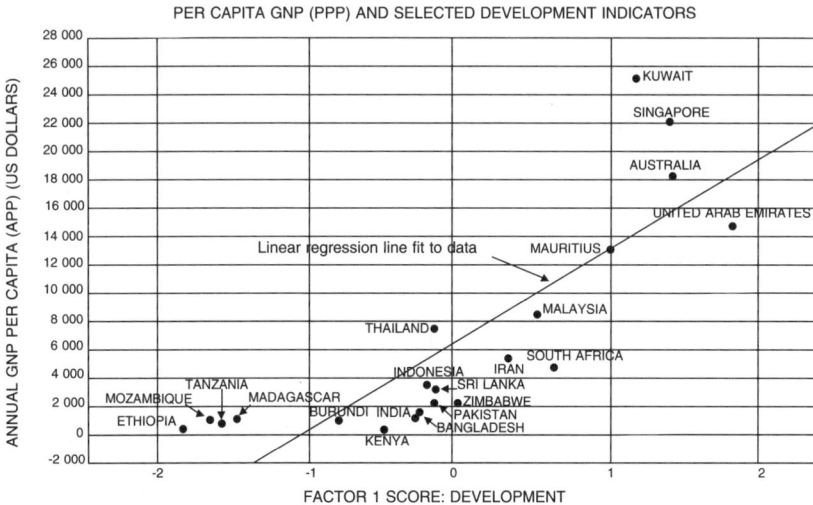

Figure A.2 *Per capita GNP and development in the IOR with trendline*

THE FIRST FRAMEWORK: TRADE PATTERNS

The first framework was constructed from the regional trade statistics provided by the *International Monetary Fund Direction of Trade Statistics Yearbook 1996* (*DOTS Yearbook*)[5]. Data concerning imports and exports was gleaned from the DOTS categories of Industrialised Nations, Developing Nations, Africa, Asia, Europe, the Middle East, the Western Hemisphere (South America and the Caribbean) and Others (Cuba and North Korea). Data was also compiled for the IOR region from individual country data in the report.

DEFINING COUNTRY GROUPS

Cluster analysis was used to define groups of similar countries in all analyses in this appendix. An example will help to illustrate why it is so necessary to get the right people to conduct such sophisticated market analysis.

Cluster analysis is an advanced multivariate statistical technique that includes many different variations or 'clustering methods'[6]. It groups countries (or products, brands, etc) by analysing similarities in their characteristics. The tree diagram output[7] (called a dendrogram) of the hierarchical cluster analysis communicates the content of clusters at a glance.

Figure A.3 below shows what can happen when a seemingly minor aspect of multivariate analysis is ignored. The figure shows a clustering dendrogram that resulted from an analysis of the DOTS raw trade statistics. The analysed data included *total* exports and imports and *sub-regional* exports and imports. However, including the total statistics creates a problem. Because the total trade figures are so much larger than the regional trade figures (and also contain the regional figures), total trade statistics dominate the cluster analysis and only two clusters emerge – large and small traders.

This may be a useful portrayal of large and small trading nations, but a much more informative picture can be teased from the same data if the total trade statistics are removed and the regional trade statistics are converted to proportions[8], as shown in Figure A.5 (page 295).

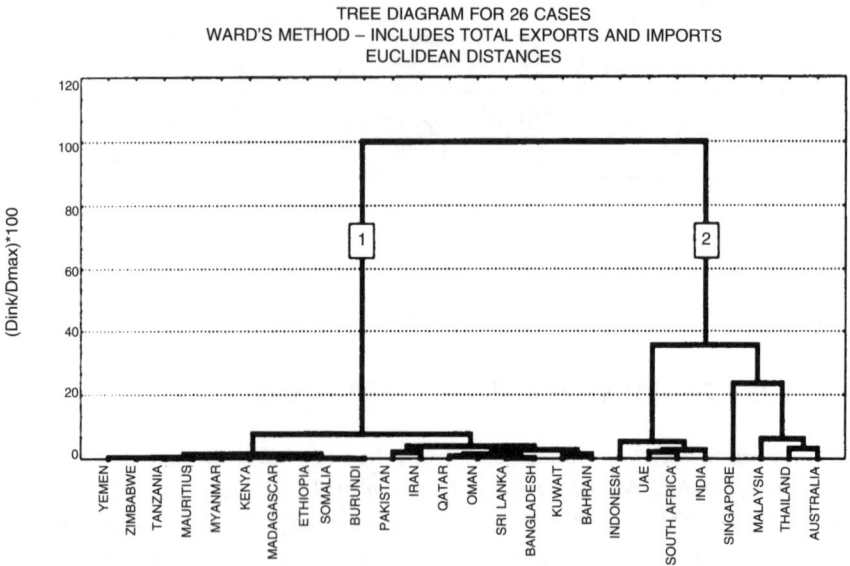

Figure A.3 Uninformative cluster analysis of raw trade statistics

SCREE PLOT OF LINKAGE DISTANCES ACROSS STEPS
EUCLIDEAN DISTANCES PROPORTIONAL STANDARDISED TRADE
STATISTICS

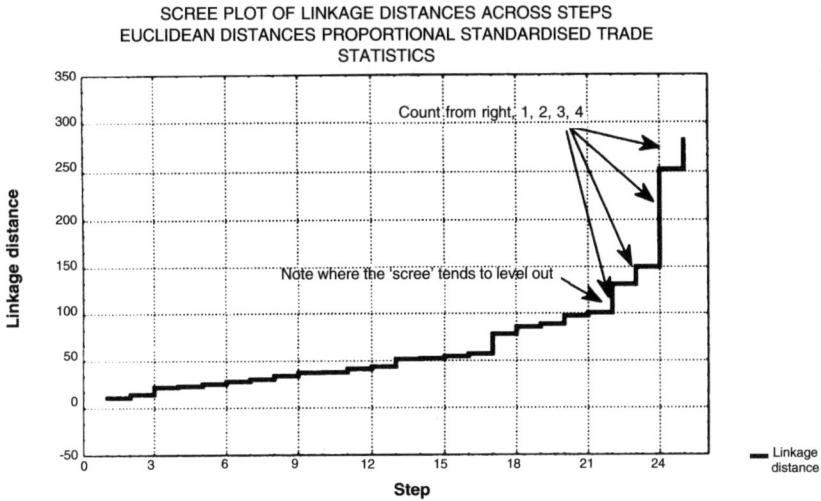

Figure A.4 A scree plot of proportional trade statistics

When analysts conduct cluster analysis, they must decide how many clusters to produce. There are some advanced statistics that can help analysts to decide, but a scree plot often suffices and can be understood by anyone. Avoiding any further statistical commentary, it is enough to say that the scree plot can be thought of as the side view of a steep rock face. Consider how rocks pile up at the bottom of a cliff (the rocks are called scree), and you will understand how this diagram came to be named. It resembles the side view of a steep rock face. The spot on the diagram 'where the rocks pile at the bottom of the cliff' usually gives a strong indication of a good cluster solution. In this case, four clusters emerge.

TREE DIAGRAM FOR 26 CASES
WARD'S METHOD – INCLUDES TOTAL EXPORTS AND IMPORTS
EUCLIDEAN DISTANCES

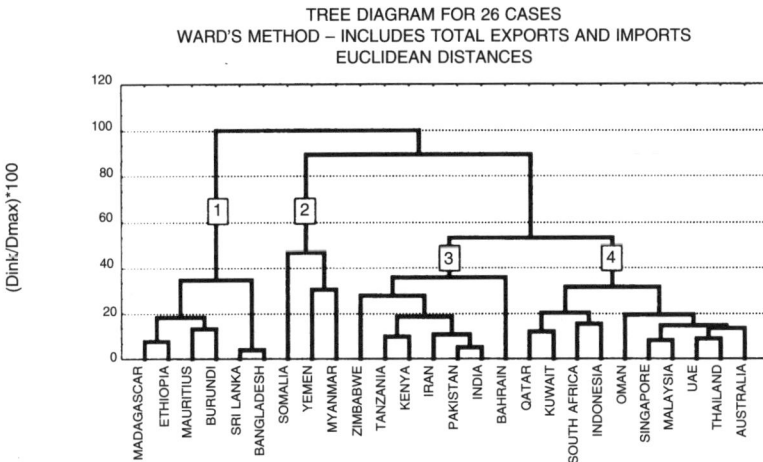

Figure A.5 A cluster analysis of proportional trade statistics

Cluster 1: The commodities exporters

The first cluster includes Madagascar, Ethiopia, Mauritius, Burundi, Sri Lanka and Bangladesh. These countries are distinguished by the highest incidence of exports to industrialised nations (82 per cent), the lowest amount of exports to the IOR (4 per cent) and developing nations (16 per cent), and the lowest amount of imports from the Middle East (5 per cent). This cluster averages $1 591 million DOTS exports and $2 764 million imports[9].

Cluster 2: The distressed

The second cluster includes Somalia, Yemen and Myanmar – all countries recently wracked by internal conflict and instability. These countries are distinguished by low exports to industrialised nations, high exports to developing nations and the Middle East, low imports from industrialised nations, and high imports from the IOR and developing nations. The 'distressed' group achieves the lowest trade, only $1 103 million exports and $1 379 imports. These three nations are not included in the second regional framework because reliable statistics concerning country characteristics are unavailable.

Cluster 3: The developing traders

The developing traders include Zimbabwe, Tanzania, Kenya, Iran, Pakistan, India and Bahrain. These countries achieve much higher average trade than the 'commodities exporters' or 'the distressed' – $10 532 million exports and $9 915 million imports. This is the only cluster where average exports exceeded imports during the period. Otherwise, these countries are relatively indistinguishable from the average IOR country. They achieve the highest exports to African nations (13 per cent) and imports from the Middle East (17 per cent), but these are not statistically significant differences from the other clusters.

Cluster 4: The IOR lions

The final cluster includes Qatar, Kuwait, South Africa, Indonesia, Oman, Singapore, Malaysia, United Arab Emirates, Thailand and Australia. Their average exports ($42 102 million) and imports ($43 290 million) dwarf the performance of the other IOR countries. They are distinguished by more balanced trade between the developing and industrialised nations, but they have the highest imports from industrialised nations (66 per cent) and the lowest exports to developing nations (32 per cent).

THE SECOND FRAMEWORK: COUNTRY CHARACTERISTICS

Although the first framework may help firms to target countries for IOR expansion, it will leave many strategists feeling frustrated. What products are these countries trading? In which countries is my product most likely to find demand? Classifying developing nations according to consumption-related criteria is an effective way to develop a framework that answers these questions.

The influence of factors such as kilometres of paved roads or access to health care can often be ignored in domestic marketing strategies, but such factors reveal much about purchase and consumption behaviour in sub-regional and international markets[10]. The United Nations, the World Bank, industry trade associations and other sources produce regular reports containing useful data. Country classification variables usually include human and infrastructural development factors that change slowly or remain constant for considerable periods.

METHODOLOGY

Selection of classification variables

The quality of an analysis depends on data quality. Choosing the right variables is very important. Variables used by Sethi and Johansson and Moinpour formed the starting list of variables for the second framework[11]. These seminal studies explored infrastructural, socio-economic and human development character-istics relevant to international marketing, and have provided a foundation for many classification studies for international marketing strategy development.

The preliminary variable list was amended after discussions with senior officials at SAFTO and the International Trade Institute of South Africa. Focused discussions with executives responsible for international trade, who were attending global marketing strategy seminars at the South African Institute of Export, completed the variable selection process. It became necessary to exclude some of the variables included in the foundation studies because they lacked validity in the regional context or because reliable data did not exist. For instance, many countries did not report reliable information regarding hospital beds, political party fractionalisation or deaths from domestic violence. The interviews and literature review suggested the inclusion of inflation, distribution of gross domestic product, and various population growth and infrastructural development statistics.

Analysts should always take care to consider prospective variables in the context of IOR lifestyles. For instance, although automobile ownership may be a good indicator of transportation development in the large industrialised regions, it may be a poorer quality indicator in a country such as Singapore (where the government incentivises the use of mass transit) or island countries such as Mauritius or Indonesia.

The final set of 61 variables was gleaned from the World Bank's World Development Report 1996 and the UN's Human Development Report 1996[12]. When data was unavailable, the widely used *Africa South of the Sahara 1996*, other current *Europa* publications and country reports from *The Economist* were consulted.

Factor analysis

The current research used factor analysis for two reasons: to understand variable structure and to provide input for the subsequent cluster analysis. It is often useful to reduce such a large number of variables to meaningful and more manageable dimensions in national classification studies[13]. Many of the variables showed large inter-relations when a correlation matrix was constructed, suggesting that the dataset was ideal for factor analysis[14].

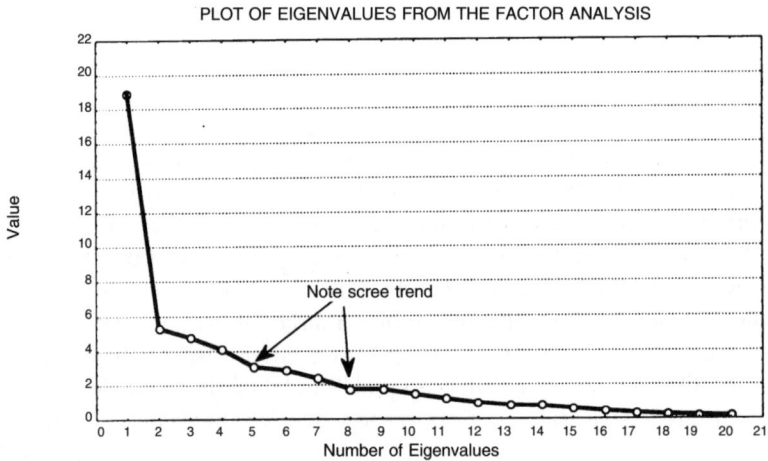

Figure A.6 *Scree plot of eigenvalues from the factor analysis*

After careful consideration of the relevant characteristics of the data and the analysis, an eight factor solution emerged from the analysis[15].

The factor loadings are the main tool for interpreting the factors. These can be thought of as the correlation of each variable with a factor and are the most important tool for interpreting the factors. More simply, the loadings express the meaning of each factor. Variables with a high positive correlation are said to load positively, and those with a negative correlation to load negatively. Negative loadings can be thought of as saying 'this is what this factor does not mean'.

The following discussion highlights those variables exceeding a loading of .70 to aid in the interpretation (those that come near this hurdle are shown in parentheses).

- *Factor 1: Development*

Loaded positively	Loaded negatively
Literacy, combined gross school enrolment ratio, life expectancy, access to health care, access to safe water, access to sanitation, daily calorie supply, real GNP per capita in PPP, energy consumption per capita, urban population, distribution of GDP to savings, GDP derived from industry, labour employed in industry, labour employed in services, newspaper copies per 100 people, televisions per capita and radios per 1000 people.	Population per doctor[16], UN capability poverty measure, distribution of GDP to private consumption, distribution of GDP to agriculture, labour employed in agriculture.

Table A.1 Factor loadings on Factor 1

The first factor accounts for 35 per cent of the total variance in the sample. It correlates with most of the indicators in the United Nations Human Development Index for industrial development and access to media. It refers to a state of having fewer people per doctor and more people living a healthy, well-nourished life; having the capability of healthy and safe reproduction and enjoying literacy and knowledge[17].

- *Factor 2: Zen industrialisation*

The second factor accounts for 10 per cent of the total variance in the sample and is hard to interpret. It combines Buddhist religious affiliation and manufacturing. The loading for telephones per capita is .68. There are no significant negative loadings.

Loaded positively	Loaded negatively
Buddhist religion, GDP derived from manufacturing and telephones per capita.	

Table A.2 Factor loading son Factor 2

- *Factor 3: Gender empowerment*

The third factor accounts for 9 per cent of the total variance. It refers to Christian and Islamic beliefs and to the empowerment of women.

Loaded positively	Loaded negatively
UN Gender Empowerment Index and Christianity	Muslim religion

Table A.3 Factor loadings on Factor 3

- *Factor 4: Ubuntu equity*

Factor 4 accounts for 7 per cent of the total variance. No variables load higher than .70 on this factor. Three variables load higher than .60.

Loaded positively	Loaded negatively
African religion	Wealth held by top 20 per cent of population, Gini Index[18]

Table A.4 Factor loadings on Factor 4

- *Factor 5: Trading and food security*

The fifth factor accounts for 6 per cent of the total variance. It refers to terms of trade, the Food Index[19] and the distribution of GDP derived from services.

Loaded positively	Loaded negatively
Terms of trade (Food Index) and GDP derived from services.	

Table A.5 Factor loadings on Factor 5

- *Factors 6 to 8*

Factors 6 to 8 account for 4 or 5 per cent of the total variance. Factor 6 refers to *Gross international reserves*, the only variable that loads positively on this factor. No variables load negatively on this factor.

GNP per capita growth loads positively on Factor 7, while kilometres of rail per million people loads negatively. This suggests *Growth through international trade*. Factor 8 is *Size*. Total GDP and area load positively on this factor.

TOWARD A TYPOLOGY OF IOR NATIONS

The rotated normalised factor scores for each country became the input for the second phase of the data analysis. The scree plot suggested a ten cluster solution as shown in Figure A.7.

SCREE PLOT OF LINKAGE DISTANCES ACROSS STEPS
EUCLIDEAN DISTANCES – IOR CHARACTERISTICS

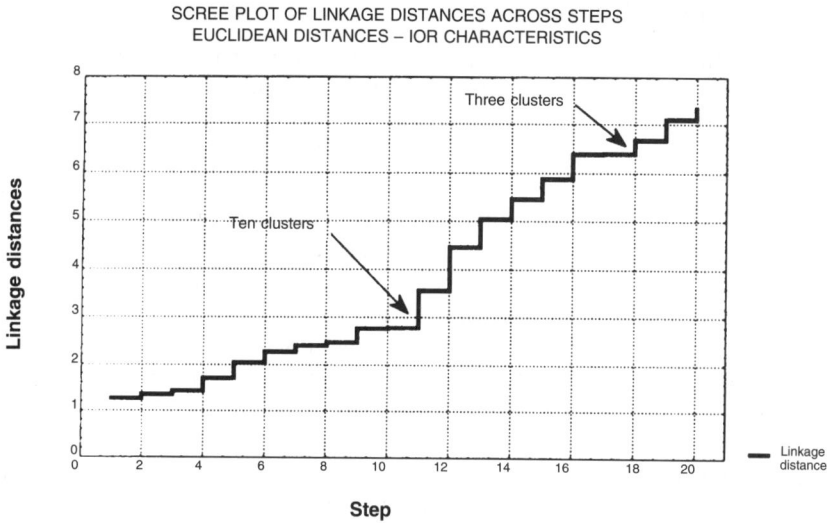

Figure A.7 Scree plot of the country characteristics amalgamation schedule

A possible three cluster solution was ignored as the solution had little strategic appeal. The ten nodes have been labelled in Figure A.8 below.

TREE DIAGRAM FOR 21 CASES
WARD'S METHOD – INDIAN OCEAN RIM CHARACTERISTICS
EUCLIDEAN DISTANCES

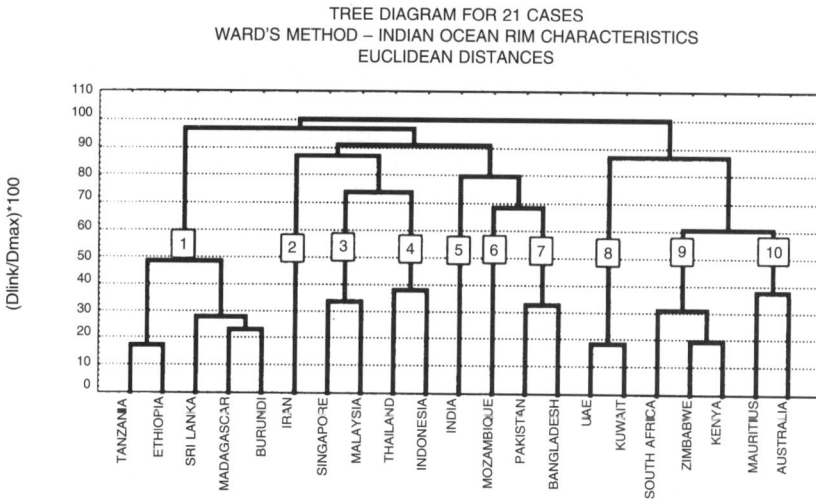

Figure A.8 Dendrogram of country characteristics cluster analysis

The following discussion briefly explores the distinctive features of each cluster of the ten cluster solution.

Cluster 1: The suffering ones

Tanzania, Ethiopia, Sri Lanka, Madagascar and Burundi are among the poorest and least developed nations in the world and they achieve the lowest score on Factor 1. Less than half the people have access to safe drinking water or sanitation. There are more than 18 000 people for every doctor.

An inordinately high proportion of GDP is derived from agriculture and the people are the least urbanised. One of every eight people professes traditional African religious beliefs. Rural lifestyles have not led to greater nutrition. Food production per capita has declined about 1 per cent per year since 1979-81 and the people have the lowest daily calorie supply of any cluster.

Although these countries have some international reserves, their consumption is generally defined by their poverty. Aid agencies and the government often buy or help finance product purchases. Companies that sell basic infrastructural products may find some opportunities in these countries. Low cost structures are important and appropriate technologies that take advantage of the available manual labour may suggest opportunities.

Cluster 2: Iran

Iran is the most differentiated country in the sample and stands alone in its own cluster. Food production per capita has been growing about 1 per cent per year since 1979-81. Exports are the most highly concentrated commodity in this oil-based economy.

Iran earns the lowest factor score on Factor 7. This is as much a result of its extensive rail network as its negative GNP growth. Some 98 per cent of the people are reported to be Muslims and the lack of Hindus is another distinguishing characteristic. Some 31 per cent of GDP goes to savings.

Iran is subject to certain trade restrictions because of its alleged support of international terrorism. The recent election of a new leader suggests that a more pragmatic relationship with the West may be in the offing. Iran's real GNP per capita or PPP (purchasing power parity) of $5 280 suggests a ready market for finished goods, agricultural products, prepared foodstuffs (compliant with Halaal traditions), clothing and textiles.

Cluster 3: The Asian tigers

Distinguished by high literacy, urbanised populations, large gross international reserves, high human development and high imports and exports, Singapore and Malaysia are symbiotic neighbours and the trading giants of the region. Twenty per cent of the population of these countries profess traditional Chinese religious beliefs and a similar proportion practise Buddhism.

A large proportion of GDP is derived from manufacturing, but this does not imply a smokestack economy – 57 per cent of the workforce is employed in services.

The Asian tigers are ready markets for most goods. Malaysia continues to have a developing character in many regions. Although its human development index (HDI) ranking dropped from 53 in the 1996 report to 60 in the 1997 report, the United Nations still classifies Malaysia as a high human development country. Malaysia has been among the most active IOR investors and was one of the leading investors in South Africa in 1996/7.

Cluster 4: The Asian tiger cubs

Thailand and Indonesia, the 'cubs', are characterised by large GNP, fast GNP growth and growing consumption of electricity. They also score highest on the Zen industrialisation factor – 47 per cent of this cluster count themselves as followers of Buddha.

Human development in Thailand is almost exactly the same as Malaysia. Indonesia lags behind in 99th place, just behind the Philippines and Botswana. Both markets have developed and developing sectors. These markets are attractive to a wide spectrum of products, including capital equipment, telecommunications and basic infrastructure, high and appropriate technology, and financial services.

Cluster 5: India

Perhaps soon to be the most populated country in the world, India stands as an independent cluster. Food production has increased almost 1.5 per cent per year since 1979-81. However, India is most distinguished by its size, GNP and Hindu population.

India is a vast country characterised in many minds as poor and struggling. Certainly India is among the poorer nations, but there is a large population that can afford sophisticated consumer goods. However, the Indian trend towards building one's home in the traditional family neighbourhood can lead to confusing distribution issues for outsiders when the upwardly mobile build a new home in a lower economic area.

India ranks 138th in the 1997 HDI ratings of 175 nations by the United Nations. However, it is a burgeoning source of high technology products such as computer software. The market presents a major opportunity for most products, and especially basic infrastructural products, education, financial services, management consulting, capital goods and raw material.

Cluster 6: Mozambique

Undergoing the beginning stages of reconstruction after decades of war and internal discord that shattered the economy, Mozambique also stands alone. Mozambique has the highest negative score on Factor 5 (trading and food security). All the indicators of human development rank among the lowest in the world and Mozambique is distinguished from other clusters by the highest capability poverty measure (i.e. access to money and other resources that alleviate poverty), poor access to safe water, low life expectancy and illiteracy. Growth in energy consumption is the lowest of all clusters.

Like 'the suffering ones', Mozambique relies on extensive foreign aid and assistance. South African business and government agriculturists are now providing some technical and management assistance, but the biggest opportunity for investors in Mozambique is the rebuilding of the Maputo port. Mozambique is also integrating more closely with the South African economy, and Maputo will soon be linked to the rich Gauteng province in South Africa by a major road which forms part of the Maputo Corridor project.

Cluster 7: The cleaving [20]

Pakistan and Bangladesh were born of the partitioning of colonial India into Islamic and Hindu portions. Originally partitioned as one country, they continue to retain similarity, although Bangladesh is the poorer of the two with a per capita GDP almost exactly the same as India and about 40 per cent less than Pakistan. Both countries appear to be re-establishing political stability after periods of uncertainty.

This cluster is characterised by Islamic religious affiliations, a high capability poverty measure and low literacy. The wealth that exists is spread quite evenly, and the cluster is distinguished by the lowest Gini coefficient and one of the lowest proportions of wealth held by the top 20 per cent of the population.

Basic health care, basic services, infrastructural products and labour-intensive manufacturing joint ventures may hold special appeal in these markets.

Cluster 8: Oil and trade

The United Arab Emirates and Kuwait are tiny giants. This cluster is distinguished by its high score on Factor 1 (development) and its high rate of human development. Access to safe water and health care, a low doctor/population ratio, high per capita GNP (PPP) and a high incidence of televisions in households characterises this cluster. Exports are concentrated on oil and the two countries enjoy a significant portion of the world's proven reserves.

Kuwait has rebuilt its oil production facilities after the Gulf War. The economies are distinguished by a distribution of GDP that favours industry and savings, and there is a higher incidence of employment in services and in labour. The UAE has diversified its industrial capacity in recent years, but there is no doubt that oil is the king of commodities in this country.

The people are mainly Muslim and wealth is concentrated in a few hands. Kuwait is a constitutional monarchy but a federation of emirates rules the UAE (where there is no voting). Women do not vote in both countries, and a group of men constituting less than 10 per cent of the population make the decisions of government. However, there has been political stability and the economies are thriving. Dubai has become an especially busy port.

Both countries have achieved the status of high human development, but their rank on per capita GDP greatly exceeds their human development index rank. This means that there are segments of the population living third world lifestyles.

These countries are small markets constituting some 4 million people in total, but their total economies are over half the size of South Africa's. Dubai is an important point of entry into neighbouring countries and most products find ready acceptance. As in most Arab economies, price negotiations can be exhausting and local customs demand careful attention.

Cluster 9: The Ubuntu triad

South Africa, Zimbabwe and Kenya are characterised by the influence of Christian and African religions, high concentrations of wealth in the hands of the top 20 per cent of the population and literacy approaching the highest levels in the Indian Ocean Rim. South Africa and Zimbabwe are classified as medium human development countries (the latter just barely), while Kenya is a low human development country. The South African economy dwarfs those of both Zimbabwe and Kenya.

Although the statistic is not reported for Kenya, South Africa and Zimbabwe have gender empowerment index rankings some 50 places higher than their GNP per capita ranks. South Africa's progress in gender empowerment is among the best in the world, surpassing France, Japan, Ireland, Greece, Israel and many other industrialised countries.

While South Africa is classified as a developing country, it offers first world lifestyles in its major cities. South Africa places emphasis on extending human development to all, and this has resulted in a high demand for telecommunications, health care, water purification, housing, roads and other basic infrastructural needs. However, South Africa also offers a ready market for high technology goods and boasts world-class industries in financial services, medicine, retailing and other fields.

This cluster boasts some of the world's last unspoiled wildernesses and tourism presents a major opportunity in all three countries. Game parks, beaches and other tourist destinations are clean and well-managed. More importantly, these countries offer destinations for many important popular interests, such as scuba diving, at very modest total holiday costs.

Cluster 10: The ocean traders

Australia and Mauritius are traders surrounded by ocean which share high human development and a wonderful potential for tourism growth. They are distinguished by the highest average score on the gender empowerment measure, fewer people per doctor, the lowest capability poverty measure, high literacy, high access to safe water, sanitation and health care, and a relatively high GNP per capita (PPP).

The ocean traders are distinguished by a high incidence of television sets and radios, high gender empowerment, high per capita GNP and Christianity (although 20 per cent of Mauritians profess to Hinduism). Australia has made good progress in agriculture, especially livestock.

Despite Australia's size (almost 8 million square kilometres), the combined population of the countries is smaller than the greater New York City metropolitan statistical area. Both countries are developed and have good potential for consumer goods, industrial products and service goods. They are also well situated to feature in logistics plans of companies that wish to set up IOR bases for operations, along with South Africa and the United Arab Emirates (mostly Dubai).

SOME CONCLUDING THOUGHTS

There is a need for increased research in these developing regions[21]. Classification schemes such as those presented in this appendix help to make the IOR region easier to understand. A better analysis would result if information was included that is known to be predictive of purchase and consumption behaviour in a particular industry. This might include information about price-sensitivity, profitability, servicing costs, product-market development stages or substitute pricing data[22].

The two frameworks discussed suggest many implications for firms considering regional marketing strategies. Although richer and poorer clusters emerged in the analyses, perhaps the most important point is the need to examine more than just geographic proximity and per capita GNP when assessing national similarity in sub-Saharan Africa.

The frameworks confirm Sethi's[23] findings regarding the lack of a 'smooth or well-defined continuum of economic development'. Rather than per capita GNP, the results suggest that development and culture variables are important aspects of regional differences. By implication, they point to the need for appropriate products and services, such as primary preventative health care products or basic education programmes, that are largely ignored by companies exporting to the region from industrialised countries. Low per capita GNP, accompanied by low penetration of basic consumer durables, suggests great potential for basic, inexpensive product designs in many industries.

The influence of *development* on national differences in the region should also interest regional policy makers. Successful countries have translated resource wealth into human development. Governments that wish to achieve sustainable living standard improvements must begin by developing national human resources.

Cultural, political, religious and socio-economic aspects of exchange in integrated regions (which are often strongly influenced by their colonial heritage) shape not only converging consumer characteristics, such as needs, values, lifestyles, and preferences, but also marketing and distribution systems. Many firms may find that the segments presented in this appendix provide a useful basis for market segmentation and further research.

The country cluster approach is appealing, whether market structure and characteristics, elaborate matrices, or deeply-rooted belief structures such as values form the basis of the analysis[24]. Marketers should remember that culturally-decentred research instruments (based on empirically meaningful emic and etic constructs linked to purchase behaviour for specific products), offer greater validity and reliability than standardised country classifications or syndicated segmentation schemes[25].

ENDNOTES

1 Quelch & Austin (1993).
2 International Monetary Fund, 1996.
3 Porter (1990).
4 The World Bank, 1992, suggests that per capita GNP may not be a useful basis for understanding living standards. For instance, people living in colder climates spend a large amount every year on winter clothing, central heating and cooling systems, heavily insulated dwellings and other expensive trappings of colder climate survival. See Liander (1967); Sethi (1971); Wind (1972); Weber (1974); Johansson (1977); Robinson (1977). The influence of culture is another important factor. Cultural influence on the hedonic and utilitarian significance of products may hold important implications to national clusters for various marketers.
5 International Monetary Fund, 1996.
6 See Milligan & Cooper (1987) for a thorough review of clustering issues. Ward's method of cluster analysis was used in all the examples presented here.
7 A dendrogram is read like a tree — the total sample is split into two nodes that split subsequently as countries become less alike. Thus, the trading patterns of South Africa and the UAE are very much alike, while Yemen and Australia are not. Nodes are not normally numbered but I have done so in this chapter to make the point clear.
8 In other words, converted to percentages of the total trade figure. This concentrates attention on the more important aspects of where each country trades.
9 Useful information, although it is not included in the cluster analysis. This was compiled by profiling the clusters after the cluster analysis.
10 See Jain (1993); Terpstra & Sarathy (1991). The higher order factors that emerge from national classification studies may also improve the usefulness of classification studies based on more specific consumption and purchase behaviours or multinational innovation diffusion patterns. For instance, see Yavas, Verhage & Green (1992/3).
11 Johansson & Moinpour (1977); Sethi (1971).
12 United Nations Development Programme (1996); World Bank (1996).
13 For instance, see Johansson & Moinpour (1977).

14 If you are interested in learning more about factor analysis method, Stewart (1981) is an excellent review article. For those with methodological interests, the reproduced correlations matrix, residual correlations matrix, the communality estimates and latent roots plots indicated that factor analysis was appropriate, and that the resulting eight factor principal components analysis was of high quality. Principal components factor analysis was used because of the desire for orthogonal rotated factors and the absence of a general factor hypothesis suggested a normalised varimax rotation. The principal components approach also makes fewer assumptions about the nature of the data. The resulting rotated normalised factor loadings fulfilled Thurstone's criteria for evaluating structural simplicity. Also see Mardia, Kent & Bibby (1979); Thurstone (1947: 335).

15 Stewart (1981) suggested combining the roots criterion and the scree plot approach for factor extraction. Eleven factors with eigenvalues higher than 1.0 emerged from the analysis and accounted for 88 per cent of the total variance in the data. The scree plot suggested eight factors. Although mindful of Cattell's (1952) suggestion about retaining one or two extra factors to retain residual information when employing rotation techniques, and Stewart's (1981) caution about extracting too few factors, the eight factor solution appeared to be the most meaningful and led to a more effective subsequent cluster analysis. In the natural sciences, analysts often retain all factors until the factors account for more than 95 per cent of the total variance. It is not uncommon for marketing researchers and other social scientists to set a 60 per cent hurdle, according to Hair Jr., Anderson, Tatham & Black (1995). The eight factors account for 80 per cent of the total variance and the communality estimates show that the factors account for more than 60 per cent of the variance of all but 3 variables, and 70 per cent of the variance of all but 8 variables.

16 Don't be confused by population per doctor. The indicator suggests that the less people per doctor the more developed the health care system.

17 The UN capability poverty measure is an index of the proportion of the population who do not live a healthy, well-nourished life, have the capability of healthy and safe reproduction and enjoy literacy and knowledge.

18 The Gini Index is a measure of the distribution of wealth in an economy.

19 Terms of trade measures the movement of export prices to import prices as compared to 1987. An index of 100 indicates that there has been no movement. The food index compares food production per capita versus the average of 1979-1981, also on a scale of 100.

20 After *Sura 82-The Cleaving* from the Koran. This sura concerns the judgement day and the guardians who look over the righteous. The cleaving of India during the transition to post-colonialism formed these countries.

21 See Douglas & Craig (1992).

22 These often emerge from a more rigorous empirical approach to variable determination for specific product market research, using techniques such as structural equation modelling or log-linear modelling.

23 Sethi (1971: 354).

24 See Herbig & Kramer (1991).

25 See Burgess (1992). The strategically equivalent segment concept recently proposed by Kale & Sudharshan (1987) provides another approach to international segmentation that many marketers will find useful.

BIBLIOGRAPHY

Aaker, D. A. (1991). *Managing Brand Equity: Capitalizing on the Value of a Brand Name.* New York: Wiley.

Aaker, D. A. (Ed.). (1993). *Brand Equity and Advertising: Advertising's Role in Building Strong Brands.* Hillsdale, New Jersey: Lawrence Erlbaum.

Aaker, D. A. (1996). *Building Strong Brands.* New York: Free Press.

Abell, D. F. (1993). *Managing with Dual Strategies: Mastering the Present, Pre-empting the Future.* New York: Free Press.

Abell, D. F. & Hammond, J. S. (1979). *Strategic Market Planning: Problems and Analytical Approaches.* Englewood Cliffs, New Jersey: Prentice-Hall.

Abratt, R., van der Westhuizen, B. I. C. & Blem, N. H. (1989). *Sales Management.* Durban: Butterworths.

Achrol, R. S. (1991). Evolution of the marketing organisation: new forms for turbulent environments. *Journal of Marketing,* 55.

Aczel, A. (1989). *Complete Business Statistics.* Homewood, Illinois: Irwin.

Agur, J. (1996). Business aviation: versatile value. *Fortune,* (28 October), Advertising supplement.

Anonymous. (1996). Globoculture creep. *Newsweek,* (30 December).

Armstrong, J. S. & Andress, J. G. (1970). Exploratory analysis of marketing data: trees vs regression. *Journal of Marketing Research,* 7 (November).

Ashton, C. (1996). GIS: the intelligent mapping system. *Asian Business Review,* (5 January).

Assael, H. & Roscoe Jr., A. M. (1976). Approaches to market segmentation analysis. *Journal of Marketing* (October).

Atrill, P. (1996). *Financial Management for Non-Specialists.* Englewood Cliffs, New Jersey: Prentice-Hall.

Bateman, T. S. & Zeithaml, C. P. (1990). *Management: Function and Strategy.* Homewood, Illinois: Irwin.

Belk, R. (1975). Situational variables and consumer behavior. *Journal of Consumer Research,* 2 (December).

Belk, R. W., Wallendorf, M. & Sherry, J. F., Jr. (1989). The sacred and profane in consumer behavior: theodicy on the odyssey. *Journal of Consumer Research,* 16 (June).

Berglund, A.I. (1989). *Zulu Thought Patterns and Symbolism.* Cape Town: David Philip.

Berry, L. L. (1995). Relationship marketing of services: growing interest, emerging perspectives. *Journal of the Academy of Marketing Science,* 23(4).

Berry, L. (1995). *On Great Service: A Framework for Action.* New York: Free Press.

Berry, L. L., Conant, J. S. & Parasuraman, A. (1991). A framework for conducting a services marketing audit. *Journal of the Academy of Marketing Science,* 19(3).

Bettis, R. A. & Hall, W. K. (1983). The business portfolio approach – where it falls down in practice. *Long Range Planning,* 16 (April).

Bishop, B. (1996). *Strategic Marketing for the Digital Age.* New York: Harper Business.

Bitner, M. J. (1995). Building service relationships: it's all about trust. *Journal of the Academy of Marketing Science,* 23(4).

Blackwell, R. D., Burgess, S. M. & Hassan, S. S. (1992). Global competitive effectiveness: a behavioural approach to sustainable growth (Working paper). Columbus, Ohio: The Ohio State University.

Blake, J. & Mouton, R. (1964). *The Managerial Grid.* Houston: Gulf.

Bolt, G. J. (1987). *Practical Sales Management.* London: Pitman.

Bonoma, T. V. (1981). Marketing success can breed 'marketing inertia'. *Harvard Business Review,* 59 (September/October).

Bonoma, T. V. & Shapiro, B. P. (1983). *Segmenting the Industrial Market.* Lexington, Massachusetts: Lexington.

Boon, M. (1996). *The African Way: The Power of Interactive Leadership.* Sandton, Johannesburg: Zebra Press.

Bosch, C. (1996). Creating data infrastructures to build better businesses. *Business Intelligence,* (November).

Brandenburger, A. M. & Nalebuff, B. J. (1996). *Co-opetition.* New York: Currency Doubleday.

Brislin, R. W. (1986). The wording and translation of research instruments. In *Field Methods in Cross-cultural Research,* 8, edited by W. J. Lonner & J. W. Berry. Beverly Hills, California: Sage.

Brislin, R. W., Lonner, W. J. & Thorndike, R. M. (1973). *Cross-cultural Research Methods.* New York: Wiley.

Brown, S. P. (1995). The moderating effects of insupplier/outsupplier status on organisational buyer attitudes. *Journal of the Academy of Marketing Science,* 23(3).

Brull, S. B. (1996). Wow! Japan's new gadgets. *Business Week,* (25 November).

Burgess, S. M. (1992). Personal values and consumer research: an historical perspective. In *Research in Marketing,* 11, edited by J. N. Sheth. Greenwich, Connecticut: JAI Press.

Burgess, S. M. & Blackwell, R. D. (1994). Personal values and South African financial services brand preference. *South African Journal of Business Management,* 25(1).

Burgess, S. M., Schwartz, S. H. & Blackwell, R. D. (1994). Do values share universal content and structure? A South African test. *South African Journal of Psychology,* 24(1).

Burns, A. C. (1986). Generating marketing strategy priorities based on relative competitive position. *Journal of Consumer Marketing,* 3 (Fall).

Buzzell, R. D. & Gale, B. T. (1987). *The PIMS (Profit Impact of Market Strategy) Principles: Linking Strategy to Performance.* New York: Free Press.

Buzzell, R. D., Gale, B. T. & Sultan, R. G. M. (1975). Market share – a key to profitability. *Harvard Business Review,* 53 (January/February).

Byars, L. L. (1991). *Strategic Management: Formulation and Implementation, Concepts and Cases.* (Third ed.). New York: Harper Collins.

Cable News Network. (1997). Larry King Live (Television programme). Atlanta: Cable News Network.

Cacioppo, J. T. & Petty, R. E. (1989). The elaboration likelihood model: the role of affect and affect-laden information processing in persuasion. In *Cognitive and Affective Responses to Advertising,* edited by P. Cafferata & A. Tybout. Lexington, Massachusetts: Lexington.

Cadbury-Schweppes (South Africa) Limited. (1997). Group audited results for the 52 weeks ended 28 December 1996. *Financial Mail,* (7 March).

Cafferata, P. & Tybout, A. (Eds.). (1989). *Cognitive and Affective Responses to Advertising.* Lexington, Massachusetts: Lexington.

California Statistical Software. (1985). *Classification and Regression Trees.* Los Angeles: California Statistical Software.

Cambridge Work-Group. (1996a). 3 com and acer form strategic alliance to integrate networking technologies. *Cambridge Work-Group Computing Report.* Boston: Cambridge Publishing.

Cambridge Work-Group. (1996b). Document management: Document Sciences and JetForm announce strategic alliance. *Cambridge Work-Group Computing Report.* Boston: Cambridge Publishing.

Cambridge Work-Group. (1996c). Internet access: HP and Verifone announce strategic alliance to develop Internet payment solutions. *Cambridge Work-Group Computing Report.* Boston: Cambridge Publishing.

Cambridge Work-Group. (1996d). Study: U.S. electronics firms converging on information superhighway; CEOs. *Cambridge Work-Group Computing Report.* Boston: Cambridge Publishing.

Castelli, J. (1996). How to handle personal information. *American Demographics* (March).

Cattell, R. B. (1952). *Factor Analysis.* New York: Harper and Brothers.

Choffray, J.-M. & Lillien, G. L. (1979). Assessing response to industrial marketing strategy. *Journal of Marketing*, 42 (April).

Christensen, H. K., Cooper, A. C. & DeKluyver, C. A. (1982). The dog business: a re-examination. *Business Horizons*, 25 (November/December).

Churchill, G., Ford, N. & Walker, O. (1997). *Sales Force Management.* (Fifth ed.). Homewood, Illinois: Irwin.

Collins, B. & Payne, A. (1991). Internal marketing: a new perspective for HRM. *European Management Journal*, 9(3).

Conklin, R. (1979). *How to Get People to Do Things: The Key to Persuading, Leading, Motivating, Selling, Supervising, Influencing, and Guiding Others.* Chicago: Contemporary Books.

Coy, P., Hof, R. D. & Judge, P. C. (1996). Has the net finally reached the wall? *Business Week*, (26 August).

Craven, D. W. (1983). *The Sales Manager's Book of Marketing Planning.* Homewood, Illinois: Dow Jones-Irwin.

Craven, D. W. (1995). Special issue on relationship marketing. *Journal of the Academy of Marketing Science*, 23(4).

Cross, R. & Smith, J. (1995). *Customer Bonding: Pathway to Lasting Customer Loyalty.* Lincolnwood, Illinois: NTC Business Books.

Curry, S. R. (1996). A world of cool companies. *Fortune*, (28 October).

Davidson, W. R., Doody, A. F. and Sweeney, D. J. (1975). *Retailing Management* (Fourth ed.). New York: John Wiley & Sons, Inc.

Davis, S. & Lawrence, P. (1978). Problems of matrix organizations. *Harvard Business Review* (May/June).

Dawis, R. V. (1992). Person-environment fit and job satisfaction. In *Job Satisfaction: How People Feel About Their Jobs and How It Affects Their Performance*, edited by C. J. Cranny, P. Cain Smith & E. F. Stone. New York: Lexington.

Day, E., Fox, R. J. & Huszagh, S. M. (1988). Segmenting the global market for industrial goods: issues and implications. *International Marketing Review*, (Autumn).

Day, G. S. (1986). *Analysis for Strategic Market Decisions.* St. Paul, Minnesota: West.

Day, G. S. (1990). *Market Driven Strategy.* New York: MacMillan.

Day, G. S. (1992). Marketing's contribution to the strategy dialogue. *Journal of the Academy of Marketing Science*, 20(4).

DeFleur, M. L. & Ball-Rokeach. S. J. (1989). *Theories of Mass Communication.* White Plains, New York: Longman.

Dichter, E. (1964). *Handbook of Consumer Motivations: The Psychology of the World of Objects.* New York: McGraw-Hill.

Dickson, P. R. (1982). Person-situation: segmentation's mission link. *Journal of Marketing*, 6 (Fall).

Dillon, W. R., Madden, T. J. & Firtle, N. H. (1994). *Marketing Research in a Marketing Environment.* (Third ed.). Burr Ridge, Illinois: Irwin.

Dixit, A. K. & Nalebuff, B. J. (1991). *Thinking Strategically: The Competitive Edge in Business, Politics and Everyday Life.* New York: Norton.

Donath, B., Dixon, C. K., Crocker, R. A. & Obermayer, J. W. (1995). *Managing Sales Leads: How to Turn Every Prospect into a Customer.* Lincolnwood, Illinois: NTC Business Publications.

Douglas, S. P. & Craig, C. S. (1992). Advances in international marketing research. *International Journal of Research in Marketing*, 9(4).

Drucker, P. F. (1994). The theory of the business. *Harvard Business Review* (September/October).

Elliott, M. (1996). Going home. *Newsweek*, (30 December).

Engel, J. F., Blackwell, R. D. & Miniard, P. W. (1995). *Consumer Behavior.* (Eighth ed.). Fort Worth: Dryden.

Engel, J. F., Kollat, D. T. & Blackwell, R. D. (1968). *Consumer Behavior.* New York: Dryden.

Engel, J. F., Warshaw, M. R. & Kinnear, T.C. (1991). *Promotional Strategy: Managing the Marketing Communications Process.* (Seventh ed.). Homewood, Illinois: Irwin.

Enis, B. M., La Grace, R. & Press, A. E. (1977). Extending the product life cycle. *Business Horizons*, 20 (June).

Evans, F. B. (1959). Psychological objective factors in the prediction of brand choice: Ford versus Chevrolet. *Journal of Business*, 32.

Fisher, R. & Ury, W. (1991). *Getting to Yes: Negotiating an Agreement Without Giving In.* London: Business Books.

Fombrun, C. (1992). *Turning Points: Creating Strategic Change in Corporations.* New York: McGraw Hill.

Frank, J. (1996). What's the score? *European Card Review*, (September/October).

Frankl, V. (1984). *Man's Search for Meaning.* (Third ed.). New York: Washington Square.

Frankl, V. E. (1986). *The Doctor and the Soul: From Psychotherapy to Logotherapy.* (Third ed.). New York: Vintage Books.

Ganitsky, J., Rangan, U. S. & Watzke, G. E. (1991). Time perspectives in international joint ventures. *Journal of Global Marketing*, 5(1).

Garguiolo, M. (1993). Two step leverage: managing constraint in organisational politics. *Administrative Science Quarterly*, 38.

Glad, E. & Becker, H. (1994). *Activity-based Costing and Management.* Cape Town: Juta.

Godfrey, D. & Bleackley, M. (1988). Strategic alliances: guidelines for success. *Long Range Planning*, 21(5).

Grant, L. (1996). Gillette knows shaving and how to turn out hot new products. *Fortune*, 134 (14 October).

Greenacre, M. J. (1993). *Correspondence Analysis in Practice.* London: Academic Press.

Greiner, L. E. (1972). Evolution and revolution as organisations grow. *Harvard Business Review* (July – August).

Guglielmo, C. (1996). Here come the super-ATMs. *Fortune* (14 October).

Hair Jr., J. F., Anderson, R. E., Tatham, R. L. & Black, W. C. (1995). *Multivariate Data Analysis with Readings.* (Fourth ed.). Englewood Cliffs, New Jersey: Prentice-Hall.

Hall, C. S. & Lindzey, G. (1970). *Theories of Personality.* (Second ed.). New York: Wiley.

Hall, W. K. (1978). SBU: hot new topic in the management of diversification. *Business Horizons*, 17 (February).

Hamel, G., Doz, Y. L. & Prahalad, C. K. (1989). Collaborate with your competitors and win. *Harvard Business Review*, 67 (January/February).

Hamel, G. & Prahalad, C. K. (1985). Do you really have a global strategy? *Harvard Business Review* (July/August).

Hamel, G. & Prahalad, C. K. (1994). *Competing for the Future.* Boston: Harvard Business School Press.

Hammond-Tooke, D. (1989). *Rituals and Medicine: Indigenous Healing in South Africa.* Johannesburg: Donker.

Hamper, R. J., & Baugh, L. S. (1990). *Strategic Market Planning.* Lincolnwood, Illinois: NTC.

Harrigan, K. R. (1988). Strategic alliances and partner asymmetries. *Management International Review*, 28(5).

Haspeslagh, P. (1982). Portfolio planning: uses and limits. *Harvard Business Review* (January/February).

Hassan, S. S. & Blackwell, R. D. (1994). Competitive global market segmentation. In *Global Marketing: Perspectives and Cases*, edited by S. S. Hassan & R. D. Blackwell. Fort Worth, Texas: Dryden.

Hassan, S. S. & Samli, A. C. (1994). The new frontiers of intermarket segmentation. In *Global Marketing: Perspectives and Cases*, edited by S. S. Hassan & R. D. Blackwell. New York: Dryden.

Haugtvedt, C. P., Petty, R. E., & Cacioppo, J. T. (1992). Need for cognition and advertising: understanding the role of personality variables in consumer behavior. *Journal of Consumer Psychology*, 1.

Hawken, P. (1988). Growing a business: Stew Leonard (Television programme). San Francisco: KQED TV Projects

Hawkins, D. I. & Coney, K. A. (1981). Uninformed response error in survey research. *Journal of Marketing Research* (August), 373.

Hayes, R. H. & Wheelwright, S. C. (1979). Link manufacturing process and product lifecycle. *Harvard Business Review* (January/February).

Hecker, S. & Stewart, D. W. (Eds.). (1988). *Non-verbal Communication in Advertising.* Lexington, Massachusetts: Lexington.

Henderson, B. D. (1973). The experience curve-review – reviewed: IV. The growth-share matrix of the product portfolio. *Perspectives*, 135. Boston: The Boston Consulting Group.

Herbig, P. A. & Kramer, H. E. (1991). International product rollout: a country cluster approach. *Journal of International Consumer Marketing*, 4 (1/2).

Heubusch, K. (1997). Big brother and the Internet. *American Demographics* (February).

Hjelle, L. & Ziegler, D. (1987). *Personality Theories: Basic Assumptions, Research and Applications.* (Second ed.). New York: McGraw-Hill.

Hlavacek, J. D. & Ames, B. C. (1986). Segmenting industrial and high-tech markets. *Journal of Business Strategy* (Fall).

Hofer, C. W. & Schendel, D. (1978). *Strategy Formulation: Analytical Concepts.* St. Paul, Minnesota: West.

Hofstede, G. (1984). *Culture's Consequences: International Differences in Work-Related Values.* Beverly Hills, California: Sage.

Holloway, R. J. & Hancock, R. S. (1968). *Marketing in a Changing Environment.* New York: Wiley.

Hornung, P. (1991). *Woody Hayes: A Reflection.* Champaign, Illinois: Sagamore.

Hunt, S. D. & Morgan, R. M. (1994). Relationship marketing in the era of network competiton. *Marketing Management*, 3(1).

Hutt, M. D. & Speh, T. W. (1992). *Business Marketing Management: A Strategic View of Industrial and Organisational Markets.* (Fourth ed.). Fort Worth, Texas: Dryden.

International Monetary Fund. (1996). *Direction of Trade Statistics Yearbook* (1996). Washington, D. C.: International Monetary Fund.

Jackson, B. B. (1985a). Build customer relationships that last. *Harvard Business Review*, 63 (November/December).

Jackson, B. B. (1985b). *Winning and Keeping Industrial Customers.* Lexington, Massachusetts: Lexington.

Jackson, R. & Wang, P. (1994). *Strategic Database Marketing.* Lincolnwood, Illinois: NTC Business Books.

Jain, S. C. (1993). *Marketing Planning and Strategy.* (Fourth ed.). Cincinnatti, Ohio: South-Western.

Jaworski, B. J. & Kohli, A. K. (1992–1993). Market orientation: antecedents and consequences. *Journal of Marketing*, 57 (July).

Johansson, J. K. & Moinpour, R. (1977). Objective and perceived similarity of Pacific Rim countries. *Columbia Journal of World Business*.

Johnson, E. M., Kurtz, D. L. & Scheuing, E. (1987). *Sales Management: Concepts, Practices, and Cases.* New York: McGraw-Hill.

Joubert, M. (1996). Profitability still rising. *Financial Mail*, 142 (15 November).

Kahle, L. R., Beatty, S. E. & Homer, P. M. (1986). Alternative measurement approaches to consumer values: the List of Values (LOV) and Values and Lifestyle (VALS). *Journal of Consumer Research*, 13.

Kale, S. H. & Sudharshan, D. (1987). A strategic approach to international market segmentation. *International Marketing Review* (Summer).

Kaplan, R. S. & Norton, D. P. (1992). The balanced scorecard: measures that drive performance. *Harvard Business Review* (January/February).

Kaplan, R. S. & Norton, D. P. (1996). *The Balanced Scorecard: Translating Strategy into Action.* Boston: Harvard Business School Press.

Kasper, H. (1996). Letter from the president: networking. *Chronicle* (Newsletter of the European Marketing Academy) (5).

Kass, G. V. (1980). An exploratory technique for investigating large quantities of categorical data. *Applied Statistics*, 29.

Katona, G. (1951). *Psychological Analysis of Economic Behavior.* New York: McGraw-Hill.

Keegan, W. & Green, M. C. (1997). *Principles of Global Marketing.* Upper Saddle River, New Jersey: Prentice-Hall.

Keller, G., Warrack, B. & Bartel, H. (1988). *Statistics for Management and Economics.* Belmont, California: Wadsworth.

Kelley, A. & Sanderson, J. (1996). Hitting the mark. *Post Magazine Insurance Week* (17 October).

Kendall, K. E. & Kendall, J. E. (1995). *Systems Analysis and Design.* (Third ed.). Englewood Cliffs, New Jersey: Prentice-Hall.

Keown, A. J., Scott, D. F. & Petty, J W (1996). *Basic Financial Management.* (Seventh ed.). Englewood Cliffs, New Jersey: Prentice-Hall.

Keppel, G. (1991). *Design and Analysis: A Researcher's Handbook.* (Third ed.). Englewood Cliffs, New Jersey: Prentice Hall.

Kerlinger, F. N. (1986). *Foundations of Behavioral Research.* (Third ed.). New York: Holt, Rinehart and Winston.

Kimball, B. (1994). *American Marketing Association Handbook for Successful Selling.* Lincolnwood, Illinois: NTC Business Books.

Klatzky, R. L. (1980). *Human Memory: Structures and Processes.* (Second ed.). New York: W. H. Freeman.

Kohli, A. K. & Jaworski, B. J. (1990). Market orientation: the constructs, research propositions, and managerial implications. *Journal of Marketing*, 54 (April).

Kolodny, H. (1981). Managing in a matrix. *Business Horizons*.

Kotler, P. (1967). *Marketing Management: Analysis, Planning and Control*. Englewood Cliffs, New Jersey: Prentice-Hall.

Kotler, P. (1991). *Marketing Management, Analysis, Planning, Implementation and Control*. Englewood Cliffs, New Jersey: Prentice Hall.

Kotler, P., Gregor, W. T. & Rogers III, W. H. (1977). The marketing audit comes of age. *Sloan Management Review*, 30 (Winter).

Kotler, P., Gregor, W. T. & Rogers III, W. H. (1989). The marketing audit comes of age: a retrospective commentary. *Sloan Management Review*, 30 (Winter).

Kotler, P. & Singh, R. (1980). Marketing warfare in the 1980s. *Journal of Business Strategy*, (Winter).

Kotter, J. P. (1988). *The Leadership Factor*. New York: Free Press.

Kotter, J. P. (1990). *A Force for Change: How Leadership Differs from Management*. New York: Free Press.

Kotter, J. P. & Heskett, J. L. (1992). *Corporate Culture and Performance*. New York: The Free Press.

Kripalani, M. (1997). You have to be pushy and aggressive: Rebecca Marks talks about how Enron bounced back. *Business Week*, 22 (24 February).

Kroenke, D. M. (1995). *Database Processing: Fundamentals, Design, and Implementation*. Englewood Cliffs, New Jersey: Prentice.

Laurent, G. & Kapferer, J.N. (1986). Consumer involvement profiles: A new practical approach to consumer involvement. *Journal of Advertising Research*, 25 (December/January).

Leenders, M. R. & Blenkhorn, D. L. (1988). Reverse Marketing: The New Buyer-Seller Relationship. New York: Free Press.

Leonhardt, D. & France, M. (1996). Absolute folly? Liquor's TV foray may create backlash against all alcohol ads. *Business Week* (25 November).

Levitt, T. (1960). Marketing myopia. *Harvard Business Review* (July/August).

Lewicki, R. J. & Litterer, J. A. (1985). *Negotiation*. Homewood, Illinois: Irwin.

Lewis, R. D. (1996). *When Cultures Collide: Managing Successfully Across Cultures*. London: Nicolas Brealey.

Liander, B., Terpstra, V., Yoshino, M. & Sherbini, A.A. (1967). *Comparative Analysis for International Marketing*. Boston: Allyn and Bacon.

Lonner, W. J. & Berry, J. W. (Eds.). (1986). *Field Methods in Cross-Cultural Research*, 8. Beverly Hills, California: Sage.

M2 Presswire. (1996a). Compaq and Cheyenne division sign enterprise storage alliance: M2 Presswire.

M2 Presswire. (1996b). Microsoft and American Institute of CPAs help CPAs expand their services: M2 Presswire.

M2 Presswire. (1996c). Tandem Computers: Retail's first integrated solution for the operation of convenience stores introduced: M2 Presswire.

Maisel, L. S. (1992). Performance measurement: the balanced scorecard approach. *Journal of Cost Management* (Summer).

Malhotra, N. K. (1993). *Marketing Research: An Applied Orientation*. Englewood Cliffs, New Jersey: Prentice-Hall.

Mandel, M. J. (1996). The triumph of the new economy: a powerful pay-off from globalization and the info revolution. *Business Week* (30 December).

Mardia, K. V., Kent, J. T. & Bibby, J. M. (1979). *Multivariate Analysis*. London: Academic Press.

Matlin, M. W. (1989). *Cognition*. New York: Holt, Rinehart and Winston.

Maynard Jr., H. B. & Mehrtens, S. E. (1993). *The Fourth Wave: Business in the 21st Century*. San Francisco: Berrett-Koehler.

McCall, J. B. & Warrington, M. B. (1989). *Marketing by Agreement: A Cross-Cultural Approach to Business Negotiations*. New York: Wiley.

McCall, R. B. (1986). *Fundamental Statistics for the Behavioral Sciences*. (Fourth ed.). San Diego, California: Harcourt Brace Jovanovich.

McCarthy, E. J. (1960). *Basic Marketing: A Managerial Approach*. Homewood, Illinois: Irwin.

McCloy, A. (1995). Digital, Microsoft alliance takes shape. *Boston Business Journal*, 15(1).

McCort, D. J. & Malhotra, N. K. (1993). Culture and consumer behavior: toward an understanding of cross-cultural consumer behavior in international marketing. *Journal of International Consumer Marketing*, 6(2).

McCracken, G. (1986). Culture and consumption: a theoretical account of the structure and movement of the cultural meaning of consumer goods. *Journal of Consumer Research*, 13(1).

McCracken, G. (1988). *Culture and Consumption: New Approaches to the Symbolic Character of Consumer Goods and Activities*. Bloomington, Indiana: Indiana University Press.

McDonald, M. (1996). *Strategic Marketing Planning*. London: Kogan Page.

McDonald, W. J. (1994). Provider perceptions of focus group research use: a multi-country perspective. *Journal of the Academy of Marketing Science*, 22(3).

McGuire, W. J. (1972). The current status of cognitive consistency theories. In *Behavioral Science Foundations and Consumer Behavior*. New York: Free Press.

McGuire, W. J. (1976). Some internal psychological factors influencing consumer choice. *Journal of Consumer Research*, 2 (March).

Menon, A., Bharadwaj, S. G. & Howell, R. (1996). The quality and effectiveness of marketing strategy: effects of functional and dysfunctional conflict in intra-organisational relationships. *Journal of the Academy of Marketing Science*, 24(4).

Miller, K. E. & Ginter, J. L. (1979). An investigation of situational variation in brand choice behavior and attitude. *Journal of Marketing Research*, 16 (February).

Miller, R. B., Heiman, S. E. & Tuleja, T. (1988). *Strategic Selling*. London: Kogan Page.

Milligan, G. W. & Cooper, M. C. (1987). Methodology review: clustering methods. *Applied Psychological Measurement*, 11(4).

Mintzberg, H. (1987). Crafting strategy. *Harvard Business Review*, 65 (July/August).

Mintzberg, H. (1994). *The Rise and Fall of Strategic Planning: Reconceiving Roles for Planning, Plans, Planners*. New York: Free Press.

Mischel, W. (1986). *Introduction to Personality: A New Look*. (Fourth ed.). New York: CBS College Publishing.

Mitchell, A. (1983). *The Nine American Lifestyles: Who We Are and Where We Are Going*. New York: MacMillan.

Monmonier, M. (1996). Maps that speak for themselves. *American Demographics* (3 January).

Moore, J. F. (1996). *The Death of Competition: Leadership and Strategy in an Age of Business Ecosystems*. New York: Harper Collins.

Moore, W. L. & Pessemier, E. A. (1993). *Product Planning and Management: Designing and Delivering Value*. New York: McGraw-Hill.

Morrall, K. (1995). Mapping plots profitable strategies. *Bank Marketing*, 27(May).

Morris, C. (1989). *Quantitative Approaches in Business Studies*. (Second ed.). London: Pitman.

Murdock, G. P. (1971). *Outline of Cultural Materials*. (Fourth revised ed.). New Haven, Connecticut: HRAF Press.

Murdock, G. P. (1975). *Outline of World Cultures*. (Fifth ed.). New Haven, Connecticut: HRAF Press.

Nadler, L. & Nadler, Z. (Eds.). (1990). *The Handbook of Human Resource Development*. New York: Wiley.

Ohmae, K. (1982). *The Mind of the Strategist: The Art of Japanese Management*. New York: McGraw-Hill.

Oliver, R. L. (1980). A cognitive model of the antecedents and consequences of satisfaction decisions. *Journal of Marketing Research*, 17 (November).

Ouchi, W. (1981). *Theory Z: How American Business Can Meet the Japanese Challenge*. Reading, Massachusetts: Addison-Wesley.

Ouchi, W. & Jaeger, A. (1978). Type Z organisations: stability in the midst of mobility. *Academy of Management Review*, 3.

Packard, V. (1957). *The Hidden Persuaders: An Introduction to the Techniques of Mass-Persuasion Through the Unconscious*. London: Longman, Green.

Packard, V. (1959). *The Status Seekers*. London: Longman, Green.

Payne, A. (1995). Relationship marketing: a broadened view of marketing. In *Advances in Relationship Marketing*, edited by A. Payne. London: Kogan Page.

Peck, H. (1995). Building customer relationships through internal marketing: a review of an emerging field. In *Advances in Relationship Marketing*, edited by A. Payne. London: Kogan-Page.

Peters, T. (1992). *Liberation Management: Necessary Disorganisation in the Nanosecond Nineties*. New York: Alfred A. Knopf.

Peters, T. J. & Austin, N. K. (1985). *A Passion for Excellence: The Leadership Difference*. London: Collins.

Petty, R. E. & Cacioppo, J. T. (1986). *Communication and Persuasion: Central and Peripheral Routes to Attitude Change*. New York: Springer-Verlag.

Pfeffer, J. (1992). *Managing with Power: Politics and Influence in Organisations*. Boston: Harvard Business School Press.

Poirier, C. C. & Houser, W. F. (1993). *Business Partnering for Continuous Improvement: How to Forge Enduring Alliances Among Employees, Suppliers and Customers*. San Francisco: Berrett-Koehler Publishers.

Porter, M. (1979). How competitive forces shape strategy. *Harvard Business Review*, (March/April).

Porter, M. (1980). *Competitive Strategy: Techniques for Analyzing Industries and Competitors*. New York: Free Press.

Porter, M. (1985). *Competitive Advantage: Creating and Sustaining Superior Performance*. New York: Free Press.

Porter, M. F. (1990). *The Competitive Advantage of Nations*. New York: Free Press.

Prahalad, C. K. & Hamel, G. (1990). The core competence of the corporation. *Harvard Business Review* (May/June).

Punj, G. & Stewart, D. W. (1983). Cluster analysis in marketing research: review and suggestions for applications. *Journal of Marketing*, 20 (May).

Puto, C. P., Patton III, W. E. & King, R. H. (1985). Risk handling strategies in industrial vendor selection decisions. *Journal of Marketing*, 49 (Winter).

Qualls, W. J. & Puto, C. (1989). Organisational climate and decision framing: an integrated approach to analyzing industrial buying decisions. *Journal of Marketing Research*, 26 (May).

Quelch, J. A. & Austin, J. E. (1993). Should multinationals invest in Africa? *Sloan Management Review* (Spring).

Quinn, J. B. (1992). *Intelligent Enterprise*. New York: Free Press.

Ramo, J. C. (1996). The next big thing. *Time* (Time Digital Supplement, 11 November), TD20-TD26.

Rappaport, A. S. & Halevi, S. (1991). The computerless computer company. *Harvard Business Review*, (July/August).

Ray, M. & Rinzler, A. (Eds.). (1993). *The New Paradigm in Business*. New York: Tarcher Perigree.

Reed, S. F. (1993). *The Toxic Executive: A Step by Step Guide for Turning Your Boss (or Yourself) from Noxious to Nurturing*. New York: Harper Business.

Reynolds, T. J. & Gutman, J. (1988). Laddering theory, method, analysis, and interpretations. *Journal of Advertising Research*, (February/March).

Ries, A. (1996). *Focus: The Future of Your Company Depends on It*. New York: HarperCollins Business.

Rink, D. R. & Swan, J. E. (1979). Product life cycle research: a literature review. *Journal of Business Research* (September).

Robbins, S. P. (1991). *Organisational Behaviour: Concepts, Controversies and Applications*. (Fifth ed.). Englewood Cliffs, New Jersey: Prentice Hall.

Robinson, G. (1986). *Strategic Management Techniques*. Durban: Butterworths.

Robinson, P.J. & Wind, Y. (1977). Multinational trade-off segmentation. In *Moving Ahead with Attitude Research edited by Y. Wind & M.B. Greenberg*. Chicago: American Marketing Association.

Rokeach, M. (1973). *The Nature of Human Values*. New York: Free Press.

Rommel, G., Kluge, J., Kempis, R.D., Diedrichs, R. & Bruck, F. (1995). *Simplicity Wins: How Germany's Mid-sized Industrial Companies Succeed*. Boston: Harvard Business School Press.

Rosenbloom, B. (1991). Introduction: the growing role for international marketing channels. *Journal of Global Marketing*, 4(4).

Samiee, S. & Jeong, I. (1994). Cross-cultural research in advertising: an assessment of methodologies. *Journal of the Academy of Marketing Science*, 22(3).

Samiee, S. & Walters, P. G. P. (1990). Rectifying strategic gaps in export management. *Journal of Global Marketing*, 4(1).

Schall, L. D. & Haley, C. W. (1988). *Introduction to Financial Management*. New York: McGraw-Hill.

Schein, E. H. (1992). *Organisational Culture and Leadership*. (Second ed.). San Francisco: Jossey Bass.

Schuchman, A. (1959). The marketing audit: its nature, purposes, and problems. In *Analyzing and Improving Marketing Performance: Marketing Audits in Theory and Practice*. New York: American Management Association.

Schwartz, S. (1992). Universals in the content and structure of values: theoretical advances and empirical tests in 20 countries. *Advances in Social Psychology*, 25.

Schwartz, S. H. (1990). Individualism-collectivism: critique and proposed refinements. *Journal of Cross-Cultural Psychology*, 21(2).

Schwartz, S. H. & Ros, M. (1995). Values in the west: a theoretical and empirical challenge to the individualism-collectivism cultural dimension. *World Psychology*, 1(2).

Sethi, S. P. (1971). Comparative cluster analysis for world markets. *Journal of Marketing Research*, 8 (August).

Shapiro, B. P. & Moriarty, R. T. (1982). *National Account Management: Emerging Insights*. Cambridge, Massachusetts: Marketing Science Institute.

313

Sharma, A. & Dominguez, L. V. (1992). Channel evolution: a framework for analysis. *Journal of the Academy of Marketing Science*, 20(1).

Sheth, J. N. & Parvatiyar, A. (1995). Relationship marketing in consumer markets: antecedents and consequences. *Journal of the Academy of Marketing Science*, 23(4).

Shimp, T. A., Samiee, S. & Madden, T. J. (1993). Countries and their products: a cognitive structure perspective. *Journal of the Academy of Marketing Science*, 21(4).

Siegel, S. & Castellan, N. J. (1988). *Non-parametric Statistics for the Behavioral Sciences*. (Second ed.). New York: McGraw-Hill.

Simon, H. (1996). *Hidden Champions: Lessons from 500 of the World's Best Unknown Companies*. Boston: Harvard Business School Press.

Skinner, B. F. (1976). *Walden Two*. (Second ed.). New York: Macmillan.

Spekman, R. E. & Gronhaug, K. (1986). Conceptual and methodological issues in buying center research. *European Journal of Marketing*, 20(7).

Spekman, R. E. & Stern, L. W. (1979). Environmental uncertainty and buying group structure: an empirical investigation. *Journal of Marketing*, 43 (Spring).

Stacey, R. D. (1991). *The Chaos Frontier: Creative Strategic Control for Business*. Oxford: Butterworth-Heinemann.

Stacey, R. D. (1993). *Strategic Management and Organisational Dynamics*. London: Pitman.

Stalk, G. (1988). Time – the next source of competitive advantage. *Harvard Business Review*, (July/August).

Steenkamp, J. B. E. M. & van Tripp, H. C. M. (1996). Task experience and validity in perceptual mapping: a comparison of two consumer-adaptive techniques. *International Journal of Research in Marketing*, 13(3).

Stevenson, H. H. (1976). Defining corporate strengths and weaknesses. *Sloan Management Review*, 17(3).

Stewart, D. W. (1981). The application and misapplication of factor analysis in marketing research. *Journal of Marketing Research*, 18 (February).

Stewart, G. B. (1991). *The Quest for Value: The EVA TM Management Guide*. New York: Harper Business.

Sweeney, T. W., Matthews, H. L. & Wilson, D. T. (1973). An analysis of industrial buyers' risk reducing behavior: some personality correlates. Paper presented at the American Marketing Association.

Tapscott, D. (1996). *The Digital Economy: Promise and Peril in the Age of Networked Intelligence*. New York: McGraw-Hill.

Tellis, G. J. & Crawford, C. M. (1981). An evolutionary approach to product growth theory. *Journal of Marketing* (Fall).

Terpstra, V. & Sarathy, R. (1991). *International Marketing*. Chicago: Dryden.

Thomas, R. R., Jr. (1991). *Beyond Race and Gender: Unleashing the Power of Your Total Work Force by Managing Diversity*. New York: American Management Association.

Thurstone, L. (1947). *Multiple Factor Analysis*. Chicago: University of Chicago Press.

Traylor, M. B. & Joseph, W. B. (1984). Measuring consumer involvement with products: developing a general scale. *Psychology and Marketing*, 1 (Summer).

Trompenaars, F. (1993). *Riding the Waves of Culture: Understanding Cultural Diversity in Business*. London: Nicolas Brealey.

Tse, D. K. & Wilton, P. C. (1988). Models of consumer satisfaction formation: an extension. *Journal of Marketing Research*, 25 (May).

United Nations. (1995). *Our GLOBAL Neighbourhood: The Report of the Commission on Global Governance*. New York: Oxford University Press.

United Nations Development Programme. (1996). *Human Development Report 1996: Economic Growth and Human Development*. New York: Oxford University Press.

Ury, W. (1991). *Getting Past No*. London: Business Books.

Usunier, J.C. & Valette-Florence, P. (1991). Personal value systems and temporal patterns (time-styles): exploratory findings (working paper). Grenoble, France: University of Grenoble, Ecole Superieure des Affaires.

Vinson, D. E., Scott, J. E. & Lamont, L. M. (1977). The role of personal values in marketing and consumer behavior. *Journal of Marketing*, (April).

von Hippel, E. (1988). *The Sources of Innovation*. London: Oxford University Press.

Vroom, V. H. & Yetton, P. W. (1973). *Leadership and Decision-making*. Pittsburgh: University of Pittsburgh Press.

Walton, M. (1986). *The Deming Management Method*. New York: Perigee.

Weber, J. A. (1974). Worldwide strategies for market segmentation. *Columbia Journal of World Business*, (Winter).

Webster Jr., F. E. (1991). *Industrial Marketing Strategy*. (Third ed.). New York: Wiley.

Weir, W. (1984). Another look at subliminal 'facts'. *Advertising Age*, 46 (15 October).

Wellins, R. S., Byham, W. C. & Wilson, J. M. (1991). *Empowered Teams: Creating Self-Directed Work Groups that Improve Quality, Productivity and Participation*. San Francisco: Jossey-Bass.

Wildstrom, S. H. (1996a). 'VCRs for the Web. *Business Week*, 8 (26 August).

Wildstrom, S. H. (1996b). Web-sites come looking for you. *Business Week*, 8 (18 November).

Wilson, D. T. (1995). An integrated model of buyer-seller relationships. *Journal of the Academy of Marketing Science*, 23(4).

Wind, Y. (1978). Issues and advances in segmentation research. *Journal of Marketing Research*, 15 (August).

Wind, Y. & Cardozo, R. (1974). Industrial market segmentation. *Industrial Marketing Management*, 3.

Wind, Y. & Douglas, S. P. (1972). International market segmentation. *European Journal of Marketing*, 6(1).

Woo, C. Y. Y. & Cooper, A. C. (1980). Strategies of effective low market share businesses. Paper presented at the Academy of Management Proceedings (August).

World Bank. (1992). *World Development Report 1992: Infrastructure for Development*. New York: Oxford University Press.

World Bank. (1994). *World Development Report 1994: Infrastructure for Development*. New York: Oxford University Press.

World Bank. (1996). *World Development Report 1996: From Plan to Market*. New York: Oxford University Press.

Yavas, U., Verhage, B. J. & Green, R. T. (1992–1993). Global consumer segmentation versus local market orientation: empirical findings. *Management International Review*, 32.

Yoshino, M. J. & Rangan, U. S. (1995). *Strategic Alliances: An Entrepreneurial Approach to Globalization*. Boston: Harvard Business School Press.

Zaichkowsky, J.L. (1985). Measuring the involvement construct. *Journal of Consumer Research*, 12 (December).

Zinkhan, G. M. & Pereira, A. (1994). An overview of marketing strategy and planning. *International Journal of Research in Marketing*, 11(3).

INDEX

stratification analysis 153, 159-62
strengths and weaknesses analysis
    151-4, 172
strong marketing unit (SMU) 269
Stussy 17
subliminal message 5
Subscriber Identity Module (SIM)
    233
superior sustainable customer solu-
    tions (see SSCS)
supply chain management 209
Suzuki 208
SWOT analysis 148
symbolic world 31, 35, 60, 141
symbolic world, categorisation 55
symbolic world, elaboration 55
symbolic world, organisation 56
systems, information technology (see
    database marketing)

Tandem Computers 209
Tapscott's twelve themes 191-2
target marketing 99, 109, 111, 230
technological environment 75, 96
teleprocessing systems 238
Teljoy 27, 93
Telkom 211
The Limited 83, 196, 200
timing 229
toxic executives 197
trade marketing 63
trade patterns (IOR) 293
TRW 146

Unilever 208
United Nations, statistical reports and
    statistics 27, 297-300
univariate analysis 104

usage, occasion, pattern and situation
    24, 61, 260

value chain, analysis, relationships
    and management 209-25, 268
values 30-31
Values and Lifestyles Study (VALS)
    37
values, Schwartz Value Survey 16,
    31, 35, 72
VanAllen Group 59
Venter, Bill 207-15
Verifone 210
Vicary, James 5
VISA 218
Vodac 93
Vodacom 93, 200
voicemail systems 234-5
VW Beetle 92

Wal-Mart 138, 186, 199
Walton, Sam 138, 199, 201
Walton's 84
wealth, consumer 26
Web radio 232
Welch, Jack 197
Westinghouse Electric 268
word-of-mouth 19
World Bank 297-8
World Wide Web 231
world-view 133, 138
world-view, competitor 135
Worthington Steel 83, 196

Xerox 207, 268

Yellow Pages 58

zero defection 251